EMBEDDING GLOBAL MARKETS

To the Memory of Ernst B. Haas
Mentor and friend

Embedding Global Markets
An Enduring Challenge

Edited by

JOHN GERARD RUGGIE
Harvard University, USA

ASHGATE

Published by
Ashgate Publishing Limited
Gower House
Croft Road
Aldershot
Hampshire GU11 3HR
England

Ashgate Publishing Company
Suite 420
101 Cherry Street
Burlington, VT 05401-4405
USA

www.ashgate.com

British Library Cataloguing in Publication Data
Embedding global markets : an enduring challenge
 1. Globalization - Economic aspects 2. International
 economic relations 3. Economics - Political aspects
 4. Liberalism
 I. Ruggie, John Gerard, 1944-
 337

Library of Congress Cataloging-in-Publication Data
Embedding global markets : an enduring challenge / edited by John Gerard Ruggie.
 p. cm.
 Includes index.
 ISBN 978-0-7546-7454-2
 1. Globalization--Economic aspects. 2. International economic relations. 3. Economics--Political aspects. 4. Liberalism. I. Ruggie, John Gerard, 1944-

 HF1359.E57 2008
 337--dc22

 2008019108

 ISBN: 978 0 7546 7454 2

Printed and bound in Great Britain by
MPG Books Ltd, Bodmin, Cornwall.

Contents

Part III   A Global Civic Order?

List of Figures and Tables

Figures

Tables

List of Contributors

Jacqueline Best is Associate Professor of Political Studies at the University of Ottawa. Her book, *The Limits of Transparency: Ambiguity and the History of International Finance,* was published by Cornell University Press in 2005.

Sean D. Ehrlich is Assistant Professor of Political Science at Florida State University. His research, which has appeared in *International Organization* and *International Studies Quarterly,* focuses on the effects of domestic institutions on economic policymaking and on the processes by which policymakers can manage public support for globalization, especially in the face of rising concerns about fair trade.

Jude C. Hays is Assistant Professor of Political Science at the University of Illinois and a Research Fellow at the Cline Center for Democracy. He has published on political economy and methodology in leading journals such as *Comparative Political Studies, Political Analysis, International Organization, World Politics* and the *American Journal of Political Science.*

Andrew Lang is a member of the Faculty of Law at the London School of Economics, where he teaches international law, specializing in the law of the World Trade Organization. He previously held a position as Research Fellow at Trinity Hall, University of Cambridge, and is one of two co-founders of the Society of International Economic Law.

Matthew Mendelsohn is currently Deputy Minister and Associate Secretary of the Cabinet, Intergovernmental Affairs, in the Government of Ontario. He is on leave from Queen's University, where he is Associate Professor in the Political Studies Department and was the Director of the Canadian Opinion Research Archive.

Clint Peinhardt is Assistant Professor in the School of Economic, Political and Policy Sciences at the University of Texas at Dallas. His recent work examines financial liberalization and foreign investment in low and middle income countries.

Salvatore Pitruzzello is Visiting Fellow at Harvard's Center for European Studies (CES). His research investigates the macro long-run historical dynamics linking the co-evolution of welfare states, economic performance and social protection. He specializes in the theory and methodology of time-series co-integration. He is the author of a forthcoming book, *Globalization and the Welfare State* (with Martin Rhodes: Polity Press).

Dani Rodrik is professor of international political economy at Harvard's John F. Kennedy School of Government and author of *One Economics, Many Recipes* (Princeton University Press, 2007).

Nita Rudra is Assistant Professor of International Affairs at the University of Pittsburgh. Her research interests include the impact of globalization on social welfare expenditures in developing countries, the political foundations of different welfare regimes, and the causes and effects of democracy in developing nations. Her most recent works appear in the *Journal of Politics*, *American Journal of Political Science*, *Studies in Comparative International Development*, *Comparative Political Studies*, *International Organization* and *International Studies Quarterly*. She has a forthcoming book with Cambridge University Press entitled: *Who Really Gets Hurt? Globalization and the Race to the Bottom Paradox in Developing Countries*. She recently completed a one-year fellowship awarded by the Council on Foreign Relations at the Social Development Department of the World Bank.

John Gerard Ruggie is Kirkpatrick Professor of International Affairs at Harvard's Kennedy School of Government and Affiliated Professor of International Legal Studies at Harvard Law. From 1997–2001 he served as UN Assistant Secretary-General for Strategic Planning. In 2005, Kofi Annan appointed him as UN Special Representative for Business and Human Rights, a post he continues to hold in the new administration of Ban Ki-moon. He has published six books and nearly 100 articles, is a Fellow of the American Academy of Arts and Sciences as well as a Guggenheim Fellow, and has won awards from the American Political Science Association and the International Studies Association. A survey in *Foreign Policy* magazine named him as one of the 25 most influential international relations scholars in the United States and Canada.

Robert Wolfe is Professor in the School of Policy Studies at Queen's University in Kingston, Ontario. A former Canadian foreign service officer, he has published widely on trade policy, the policy process, and on international institutions, notably the World Trade Organization.

Acknowledgements

The editor and publishers wish to thank the following for permission to use copyright material.

Andrew T.F. Lang, "Reconstructing Embedded Liberalism: John Gerard Ruggie and Constructivist Approaches to the Study of the International Trade Regime", *Journal of International Economic Law*, 9 (March 2006), 81–116, by permission of Oxford University Press.

Jacqueline Best, "Hollowing Out Keynesian Norms: How the Search for a Technical Fix Undermined the Bretton Woods Regime", *Review of International Studies*, 30 (July 2004), 383–404, © British International Studies Association, published by Cambridge University Press, reprinted by permission.

Salvatore Pitruzzello, "Trade Globalization, Economic Performance, and Social Protection: Nineteenth-Century British Laissez-Faire and Post-World War II U.S.-Embedded Liberalism", *International Organization*, 58 (Fall 2004), 705–744, © International Organization Foundation, published by Cambridge University Press, reprinted by permission.

Dani Rodrik, "Why Do Open Economies Have Bigger Governments?", *Journal of Political Economy*, 106 (No 5, 1998), 997–1032. © 1998, The University of Chicago Press.

Jude C. Hays, Sean D. Ehrlich, Clint W. Peinhardt, "Government Spending and Public Support for Trade in the OECD: An Empirical Test of the Embedded Liberalism Thesis", *International Organization*, 59, Spring 2005, 473–494, © International Organization Foundation, published by Cambridge University Press, reprinted by permission.

Nita Rudra, "Globalization and the Decline of the Welfare State in Less-Developed Countries", *International Organization*, 56:2 (Spring, 2002), 411–445, © 2002 by the IO Foundation and the Massachusetts Institute of Technology.

Robert Wolfe, Matthew Mendelsohn, "Values and Interests in Attitudes toward Trade and Globalization: The Continuing Compromise of Embedded Liberalism", *Canadian Journal of Political Science/Revue canadienne de science politique*, 38 (01); 45–68, (2005) © *Canadian Journal of Political Science*, published by Cambridge University Press, reprinted with permission.

"Taking Embedded Liberalism Global: the Corporate Connection" David Held and Mathias Koenig-Archibugi, eds, *Taming Globalization: Frontiers of Governance*, 2003, published by Polity Press, reprinted with permission.

Every effort has been made to trace all the copyright holders, but if any have been inadvertently overlooked the publishers will be pleased to make the necessary arrangement at the first opportunity.

Introduction:
Embedding Global Markets

John Gerard Ruggie

One of the most striking features of the United States' financial sector meltdown in the spring of 2008 is how eerily familiar it felt to the historically minded: rapidly mounting transactions in markets lacking transparency and oversight, threatening not only financial institutions but the economy as a whole. In 1930, it had been commercial banks. In 2008, it was "shadow banks", well beyond regulators' reach, engaged in the private trading of complex instruments like collateralized debt obligations, blessed by rating agencies but impossible to value accurately, and coupled with hedges that no one understood in their totality while they were shuffled like hot potatoes among players that were leveraged on average 30:1 or more. The market for one of the hedging instruments alone – credit default swaps – had reached $40 trillion, most of it in a span of just two years (Schwartz and Creswell 2008). When this bubble burst in a credit market freeze, it generated the equivalent of old-fashioned runs on the banks that required federal bailouts to prevent systemic collapse.

At the same time, in the Democratic presidential primaries the two contenders promised little more as a solution to an Ohio electorate hemorrhaging manufacturing jobs for years than that they would consider renegotiating the North American Free Trade Agreement. To be sure, this was not yet Smoot-Hawley territory, the protectionist legislation the U.S. Congress adopted in 1930 that sent world trade into a death spiral. But even though NAFTA was hardly the cause of working American's plight, it had become a foil for frustration. Let it be noted, in the interest of equal time, that the major economic proposal of their Republican opponent was to make temporary tax cuts favoring upper income brackets permanent.

All the while, the world's geo-economic landscape was transforming significantly. The legal rights enabling transnational corporations to operate as globally integrated systems have expanded rapidly in the past generation through various forms of investor protections, some permitting foreign firms to sue states under binding international arbitration (Stone Sweet 2006, Van Harten 2005). Off-shore production has turned China into a giant factory supplying Western consumers with every imaginable product, while also creating enormous hazards to itself and occasionally to people and pets abroad. The so-called BRIC countries – Brazil, Russia, India and China – have emerged as major global economic powerhouses, and some leading analysts have the audacity to point out that none has done so by following the prescriptions of the so-called Washington consensus (Rodrik forthcoming) – or when they did briefly, as in the case of Russia and Brazil, they ran into deep economic trouble.

In short, before the end of the new century's first decade a serious disjuncture had erupted in the world political economy: between the scope and impact of economic forces and actors, and the ideational and institutional capacity of societies to manage them.

This book is intended to help elucidate the nature of this disjuncture by focusing on a core element we once understood but, willfully or otherwise, seem to have forgotten: markets work optimally only if they are embedded within rules, customs and institutions (McMillan 2002). Markets themselves require these to survive and thrive, while society needs them to manage the adverse effects of market dynamics and produce the public goods that markets undersupply. Indeed, history teaches us that markets pose the greatest risks – to society and business itself – when their scope and power far exceed the reach of the institutional underpinnings that allow them to function smoothly and ensure their political sustainability. This is such a time.

This book represents an archeological dig, metaphorically speaking, to restore what we once knew in the hope that we can update its lessons and build upon them to secure a more stable and sustainable economic future.

Embedded Liberalism

I introduced the concept of embedded liberalism in a 1982 article that has become one of the most frequently cited sources in the study of international political economy (Ruggie 1982). The article had two aims. One was to describe and explain the institutional framework through which the capitalist countries after World War II sought to reconcile the efficiency of markets with the broader values of social community – "embedding" markets, in short.[1] Liberalization and the quest for domestic stability were coupled and even conditioned upon one another, I argued.

The other aim was to show that this institutional framework reflected not merely the configuration of state power and interests, but also prevailing social expectations, norms and economic ideas that were widely shared among the capitalist countries – employing, thereby, a type of analysis that has since become known as "social constructivism" (Ruggie 1998).

The article was written in a particular intellectual context, and in refutation of prevailing orthodoxy. Two premises framed the mainstream academic study of international political economy at the time. Both stemmed from the so-called hegemonic stability theory made popular by Charles Kindleberger's (1973) important study of why the Great Depression was so deep and lasted so long: Britain couldn't and America wouldn't provide leadership was his answer, in short. One premise was that the U.S.-led post-World War II order essentially was much the same in its "liberalism" as the British-led laissez-faire order in the late nineteenth century – and that what I considered its "embeddedness" merely constituted cheating, especially in trade. The other premise was that the United States was in decline and that the liberal or open international economic order would soon become the victim of a resurgent

---

1   I adapted this term from Polanyi (1944).

protectionism. I contended then and demonstrated in greater detail subsequently that neither premise was valid (Ruggie 1993, 1995).

Both the concept of embedded liberalism and the analytical perspective of social constructivism soon gained currency among international relations scholars. The idea of embedded liberalism reached beyond this niche in the 1990s when it was discovered by economists and others interested in the impact of economic globalization on domestic social protection (for example, Rodrik in this volume, and 1997). Social constructivism in the political economy context was taken up more recently by international trade lawyers trying to understand better the role of normative and ideational factors in managing the evolving global trade regime (see Lang in this volume).

Challenges to Embedded Liberalism

The need to embed markets in shared values of social community while, at the same time, remaining committed to international liberalization, did not come easily or rapidly to policymakers. It took the collapse of the Victorian era's variant of globalization – followed by, though not precisely in this order, World War I, extreme left wing revolution in Russia, extreme right wing revolutions in Italy and Germany, militarism in Japan, unprecedented international financial volatility, the shriveling up of world trade and the Great Depression. Nor was that the end of it. The social strains produced by *those* upheavals were so powerful that the world descended into yet a second world war in the span of a single generation.

The post-World War II compromise of embedded liberalism, of course, reflected international power relations: had the Soviet Union or Nazi Germany ended up as the world's hegemon – or had the United Kingdom, for that matter – the outcome would have been different (Ruggie 1992). In the event, the United States was paramount, with the UK as its junior negotiating partner. The structure of the postwar economic order also reflected interests: in the simplest terms, the ever-present quest by dominant forms of capital for liberalization, and declining forms for protection.

But the postwar order also reflected shared values and understandings concerning the legitimate role of the state in managing economic relations at home and abroad – a vision that grew out of the earlier experiences. This understanding was described by different names in different countries: the New Deal state in the United States, and social democracy or the social market economy in Europe. But the underlying idea was the same: a grand social bargain whereby society agreed to liberalize markets, which in some cases had become heavily administered if not autarchic in the 1930s, but *also* to share the social adjustment costs that open markets inevitably produce.

Governments played a key role in enacting and sustaining the embedded liberalism compromise: moderating the volatility of transaction flows across borders and providing social investments, safety nets, and adjustment assistance – and all the while pushing international liberalization within a framework of multilateral principles, norms and institutions relations.

In the industrialized world, this grand bargain formed the basis of one of the longest and most equitable periods of economic expansion in human history, from the 1950s into the 1990s. And it provided the institutional foundation for the newest wave of globalization, which has been far broader in scope and deeper in reach than its nineteenth century antecedent.

Today, two transformations have eroded the embedded liberalism framework, one in the domestic political economies of capitalist countries, the other in their global context. On the domestic front, the broadly Keynesian macroeconomic policy tools with which the compromise was associated succumbed long ago to attacks from monetarism, rational expectationism, supply side economics, and other approaches more consistent with neoliberal and even laissez-faire views and preferences. As Blyth (2002: 126) put it, "attacking embedded liberalism meant attacking Keynesian ideas" – though there was no inherent reason why technical defects in the policy tools should have undermined underlying preferences (see Best in this volume).

That link, in turn, is best accounted for by the fact that the domestic political coalitions on which the compromise rested, expressing the different ways in which countries accommodated the new relationships among capital, labor, and the state, have weakened or, as in the case of the United States, almost unraveled altogether.

The embedded liberalism framework has also been challenged on a second front. It was predicated on the existence of separate and distinct national economies, engaged in *external* transactions, conducted at *arm's length,* which governments could buffer effectively at the *border* by point-of-entry measures like tariffs, non-tariff barriers and exchange rates. But markets and firms have gone increasingly global, threatening to leave behind merely national social bargains (Ruggie 2004). Many developing countries are doubly disadvantaged, having never enjoyed the privilege of cushioning the adverse domestic effects of international market exposure in the first place, and lacking the resources, institutional capacity, and, in some cases, the interest on the part of their ruling elites to rise to the new challenges of globalization.

Socially Sustainable Globalization

The 1980s first witnessed the emergence of greater skepticism about the domestic interventionist state, especially in the United States and Britain. For example, although public spending continued to rise, it did so at a decreasing pace (Tanzi and Schuknecht 2000).

More telling, Garrett and Mitchell (2001) found that before the 1990s greater exposure to trade had been an important contributor to domestic fiscal expansion, consistent with the embedded liberalism compromise. But thereafter, marginal increases in trade exposure began to lead to lower government spending, reversing the traditional relationship. Similar results hold for marginal increases in financial openness. The magnitudes remained small but seemed to indicate the beginnings of a shift in the domestic role of the capitalist state: away from a *compensatory* posture vis-à-vis globalization under embedded liberalism, to a *competitive* one, allowing the effects of global market forces to be imposed more directly on domestic factors of production, especially labor. The Blair and Clinton administrations sought to chart a "third way," with mixed results (Giddens 2000). By and large, neoliberalism gained broad ascendancy in policy circles by century's end.

But by the late 1990s, serious concerns about globalization had also arisen. From the left, the anti-globalization backlash focused scrutiny and pressure on multilateral economic institutions. The legitimacy crisis faced by the WTO and ongoing protests against the Bretton Woods institutions resulted from the perception that they abandoned their earlier mandates, which included securing social stability and social inclusion as well as market expansion and deepening, and that they failed to embrace quickly and firmly enough such newer concerns as environmental sustainability. Fears about lost jobs, the belief that others practice unfair trade, and more primal reactions against the social and cultural dislocations wrought by globalization began to drive populist agendas on the political left and right in many parts of the world.

The past is never inevitably prologue. But here is how United Nations Secretary-General Kofi Annan assessed the state of play at the Davos World Economic Forum in January 1999, ten months before anti-globalization protesters and the authorities waged the so-called Battle of Seattle at the ill-fated ministerial meeting of the World Trade Organization:

> Our challenge today is to devise a similar [to embedded liberalism] compact on the global scale, to underpin the new global economy. ... Until we do, the global economy will be fragile and vulnerable – vulnerable to backlash from all the "isms" of our post-cold-war world: protectionism, populism, nationalism, ethnic chauvinism, fanaticism and terrorism (Annan 1999).

Thus, reconstituting some form of embedded liberalism is desirable. But is it possible?[2]

The magnitude of the task we face as a world community is monumental. The aim of this book is to convey to scholars, policymakers, and the public at large what it involves and why it matters. We hope that our doing so will inspire the development of new twenty-first century solutions to an enduring challenge.

Book Outline

The book is divided into three parts: (1) the analytics of embedded liberalism; (2) a survey of macro-patterns in the industrialized countries and beyond that demonstrate the benefits of embedded liberalism in practice; and (3) an exploration of some possible building blocks for a more inclusive globalization.

I. The Idea of Embedded Liberalism

The original embedded liberalism article is not reproduced in this book because Andrew Lang's chapter does an excellent job summarizing it. Lang also shows how the constructivist elements of the embedded liberalism argument help elucidate the evolution of the global trade regime – and how that regime continues to be shaped by the generative grammar, as it were, of the postwar compromise even as it is challenged by other pressures.

---

2   This question is also addressed in Bernstein and Pauly (2007).

In contrast, the monetary regime took a different turn early on.[3] Jacqueline Best, in this book's second chapter, traces the steps through which the International Monetary Fund (IMF) "hollowed out" its original Keynesian norms and increasingly became a marginal player in managing the evolving monetary order – except where countries depended directly on its assistance, and that pool of clients shrank significantly over time. Whatever its other virtues may be, the international monetary system has been subject to repeated crises as a result – in Asia, Russia, and Latin America – successively "fixed" by ad hoc measures and coalitions led by the U.S. Treasury, a far cry from the postwar designs.

II. Embedded Liberalism in Practice

The next four chapters illuminate the practice of embedded liberalism and its consequences for economic performance and social protection. Each is based on detailed statistical analyses of comprehensive data sets. Their conclusions reinforce the desirability of reconstituting a twenty-first century version of the embedded liberalism compromise.

Salvatore Pitruzzello compares patterns of outcomes in the nineteenth century British-led laissez-faire economic order and the post-World War II U.S.-led embedded liberalism order. He demonstrates that the complementarity of market and state under embedded liberalism generated both better long-term economic performance and social protection than its laissez-faire predecessor.

Dani Rodrik was one of the first economists to explore the embedded liberalism thesis, initially in a monograph in which he asked the heretical question – for a mainstream economist – whether globalization had gone too far (Rodrik 1997). In the chapter included in this book, Rodrik examines the link between open economies and government spending across more than 100 countries. Cameron (1978) had found a positive correlation among the OECD countries and Katzenstein (1983) among the small European democracies. Rodrik confirms the positive relationship. And he then tests the hypothesis, with good results, that government spending plays a risk-reducing role in economies that are exposed to significant external risk through trade.

Whereas Rodrik's sample is global, Hays, Ehrlich and Peinhardt focus on the OECD countries. They examine whether government programs designed specifically to protect individuals harmed by imports reduce opposition to free trade. They find strong micro-level empirical support that this is, indeed, the case – a result that also continues to be borne out in public opinion surveys (see Wolfe and Mendelsohn in this book).

However, many developing countries lack the capacity to compensate for the risks and dislocations associated with open markets. Nita Rudra's chapter is one of

---

3 References to IMF conditionality in the form it subsequently took are nowhere to be found in its Articles of Agreement. At the insistence of the United States, the Executive Directors adopted an "interpretation" of the Articles in 1947, to the effect that the Fund could challenge, postpone, or reject requests for assistance, or accept them "subject to conditions" (Horsefield 1969).

the few systematic studies to have addressed this issue. She examines the impacts of capital and trade flows on government welfare spending in 53 developing countries. Her results indicate that when the proportion of low-skilled workers in a nation is high, globalization will lead to a decline in welfare spending. Most significantly, she finds that in countries where labor-market institutions are not yet well developed, government social-welfare spending is constrained by international market forces. Although Rudra doesn't say so, IMF and World Bank conditionality provisions often reinforce this constraint on developing countries rather than help to manage it.

III. A Global Civic Order?

There exists no single silver bullet for reconstituting a functional equivalent to embedded liberalism in the context of globalization. All social actors – states, business, and civil society – will have to learn to do many things differently if the disjuncture identified earlier is to be set right. As always, the main drivers have to be states. But states themselves are constrained by collective action problems – competing for investments, protecting their transnational firms, or finding that the interests of those who govern are served very nicely by current arrangements. So where else, in addition, can one look for building blocks?

Ironically, it seems that the public has never abandoned the social expectations and aspirations expressed in the embedded liberalism compromise. In-depth analyses of Americans' attitudes toward trade have consistently shown that the public is not protectionist – but that it feels the average worker is not getting a fair deal. "This is a bipartisan consensus," concludes Steven Kull, who has conducted several such surveys (2004: 3).[4]

Wolfe and Mendelsohn constructed a survey instrument to explore corresponding attitudes among Canadians. As they report in their contribution to this book, the Canadian public strongly supports trade agreements, as well as more international cooperation across a broad variety of fields. But when it comes to protecting their own labor and workplace standards, and even more so their domestic social programs, Canadians overwhelmingly want the responsibility to remain in the hands of their own government, fearing that they would be less well protected otherwise. The authors also find that individual values and ideology offer a better explanation of attitudes toward trade liberalization and globalization than self-interest.

In short, at least among these publics, preferences and attitudes remain broadly consistent with the underlying principles of embedded liberalism, and therefore can be tapped in formulating a new institutional framework. There is no reason to believe that Europeans' attitudes differ significantly.[5]

---

4 The University of Maryland's Program on International Policy Attitudes has conducted these surveys periodically: http://www.pipa.org/archives/us_opinion.php.

5 A cross-national survey of the U.S., Britain, France, and Germany, conducted by the German Marshall Fund of the USA, found generally similar patterns. The only significant deviation was in France, where a majority of respondents opposed globalization, though only eight percent favored raising tariffs in response (de Jonquières 2004).

The final chapter in this book turns to the dynamic interplay between global civil society and transnational corporations in the domain of corporate social responsibility as another potential piece of the puzzle. For more than a decade now major firms, especially in large footprint and brand-sensitive industries, have been pressured by civil society actors toward adopting higher standards in core labor rights, health, safety, and environmental practices, and to engage in programs to advance anti-poverty agendas in developing countries. More recently, governments, too, have begun to promote such approaches.

Although voluntary initiatives undertaken by a relatively small number of large companies cannot meet systemic challenges on their own, Ruggie suggests that they can generate positive consequences. Improving those companies' social and environmental performance has direct benefits for their employees and surrounding communities. Equally important is their potential for generating positive spillover effects. In the developing world, the adoption of good practices by these firms may exert an upward pull on the performance of local enterprises in the same sector. In the industrialized countries, the diffusion of good practices by major companies' social and environmental performance abroad may lessen the fear that a global "race to the bottom" will undermine their own policy frameworks for achieving social inclusion and economic security at home. Furthermore, as companies engage more extensively in efforts to strengthen the social and environmental pillars of globalization, they also may give governments greater impetus and courage to do what only they can do: to govern, and to govern in the public interest.

References

Annan, Kofi (1999). "Secretary-General Proposes Global Compact on Human Rights, Environment, in Address to World Economic Forum in Davos," http://www.un.org/News/Press/docs/1999/19990201.sgsm6881.html.

Bernstein, Steven and Pauly, Louis W., eds (2007) *Global Liberalism and Political Order: Toward a New Grand Compromise?* (Albany, NY: SUNY).

Blyth, Mark (2002). *Great Transformations: The Rise and Decline of Embedded Liberalism* (New York: Cambridge).

Cameron, David (1978). "The Expansion of the Public Economy: A Comparative Analysis," *American Political Science Review*, 72 (December): 1243–1261.

de Jonquieres, Guy (2004). "Survey Shows Cautious Support for Global Trade," *Financial Times*, July 14: 11.

Giddens, Anthony (2000). *The Third Way and Its Critics* (Cambridge: Polity).

Horsefield, J. Keith (1969). *The IMF, 1945–1965*, vol. 3 (Washington, DC: IMF).

Katzenstein, Peter J. (1983). "The Small European States in the International Economy," in John Gerard Ruggie, ed., *The Antinomies of Interdependence* (New York: Columbia).

Kindleberger, Charles P. (1973). *The World In Depression, 1929–1939* (Berkeley: University of California Press).

Kull, Steven (2004). "Election Year Politics and American Attitudes Toward the Global Economy," Columbia University Business School, APEC Study Center, 7 April.

McMillan, John (2002). *Reinventing the Bazaar: A Natural History of Markets* (New York: Norton).

Polanyi, Karl (1944). *The Great Transformation* (Boston: Beacon).

Rodrik, Dani (1997). *Has Globalization Gone Too Far?* (Washington, DC: Institute for International Economics).

Rodrik, Dani (forthcoming). "Goodbye Washington Consensus, Hello Washington Confusion?" *Journal of Economic Literature.*

Ruggie, John Gerard (1982). "International Regimes, Transactions, and Change: Embedded Liberalism in the Postwar Economic Order," *International Organization,* 36 (Spring): 195–231.

Ruggie, John Gerard (1992). "Multilateralism: The Anatomy of an Institution," *International Organization,* 46 (Summer): 561–598.

Ruggie, John Gerard (1993). "Unravelling Trade: Global Institutional Change and the Pacific Economy", in Richard Higgott, Richard Leaver and John Ravenhill, eds, *Pacific Economic Relations in the 1990s* (Boulder, CO: Lynne Rienner).

Ruggie, John Gerard (1995). "At Home Abroad, Abroad at Home: International Liberalization and Domestic Stability in the New World Economy", *Millennium: Journal of International Studies,* 24 (Winter): 507–526.

Ruggie, John Gerard (1998). "What Makes the World Hang Together? Neo-Utilitarianism and the Social Constructivist Challenge," *International Organization,* 52 (Autumn): 855–885.

Ruggie, John Gerard (2004). "Reconstituting the Global Public Domain: Issues, Actors, and Practices," *European Journal of International Relations,* 10 (December): 499–531.

Schwartz, Nelson D. and Creswell, Julie (2008). "What Created This Monster? Yes, the Markets Can Bite Back," *New York Times,* March 23: Business Section 1, 7.

Stone Sweet, Alec (2006). "The New *Lex Mercatoria* and Transnational Governance," *Journal of European Public Policy,* 13 (August): 627–646.

Tanzi, Vito and Schuknecht, Ludger (2000). *Public Spending in the 20th Century* (New York: Cambridge).

Van Harten, Gus (2005). "Private Authority and Transnational Governance: The Contours of the International System of Investor Protections," *Review of International Political Economy,* 12 (October): 600–623.

PART I
The Idea of Embedded Liberalism

Chapter 1

Reconstructing Embedded Liberalism: John Gerard Ruggie and Constructivist Approaches to the Study of the International Trade Regime

Andrew T.F. Lang

Introduction

In 1982, John Gerard Ruggie published a study of the postwar international trade and monetary regimes entitled 'International Regimes, Transactions and Change: embedded liberalism in the postwar economic order' (*International Regimes, Transactions and Change*).[1] Against the prevailing idea that the postwar international economic order was 'orthodox liberal' in character, Ruggie argued on the contrary that it was characterized by a political commitment to what he called 'embedded liberalism'.

The story of embedded liberalism was described early on as 'highly original'[2] and, in Ruggie's own words, encountered 'some initial scepticism'.[3] But it was a compelling narrative, and it quickly began to gain currency, at least within the fields of political science and international relations. Then, from the mid-1990s, Ruggie's notion of embedded liberalism seemed to catch the imagination of scholars in other fields. It proved to be a particularly useful explanatory concept for economists and others interested in the effects of trade liberalization (and global economic integration more generally) on social protection in advanced economies.[4] International trade

---

1   J. G. Ruggie, 'International Regimes, Transactions, and Change: Embedded Liberalism and the Postwar Economic Order', in S. D. Krasner (ed.), *International Regimes* (Ithaca, NY: Cornell University Press 1983) 195. The same article was also published in a slightly edited form in Ruggie's 1998 collection of earlier writings: J. G. Ruggie, *Constructing the World Polity: Essays on International Institutionalisation* (1998). Throughout this article, I will be referring almost exclusively to the 1983 version.

2   S. D. Krasner, 'Structural Causes and Regime Consequences: Regimes as Intervening Variables', in S. D. Krasner (ed.), *International Regimes* (Ithaca, NY: Cornell University Press 1983) 1 at 17.

3   Ruggie, *Constructing the World Polity*, above n 1, at 62.

4   See below n 34–35 and accompanying text.

lawyers, too, began to show an interest in embedded liberalism. A series of articles by Dunoff have been most influential in introducing the concept of embedded liberalism to trade lawyers.[5] Since then, references to embedded liberalism in the writing of trade lawyers have been steadily increasing, to the extent that a familiarity with the basic contours of Ruggie's concept is now often assumed.[6] While it is still relatively early in the process, there seems to be every reason to think that Ruggie's article, and the concept of embedded liberalism which it introduced, has already had a significant impact on the way trade lawyers understand the object of their study.

This growing interest in *International Regimes, Transactions and Change* encouraged me to spend some time exploring that article, as well as the related work of Ruggie and some of his like-minded colleagues.[7] The experience left me with the clear conviction that as trade lawyers we have a great deal to learn from the insights which Ruggie sets out in International Regimes, Transactions and Change. For one thing, those insights challenge some of the key assumptions upon which our major debates are based: the 'received wisdom' which Ruggie destabilized back in 1982 still has a hold over the imagination of many of us. Moreover, Ruggie's article draws attention to significant gaps in our research programmes. But the experience also left me with the strong sense that the most important insights which Ruggie has to offer have been misunderstood or at least neglected by the treatment of his work in the writing of many trade lawyers. In particular, while the narrative of embedded liberalism itself has been relatively well reproduced, the theoretical framework on which it is based has been neglected.

In the decades since *International Regimes, Transactions and Change* was written, Ruggie has emerged as one of the most important figures in the development of so-called constructivist theoretical approaches to the study of international regimes. Trade lawyers have on the whole been heavily influenced by liberal, and particularly

---

5   J. L. Dunoff, ' "Trade and": Recent Developments in Trade Policy and Scholarship – And Their Surprising Political Implications', 17 (2/3) *Northwestern Journal of International Law and Business* 759 (1997); J. L. Dunoff, 'Rethinking International Trade', 19 (2) *University of Pennsylvania Journal of International Economic Law* 347 (1998); J. L. Dunoff, 'The Death of the Trade Regime', 10 (4) *European Journal of International Law* 733 (1999).

6   See, for example, J. H. Knox, 'The Judicial Resolution of Conflicts Between Trade and the Environment', 28 (1) *Harvard Environmental Law Review* 1 (2004).

7   For a selection of Ruggie's work, see the material referred to in n 1 above, as well as J. G. Ruggie and F. Kratochwil, 'International Organization: a State of the Art on an Art of the State', 40 (4) *International Organization* 753 (1986); J. G. Ruggie, 'Embedded Liberalism Revisited' in E. Adler and B. Crawford (eds), *Progress in Postwar International Relations* (1991) 202; J. G. Ruggie (ed.), *Multilateralism Matters: The Theory and Praxis of an Institutional Form* (1993); J. G. Ruggie, 'At Home Abroad, Abroad at Home: International Liberalisation and Domestic Stability in the New World Economy', 24 (3) *Millennium* 507 (1994); J. G. Ruggie, 'Trade, Protectionism and the Future of Welfare Capitalism', 48 (1) *Journal of International Affairs – Columbia University* 1 (1994); J. G. Ruggie, 'Globalization and the Embedded Liberalism Compromise: The End of an Era?', in W. Streeck (ed.), *Internationale Wirtschaft, Nationale Demokratie* (1998); J.G. Ruggie, 'Taking Embedded Liberalism Global: The Corporate Connection', in D. Held and M. Koenig-Archibugi (eds), *Taming Globalization: Frontiers of Governance* (2003).

liberal institutionalist, approaches to the study of the trade regime. We have also, at some level, internalized many of the core insights of (neo)realist thought. But we have been very slow to draw on constructivist insights.[8] One of the great values of *International Regimes, Transactions and Change*, then, is that it represents an extended and highly accessible treatment of the trade regime – one which already has traction among a growing number of trade lawyers – by one of the titans of constructivist thinking. While it is not my intention to introduce trade lawyers to constructivism generally,[9] one of my central aims was nevertheless to excavate the theoretical framework which underpins *International Regimes, Transactions and Change* and to explore some of the implications this framework has for the way trade scholars go about their work.

This chapter is structured as follows. In section I, I summarize *International Regimes, Transactions and Change*, with the intention, as far as possible, of letting Ruggie's article speak for itself. Section II describes the resurgent interest in embedded liberalism from the middle of the 1990s and gives a flavour of the different ways in which embedded liberalism has been used in the writing of trade scholars. In section III, I offer some comments on the lessons which trade lawyers have so far attempted to draw from Ruggie's article. First, I argue that the story of embedded liberalism usefully challenges prevailing assumptions about the underlying objectives of the trade regime and reminds us that different kinds of open, liberal trading systems are possible. Second, I show that embedded liberalism provides a framework within which to reformulate the terms of current debates about the trade regime. Instead of arguing primarily about how open the trading system should be – that is, how far down the road of trade liberalization we want to go – Ruggie shows us that we should also be debating what 'social purpose' we want the trade regime to embody. Third, I voice some concerns about the common tendency to see in embedded liberalism an attractive normative vision for the contemporary trade regime. I argue that this use of Ruggie's concept risks constraining our collective imagination, and tying us to the institutional forms, ideational frameworks and political priorities of the past. I also argue that the postwar period of embedded liberalism has to some extent been mystified and eulogized and that we should remember those whose voices and concerns which were marginalized during that time.

---

8   Important exceptions include K. W. Abbott, ' "Economic" Issues and Political Participation: The Evolving Boundaries of International Federalism', 18 (3) *Cardozo Law Review* 971 (1996) and perhaps Drake and Nicolaïdis, 'Ideas, Interests and Institutionalization: "Trade in Services" and the Uruguay Round', 46 (1) *International Organization* 37 (1992). As I understand it, R. Howse, 'From Politics to Technocracy – and Back Again: The Fate of the Multilateral Trading Regime', 96 (1) *American Journal of International Law* 94 (2002) also owes an intellectual debt to various versions of constructivist thought, as do various publications of Jeffrey Dunoff, referred to below.

9   Some important steps down that road have already been made by Nichols, who has, with great clarity, introduced trade lawyers to the schools of historical and sociological institutionalism, both of which (particularly the latter) are intellectual cousins of constructivist approaches in IR, see P. M. Nichols, 'Forgotten Linkages – Historical Institutionalism and Sociological Institutionalism and Analysis of the World Trade Organization', 19 (2) *University of Pennsylvania Journal of International Economic Law* 461 (1998).

In section IV, which is the longest and most important section, my aim is to draw attention to the theoretical framework of Ruggie's article. *International Regimes, Transactions and Change* is predicated upon an approach to the study of international regimes which is in many respects fundamentally different from that which most trade lawyers tend to use. My aim is to show how this constructivist approach can augment our understanding of the trade regime and trade law in important ways. First, I show how it alerts us to dimensions of the trade regime to which we typically pay scant attention: the shared narratives that it embodies, the constitutive[10] rules that it establishes, and the communicative and cognitive processes that take place within it. Second, I make the claim that constructivist approaches can enhance our understanding of the *determinants* of the trade regime and of institutional change in the WTO. Our current preoccupation with materialist and interestbased analyses should be accompanied by attention to the role of ideational and cognitive factors in making the trade regime what it is. Third, I argue that our understanding of the *consequences* of the trade regime – its effects on behaviour and outcomes – can be similarly developed. The trade regime, constructivist scholars remind us, does not just regulate actor behaviour, it also partly constitutes it, at the same time as partly constituting actors' identities and interests. In each of these areas, I show how these insights have the potential to change the questions we ask about trade law and the role that we play as trade lawyers.

I. International Regimes, Transactions and Change: Embedded Liberalism in the Postwar Economic Order

International Regimes, Transactions and Change was originally published as part of a special issue of *International Organization* addressing the topic of international regimes.[11] This volume has become something of a foundational text for the study of regimes in the field of international relations and prefigured a number of different theoretical approaches which have developed more fully since then. At heart, the contributors to this volume sought to determine 'whether regimes make any difference',[12] and if so, in what way. Ruggie's study of the postwar regimes for money and trade offers a distinctive response to this question.

Ruggie begins by briefly setting out his 'basic approach' to the study of international regimes. International regimes, Ruggie notes, are social institutions 'around which actor expectations converge'. Since regimes take shape in the form of converging expectations, he argues, they have 'an intersubjective quality' like a language. When we study international regimes, therefore, we cannot limit ourselves to their 'concrete

---

10 When, in this chapter, I describe rules, ideas, narratives or particular social processes as 'constitutive' of behaviour, I mean that these rules and the like provide the conditions in which such behaviour is given meaning and made thinkable and (therefore) possible. This is different from a situation in which rules etc. regulate the pursuit of pre-constituted interests. See further section IV(A).

11 The special issue was published later as an edited collection: S. D. Krasner (ed.), *International Regimes* (Ithaca, NY: Cornell University Press 1983).

12 Krasner, above n 2, at 1.

elements'; we must also pay attention to their 'phenomenological dimension'. In other words, we must understand the trade regime as, above all, an 'intersubjective framework of meaning'.[13] I will explain the concept of intersubjectivity in section IV below and argue that this basic insight into the nature of the trade regime is potentially the most valuable lesson for trade lawyers in Ruggie's article.

From this vantage point, Ruggie develops his core theoretical argument about the trade regime.[14] This argument, it is important to note, was framed as a response to hegemonic stability theory, which was probably the dominant theoretical model of the international economic order at the time. Hegemonic stability theory sees the international economic order as closely related to the prevailing distribution of power in the international system. For present purposes, the key prediction of this theory is that the presence of an economic hegemon – provided it is committed to liberal goals – 'is likely to result in an open trading structure'.[15] Conversely, a 'decline in hegemonic power should ... be associated with a weaker, less open' trading structure.[16] This is in part because a stable open economic order requires heavy investment in institutional infrastructure and thus an extraordinarily powerful hegemon willing to pay the costs of the provision of this 'public good'.[17]

Contrary to hegemonic stability theory, Ruggie saw the international economic order as determined by 'a fusion of power and legitimate social purpose'.[18] To say anything sensible about the character of the international economic order, as opposed to merely its form, he argues, 'it is necessary to look at how power and legitimate social purpose become fused to project political authority into the international system'.[19] (This emphasis on the dimension of 'shared social purpose' should be understood as going hand in hand with his emphasis on the 'phenomenological dimension' of regimes.) He illustrates this argument by drawing a distinction between the open trading order which existed pre-WW1 and that which existed post-WW2. While a hegemonic power existed in both periods, the two trading orders differed along the axis of social purpose. The former, he argues, was characterized by a shared commitment to 'orthodox liberalism' or 'laissez-faire liberalism'. The

---

13 All citations in this paragraph are to Ruggie, 'Embedded Liberalism', above n 1, at 196.

14 In fact, Ruggie sets out three different theoretical arguments at this point, but as he himself notes all three 'stand or fall together', as they all ultimately 'lead back to [his] depiction of international authority as reflecting a fusion of power and legitimate social purpose'. Ibid, at 200.

15 S.D. Krasner, 'State Power and the Structure of International Trade', 28 *World Politics* 317 (1976), at 318; see also C. Lipson, 'The Transformation of Trade: the Sources and Effects of Regime Change' in S.D. Krasner (ed.), *International Regimes* (Ithaca, NY: Cornell University Press 1983) 233 at 254.

16 Lipson, above n 15, at 254. To be clear, Lipson is not an advocate of hegemonic stability theory, he is merely explaining its contours in the cited passage.

17 This short summary of hegemonic stability theory (HST), while fairly standard in the literature, inevitably fails to capture the theory's subtleties. For the seminal work on HST, see C. P. Kindleberger, *The World in Depression, 1929–1939* (1973).

18 Ruggie, 'Embedded Liberalism', above n 1, at 201.

19 Ibid, at 198.

latter grew out of a commitment to something different, which he calls 'embedded liberalism'.[20]

The bulk of the article shows how the international economic order has historically varied according to changes in collective ideas about the 'legitimate social purposes' for which power can be exercised. Shared ideas at the international level, Ruggie suggests, are in part a function of changes in ideas at the domestic level. Particularly important, as far as the international trade regime is concerned, are changes in ideas about the purposes 'in pursuit of which state power was expected to be employed in the domestic economy'.[21] Drawing heavily on the work of Polanyí,[22] Ruggie shows how the rise of free trade policies in the nineteenth century reflected a fundamental redefinition of ideas about state–society relations at the domestic level. The liberal international economic order of the time, he observes, rested on the internationalization of these ideas: the nineteenth century Pax Britannia was therefore a result not just of Britain's hegemony, but also of the fact that this 'new balance of state society relations ... expressed a *collective* reality'.[23] In the period after WW1, Ruggie suggests (again following Polanyí), there was a mass social reaction against market rationality across Europe and in the United States, and this transformation in ideas about the proper social purpose of power was reflected in the form of the international economic order. Efforts to reconstruct an orthodox liberal economic order in the interwar period failed, according to Ruggie, 'not because of the lack of a hegemon, [but] because they stood in contradiction to the transformation in the mediating role of the state between market and society, which altered fundamentally the social purpose of domestic and international authority'.[24]

This sets the stage for the emergence after WW2 of a new liberal economic order, different in kind from that which had gone before. None of the negotiators at Bretton Woods, Ruggie notes, were doctrinaire-free-traders. The regime that they created was predicated on a shared sense of the necessity, and legitimacy, of governmental intervention into the market for the purposes of securing domestic stability. Thus, the set of objectives which came to be embodied in the postwar trade regime – that is, the underlying shared vision which constituted the trade regime – was double-pronged: the aim was 'to devise a framework which would safeguard and even aid the quest for domestic stability without, at the same time, triggering the mutually destructive external consequences that had plagued the interwar period'.[25] On the one hand, this entailed a turn away from discrimination in trading relations – this half of the plot is the one that 'we tend to remember more vividly today'.[26] But on the other hand, it also entailed a commitment to domestic interventionism. Thus, the international trade regime contained elements which were designed to enable intervention in support of domestic stability. A balance was struck: a variety of forms of domestic

---

20 Ibid.
21 Ibid, at 202.
22 K. Polanyí, *Origins of Our Time: the Great Transformation* (1945).
23 Ruggie, 'Embedded Liberalism', above n 1, at 202.
24 Ibid, at 208.
25 Ibid, at 209.
26 Ibid.

cushioning were permitted, provided that such measures were 'commensurate with the degree of external disturbance and compatible with the long-term expansion of international transactions'.[27] It is this complex vision, founded in new understandings about the social purposes for which power may legitimately be exercised, that Ruggie called 'embedded' liberalism. His use of the term 'embedded' recalled Polanyí's notion of the disembedding of economic from social life and reflected the fact that, in the postwar GATT, the liberalism of freer trade was embedded within a deeper commitment to an interventionist programme of governmental social action.

This shared vision was reflected in the texts of the GATT itself. Ruggie notes that while the principles of multilateralism and tariff reduction were affirmed in the texts, multilateralism ultimately 'meant non-discrimination above all', and commitments on tariff reduction were, at least at the start, relatively weak. Furthermore, the texts contained a wide variety of 'safeguards, exemptions, exceptions and restrictions' – such as those relating to balance of payments restrictions, preferential trading agreements, emergency safeguards and others – which were designed to facilitate and protect 'a variety of domestic social policies'.[28] Thus, while the GATT was a liberal trade regime, it was a particular kind of liberal trade regime, one in which 'multilateralism and the quest for domestic stability were coupled and even conditioned by one another'.[29] This character, in turn 'reflected the shared legitimacy of a set of social objectives to which the industrial world had moved, unevenly, but "as a single entity."'[30]

The final sections of the article turn to the question of regime change.[31] At that time, observers of the trade regime were concerned with the proliferation of new forms of trade barriers – the 'New Protectionism' of the 1970s. Many saw this trend as evidence of a decline in the strength of the trade regime and attributed it to a decline in US hegemony. Ruggie interpreted the trend differently. He saw the New Protectionism as evidence of continuity, not change: it was a way of giving effect to embedded liberalism in changed global economic conditions. He shows how the new protectionist measures were of precisely the kind that might be expected within the model of embedded liberalism – they did not afflict the entire trading order, but rather represent limited and relatively modest measures to 'slow down structural change and minimize the social costs of domestic adjustment'.[32] This is not to say, of course, that embedded liberalism is necessarily an enduring part of the trade regime. Ruggie concludes his article by foreshadowing the possibility of a new chapter in the social purpose story. In part because of the stresses caused by the embedded liberalism bargain itself, Ruggie notes, the 'foremost force for discontinuity at present' may

---

27 Ibid, at 221.
28 Ruggie, 'Embedded Liberalism', above n 1, at 212.
29 Ibid, at 214.
30 Ibid, footnote in original omitted.
31 For the purposes of this summary, I have skipped over Part 3 of Ruggie's article, which essentially describes how the character of international trade flows themselves seemed to reflect and facilitate the vision of embedded liberalism: Ibid, at 214.
32 Ibid, at 228. Ruggie develops this argument in later articles, see n 7 above.

be 'the resurgent ethos of [neo]liberal capitalism'.[33] The survival of embedded liberalism, he concludes, depends not only on 'renegotiating ... forms of domestic and international social accommodation', but also on retaining an awareness of the need for the trade regime to find a way to accommodate both halves of the grand compromise of embedded liberalism.

II. Revisiting Embedded Liberalism in the Age of Globalization

From about the middle of the 1990s, there was something of a resurgence of interest in Ruggie's notion of embedded liberalism. Much of this interest has come from economists and others interested in the pressure that global economic forces were bringing to bear on traditional measures of social protection. Some of these commentators are motivated by a concern with what they see as the increasing unwillingness or inability of many advanced country governments to pursue measures to ensure domestic stability in global economic conditions. They see this as the unravelling of the embedded liberalism compromise, according to which international economic liberalization had gone hand in hand with domestic measures of social protection. This unravelling is a matter of concern, it is commonly argued, because it may prefigure an erosion of support for the liberalization of trade. Rodrik, for example, whose work has been highly influential in this area, argues for the need to sustain, reinvent and reinvigorate the embedded liberalism compromise in the contemporary economic and political climate.[34] Similar calls can be found throughout the international economic literature, including in a series of articles which Ruggie himself has written, in which he revisits and updates the embedded liberalism story.[35]

In legal trade scholarship, two figures in particular stand out as having drawn most extensively on Ruggie's work. First, in a series of influential articles from 1996 to 1999, Dunoff examined three different theoretical models of the trade regime, of which embedded liberalism was one.[36] In his description of embedded liberalism, he emphasizes the complex and multiple objectives of the postwar trade regime, and the way it facilitated – and was predicated on – governmental intervention to protect

---

33 Ruggie, 'Embedded Liberalism', above n 1, at 229.

34 See, e.g., D. Rodrik and Institute for International Economics, *Has Globalization Gone Too Far?* (1997), also Rodrik's contribution in J. S. Nye and J. D. Donahue, *Governance in a Globalizing World* (2000).

35 E. B. Kapstein, 'Workers and the World Economy', 75(3) *Foreign Affairs* 16 (1996); J. Bhagwati, 'Fear Not: The Global Economy and American Wages', *The New Republic* 36 (1997) and R. O. Keohane, 'The World Political Economy and the Crisis of Embedded Liberalism', in J. H. Goldthorpe (ed.), *Order and Conflict in Contemporary Capitalism* (1984) 15 offer similar readings (at least for these purposes) as Rodrik. Ruggie has revisited the embedded liberalism story in at least five articles since the 1990s; see n 7 above.

36 See the three articles referred to in n 5 above as well as J. L. Dunoff, 'The Global Market as Friend or Foe of Human Rights', 25 (1) *Brooklyn Journal of International Law* 125 (1999).

domestic social interests.[37] He argues, however, that changes in the global economy as well as changes in the trade regime itself fundamentally call into question the ongoing relevance of the embedded liberalism model. As new trade rules reach into areas once considered domestic, he suggests, the domestic policy autonomy which was a constituent element of the embedded liberalism is eroded. Furthermore, he echoes the concern that the ability of national governments to continue to provide social protection threatens to unravel the embedded liberalism bargain. In Dunoff's view, new conditions call for a 'new model' of the trade regime.[38] Second, Howse draws heavily on Ruggie's account in a 2002 article, entitled 'From Politics to Technocracy – And Back Again'.[39] Beginning with a re-telling of Ruggie's story about the GATT's origins ('trade liberalization was embedded within a political commitment, broadly shared among the major players in the trading system of that era, to a progressive, interventionist welfare state'[40]), Howse narrates a story of embedded liberalism's disintegration. Over the first two decades of the GATT, he suggests, the shared vision of embedded liberalism became increasingly hidden, partly as a result of the increasingly technocratic ethos of the regime. Then, from the 1970s, it came under sustained challenge: on the one hand from the 'ascendant economic neo-Right',[41] and on the other from those on the Left who were concerned that the ongoing evolution of the trading system threatened the forms of social protection to which they had traditionally attached importance. Howse is interested primarily in contemporary responses to this disintegration. He critiques a variety of responses offered by those he calls WTO 'insiders', praises the Appellate Body for its first steps in crafting new kinds of consensus and offers a fascinating new vision of his own for the trade regime on the basis of the notions of subsidiarity, participation and an enabling approach to domestic adjustment.[42]

But, quite apart from detailed treatments of this kind, briefer references to embedded liberalism have started frequently to appear in the writings of trade lawyers.[43] A few examples will serve to convey their flavour. Kalderimis, for example, has used embedded liberalism to argue for a particular interpretive approach to trade agreements. He argues that WTO texts reflect the balanced political vision evoked by the notion of embedded liberalism and cautions the trade regime to stay true to this balance if it is to maintain its legitimacy.[44] Steinberg, in a similar discussion of

---

37 See, e.g., Dunoff, 'The Death of the Trade Regime', above n 5, at 738.

38 Dunoff, 'Rethinking International Trade', above n 5, at 377ff.

39 Howse, above n 8.

40 Ibid, at 97.

41 Ibid, at 101.

42 See also R. Howse and K. Nicolaïdis, 'Legitimacy through "Higher Law"? Why Constitutionalizing the WTO is a Step Too Far', in T. Cottier and P. C. Mavroidis (eds), *The Role of the Judge in International Trade Regulation: Experience and Lessons for the WTO* (2003) 307 for an expanded account of this vision.

43 By way of illustration: a Lexis search on the phrase 'embedded liberalism' yields about 70 results, of which about half are substantive (more than passing) references to Ruggie's article.

44 D. Kalderimis, 'Problems of WTO Harmonization and the Virtues of Shields over Swords', 13 (2) *Minnesota Journal of Global Trade* 305 (2004), at 314.

the relevance of the 'object and purpose' of WTO agreements to their interpretation, rejects the assumption that they are purely 'liberal agreements' in favour of the 'more nuanced view' – explicitly based on embedded liberalism – that 'their purposes are mixed'.[45] Knox uses embedded liberalism in a descriptive rather than normative way to support his contention that the WTO does not single-mindedly pursue free trade, but rather 'carefully balance[s] … [Members'] commitment to free trade' with their other interests.[46] Winickoff *et al*. argue that the interpretation and evolution of the SPS agreement should be 'consistent with the original goals of the international trading regime', which (referring to Ruggie) they characterize as embodying 'the idea that free trade cannot be pursued at the expense of other important goals'.[47] Gathii argues that both 'embedded liberalism' and 'neoliberalism' have co-existed in the trade regime from its beginning and that present attempts to constitutionalize the trade regime represent an attempt to undermine what remains of the hold of embedded liberalism over the trade regime.[48] Cho, like many others, uses Ruggie's account in the context of the linkage debate, suggesting that embedded liberalism constituted an 'initial linkage' between trade and non-trade issues in the trade regime.[49]

Embedded liberalism, then, has entered the vocabulary of trade lawyers and occupies an important place on our conceptual horizon. In my view, this is in many respects a promising development: as I will show, attention to Ruggie's insights promises to significantly augment our understanding of the trade regime and trade law. In the next section, I identify those lessons which trade lawyers tend to draw from embedded liberalism, both to make explicit the genuine utility of this work and at the same time to draw attention to the ways in which it might lead us astray.

III. The Dimension of 'Legitimate Social Purpose'

Trade lawyers who draw on Ruggie's work have so far tended to pay most attention to his argument about the 'social purpose' embodied in the postwar trade regime. There are at least three different ways in which this argument has been deployed in contemporary debates among trade lawyers.

---

45 R. H. Steinberg, 'Judicial Lawmaking at the WTO: Discursive, Constitutional, and Political Constraints', *American Journal of International Law* 247 (2004), at 262.

46 Knox, above n 6, at 47. This is advanced as part of his broader argument that trade jurisprudence has become 'greened' in part because of the Appellate Body's responsiveness to a variety of state interests.

47 D. Winickoff *et al*., 'Adjudicating the GM Food Wars: Science, Risk, and Democracy in World Trade Law', 30 *Yale Journal of International Law* 81 (2005), at 107.

48 J. T. Gathii, 'Re-characterizing the Social in the Constitutionalization of the WTO: A Preliminary Analysis', 7 *Widener Law Symposium Journal* 137 (2001).

49 S. Cho, *Free Markets and Social Regulation: A Reform Agenda of the Global Trading System; Toward a New International Economic Law* (2003) 629 and n9. Two other early references to embedded liberalism are Abbott, above n 8 (on which I will draw later), and in G. R. Shell, 'Trade Legalism and International Relations Theory: an Analysis of the World Trade Organization', 44 (5) *Duke Law Journal* 829 (1995).

A. Destabilizing Common Assumptions About the Philosophical and Normative Underpinnings of the Trade Regime

When he wrote *International Regimes, Transactions and Change*, Ruggie noted a tendency among commentators to assume that the postwar trading regime was an 'orthodox liberal regime' (by which he meant something roughly analogous to the variant of *laissez-faire* liberalism of the nineteenth century). One of the main purposes of his article was to expose the inaccuracy of that assumption:

> ... the common tendency to view the postwar regimes as liberal regimes, but with lots of cheating taking place on the domestic side, fails to capture the full complexity of the embedded liberalism compromise.[50]

This lesson is just as relevant today as it was in 1982. The tendency to assume that the current trade regime is an orthodox liberal regime – or more accurately, to see it as a 'liberal' trade regime and to take a particular notion of liberal as self-evident – remains very strong, particularly among trade lawyers.[51] Discussions between supporters and critics of the trade regime, moreover, are often carried out on the (rarely explicitly justified) basis that it is a neoliberal, or quasi-neoliberal, institution. No doubt this is in part because we are, by and large, taught to see liberal trade theory as the fundamental philosophical and theoretical basis on which the regime rests. This tendency to tacitly assume that the trade regime has orthodox (neo)liberalism as its philosophical underpinning is important for at least three reasons. First, it can orient judicial interpretation of WTO texts.[52] There are a number of commentators who have taken exception to the ways in which WTO Panels and the Appellate Body have on occasion appeared to interpret the agreements on the assumption that their object and purpose is solely and simply the liberalization of trade.[53] Second, it has had the result that there is still very little sustained attention devoted to understanding the shared social purpose which characterizes the trade regime or to carefully analysing the kind of liberalism which animates it. Third, even to the extent that the assumption is correct, it is dangerous because it can lead us to conclude that the trade regime is necessarily that way, rather than contingently so. One of the great values of the notion of embedded liberalism, then, is that it destabilizes our assumption that the trade regime is built upon orthodox liberalism. In doing so, it reminds us that many different kinds of open, liberal trading regimes are possible. It re-opens imaginative space to conceive of different forms that a fully liberal trading system may take.[54]

---

50 Ruggie, 'Embedded Liberalism', above n 1, at 214.

51 See Howse, above n 8, at 110.

52 See ibid; also Steinberg, above n 45.

53 See, e.g., R. Howse, 'The Canadian Generic Medicines Panel – A Dangerous Precedent in Dangerous Times', 3 (4) *Journal of World Intellectual Property* 493 (2000).

54 Ilg shares this emphasis of mine on the way embedded liberalism opens up what it is possible to imagine: 'Embedded liberalism reflects a shared belief in the need to promote international stability through transparency and predictability, while at the same time maintaining the ability of states to pursue what Ruggie terms "legitimate social purpose." While policymakers have given up on the ideal of compromise, it is possible to conceive of

There are two reasons why I describe this use of embedded liberalism as *destabilizing*. On the one hand, it is destabilizing for the simple reason just mentioned, that by providing an alternative account of the normative underpinnings of the trade, it tends to undermine and challenge the orthodox account and all the assumptions that go with it. But it is also (more profoundly) destabilizing in that its whole purpose is to uncover ongoing contradictions and tensions within the trade regime. Because Ruggie uses the language of 'consensus' and 'shared understanding', it is easy to forget that, within the world that he paints, conflict, dissonance and contradiction are *prior to* consensus and are the fundamental characteristics of social life. Ruggie's story of embedded liberalism begins by highlighting the fundamentally competing objectives of the postwar trade regime: the preservation of domestic stability and the pursuit of multilateralism in trade. He thus suggests that, in an important sense, the trade regime rests on, and is constituted by, such contradictory impulses. Embedded liberalism is the name he gives for the compromise which evolved between these two impulses, but it is clear that he does not conceive of this as a stable equilibrium or a final resolution. It is only that as long as the major players broadly shared a commitment to embedded liberalism the contradiction on which the trade regime was built could be largely hidden from view.[55]

One of the effects of the rediscovery of embedded liberalism by contemporary trade scholars, then, is that this submerged and unresolved ambiguity is brought back to the surface – a light is shone on some fundamental tensions which the trade community as a whole has for so long been able to ignore. Finnemore refers to the process by which '[u]nresolved normative tensions in a set of social compromises at one time may be the mobilizing force for attacks on that set of social arrangements later'.[56] In my understanding, it is precisely to this end, as a mobilizing force for the destabilization of contemporary arrangements, that embedded liberalism is being deployed by many contemporary trade lawyers.

Dunoff's notion of 'embedded legalism' is a good example.[57] This is a concept which Dunoff has developed in the context of debate about reform of the WTO's dispute-settlement mechanism and in particular debate about private enforcement of WTO laws. He challenges the prevailing assumption among trade lawyers that the overarching and unitary objective of the dispute-settlement mechanism is strict enforcement of WTO obligations. Compliance, he suggests, has never been the sole nor even the highest value of dispute-settlement processes in the WTO. Instead, he suggests, we should see such processes as a compromise between the need to ensure compliance and the need to provide a degree of flexibility – a complex and evolving

---

a system that has been built on socially determined policies instead of one that competitively strips them away'. See M. Ilg, 'Environmental Harm and Dilemmas of Self-Interest: Does International Law Exhibit Collective Learning?', 18 *Tulane Environmental Law Journal* 59 (2004), at 92.

55 Cf. Howse, above n 8.

56 M. Finnemore, *National Interests in International Society* (1996) 135.

57 Dunoff, 'Death, Dumping and Domestic Courts: Private Enforcement of WTO Norms', forthcoming. These ideas were also presented by Professor Dunoff at the British Institute's International and Comparative Law's Fifth Annual WTO Conference, 17 May 2005.

compromise between legalism and pragmatism, between rule- and power-based approaches to dispute settlement. In a creative reference to Ruggie's work, Dunoff calls this the 'compromise of embedded legalism'. What is important in the present context is the underlying impulse of Dunoff's argument: like Ruggie, he seeks to recover the unresolved and constitutive ambiguity on which the trade regime (or some element of it) is based. And he does this in order to destabilize the current 'solution' to this ambiguity, to revisit the processes by which it was temporarily hidden from view, and thereby to open up imaginative and rhetorical space for the formation of a new grand compromise.

This form of scholarship may be contrasted with those commentators who take the lesson of embedded liberalism one step further. There are some who argue that embedded liberalism not only represents the normative vision which underlay the trade regime at its inception, but – at least to the extent that the agreements are unchanged – it *remains* so.[58] In my view, this is almost certainly a misleading conclusion. For one thing, it overestimates the extent to which the normative vision of the trade regime is deducible from the text of trade agreements. It also underestimates the extent to which the trade regime (like any social institution) is characterized by continuing contradiction and tension, as just explained. And it underestimates the extent to which the 'social purpose' on which the trade regime is predicated varies with changes in underlying ideational, political, social and material conditions. Indeed, as I mentioned earlier, there are by now numerous commentators who have charted the various ways in which embedded liberalism has at least partially disintegrated as a shared political vision. I therefore prefer a more modest formulation of the lesson to draw from *International Regimes, Transactions and Change*. We cannot make assumptions about the character of the present trade regime. Nor can we simply deduce its underlying character from its concrete elements, such as the text of its constituent agreements. Rather, understanding and specifying the social purpose contingently embodied in the present trade regime requires sustained, direct analysis. More particularly, any claim that the present regime is 'neoliberal' (or any analogous claim) must be accompanied by an account of precisely how, if at all, embedded liberalism endures – and if it does not, a compelling explanatory account of its demise and replacement.[59]

It is a legitimate question how precisely lawyers are to conduct a direct analysis of 'intersubjective understandings' embodied in the trade regime and what skills we might bring to the task. No doubt this is in part a question which must be answered pragmatically, in the course of an attempted answer. But, as I elaborate further below, it may not be as unfamiliar a task as it appears, particularly once we realize that legal discourse is a key site in which such intersubjective understandings are formed. We are, after all, trained to read law not just as a set of rules or texts, but as a living jurisprudence. We are accustomed to identifying deeper trends and

---

58 See, e.g., Kalderimis, above n 44; Steinberg, above n 45; Winickoff *et al.*, above n 47, as well as the remarks of Sanford Gaines referred to in F. M. Abbott, 'International Trade and Social Welfare: The New Agenda', 17 *Comparative Labor Law Journal* 338 (1996).

59 Howse, above n 8, is clearly the outstanding example of this kind of account in current trade law scholarship.

conceptual structures in bodies of law which give them their coherence and govern their evolution. When members of the Appellate Body make decisions, and when lawyers interpret and critique those decisions, we all necessarily draw on generally shared ideas concerning what the trade regime is all about, what its core objectives and values are and so on. In many ways, the task set out in the previous paragraph is no more than making such understandings themselves the object of our analysis and the subject of our critique.

B. Reformulating the Terms of Current Debates Among Trade Lawyers

If embedded liberalism can help us better to understand what the trade regime *is* (or at the very least *was*), it also helps us to engage more productively with the question of what the trade regime *should* be. Ruggie took issue with hegemonic stability theory for the narrowness of its analytical optic. It tended to analyse the international economic order along only a single axis of change – either more open or more closed, depending on the existence of an economic hegemon. Ruggie introduced the concept of social purpose, therefore, as a second axis of change, to help us understand the character of the trading system in a more nuanced way.

The introduction of this second axis of analysis can be used to enrich and re-orient contemporary debates about what the current trade regime should be like. To a very large degree, current debates about the trade regime are understood by many to be about *how open* the international trading system should be. For example, there is much discussion about whether and how the trade regime should balance its trade liberalization objectives against other legitimate objectives, such as the protection of the environment or of human rights.[60] These other legitimate objectives are said to have a bearing on how far we should go down the road of liberalizing trade, how quickly we should go down it and what other measures we should be pursuing while we do. Overwhelmingly, these debates are framed as a search for the appropriate 'boundaries'[61] or 'limits'[62] of trade liberalization. While the 'how open?' question is obviously an important one, Ruggie's notion of social purpose reminds us that there is another debate we should be having. We should be discussing not only how open the trading regime should be, but also on what shared social purpose it should be predicated. To put the same point differently: not only should we be asking how far we should travel down the road to an imagined 'endpoint' of free trade, we should

---

60 I am referring here to the so-called 'linkage' debate. There is a very large literature on linkage issues, but important published symposia include: 'The Boundaries of the WTO' 96 (1) *American Journal of International Law* (2002); 'Linkage as Phenomenon: Linking the Trade Linkage Debate' 19 *University of Pennsylvania Journal of International Economic Law* (1998); 'Institutional Conundrums of an Expanded Trade Regime' 7 *Widener Law Symposium Journal* (2001), among others.

61 See, e.g., the Symposium entitled 'The Boundaries of the WTO', papers from which are published in 96 (1) *American Journal of International Law* (2002).

62 See, e.g., F. M. Abbott, T. Cottier and J. H. Jackson, 'The Limits of International Trade: Workers' Protection, the Environment and Other Human Rights', *Proceedings of the American Society of International Law 2000* (2000), 219.

also be questioning the particular endpoint we have in mind. There is more than one possible vision of what free trade means – more than one vision of what trade liberalization is all about – depending on (among other things) the shared social purpose which constitutes it.

This point, it should be noted, is rarely made explicit in the work of trade lawyers drawing on embedded liberalism, and in fact in my view is positively obscured in much of it. It is common to re-tell embedded liberalism as a milder or more restrained version of orthodox liberalism. Steinberg, for example, draws from embedded liberalism the lesson that WTO agreements 'embody both liberal and protectionist elements', rather than a different form of liberalism.[63] This is a way of talking which (at least on the surface) buys into the pervasive, and surprisingly powerful, myth that criticism of the current trade liberalization project indicates a sympathy with protectionism and that any toleration by the trade regime of what is currently perceived as a trade barrier represents a concession to protectionism. It is precisely this myth which Ruggie's account requires us to question. Embedded liberalism teaches us that no one group has a monopoly on what it means to support free trade and therefore that advocating change is not necessarily the same thing as advocating a weakening of our commitment to free trade.

A point of clarification may be necessary here, to avoid some confusion. The argument I make in the previous paragraphs appears to assume that the degree of openness of an international economic order, and the social purpose which is embodied in it, are independent variables. In fact, while neither is fully dependent on (determined by) the other, nor are they fully independent of one another. Ruggie makes it clear that embedded liberalism involved sacrificing some potential gains from trade, slowing the process of liberalization, shaping it in certain ways, and confining it within certain limits.[64] In other words, a movement along the 'social purpose' axis, from orthodox liberalism to embedded liberalism, did seem to entail a small but significant move along the 'openness' axis, away from greater openness. But this does not alter the crucial point that (contrary to the apparent assumptions of much contemporary debate) disagreements about the proper nature and form of the trade regime cannot be boiled down to questions about the optimum degree of openness. The salient and essential difference between the Pax Britannia and the postwar trade regime, just like the salient difference between the postwar trade regime and the current one, is not in their degree of openness. The essence of the difference is, in Ruggie's terms, in their 'social purpose'. One choice we have when designing an international economic order is the level of openness it is to entail. Another choice is the shared social purpose we want it to embody. They are not fully independent choices, but they are different. Another value of Ruggie's notion of embedded liberalism, then, is that it helps us to reformulate the terms of critical debate, so as to concentrate more directly on the latter. It encourages us to discuss and define a vision of social purpose which is appropriate for the trade regime in the contemporary age.

---

63 Steinberg, above n 45, 262.
64 Ruggie, 'Embedded Liberalism', above n 1 at 213.

C. Recovering the Spirit of Embedded Liberalism

This brings me to a third lesson which many commentators draw from Ruggie's discussion of social purpose. For many who are attracted to the concept of embedded liberalism, its most important feature is that it offers a vision of the trade regime in which a commitment to social protection was combined with, indeed inseparable from, efforts to liberalize international trade. The genius of the postwar negotiators who devised embedded liberalism, on this view, is not only that they managed to combine the two, but that they realized that the two must be combined if trade liberalization is to be sustainable in the long term. We need, so the story continues, to relearn that lesson. We need to reinvent embedded liberalism for the global age by finding new ways and new forms through which to combine social protection with a continuing commitment to liberal trade. For many, this is *the* lesson to be drawn from the concept of embedded liberalism. Interestingly, while Ruggie explicitly declined to make these claims in *International Regimes, Transactions and Change*, he has since done so in later articles.[65]

It is important to register the nature, and the ambition, of this use of Ruggie's original concept. These commentators are, quite clearly, not simply advocating a return to the past. Embedded liberalism is being used here as an ideational frame for the production of new policy ideas, just as the notion of 'reinventing embedded liberalism' is being used to focus and direct creative energies and ideas. The historical rise and fall of embedded liberalism, furthermore, is being used as a narrative through which such proposals are given political significance. Ruggie's historical work on the trade regime gives these policy ideas an important theoretical and empirical foundation, while the narrative of embedded liberalism serves as an ideational 'focal point'[66] for the generation of new political coalitions. In short, the story of embedded liberalism is seen by these commentators as a conceptual tool for facilitating, energizing and crystallizing 'new trade thinking' in the broadest sense. While I fully appreciate the crucial role that such 'big ideas' can play in progressing policy debates, I am concerned that thinking in terms of reinventing embedded liberalism may actually *constrain* the generation of useful policy proposals, rather than facilitate it. This is for three related reasons.

First, there is a risk that our imagination will be limited by the past institutional forms of embedded liberalism. This may seem an unwarranted concern, given the emphasis which is typically placed precisely on designing new institutional forms in which to clothe the new embedded liberalism. But to some degree, there is already evidence of this imaginative constraint. The era of embedded liberalism was predicated upon the institutional forms of the welfare state, and the function of social protection was largely carried out through those forms. As a result, embedded liberalism shaped the trade regime in a largely negative way: by creating a *permissive*

---

65 Ibid at 238. But compare his later writings, n 7 above.

66 J. Goldstein and R. O. Keohane, 'Ideas and Foreign Policy: An Analytical Framework', in J. Goldstein and R. O. Keohane (eds), *Ideas and Foreign Policy: Beliefs, Institutions, and Political Change* (1993) 3 at 17.

environment for the pursuit of social protection through the welfare state.[67] While it is true that the trade regime also played an enabling role in respect of welfare state policies, this role was more diffuse and tends to be remembered less today.[68] There is risk, then, that reinventing embedded liberalism for the trade regime may come simply to mean recreating a permissive environment in the trade regime for the pursuit of (new and old) domestic measures of social protection – the creation of new 'exceptions, qualifications safeguards' and so on.[69] Already this seems to be the tendency in much of the work by trade lawyers.[70] But, as Howse has already noted, there are indications that a more positive, facilitative role for the trade regime may be necessary in present conditions, particularly with respect to developing countries.[71] To the extent that some of the traditional tools of social protection are less effective or no longer available for some governments, it may be that the trade regime has a positive role to play in regenerating that capability. Thinking in terms of 'reinventing embedded liberalism' may direct our attention away from creating such a positive role for the WTO.

Second, there is a risk that our imagination will be limited by the past ideational forms of embedded liberalism. The story of embedded liberalism is based on a series of constitutive ideas. For example, Dunoff notes that it is predicated upon a particular distinction between matters of domestic and international concern, between matters of trade policy and social policy, and between matters of a public and private nature.[72] The notion of 'social protection' itself, central to defining embedded liberalism, rests on particular ideas about who is in need of protection, who bears the responsibility of protection and what kinds of risks are worthy of protection. As Blackett observes, the embedded liberalism narrative tends to answer these questions within limited confines of a single-nation optic.[73] While it is admittedly perfectly possible to reconceive such constitutive ideas, my concern is that thinking in terms of 'reinventing embedded liberalism' will not help us to do so. Our thinking may instead come to conform to categories which risk no longer being relevant. In other words, reinventing embedded liberalism may implicitly encourage us to base our thinking on an outdated and impractical version of (say) the distinction between international and domestic matters. It may likewise encourage us to continue conceiving of distributive justice concerns primarily within a single-nation optic, rather than on a broader foundation.

---

67 See Ruggie, 'Embedded Liberalism', above n 1, at 213. The argument that I am making here mirrors that of Howse, above n 8, at 116.

68 Howse does make the important point, however, that this enabling role did exist: Howse, above n 8, at 95.

69 Ruggie, 'Embedded Liberalism', above n 1, at 213.

70 An important example might be P. M. Nichols, 'Trade Without Values', 90 (2) *Northwestern University Law Review* 658 (1996).

71 Howse, above n 8, at 116.

72 See, e.g., Dunoff, 'The Death of the Trade Regime', above n 5, at 751.

73 A. Blackett, 'Toward Social Regionalism in the Americas', 23 *Comparative Labor Law and Policy Journal* 901 (2002), at 911.

Third, I am concerned that our imagination may be constrained by past political priorities. As Ruggie and others since him have told it, the story of the trade regime has 'two themes', the first relating to 'multilateralism' and the second relating to 'domestic stability'.[74] Stylized, the story of embedded liberalism is about the marriage of these two themes in the postwar order, the disintegration of the marriage with the demise of social protection and its subsequent rejuvenation in the future. It is important to remember that this collective sense of what the trade regime was all about responded to – was a creation of – contemporary perceptions about the most pressing political priorities of the time. But, from a twenty-first century perspective, there are some deafening silences in this story. There is, above all, no development theme in the embedded liberalism story: development does not figure in the self-understanding of the trade regime and facilitating development does not count high among its purposes. The story leaves out, in Dillon's words, 'vestiges of colonialism, global racism, and a long past of global exploitation'[75] – as well as more positive understandings of how the trade regime figured in postwar development efforts. Similarly, there is no explicit environment plot and no account of how environmental trends and values have shaped the self-understanding of the trade regime.

It is not sufficient to respond that embedded liberalism is only one story among many and only purports to address some aspects of the trade regime. We shall see below that the stories we tell about the trade regime are partly constitutive, in that they contribute to the creation of a shared sense of what the trade regime is about and in doing so transform the trade regime itself. For this reason, silences in a story can lead to inattention at the level of policy. It will come as no surprise, then, that the era of embedded liberalism has been criticized by numerous scholars – Ruggie included – for the way in which it tended to purchase domestic stability in industrialized countries by externalizing the costs of adjustment to developing countries.[76]

More generally, it is important not to eulogize the period of embedded liberalism in the history of the trade regime. Although Ruggie talks of consensus and shared vision, we must remember that the creation of a shared framework is often bought at the cost of marginalizing and silencing important concerns and important groups. The relative absence of a vision for development in the original trade regime, for example, is thrown into some relief by Keynes' words, spoken at the Bretton Woods conference:

> Twenty-one countries have been invited which clearly have nothing to contribute and will merely encumber the ground, namely, Colombia, Costa Rica, Dominica, Ecuador, Salvador, Guatemala, Haiti, Honduras, Liberia, Nicaragua, Panama, Paraguay, Philippines,

---

74 Ruggie, 'Embedded Liberalism', above n 1, at 209.

75 S. Dillon, 'A Farewell to "Linkage": International Trade Law and Global Sustainability Indicators', 55 (1) *Rutgers Law Review* 87 (2002), at 152.

76 L. Anell and B. Nygren, *The Developing Countries and the World Economic Order* (1980); Ruggie, 'Embedded Liberalism', above n 1, at 229; D. Tussie and D. Glover, *The Developing Countries in World Trade: Policies and Bargaining Strategies* (1993); J. Hills, 'A Global Industrial Policy: US Hegemony and the GATT', 1 (2) *Review of International Political Economy* 257 (1994); and Tussie's contribution in C. Murphy and R. Tooze, *The New International Political Economy* (1991).

Venezuela, Peru Uruguay, Ethiopia, Iceland, Iran, Iraq and Luxembourg – the most monstrous monkey-house assembled for years.[77]

We are still living with the legacy of attitudes and decisions, formed and made decades ago that certain kinds of issues could safely and legitimately be ignored – chief among them the distributional consequences of trade, development, and to a lesser extent the labour and employment consequences of trade liberalization. In my view, focusing too much on reinvigorating embedded liberalism runs a significant risk of perpetuating the marginalization of the same issues and groups. In my view, we should not 'reinvent embedded liberalism', but rather (to speak with Dunoff[78]) 'rethink international trade' altogether. Embedded liberalism was a useful response to (and product of) some of the most pressing social issues facing influential founding members at the GATT's inception. But we now have a different set of pressing issues and perhaps we need a wholly new story to respond to them.

IV. The Constructivist Theoretical Framework of Embedded Liberalism

I now come to what I believe to be the most important aspect of Ruggie's work on the trade regime, an aspect which has so far received very little attention from most trade scholars. *International Regimes, Transactions and Change* is routinely cited by international relations scholars as an early example of a constructivist (or reflectivist[79]) approach to the study of international institutions. In 1982, of course, the term 'constructivism' did not exist in this context,[80] and the constructivist challenge to prevailing theories of international relations had yet to be rigorously formulated. But in the decades since then, Ruggie has played a central role in the development of constructivist thinking, and *International Regimes, Transactions and Change* has come to be seen as an important milestone in the progress of his ideas.

Constructivist thinking has developed in dialogue with modern variants of both realist and liberal approaches to the study of international relations. It takes issue with what it sees as their common materialist and rationalist (or functionalist) foundation and prefers to place emphasis instead on ideational and cognitive dimensions of social life. While there are many variants of constructivist thought, Ruggie's description of its core elements (written in 1998) represents a useful summation:

At bottom, constructivism concerns the issue of human consciousness: the role that it plays in international relations, and the implications for the logic and methods of social inquiry of taking it seriously. Constructivists hold the view that the building blocks of international reality are ideational as well as material; that ideational factors have normative as well as instrumental dimensions; that they express not only individual but

---

77 G. M. Meier, *Emerging from Poverty: the Economics that Really Matters* (1984) 11.

78 Dunoff, 'Rethinking International Trade', above n 5.

79 The term 'reflectivist' was coined by Keohane in 'International Institutions: Two Approaches', 32 *International Studies Quarterly* 379 (1988), but constructivist is more commonly used today.

80 It was, by all accounts, first used in relation to IR theory by Onuf in *World of Our Making: Rules and Rule in Social Theory and International Relations* (1989).

also collective intentionality; and that the meaning and significance of ideational factors are not independent of time and place.[81]

This leads to a unique approach to the study of international institutions. Perhaps, its most distinct contribution is to our understanding of the nature of regimes – in particular, their intersubjective quality. This leads, in turn, to an enriched understanding of the determinants of regimes (how they originate, what constitutes them and by what processes they change) and their consequences (the way they impact on behaviour and outcomes).

To my mind, perhaps the most valuable and least well understood feature of *International Regimes, Transactions and Change* is that it sets out many of the core features of constructivist analysis of institutions and illustrates them through an investigation of the postwar trade regime. In the sections which follow, I try to set out some of its core features, and demonstrate some of the ways in which attention to constructivist insights have the potential to enhance trade lawyers' understanding of trade law and the trade regime, enrich our research programme and change the way we think about what it is that we as lawyers do.

A. The Nature of International Institutions: The Trade Regime as an 'Intersubjective Framework of Meaning'

The standard definition of regimes describes them as 'sets of implicit or explicit principles, norms, rules, and decision-making procedures around which actors' expectations converge in a given area of international relations'.[82] At the start of *International Regimes, Transactions and Change*, Ruggie reflects on this definition in a passage which it is worth setting out in full:

> International regimes have been defined as social institutions around which actor expectations converge in a given area of international relations. Accordingly, as is true of any social institution, international regimes limit the discretion of their constituent units to decide and act on issues that fall within the regime's domain. And, as is also true of any social institution, ultimate expression in converging expectations and limited discretion gives international regimes an intersubjective quality. To this extent, international regimes are akin to language; and language is inherently "dialogical", in that it must be shared to be effective. The constituent units of a regime, like speakers of a common language, generally have little difficulty in determining what even an entirely new usage signifies. Should it be technically inappropriate or incorrect, they nevertheless may still "understand" it – in the dual sense of being able to comprehend it and willing to acquiesce in it.

> Thus, it follows that we know international regimes not simply by some descriptive inventory of their concrete elements, but also by their generative grammar, the underlying principles of order and meaning that shape the manner of their formation and transformation. Likewise, we know deviation from regimes not simply by a categorical description of acts

---

81 Ruggie, 'Embedded Liberalism', above n 1, at 33.
82 Krasner, above n 2, at 2.

that are undertaken, but also by the intentionality and acceptability others attribute to those acts in the context of an intersubjective framework of meaning.[83]

This fundamental theoretical move, of emphasizing the nature of regimes as 'intersubjective frameworks of meaning', is one of foundational elements of constructivist approaches to the study of international institutions,[84] and it is worth pausing to elaborate it.

How and why, first of all, does Ruggie use the word 'intersubjective'? Most simply, he uses it to stress that regimes are mental phenomena – this much is obvious, given that regimes consist of sets of shared expectations (beliefs) about how actors will and should behave in their trade relations with one another. More importantly, Ruggie is emphasizing that the trade regime is made up of 'shared' beliefs – but here shared is used in a very specific sense. They are not only shared in the simple sense that they are beliefs which are the same across a number of different individuals, but they are also shared in the sense of collective. In other words, the beliefs or expectations which make up the trade regime exist in individuals' minds not in the form 'I believe' but in the form 'we believe' or 'I believe only as part of our believing'.[85] They express collective not individual intentionality, and in that sense are 'intersubjective'. This intersubjective nature gives regimes some distinctive qualities. For one thing, they exist and take the form that they do, precisely because the relevant actors believe that they do and act accordingly. For another, they change as those actors' shared ideas about them change. Moreover, because they are based on collective intentionality (a sense of 'we-feeling'[86]) they are dialogic in character, in the sense that they are produced by constitutive processes of communication and interpretation.[87] As I explain below, these qualities have implications for the way we study the trade regime and the questions we ask about it.

What, secondly, is meant by a 'framework of meaning'? Ruggie is keen to correct the common tendency to see regimes as fully specified by an 'inventory' of the rules of conduct and decision-making processes that they establish. Treating the trade regime in this way, he believes, 'omits a great many things that regimes are and do in addition to embodying regulative rules'.[88] Two are particularly important. First, the trade regime does not just regulate behaviour, it provides cognitive scripts which give meaning to behaviour, and thus make social action (including international co-operation) possible:

---

83 The passage I use here is a very slightly modified version included in Ruggie's 1998 collection of his own essays: Ruggie, *Constructing the World Polity*, above n 1, at 63. While the changes are minor (less than ten words and the inclusion of a new paragraph break), they tend to make the passage clearer.

84 B. A. Simmons and L. L. Martin, 'International Organizations and Institutions', in W. Carlsnaes, T. Risse-Kappen and B. A. Simmons (eds), *Handbook of International Relations* (2002) 192 at 198.

85 I take this formulation from Ruggie, *Constructing the World Polity*, above n 1, at 20.

86 Ibid, at 37.

87 See also A. Wendt, *Social Theory of International Politics* (1999) 160 and surrounding for a useful discussion of intersubjectivity and related concepts.

88 Ruggie, *Constructing the World Polity*, above n 1, 96.

... the Bretton Woods monetary negotiations and the corresponding negotiations to establish an international trade regime produced more than standards of behaviour and rules of conduct. They also established intersubjective frameworks of meaning that included a shared narrative about the conditions that had made these regimes necessary and what they were intended to accomplish[.][89]

The trade regime, therefore, consists in part of a set of collectively agreed answers to questions about why the regime itself exists and what is its domain of operation, about the kinds of roles that member states are expected to play, the objectives they are expected to pursue, and so on. Ruggie's story of embedded liberalism should therefore be understood as, in large part, an attempt to specify this framing narrative as it stood in the early 1980s.

Second, the trade regime consists not only of regulative rules, but also of 'constitutive rules'.[90] Where regulative rules regulate (prohibit, require and constrain) antecedently-existing social activity or behaviour, constitutive rules create the very possibility of a social activity. The rules of chess are a good example: it is not the case that 'there were a lot of people pushing bits of wood around on boards, and in order to prevent them from bumping into each other ... [so that] we had to regulate the activity'.[91] Rather, the rules of chess create the possibility of 'playing chess'. Constitutive rules define the rules of the game – who plays, what the objectives are, what roles are to be assumed, what particular kinds of activity count as in the context of the game.[92] Constitutive rules are logically prior to regulative rules, because they define the domain in which regulative rules take effect. To say that the trade regime embodies not just regulative but also constitutive rules, then, is to say that the trade regime does not just regulate trade policy, but sets the conditions of possibility of international economic co-operation, by setting out the 'rules of the game' by which actors understand what it is that they are doing. Again, *International Regimes, Transactions and Change* highlights precisely this constitutive dimension of the trade regime. It describes, through the lens of embedded liberalism, the rules of the game which were established in the postwar era.

Finally, where rationalist theories of international institutions tend to focus on behavioural dynamics (describing and explaining patterns of behaviour among regime participants), constructivist approaches focus on their communicative dynamics.[93] Participants in the trade regime do not just act and respond to others' actions. They also communicate their intentions and beliefs, and interpret the behaviour of other participants. For constructivists, the trade regime cannot properly be understood without attention to this communicative and cognitive dimension, because 'interpretations of actions by actors are an irreducible part of their collective existence'.[94] Indeed, precisely because of regimes' intersubjective character,

---

89 Ibid, at 21.

90 This terminology is relatively widely used; a good discussion is ibid, at 22.

91 This example comes from the work of John Searle, referred to in ibid, at 22.

92 Ibid.

93 By separating these two, I am not suggesting that they do not mutually influence one another (indeed, that is the whole point). See generally, ibid, at 12.

94 F. Kratochwil, 17 (2) *Millennium Journal of International Studies* 263 (1988), at 277.

'communicative dynamics may tell us far more about ... a regime ... than overt behaviour alone'.[95] Again, this is one of the most important lessons of *International Regimes, Transactions and Change* (made explicit in Ruggie's re-interpretation of the New Protectionism), but it is one which has gone largely unnoticed by trade lawyers.

Why are these insights important for trade lawyers? For one thing, we are necessarily students of the trade regime, not just of 'trade law' narrowly conceived. *International Regimes, Transactions and Change* opens our eyes to important and under-explored dimensions of our subject of study and provides a rigorous theoretical framework for their examination.[96] But there is also a more immediate relevance to the study of trade law itself. Since trade law is as much a social institution as the trade regime (we may conceive of them as analytically distinct but overlapping, and perhaps mutually constitutive, social institutions), then insights into the nature of the trade regime apply equally to trade law. Like the trade regime, we may expect trade law to have not just a regulative but a constitutive function. One lesson we may learn from *International Regimes, Transactions and Change*, therefore, may be the need to pay greater attention to specifying constitutive rules and explaining changes to them over time. We may enquire the part that trade law plays in generating, sustaining and transforming the shared narratives which form a constitutive part of the trade regime. Conversely, we may seek to determine what role this shared narrative plays in the ongoing interpretation and administration of legal rules and norms. We may be prompted, moreover, to enquire into the communicative dynamics of trade law (and trade lawyers) and analyse their relationship to the communicative dynamics of the trade regime as whole, rather than focusing only on trade law's effects within the realm of behaviour.[97] Constructivist insights into the fundamental nature of the trade regime, in sum, facilitate insights into the nature and operation of trade law and promise to significantly expand our research agenda as trade lawyers. The next two sections try to spell out some of these general implications in more detail.

B. The Determinants of the Trade Regime: Explaining and Shaping Institutional Change in the Trade Regime

Taken as a whole, trade lawyers' understanding of the determinants of the trade regime owes much to various versions of (neo)realist, institutionalist and (neo)liberal theories of international relations.[98] We have internalized the core realist insight that

---

95 Ruggie, *Constructing the World Polity*, above n 1, at 98.

96 For example, it is possible to see the linkage debate as an attempt by trade lawyers to talk about the intersubjective dimension of the trade regime. That debate is characterized by talk of the 'ethos', 'spirit' and 'values' of the regime. Attention to Ruggie's theoretical framework can help us to identify precisely what it is that we are talking about.

97 For a fascinating argument grounded in a concept of law as communicative practice, see S. Cho, 'The WTO's Gemeinschaft', 56 *Alabama Law Review* 483 (2004).

98 This observation has been made on a number of occasions by other commentators: J. Goldstein, 'Ideas, Institutions, and American Trade Policy', 42 (1) *International Organization* 179 (1988), at 180; J. Goldstein, *Ideas, Interests, and American Trade Policy* (1993) 238; Abbott, above n 8.

the distribution of capability in the international system is a powerful explanatory variable for behaviour. While this does not mean that we see the trade regime as purely epiphenomenal, it does mean that we tend to see many features of the trade regime as reflecting the interests of powerful nations.[99] (Moreover, in this context, we understand power primarily in material, economic terms.) This in turn shapes the research that we carry out: trade lawyers have spent a lot of time, for example, analysing the ways in which WTO rules and decision-making procedures marginalize – or not – the interests of less-powerful developing countries and arguing for institutional changes to redress the perceived imbalance. To follow Krasner's analysis, we see the trade regime in this context as an independent 'source of power' which feeds back into, and modifies, the underlying distribution of capabilities on which it is based.[100]

Trade lawyers have also incorporated institutionalist approaches – particularly, in the rational choice tradition – into our basic understanding of the WTO. Game theoretic explanations of the trade regime, focusing on patterns of incentives among rational self-interested actors, are relatively common. Furthermore, we have been adept at taking on board some of the primary lessons of liberal international relations theories. We routinely look inside the border and understand trade policy choices by governments as a function of the demands made by domestic pressure groups.[101] More generally, we are comfortable with a framework which sees sub-state and non-state actors as heavily involved in influencing the character and form of the international trading system. This has also significantly influenced our work on institutional design: there is a very large and growing body of work by trade lawyers focusing on the question of participation in WTO decision-making as a primary mode of institutional change – the question of which actors and which interests should have a direct influence on WTO decisions.

We have, however, been less efficient in incorporating constructivist insights into our understanding of how the WTO evolves and is shaped. This is, it should be noted, in contrast with international lawyers working in other areas, some of

---

99 See, e.g., A. M. Slaughter, A. S. Tulumello and S. Wood, 'International Law and International Relations Theory: A New Generation of Interdisciplinary Scholarship', 92 (3) *American Journal of International Law* 367 (1998), at 376; Steinberg, above n 45; F. M. Abbott, 'The WTO Medicines Decision: World Pharmaceutical Trade and the Protection of Public Health', 99 (2) *American Journal of International Law* 317 (2005). It is worth noting also that there are few realists nowadays who see international institutions as purely epiphenomenal.

100 S. D. Krasner, 'Regimes and the Limits of Realism: Regimes as Autonomous Variables', in S. D. Krasner (ed.), *International Regimes* (Ithaca, NY: Cornell University Press 1983) 355 at 364.

101 Goldstein, 'Ideas, Institutions', above n 98, at 180; H. V. Milner, 'International Trade', in W. Carlsnaes, T. Risse-Kappen and B.A. Simmons (eds), *Handbook of International Relations* (2002) 448 at 450; Abbott, above n 8. A distinction should be drawn between what I am referring here to as liberal IR theorists and their 'neo' counterparts, who are often criticized for 'black-boxing' the state. See Finnemore, above n 56, 143. (There is also the question of how those interests are mediated by different domestic political institutions – which may give greater or lesser scope for pressure groups to affect decision-making.)

whom have drawn considerably and explicitly on constructivist literature.[102] One consequence of this is that scholars of the trade regime typically emphasize material factors over ideational factors in our explanations of the trade regime.[103] It is true that in recent years a number of liberal IR scholars have attempted to address this imbalance and give greater attention to ideational factors in their work. Goldstein's fascinating research on the role of ideas in the formation of US trade policy stands out in this regard.[104] Dunoff has already called for trade lawyers to pay more attention to this important body of work, and (much as I see great value in it) I do not intend to reiterate that call here.[105] The work of these theorists is different from that of constructivists, in that it still operates largely within a rational choice framework. That is to say that these theorists still tend to explain behaviour in terms of the interaction of preference-maximizing, pre-constituted actors[106] and they still largely see international institutions as functionally determined. My focus in this section, then, is on the distinctive insights which constructivist theories yield into the role of ideational factors in shaping the character of the trade regime, as exemplified in *International Regimes, Transactions and Change*. My claim is that attention to the constructivist underpinnings of embedded liberalism can augment our understanding of what makes the trade regime the way it is and therefore expand the ways we currently go about explaining, generating and shaping institutional change at the WTO.

Since, as was set out in the previous section, the trade regime is at base a mental phenomenon, or cognitive construct, it follows that the trade regime is in a quintessential sense *made up of* ideas. The intersubjective framework of meaning embodied in the trade regime, according to constructivist thinking, is constituted by a set of ideas about how the world is and how it works. Kenneth Abbott makes this point clear:

---

102 For a small selection, see Slaughter, Tulumello and Wood, above n 99; K. W. Abbott, 'International Relations Theory, International Law, and the Regime Governing Atrocities in Internal Conflicts', 93 (2) *American Journal of International Law* 361 (1999); J. Brunnee and S. J. Toope, 'International Law and Constructivism: Elements of an Interactional Theory of International Law', 39 (1) *Columbia Journal of Transnational Law* 19 (2000) as well as various contributions to O. A. Hathaway and H. H. Koh, *Foundations of International Law and Politics* (2005).

103 I take the terms 'material' and 'ideational' from standard terminology in debates common to IR theory (e.g., Wendt, above n 87, at 32).

104 Goldstein, '*Ideas, Institutions*', above n 98; Goldstein, Ideas, Interests, above n 98; J. Goldstein and R. O. Keohane, *Ideas and Foreign Policy: Beliefs, Institutions, and Political Change* (1993). Others include R. Jervis, *Perception and Misperception in International Politics* (1976); R. Little, S. Smith and A British International Studies (eds), *Belief Systems and International Relations* (1988); B. Weingast, 'A Rational Choice Perspective on the Role of Ideas: Shared Belief Systems and State Sovereignty in International Co-operation', 23 *Politics and Society* 449 (1995); N. Woods, 'Economic Ideas and International Relations: Beyond Rational Neglect', 39 *International Studies Quarterly* 161 (1995).

105 Dunoff, 'Rethinking International Trade', above n 5, 377.

106 See Goldstein, *Ideas, Interests*, above n 98, at 9; Ruggie, *Constructing the World Polity*, above n 1, 17; Wendt, above n 87, 118.

Economic and political structures are not corporeal things; they owe their existence to
constitutive ideas, constitutive in the sense of defining or creating a social institution ...
that would otherwise not exist ... [This] is true of ... social constructs like ... international
regimes. ... As the underlying ideas change, the norms, rules and institutions that embody
them, at all levels of political activity, evolve along with them.[107]

In *International Regimes, Transactions and Change*, Ruggie selects one subset of
these constitutive ideas – namely 'legitimate social purpose', or ideas about the
proper role of the state in relation to the market – and shows how they came to be
embodied in the postwar regime. He shows how the trade regime rested also on a
constitutive idea about what trade liberalization was: trade liberalization, in his view,
was understood fundamentally as 'non-discrimination'.[108] (In fact, to be clear, the
relationship between such ideas and the regimes is one of *mutual* constitution: it is true
that the shared narrative of embedded liberalism rests on a particular understanding
of what 'trade liberalization' means, but it is also true that the embedded liberalism
was the framework within which the notion of trade liberalization was given meaning
in the postwar era.)

Other commentators have provided similar insights. Kenneth Abbott has shown
how the trade regime is constituted by an evolving idea of what is an 'economic'
issue.[109] Goldstein has observed that such foundational concepts as 'free trade'
and 'protectionism' have changed significantly over time, and that such changes
have been reflected in institutions related to trade policy.[110] The key point is that
we cannot explain change in the trade regime without attention to the evolution of
the ideational determinants of the trade regime. The same is true for our proposals
for institutional change: it may not be enough to alter the configuration and relative
power of actors involved in decision-making, without simultaneously altering the
ideational framework which tells these actors why they are there and what they are
supposed to be doing.

Two brief examples may be useful. First, it is common among trade lawyers
to explain the expansion of the trade regime to cover services trade, rather than
solely goods trade, by reference to, on the one hand, a change in material conditions
(the fact that services came to represent an increasingly large proportion of the
domestic product of the most powerful GATT Members), and, on the other hand,
pressure group politics (a well co-ordinated campaign of action by domestic service
industries to put their concerns on the agenda of the trade regime). But, as Drake and
Nicolaïdis have demonstrated, this story is seriously incomplete without an account
of the conceptual revolution by which particular kinds of economic activity came to
be redefined as 'trade in services'.[111] Unless one adheres to a very strong form of the
view that ideas arise according to functional need, interest-based analyses can tell us

---

107 Abbott, above n 8, 974.
108 Ruggie, 'Embedded Liberalism', above n 1, at 213.
109 Abbott, above n 8.
110 Goldstein, *Ideas, Interests*, above n 98, at 240. Goldstein is referring to change in
these meanings in the context of a discussion of domestic institutions, but the same point is
applicable.
111 Drake and Nicolaïdis, above n 8.

little about this change. They say nothing, for example, about the crucial processes by which a particular meaning of trade in services came to be shared and accepted as legitimate by all relevant actors.

Second, the trade regime's change of emphasis from border measures to 'behind the border' trade barriers is also typically explained as a response to a change in underlying political and material conditions. As border barriers were gradually reduced and eliminated, so the story goes, and as governments experimented with new forms of regulatory measures, so domestic regulation came to be a more significant impediment to private traders' activities.[112] As a result of pressure from such private actors, governments began to pay greater attention to disciplining domestic regulation within the trade regime. But, again, this story fails to capture an important dimension. A world in which (say) domestic regulation on the use of asbestos could be challenged within the WTO entails a fundamental reconfiguration of shared ideas about what constitutes a 'trade barrier' and 'trade policy', and a re-conceptualization of shared understandings about the domain in which the trade regime operates. As it stands, little direct attention has been paid to the social processes by which this occurred.

If it is true that the trade regime is an expression not only of the prevailing distribution of power and interests, but also of prevailing ideas, then we need to pay closer attention to the social processes by which ideas are generated in and around the trade regime. In *International Regimes, Transactions and Change*, Ruggie highlights two different loci for such processes. On the one hand, the trade regime is a product of evolving ideas and social values at the domestic level – particularly of the changing centrality of the 'captivating social metaphor' of the market in the public imagination.[113] On the other hand, the trade regime is constituted by discursive practices – that is to say, communicative behaviours, modes of cognition, characteristic vocabularies, and so on – which exist or occur at the international level. It was, Ruggie suggests, in large part through negotiations and discussions between actors at the international level that the intersubjective framework of embedded liberalism came about.

Ikenberry, in an article which builds on Ruggie's analysis, elaborates this insight further. He shows how the intersubjective understandings which constitute embedded liberalism were, in significant part, the product of interactions among a community of economic experts, inspired by Keynesian economic ideas, who 'fostered agreement by altering the political debate about postwar policy, by crystallizing areas of common interest between ... governments, and by elaborating a set of politically resonant ideas that served to build larger coalitions within and between governments'.[114] More

---

112 This is a very common story. For a typical example, see G. Verhoosel, *National Treatment and WTO Dispute Settlement: Adjudicating the Boundaries of Regulatory Autonomy* (2002) 4.

113 Ruggie, 'Embedded Liberalism', above n 1, at 202. For a similar argument in a different context, see D. H. Lumsdaine, *Moral Vision in International Politics: the Foreign Aid Regime, 1949–1989* (1993).

114 G. J. Ikenberry, 'A World Economy Restored: Expert Consensus and the Anglo-American Postwar Settlement', 46 (1) *International Organization* 289 (1992), 318. See also,

generally, the literature on 'epistemic communities' has demonstrated the important role that networks of authoritative experts, who share a common set of causal beliefs and share particular ideas about the proper construction of social reality, play in formulating states' interests and designing strategies to pursue them.[115] This point, it is worth noting, is obscured in many contemporary retellings of the story of embedded liberalism. Such retellings often portray embedded liberalism solely as the product of interest group politics – an attempt, that is, to simultaneously satisfy those groups in favour of liberal trade and those groups who would suffer from it in the short term.[116]

Legal discourse is one of the many forms of communicative practice through which the trade regime is produced, and lawyers play a crucial role as an 'epistemic community' in the context of the international trade regime. It would seem useful, therefore, to investigate the ways in which trade law is bound up in constituting and reconstituting the intersubjective framework of meaning which is the trade regime. Enquiry of this sort may, on the one hand, be applied to the formal jurisprudence of the WTO. For example, there is an oft-cited line of cases – including *Asbestos, Shrimp/Turtle, Tuna/Dolphin, Gambling* and others – in which the Appellate Body confronts the task of balancing the goal of trade liberalization with other apparently legitimate goals. At present, trade lawyers tend to analyse those cases for the way they interpret and shape the regulative rules embodied in WTO agreements. But such cases also serve an important constitutive function: what the Appellate Body implicitly and explicitly says about the trade regime in these cases helps to shape intersubjective understandings about the objectives and values which the trade regime embodies. Driesen's work on this line of cases, in which he identifies three alternative ideas of 'free trade' in play, would seem like a useful point of departure for further scholarship.[117]

---

at 297: 'Although these experts shared a set of economic beliefs, it was only in the process of planning and negotiation that they came to possess a common identity and purpose'.

115　The literature on epistemic communities is most closely associated with the work of Peter Haas, see, e.g., P. M. Haas, 'Introduction. Epistemic Communities and International Policy Co-ordination', 46 (1) *International Organization* 1 (1992), as well as the contributions to that entire issue of *International Organization*.

116　A good example of the way embedded liberalism has be retold through a functionalist paradigm might D. Zaring, 'International Law by Other Means: The Twilight Existence of International Financial Regulatory Organizations', 33 (2) *Texas International Law Journal* 281 (1998), at 311: 'under this analysis [ie, analysis drawing on embedded liberalism], each state balances the interests of groups opposed to and in favor of free trade and is willing to participate in international economic institutions because free trade structures are embedded within an international framework recognizing the need for states to exercise political control over the distributional consequences of global economic change'. Other examples include: A. Maravel, 'Constructing Democracy in the North American Free Trade Area', 16 (3) *Northwestern Journal of International Law and Business* 331 (1996), at 406; Gathii, above n 48, 149.

117　In Driesen's schema, free trade may firstly be understood as 'trade free from discrimination'. He identifies this concept of 'non-discriminatory trade' as underpinning, e.g., GATT Article III. Secondly, free trade may be understood also as trade free from economic

The same questions might also be asked, on the other hand, about legal scholarship, by which I mean all the formal and informal discursive practices in which academic trade lawyers are engaged. How do we produce the trade regime in what we say and write? A prominent example might be the linkage debate, in which trade scholars have set themselves the task of discussing and debating the proper relationship between 'trade' and 'non-trade' issues, values and objectives.[118] How, we may ask, does this debate produce or sustain particular ideas of what trade and non-trade mean?[119] Another example might be the 'constitutionalist' literature on the trade regime. Might it be that, whether or not it is accurate to describe the current WTO as constitutional in any sense, commentators in this debate are 'generating a process where we come to under the WTO as a constitutional entity'?[120] If it is true that what we do is partly constitutive of the trade regime, then this may change what we understand our task to be. It opens up the possibility of being more self-conscious in this role: perhaps we could spend as much time telling compelling stories about the trade regime as we do interpreting and arguing about its regulative rules. One might even expect lawyers to have something of a comparative advantage in this area, given our expertise in interpretive methodology. One need only look at the power which the narrative of embedded liberalism has already had to spark imagination, charge debate and transform contemporary understandings of the trade regime, to see the potential in such a form of scholarship.

There is one final important point to be made. I have claimed that we need to look not only to actors, interests and power to understand why the trade regime is the way it is, but also to ideas and shared understandings. Clearly, these two lines of enquiry are intimately connected. It is a common criticism of certain kinds of ideational research that ideas and intersubjective meaning seems to arise out of nowhere, to be taken for granted. It is important to recognize that ideas are generated and shaped by political contest, by struggles between influential actors, just as much as the reverse. The point that I am making here is simply that, while the evolution of ideas is closely related to the question of participation, neither can be reduced to the other.

C. How the Trade Regime Impacts Behaviour and Outcomes

Finally, let us turn our attention to the *consequences* of the trade regime and trade law, in terms of their effects on actor behaviour. In fact, Ruggie scarcely addresses this

---

burden: 'trade free of national regulation … unencumbered by national laws that might increase prices'. Driesen refers to this as the 'laissez-faire concept' of free trade. Finally, free trade may be understood as 'trade free from international coercion', or, in other words, trade free from sanctions designed to coerce other countries into adopting particular policies or positions. He sees this concept of free trade in the Appellate Body's *Shrimp/Turtle* decisions. See D. M. Driesen, 'What is Free Trade?: The Real Issue Lurking Behind the Trade and Environment Debate', 41 (2) *Virginia Journal of International Law* 279 (2001), at 300.

118 See above n 60.

119 See Lang, 'Whose Trade Values? What Trade Issues? Dereifying the Trade Linkage Debate', forthcoming.

120 I owe this point to Professor Dunoff, personal communication, 9 September 2005, referring to his forthcoming paper.

question directly in *International Regimes, Transactions and Change*. Nevertheless, constructivist thinking in this area is based on precisely the same core insights that he set out in that article – namely, an emphasis on the nature of regimes as intersubjective frameworks of meaning and close attention to cognitive and discursive processes in social life – and it is worth briefly drawing attention to some of the lessons that trade lawyers may find useful in it.

Most trade lawyers tend implicitly to talk about the causative effects of the trade regime as if it were an 'intervening causal variable'.[121] That is, while the behaviour of actors – and thus related outcomes – is primarily determined by basic causal variables such as power and interests, the trade regime affects outcomes by limiting the freedom of these actors to pursue particular policy options when they otherwise might do so. The trade regime has such a significant impact on outcomes, on this view, because the constraints it imposes are backed by a strong enforcement mechanism, and thus the regime significantly alters the cost–benefit calculus actors use to determine their behaviour. (This view of regimes as intervening causal variables, it will be clear, corresponds closely with a view of trade law as collection of regulative rules.) While this model has considerable explanatory power, constructivists argue that it leaves out of account some of the most important ways in which regimes affect behaviour. In particular, they draw attention to the constitutive role that international institutions like the trade regime play in the social formation of actors' identities and interests, as well as more directly in the social construction of behaviour.[122]

First of all, the trade regime constitutes actor *behaviour* in the sense that it provides the intersubjective framework of meaning within which such behaviour takes on significance, and through which it is interpreted by others. A good example might be the way some forms of governmental practice come to be seen an 'intervention' in trade flows, while others are seen as part of the political and cultural context within which trade is carried out. Whether or not a regulation banning the sale and importation of asbestos products is in truth, an intervention into trade flows depends not just on the nature of the measure, and the beliefs and intention of the policymakers, but also crucially upon shared intersubjective understandings that constitute it as an 'intervention'.[123] The same practice would not be an 'intervention', in other words, in the absence of the intersubjective beliefs which make it so. This is important because the meaning attributed to behaviour changes the conditions under which states which choose to engage in it, and changes the way they respond to such behaviour in their trading partners. This may have important consequences for the kinds of questions that we as trade lawyers ask about WTO law. While we spend a great deal of time analysing which kinds of measures are prohibited by trade law and which are not, we spend little time analysing the separate question of which kinds of measures trade law helps to constitute as an intervention (or as a 'barrier',

---

121 This terminology is taken from Krasner, above n 2. In addition, most commentators would, if pressed, agree with the limited circumstances in which the trade regime acts as an independent or autonomous causal variable; Krasner, above n 100.

122 See generally, Ruggie, above n; Slaughter, Tulumello and Wood, above n 99; Wendt, above n 87; Simmons and Martin, above n 84 for some general descriptions of constructivist approaches to this issue.

123 Wendt, above n 87, at 176.

or as 'protectionism', or whatever) and the processes by which it does so. I am not referring here to the kinds of definitional discussions common in legal commentary, but rather to the categories into which trade law encourages us to divide the world. If constructivists are right, this constitutive function of trade law, by which we learn to attribute particular meanings to behaviour, may represent a far more important way in which trade law affects outcomes in the international trading system.

Secondly, the trade regime may also affect behaviour and outcomes indirectly by constituting actors' *identities* and *interests*. Constructivists remind us that our preferences are not wholly material-based, but also have a cognitive element: 'we want what we want', in Wendt's words, 'because of how we think about it'.[124] Preferences (whether of individuals or of states) arise in the context of 'scripts' or 'frames' which tell us something of how the world is, and what it is appropriate and legitimate to desire.[125] Through such scripts, we come to see ourselves as having particular identities, with particular kinds of preferences. Furthermore, a number of scholars have shown how the identities and interests of states can be reconstituted through discursive processes of learning, persuasion and deliberation.[126] Again, this theoretical framework could help trade lawyers understand how trade law and legal discourse affects outcomes in international trade. Some creative lines of enquiry can be imagined. While there is certainly a material basis to the basic preference for liberal trade (and the wealth maximization to which it is directed), it would be fruitful to enquire whether and how the trade regime helps to construct the kinds of states which place particular emphasis or priority on liberal trade objectives. We may also wonder to what extent the shared narrative embodied in the trade regime encourages governments to understand their primary role in international economic life as facilitators of transnational commerce, rather than some other role. This kind of thinking may be particularly relevant for those trade lawyers interested in the issue of regulatory autonomy: the clear message is that we should not only be interested in the way the trade regime prohibits certain kinds of regulation, we should also pay attention to the ways in which, by the operation of intersubjective understandings, states come to see certain kinds of regulation as not in their own interest.

There is already research in this vein from which trade lawyers can draw inspiration. Both Tarullo and Kennedy, for example, have shown how trade law communicates ideas of what a 'normal' trading nation is and does.[127] This raises the possibility of research into how these ideas structure states' self-understandings and conceptions of appropriate behaviour within the trade regime. Finnemore, as

---

124 Ibid, at 119.
125 I take this formulation from ibid, at 122.
126 E. B. Haas, 'Words can hurt you; or, who said what to whom about regimes', in S. D. Krasner (ed.), *International Regimes* (Ithaca, NY: Cornell University Press 1983) 23; E. B. Haas, *When Knowledge is Power: Three Models of Change in International Organizations* (1990); Wendt, above above n 87, 12ff; Simmons and Martin, above n 84, at 198, among many others.
127 D. K. Tarullo, 'Logic, Myth, and the International Economic Order', 26 *Harvard International Law Journal* 533 (1985); D. Kennedy, 'Turning to Market Democracy: A Tale of Two Architectures', 32 (3) *Harvard International Law Journal* 373 (1991).

well, has produced extensive research on the ways in which international institutions facilitate the diffusion of standards of what it means to be a modern state – effectively 'teaching' states that to be modern states means to have certain things.[128] It takes little imagination to suppose that the trade regime plays a similar role, diffusing norms about the kinds of economic and trade policies which 'modern' states employ. One of the most prominent venues for this must be accession negotiations, in which both current and prospective WTO Members engage in a process of teaching and learning what it means to be a WTO Member, and by extension what it means to be a responsible member of the international economic community. At least during the first five or so years of the WTO, during which time a number of former Eastern European transition economies joined the WTO, there is a strong argument to be made that the accession process was a powerful force for the 'globalization of market rationality'.[129] The Trade Policy Review Mechanism, in which WTO Members collectively comment on the economic policies of individual Members, also suggests itself as an important venue in which discursive processes are at work, teaching states standards of appropriate behaviour, providing cognitive scripts, assigning roles and constituting interests.

Conclusion

A large and growing number of international trade scholars are finding Ruggie's concept of embedded liberalism an appealing one. Some, no doubt, find it useful because it explains the elements of the trade regime for which more orthodox theories fail to account. Others, particularly progressive trade lawyers, clearly see it as an attractive normative vision for what the trade regime might once again come to be. My aim in this chapter has been, in part, to trace the impact that embedded liberalism has started to have on legal trade scholarship and to set out clearly and explicitly the different ways in which it has been brought to bear in contemporary debates. My motivation for doing so has been a belief that what Ruggie teaches us in this article is peculiarly relevant to current scholarship and a conviction that it is time to make some of those lessons more explicit.

In essence, the value I see in Ruggie's account is twofold. First, I see embedded liberalism playing a crucial *destabilizing* role. By this, I mean that it serves to destabilize common assumptions about the objectives of the trade regime, its philosophical and normative underpinnings, and thereby to expand our conceptions of what a liberal trade regime might plausibly look like. It can also be used to destabilize the terms of current debates about the trade regime, which are narrowly focused on the optimal extent, rather than the nature, of trade liberalization. I understand this destabilizing role to be very different from the view of embedded liberalism as a viable, substantive normative vision for the trade regime. I do not

---

128　Finnemore, above n 56; M. Finnemore, 'Norms, Culture, and World Politics: Insights from Sociology's Institutionalism', 50 (2) *International Organization* 325 (1996). See also Ruggie, *Constructing the World Polity*, above n 1, at 15.

129　Ruggie, *Constructing the World Polity*, above n 1, at 19.

share the enthusiasm of many who see in embedded liberalism a fruitful way of re-imagining a future trade regime. My sense is that the use of embedded liberalism in this way closes off more imaginative possibilities than it opens. I also think we need to be more critical of the period of embedded liberalism and pay more attention to the voices and concerns that were marginalized in its creation.

Second, I suggested that probably the most important insight of *International Regimes, Transactions and Change* is its characterization of the trade regime as an intersubjective framework of meaning. We should think of embedded liberalism as, above all else, a name for the framework of meaning which was the postwar trade regime. I have tried to give a sense, within the confines of this short chapter, of the immense potential that constructivist approaches to the study of the trade regime have to reorient and enrich the work that trade lawyers do. Because it is one of the foundational texts for constructivist theorists of international institutions, and because it already has traction within the community of international trade scholars, *International Regimes, Transactions and Change* can be fruitfully used as an entry point into constructivist literature.

Chapter 2

Hollowing out Keynesian Norms: How the Search for a Technical Fix Undermined the Bretton Woods Regime

Jacqueline Best

In the realm of macro-economics, at least, problems and issues were coming to be treated as technical rather than ideological

James Tobin, *The New Economics One Decade Older*[1]

After a decade of financial crises, international economic leaders have begun to talk about the need for reform. Yet, while they speak in dramatic terms of a 'new financial architecture', in practice, they seem more interested in more limited renovations to the international monetary system. Arguing that 'A lack of reliable data ... was critical to [recent] crises', the International Monetary Fund has, for example, emphasised the importance of better data-gathering systems and greater surveillance.[2] By defining the cause of the crises as informational rather than systemic, Fund leaders thus justify a limited solution: in Michel Camdessus' words, what is needed is 'no new machinery, no new heavy public intervention', but rather a series of limited technical fixes.[3] This is not the first time that international financial leaders have succumbed to the seduction of technique. Four decades ago, as the Bretton Woods system struggled through an escalating series of monetary crises, state and global policymakers chose a similar path of technical expediency, opting for limited reforms. As we now know, those strategies ultimately proved to be inadequate to the task of rescuing the postwar monetary order. In this chapter, I revisit that regime and its collapse, examining the roots of the contemporary search for technical fixes.

In re-examining the collapse of the Bretton Woods regime, I engage with two interconnected puzzles, one empirical and one theoretical. The first of these puzzles can be articulated as a simple question: why did the Bretton Woods regime collapse when it did? In responding to that question, I draw on a perspective that emphasises the role of norms and ideas in fostering both the success and the ultimate failure of

---

1 James Tobin, *The New Economics One Decade Older* (Princeton, NJ: Princeton University Press, 1974), p. 5.

2 IMF, *Reforming the International Financial Architecture: Progress through 2000* (Washington, DC: International Monetary Fund, 2001).

3 Michel Camdessus, *From Crisis to a New Recovery: Excerpts from Selected Addresses by Michel Camdessus* (Washington, DC: International Monetary Fund, 1999), p. 6.

that regime, focusing in particular on the role of economic theory in defining possible policy responses. This chapter thus contributes to a growing body of scholarly literature that focuses on the role of norms and ideas in international political economy.[4] Yet that very literature is itself the source of the second, theoretical, puzzle. Among the most persuasive of the writings in this field are the contributions by John Gerard Ruggie and Eric Helleiner.[5] Both seek to complicate the dominant neoliberal institutionalist and power-based analyses by emphasising the importance of the postwar embedded liberal consensus in supporting the early Bretton Woods regime. Yet each provides a very different account of the nature of those norms in the declining days of the regime: Ruggie suggests that there was a continuity of embedded liberal norms before and after the Bretton Woods system's collapse, while Helleiner argues that there was a significant shift away from those norms and towards neoliberalism immediately before the collapse. How might we reconcile these two conflicting accounts?

In this chapter, I suggest that the solutions to these empirical and theoretical puzzles are inextricably connected. The second puzzle becomes clearer if we see both Ruggie and Helleiner as only partly correct: I will suggest that there was neither a clear continuity nor a breach in the norms that supported the Bretton Woods regime – instead, there was gradual process of hollowing out, as the Keynesian ideas that had informed the original agreement came to be replaced with the neoclassical synthesis. This reinterpretation allows us to begin fitting some new pieces into our first puzzle: it was this process of hollowing out which shaped policymakers' strategies for responding to the crisis at hand, encouraged their adoption of limited, technical solutions, and thus ultimately contributed to the regime's decline.

Narrating the Global Economy: Why and How Ideas Matter

Scholars return to great events such as the collapse of the Bretton Woods regime not only to gain new insights for contemporary practices but also to test new theories. Whereas constructivist theorists are relative newcomers to this endeavour, neoliberal institutionalist and power-based theorists have had a long history of such analyses. In recent years, neoliberal analyses have acquired an institutionalist inflection, emphasising the central role played by certain key technical problems – such as the failure of the adjustable peg exchange rate and the weakness of the dollar-exchange

---

4   See Peter Hall, 'Policy Paradigms, Social Learning and the State', *Comparative Politics*, 25:3 (1993), pp. 275–92; Kathleen McNamara, *The Currency of Ideas: Monetary Politics and the European Union* (Ithaca, NY: Cornell University Press, 1998); Kathryn Sikkink, *Ideas and Institutions: Developmentalism in Brazil and Argentina* (Ithaca, NY: Cornell University Press, 1991); Mark Blyth, *Great Transformations: The Rise and Decline of Embedded Liberalism* (Cambridge: Cambridge University Press, 2002).

5   Eric Helleiner, *States and the Reemergence of Global Finance: From Bretton Woods to the 1990s* (Ithaca, NY: Cornell University Press, 1994); John Gerard Ruggie, 'International Regimes, Transactions and Change: Embedded Liberalism in the Postwar Economic Order', *International Organization*, 35:2 (1982), pp. 379–415.

system – as central factors in the regime's decline.[6] Power-based theorists, on the other hand, have traditionally emphasised the role of political conflict, focusing on the hegemonic position of the United States and arguing that shifting US interests ultimately undermined the system.[7] In spite of their considerable differences, both dominant theoretical approaches suffer from a common weakness: while both identify a crucial contributing factor – failed economic policies or changing political interests – they ultimately fail to explain the logic which produced these outcomes. Why were these policies pursued and these interests defined as they were? To answer that question, we must examine the social context within which these actions took place and examine the norms and ideas through which institutional and political possibilities were defined and articulated.

Why do ideas matter? Because the realm of financial governance is one made up of 'institutional facts' – to borrow John Searle's term – facts that cannot be understood without reference to their social and discursive context.[8] The very meaning of the green pieces of paper that wield so much power in the modern world depends on our perception of – and faith in – their value.[9] Our diagnosis of the crises that ail us (in fact our very definition of a set of circumstances as a crisis) depends in part on the theoretical tools through which we define them and the vocabularies through which we narrate their possible solutions.[10] These ideas and norms thus play a key role in enabling both cooperation and contestation, by providing the tools for building or dismantling international institutions.[11] The architects of the Bretton Woods Agreement sought to create a postwar financial regime that would avoid the perceived problems of the previous Gold Standard system. Underpinning and reinforcing the various concrete policies and institutions of the postwar order was a particular set of norms and ideas which has come to be known, following Ruggie, as embedded liberalism.

---

6   Michael Bordo, 'The Bretton Woods International Monetary System: A Historical Overview', in Michael Bordo and Barry Eichengreen (eds), *A Retrospective on the Bretton Woods System: Lessons for International Monetary Reform* (Chicago, IL: University of Chicago Press, 1993), pp. 83–4; Barry Eichengreen, 'Epilogue: Three Perspectives on the Bretton Woods System', *Retrospective*, pp. 641–2; Barry Eichengreen, *Globalizing Capital: A History of the International Monetary System* (Princeton, NJ: Princeton University Press, 1996).

7   Robert Gilpin, *The Political Economy of International Relations* (Princeton, NJ: Princeton University Press, 1987); Joanne Gowa, *Closing the Gold Window: Domestic Politics and the End of Bretton Woods* (Ithaca, NY: Cornell University Press, 1983); Robert O. Keohane and Joseph S. Nye, *Power and Interdependence* (Boston, MA: Little, Brown, 1977).

8   John Searle, *The Construction of Social Reality* (New York: Free Press, 1995). See also: William Connolly, 'Essentially Contested Concepts in Politics', *The Terms of Political Discourse*, 2nd ed. (Princeton, NJ: Princeton University Press, 1983), pp. 9–45; Michel Foucault, 'Two Lectures', in Colin Gordon (ed.), *Power/Knowledge: Selected Interviews and Other Writings, 1972–1977* (Brighton: Harvester Press, 1980), pp. 92–108.

9   Jonathan Kirshner, 'The Study of Money', *World Politics*, 52 (2000), pp. 407–36.

10 Colin Hay, 'Narrating Crisis: The Discursive Construction of the "Winter of Discontent"', *Sociology*, 30 (1996), pp. 253–77.

11 Blyth, *Great Transformations*.

How did these ideas matter? What role did they play in the ultimate demise of the regime? As I suggested above, when we look at some of the literature on the role of norms in financial governance, we find two very different answers to that question. In his influential 1982 article on embedded liberalism, Ruggie argues that the collapse of the Bretton Woods exchange system did not constitute a fundamental regime change because the same norms that shaped the creation of that system – the embedded liberal compromise – also informed the new mechanisms that replaced it.[12] In *States and the Reemergence of Global Finance*, Eric Helleiner takes a rather different approach to the role of norms and ideas, arguing that the collapse of the Bretton Woods regime was fostered in part by a significant change in the norms governing finance. Helleiner combines this concern with the role of changing norms with a focus on political contestation, emphasising the central role played by the US in defeating any attempts at reform. He argues that there had been an important shift in the political-economic philosophy that animated the US approach to international finance to a full-hearted embrace of free-market principles.[13] This intellectual shift was not yet widespread, but it was nonetheless capable of altering the international landscape by changing the US stance on a new international monetary order. Without the US's support, he argues, the deal was impossible. Thus, where Ruggie argues that this period was marked by continuity in the norms governing international finance, Helleiner points to a significant breach.

To understand this tension between these two analyses, we need to take a closer look at the nature of the norms that characterised the Bretton Woods regime. In the first section of this article, I will therefore examine these norms, focusing on the influence of the economic theories of that era. I will suggest that there were in fact some important changes between the signing of the Bretton Woods agreement in 1944 and its golden era during the 1960s. While the original Bretton Woods agreement bore Keynes' intellectual imprint, its interpretation and implementation in the 1960s was informed by later variations of Keynesian thought, most notably that of the neoclassical synthesis. As James Tobin suggests in the quote at the beginning of this chapter, advocates of the neoclassical synthesis treated economic problems as 'technical rather than ideological'.

This kind of technical approach sought to separate economic questions from the complications of politics and ideas. Such faith in the neutrality of technique also rested on a further assumption that the market itself was essentially rational. Such assumptions are of course very familiar, as they remain today the bread and butter of neoliberal economic theory and practice. Yet, at the time, this kind of belief in the neutrality of technique was a departure from Keynes' own theory, which emphasised the intersubjective nature of economic activity – the centrality of expectation and convention and the powerful role of economic ideas. It was this recognition of the power of ideas – what I have elsewhere called the self-reflexivity

---

12 Ruggie, 'International Regimes'.
13 Helleiner, *States and the Reemergence of Global Finance*, pp. 111–22.

of the Keynesian social purpose – that was hollowed out in the transition to the neoclassical synthesis.[14]

Did this shift in political economic ideas have an impact on the forms of financial governance? In the second section of this article, I will tackle this difficult question by considering the failure of policymakers to address growing pressures on the regime throughout the 1960s. I will focus in particular on financial policy decisions governing the domestic and international regulation of capital movements – movements that were to play a key role in successive currency crises in the final years of the regime. By tracing the logic of policies adopted by the United States and international institutions such as the International Monetary Fund and Bank for International Settlements, I will suggest that there was a significant shift in policy marked by an increasing turn towards technical fixes. Losing sight of Keynes' insight into the intersubjective nature of financial behaviour, policymakers downplayed the structural and psychological roots of growing market volatility, opting for a series of short-term technical strategies. Their limited response to the challenge of speculation ultimately helped to foster the conditions for financial crisis and severely constrained the international system's ability to respond. The hollowing out of the Keynesian norms that had sustained the postwar regime thus created the conditions for the eventual collapse of the Bretton Woods regime.

Hollowing out Keynesian Norms: Changing Economic Ideas

If we are to understand the nature of the ideas and norms that helped to shape the Bretton Woods regime, we can learn much from the study of the economic theories of the era. In this first section of the chapter, I will therefore take a closer look at the economic ideas that dominated the early and later postwar years. Where others have focused on two central schools of thought – Keynesianism and monetarism – I will focus on three. Moreover, I will suggest, it was the third of these theoretical traditions, that of the neoclassical synthesis, which played the most important role in the later years of the Bretton Woods regime.

Keynesianism and the Bretton Woods Agreement

Johnathan Kirshner has suggested that the authorship of this particular 'compromise of market forces and social contract' should be attributed to John Maynard Keynes, both the most influential economic thinker of his era and one of the architects of the Bretton Woods Agreement.[15] Keynes' proposed compromise was based on a radical theoretical proposition: that the central tenets of classical economic theory

---

14 Jacqueline Best, 'From the Top Down: The New Financial Architecture and the Re-embedding of Global Finance', *New Political Economy*, 8:3 (2003), pp. 363–84.

15 Jonathan Kirshner, 'Keynes, Capital Mobility and the Crisis of Embedded Liberalism', *Review of International Political Economy*, 6:3 (1999), p. 314.

only applied to a special case – the rarely occurring situation of full-employment.[16] Keynes' own theory, on the other hand, sought to explain the logic that shaped economic relations at all other times.

Keynes' analysis rested on a key insight into the intersubjective nature of the free market system. Investment, for Keynes, was crucial. And decisions to invest, he argued, depend on expectations of future growth. Investment will occur if the marginal efficiency of capital is greater than the rate of interest – in other words, if investors think that they will get a sufficient rate of return.[17] Yet none of these factors is easily predicted, since they depend on the behaviour of other investors. Each investor must therefore guess what others will do, so that expectations and mass psychology play central roles in investment decisions.[18] Keynes thus likened the strategy of the investor to a newspaper competition in which contestants were successful if their selection of the six prettiest faces from a hundred photographs was closest to the average: 'We have reached the third degree where we devote our intelligences to anticipating what average opinion expects the average opinion to be'.[19]

An economic system that relied on such uncertain forces to allocate its resources, he argued, was unlikely to provide particularly stable day-to-day economic conditions, since '*conventional* judgment' is a fickle thing.[20] Keynes therefore saw economic crises as central to a capitalist economy – and he identified the intersubjective nature of investing behaviour as central to those cycles. Booms tend to produce over-optimism, given the psychology of investors and the problem of insufficient information.[21] Yet as long as booms are driven by such 'animal spirits', they are doomed to end eventually, giving way to recession or depression. In such situations, the market alone could not bring the economy out of its slump. Instead, it was the responsibility of the state to foster the consumption and investment necessary to obtain a full-employment equilibrium. Keynes' proposals for a postwar financial order sought to create an international financial system that would enable states to pursue such active economic policies. Above all, he insisted, the postwar financial system must limit the power of disequilibrating capital flows, through comprehensive exchange rate and cooperative controls if necessary.[22]

---

16 Keynes sets out this claim in the very first chapter of his *General Theory*. John Maynard Keynes, *The General Theory of Employment Interest and Money* (New York: Harcourt Brace, 1964).

17 Keynes, *General Theory*, p. 145.

18 Ibid., pp. 46, 161–2.

19 Ibid., p. 156.

20 Keynes, 'The General Theory of Employment', *The Quarterly Journal of Economics* (February 1937), reproduced in Donald Moggridge (ed.), *The Collected Works of John Maynard Keynes: The General Theory and After*, vol. XIV (London: Macmillan, 1973), pp. 114–15. Italics in original.

21 Keynes, *General Theory*, pp. 315–16.

22 Keynes, 'Proposals for an International Clearing Union (April 1943)', in J. Keith Horsefield (ed.), *The International Monetary Fund 1945–1965: Documents*, vol. III (Washington, DC: International Monetary Fund, 1969), p. 31; Donald Moggridge, *Maynard Keynes: An Economists' Biography* (London: Routledge, 1992), pp. 575, 672–3. On Keynes

While Keynes' ultimate practical goal may not have been particularly radical – he did seek to rescue rather than to revolutionise capitalism – his theoretical premises were. He directly challenged the ability of classical theory to explain financial activity, arguing, 'the fact that our knowledge of the future is fluctuating, vague and uncertain, renders wealth a peculiarly unsuitable subject for the methods of classical economic theory'.[23] At the same time, he replaced the classical theorists' perfectly rational *homo economicus* with a far more complex conception of a socially embedded, communicating economic actor whose expectations about the future are shaped by convention. These twin aspects of Keynes' theory – its radical critique of classical theory and its insistence on the role of mutual perception and expectations – have often been downplayed, as we perceive him through the lenses of his later more conservative revisers. Yet there does exist a tradition of emphasising this aspect of his work, a tradition that has recently gained new attention.[24] By rediscovering this aspect of Keynes work – by reclaiming the importance of its philosophical core – we can also better understand the logic of the international financial proposals that it informed.

Keynes' insight into the intersubjective nature of investment has two principal implications for economic policy. The first is primarily negative: financial markets cannot be relied on to create an equilibrium that meets the social needs of a modern economy. Internationally, this market pathology is likely to manifest itself most destructively in the form of volatile capital movements. The second implication of Keynes' philosophical insights is more positive: because economic judgment is conventional, it is amenable to influence and education.[25] While he recognised that this is not an easy task, Keynes nonetheless attempted this very challenge, describing himself as 'a free individual man endeavouring, no longer to mould directly the course of events, but to influence the opinion which in the long run determines things'.[26] Together, these two insights encouraged a particular kind of economic governance – an approach that believed in the value of regulation, all the while recognising the limits of technical solutions in the face of radical uncertainty.[27] Keynes recognised what we might describe today as the essential ambiguity of economic activity – the

and Harry Dexter-White's proposals for cooperative controls, see Helleiner, *States and the Reemergence of Global Finance*.

23 Keynes, *The General Theory and After*, p. 113.

24 Allan Meltzer, 'Keynes' *General Theory*: A Different Perspective', *Journal of Economic Literature*, 19 (March 1981), pp. 34–64; Christopher Torr, *Equilibrium, Expectations and Information* (Cambridge: Polity Press, 1988); Robert Skidelsky, *John Maynard Keynes: A Biography*, vol. III (New York: Viking, 2001); Blyth, *Great Transformations: The Rise and Decline of Embedded Liberalism*.

25 For example, Roger Middleton discusses Keynes' belief in the possibility of changing conventional business perception of deficits as 'unsound finance' in the context of his 1930s-era debate with the British Treasury over the role of psychological expectations. Roger Middleton, *Towards the Managed Economy: Keynes, the Treasury and the Fiscal Policy Debate of the 1930s* (London: Methuen, 1985).

26 Donald Moggridge (ed.), *The Collected Works of John Maynard Keynes: Activities 1931–1939*, vol. XXI (London: Macmillan, 1973), p. 47.

27 Keynes, *The General Theory and After*, pp. 112–14.

Embedding Global Markets

centrality of mutual interpretation to economic decisions and the often-surprising unpredictability that is its result.[28] The Bretton Woods Agreement that this insight inspired sought to respond to these challenges by limiting speculation and by working to entrench a new set of economic conventions – all the while seeking to remember the fragility of economic stability.

The Neoclassical Synthesis

While Keynes' theories and the institutions that they had helped to create outlived his death in 1946, they were soon revised and reinterpreted by his successors, the advocates of the neoclassical synthesis. In 1961, Paul Samuelson argued in the fifth edition of his tremendously popular economics textbook that this new synthesis 'is accepted in its broad outlines by all but a few extreme left-wing and right-wing writers'.[29] While the neoclassical synthesis drew its inspiration from Keynes' writings, it possessed a number of crucial differences: most significantly, it ignored the intersubjective nature of economic activity, and thus drew very different conclusions about the challenges facing economic governance and the solutions that should be devised.

Together with fellow economists Robert Solow, James Tobin, James Meade and J.R. Hicks, Samuelson had worked to adapt Keynes' insights so that they fit within the broad outlines of the classical framework.[30] Rejecting the classical presumption of automaticity, they argued that it was entirely possible for an economy to attain an equilibrium that involved a significant level of involuntary unemployment. Like Keynes, they saw the gap between savings and investment as a crucial cause of this problem: savings do not necessarily translate into investment. Since any money saved is not spent today, it does not create a demand for goods and services. This gap between what people earn and what they consume will put deflationary pressure on an economy unless it is counterbalanced by an equivalent level of investment. However, investment does not automatically reach the right level – hence the need for government policy.

While this argument bears considerable similarities to that presented by Keynes in the *General Theory*, it also contains significant differences: where Keynes emphasised the role of intersubjective expectations in explaining the volatility and irrationality of investment, Samuelson and his cohort focused instead on institutional and exogenous factors. They blamed short-run imperfections in the market, such as

---

28 I take up this question the role of ambiguity in international financial governance far more extensively in Jacqueline Best, *Uncertain Economies: The Politics of Ambiguity in International Finance* [working title] (Ithaca, NY: Cornell University Press, forthcoming 2005).

29 Paul A. Samuelson, *Economics: An Introductory Analysis*, 5th ed. (New York: McGraw-Hill, 1961), p. 242.

30 See, for example: James E. Meade, 'A Simplified Model of Mr. Keynes' System', *Review of Economic Studies*, 4:2 (1937), pp. 98–107; Paul A. Samuelson and Robert M. Solow, 'Analytical Aspects of Anti-Inflation Policy', *The American Economic Review*, 50:2 (1960), pp. 177–94; James Tobin, 'Inflation and Unemployment', *American Economic Review*, 62:1/2 (1972), pp. 1–18.

asymmetric information and price stickiness to explain the failure of the system to reach a full-employment equilibrium on its own. Keynes' more fundamental challenge to the assumptions of classical theory was therefore set aside in favour of an analysis which sought to correct far more technical problems. With this assessment of the causes of unemployment and inflation came a series of technical solutions: the right combination of fiscal and monetary policy could alter demand sufficiently to eliminate inflationary or deflationary gaps between current and full-employment equilibria.[31]

Although they had proven that the classical assumption of a *perfect* market was false, these neoclassical synthesists nonetheless subscribed to a belief in the *perfectibility* of the market. Keynes, too, sought to develop the theories and policies necessary to transform the real economy into one that would follow the rules of the classical economists; yet he saw that task as far more daunting than did his neoclassical successors. Keynes' prescriptions for government policy were therefore more complex than those of Samuelson and his ilk. Fiscal and monetary policy alone could not tame the wild economic swings produced by speculative expectations, Keynes argued, hence his emphasis on socialising the conditions of investment and strictly controlling capital flows. Neoclassical synthesists ignored such insights. For them, more limited, technical solutions were enough. Consequently, they spent much of the 1960s and early 1970s developing ever more precise models for finding and implementing such solutions – at both national and international levels.

The Monetarist Challenge

Although the neoclassical synthesis defined the mainstream of economic theory and policy, it was not without its challengers. There was a final set of economic ideas and norms that played a role in the debates of this era: monetarism. Milton Friedman used the basic postulates of monetarist theory to attack the neoclassical synthesists' faith in the ability of public policy to compensate for economic imbalances, whether in the form of domestic fiscal policy or the international management of exchange rates and capital flows.

At the heart of monetarism is the quantity theory of money which states that there is an exact relationship between changes in the quantity of money and the general price level: an increase in the money supply will cause an increase in the level of prices. Monetarists argued that changes in the stock of money are the principal determinants of spending patterns, and thus of economic activity as a whole. Fiscal policy is unlikely to have much effect on the level of output, and is in fact likely to

---

31 In 1958, A. W. Phillips published a paper that suggested that there had historically existed a negative relation between levels of unemployment and inflation in the United Kingdom. Two years later, Samuelson and Solow published a paper that formalised the 'Phillips curve', offering governments the opportunity to determine the precise trade-off they were willing to accept between levels of unemployment and inflation. A. W. Phillips, 'The Relation between Unemployment and the Rate of Change of Money Wage Rates in the United Kingdom, 1861–1957', *Economica*, 25 (1958), pp. 283–99; Samuelson and Solow, 'Anti-Inflation Policy'.

'crowd out' private investment if it involves taxing or borrowing from the public.[32] Government policy, they argued, should therefore focus on managing the money supply, rather than on managing demand as the neoclassical synthesis suggested. Yet, even here, monetarists were wary of discretionary monetary policy: they argued that because of short-run lags between a change in monetary policy and individuals' recognition and adaptation to the change, short-run stabilisation policies are likely to prove counter-productive. While money is neutral in the long run, they argued, in the short run changes to the money supply can have destabilising effects on the 'real economy' while the system adjusts to the new level of prices. Hence monetarists argued that discretionary monetary policy should be abandoned in favour of a rigid rule governing the gradual expansion of the money supply.[33] Active public economic policy is therefore either redundant or, more likely, perverse.

The Hollowness of the Neoclassical Synthesis

Given their very different conceptions of the role of government policy, it is not surprising that neoclassical synthesists and monetarists argued energetically over the direction of international financial governance. Nonetheless, as I will discuss further below, in public policy circles these debates were consistently won by the proponents of the neoclassical synthesis – at least until the mid-1970s. If the roots of the weakening of the Bretton Woods monetary regime are to be found in the arena of norms and ideas, we will therefore need to concentrate on the influence of the neoclassical synthesis. The intuitive approach to studying the neoclassical synthesis is to assume that it is very much like Keynes' own theory – not least because its proponents have tended to read Keynes through their own technically oriented lenses. Yet, if we take seriously Keynes' insight into the intersubjective nature of economic activity, we find that advocates of the neoclassical synthesis had far more in common with monetarists than one would initially believe.

At one level, it is hard to imagine less compatible theories: the neoclassical synthesists put government policymakers at the centre of their economic system, while monetarists sought to strip the role of public policy to a single rule. Yet, by rejecting Keynes' more critical insights, the neoclassical synthesists did move far closer to their monetarist opponents. Unlike Keynes, both neoclassical synthesists and monetarists assume that it is possible to participate in the economy without the complications of mutual interpretation: the economy is transparent to the analyst's

---

32 By the late 1960s, Friedman and Edmund Phelps had also developed a significant challenge to the Phillips' curve (see n. 31), arguing that, in the long run, the curve became a vertical line – so that rather than a trade-off between higher inflation and lower unemployment, policymakers were instead faced with the prospect of increasing the rate of inflation without having any impact on the level of unemployment, as it inevitably gravitated towards its 'natural rate'. Milton Friedman, 'The Role of Monetary Policy', *American Economic Review*, 58 (1968), pp. 1–17; Edmund S. Phelps, 'Phillips Curves, Expectations of Inflation and Optimal Unemployment over Time', *Economica*, 34 (1967), pp. 254–81.

33 Thomas M. Humphrey, 'The Quantity Theory of Money: Its Historical Evolution and Role in Policy Debates', *Federal Reserve Bank of Richmond Economic Review*, 60:3 (1974), pp. 2–19; Milton Friedman, *Monetarist Economics* (London: Basil Blackwell, 1991).

gaze. Both monetarists and neoclassical synthesists therefore tend to ignore the intersubjective nature of economic activity. Instead, both schools focus on the role of technical uncertainties, although they treat them very differently.[34] For neoclassical synthesists, short-term uncertainties produced by informational or institutional limitations can be corrected by the application of governmental expertise. For monetarist theorists, however, short-term uncertainties, which take the form of time lags, pose a greater problem to economic stability, for they make it very difficult for policymakers to predict the effects of their actions. The only significant conceptual difference between the two theories' treatment of uncertainty is their definition of its magnitude and their belief in the capacity of discretionary policy to compensate for it.

The neoclassical synthesis sought to adapt Keynes' insights to fit within the classical framework by treating the problems of involuntary unemployment and business cycle volatility as the effects of short-run uncertainties – rather than of the more complex and persistent phenomenon of intersubjectivity. By focusing on the inability of classical theory to account for or address such short-run phenomena, their theory did pose a challenge to the monetarist claims. Yet to achieve this tidy synthesis, they had sacrificed Keynes' intersubjective insights, relying solely on their theory's ability to find technical solutions. What was the appeal of this emphasis on technique? No doubt part of the answer is disciplinary: as economic theory became increasingly mathematical, so did economic practice. Yet the seduction of technique was practical as well as intellectual for it appeared to provide a means of transcending subjectivity and even politics.[35] The search for such solutions led them towards increasingly quantitative approaches, in an effort to develop objective forms of measurement and intervention. Yet once started on this path, they had already begun to grant strategic ground to the monetarists. Income, consumption and investment aggregates were far messier to measure – and more politically fraught to manage – than the money supply. The monetarists' lean and parsimonious theory appeared to provide an even more objective means of solving technical problems. In many ways, the neoclassical synthesis thus set the stage for its own eventual defeat. But first it would play a role in shaping the international financial community's response to the challenges facing the late Bretton Woods regime.

---

34 For a fuller discussion of the nature of technical uncertainty and its difference from a mere form of intersubjective ambiguity, see Jacqueline Best, 'The Politics of Transparency: Ambiguity and the Liberalization of International Finance', in James Busumtwi-Sam and Laurent Dobuzinskis (eds), *Turbulence and New Directions in Global Political Economy* (Basingstoke and New York: Palgrave, 2003), pp. 126–44.

35 The victory of technical modes of financial governance is part of a much broader rise of technique and expertise as privileged modes of social management. For an interesting perspective on this history, see: Michel Foucault, 'Governmentality', in Graham Burchell, Colin Gordon and Peter Miller (eds), *The Foucault Effect: Studies in Governmentality* (London: Harvester Wheatsheaf, 1991), pp. 87–104.

The Neoclassical Synthesis and Monetary Policy

As the popularity of Paul Samuelson's economic textbook attests, by the 1960s the neoclassical synthesis had become dominant in the realm of economic theory. What of the realm of practice? If we examine the policies of the most influential state in the international monetary system during the 1960s,[36] we find evidence of an 'economic experiment' of sorts under way.[37] As John Kenneth Galbraith argues, while Keynesianism came to the United States through the universities, it eventually came to exercise an enormous influence on policy – most notably during the administrations of Kennedy and Johnson in the early 1960s.[38] Yet the Keynesianism of the Kennedy administration was of a very particular sort: at the beginning of his term, Kennedy appointed a task force under the leadership of Paul Samuelson.[39] As Robert Solow, another member of the group noted, 'we were believers in what is usually called "the neoclassical synthesis"'.[40] If Kennedy was 'the first Keynesian President',[41] he was decidedly of a neoclassical bent. Thus the era of 'new economics' was born in America.

Kennedy went on to appoint a number of prominent advocates of the neoclassical synthesis to his Council of Economic Advisers (CEA), beginning with Walter Heller and James Tobin in 1961.[42] The CEA introduced a wealth of neoclassical synthesist policies, including counter-cyclical fiscal and monetary policy, deficit-financing, a full employment goal and a major tax cut.[43] In the area of international economic policy, the CEA shared its influence with the more cautious Undersecretary for Monetary Affairs, Robert Roosa. Roosa was not a card-carrying member of the neoclassical synthesis tribe, and yet the policies that he introduced were very much a product of the era of 'new economics'. While Roosa was more concerned with

---

36 I will focus here on the United States as a key player in the international financial system of the era. As Kathleen McNamara points out, Keynesianism also took hold in much of Europe, although there was considerable variation in the degree to which European states adopted Keynesian macroeconomic policy: McNamara, *The Currency of Ideas*. Nonetheless, as far as external financial policies were concerned, the adoption of capital controls and fixed exchange rates was widespread. See n. 54 for details.

37 Thomas Karier, *Great Experiments in American Economy Policy: From Kennedy to Reagan* (Westport, CT: Praeger, 1997).

38 John Kenneth Galbraith, 'How Keynes Came to America', in F. Hamouda and B.B. Price (eds), Keynesianism and the *Keynesian Revolution in America* (Cheltenham, UK: Edward Elgar, 1998), pp. 8–17.

39 Donald Winch, *Economics and Policy: A Historical Study* (London: Hodder and Stoughton, 1969), p. 303.

40 Robert M. Solow, 'The Kennedy Council and the Long Run', in George L. Perry and James Tobin (eds), *Economic Events, Ideas, and Policies: The 1960s and After* (Washington, DC: Brookings Institution Press, 2000), pp. 121–2.

41 Arthur M. Schlesinger Jr., *A Thousand Days: John F. Kennedy in the White House* (Boston, MA: Houghton Mifflin, 1965), p. 549.

42 George L. Bach, *Making Monetary and Fiscal Policy* (Washington, DC: The Brookings Institution, 1971), p. 112.

43 For a discussion of the economic rationale behind the CEA's recommendations, see Tobin, *New Economics*, pp. 6–16.

the US balance of payments deficit than most members of the CEA, his strategies for reducing it were consistently framed by the desire to balance such international pressures with the domestic priorities of demand management and full employment. Like his more Keynesian colleagues, Roosa emphasised the central role of government, insisting that 'there must be some reliance upon the judgment of men, expressed through governmental action' in managing the economic challenges of the era.[44] Together, the Treasury and CEA developed a series of strategies designed to reconcile domestic and international needs. These efforts combined a conviction in the priority of domestic stability, a belief in the economic role of government and a faith in short-term, technical solutions. In so far as the US played a key role in the fate of the Bretton Woods regime, its actions reflected the growing influence of the neoclassical synthesis.

Nor were IMF staff members immune from the growing influence of the 'new economics'. Over time, the institution opted for a particular hybrid of Keynesian and monetarist ideas, combining the neoclassical synthesis' emphasis on demand management with the monetarist preference for monetary targets. In his study of the IMF policy paradigm, Wilfred David argues that the basic assumption that animated Fund financial stabilisation programmes was that balance of payments disequilibria in developing economies were generally caused by expansions in demand relative to supply, producing inflation and an external deficit. In response the IMF would impose ceilings on domestic credit and external borrowing in order to limit the government's ability to finance any budget deficit.[45] On the one hand, IMF staff accepted the central elements of the neoclassical synthesis, emphasising the importance of a government-managed recovery. On the other, in their search for increasingly objective targets appropriate to the Fund's role as the provider of 'purely technical' assistance, IMF staff found the simplicity of the monetarist approach appealing.[46] The Fund thus developed a particular hybrid of Keynesian neoclassical and monetarist approaches to payments imbalances, combining a focus on demand-management with a set of targets that relied on controlling the money supply.[47]

In its final decade, the Bretton Woods regime was thus still largely defined by Keynesian economics – but it was a Keynesianism with a rather classical inflection. While major policy initiatives were introduced under the banner of Keynesianism, the strategies of US and IMF policymakers were not only more cautious than Keynes in their identification of the limits of the market mechanism; they were also increasingly tied to kinds of econometric and statistical methods which, as Donald Winch suggests, were at odds with 'the casual, if inspired, empiricism' of Keynes.[48]

---

44 Robert Roosa, *The Dollar and World Liquidity* (New York: Random House, 1967), pp. 66, 68, 139.

45 Wilfred L. David, *The IMF Policy Paradigm: The Macroeconomics of Stabilization, Structural Adjustment, and Economic Development* (New York: Praeger, 1985), pp. 33–43, 52–9.

46 Margaret De Vries, *The International Monetary Fund 1966–1971: System under Stress*, vol. I (Washington, DC: International Monetary Fund, 1976), pp. 364–5, 582.

47 De Vries, *The International Monetary Fund 1966–1971*, p. 363.

48 Winch notes, 'Keynes himself was unsympathetic towards this type of mathematical and statistical exercise'. Winch, *Economics and Policy*, p. 314.

Thus, while the basic Keynesian belief in the central role of public economic policy remained, the form of that policy was gradually stripped of many of its Keynesian attributes. This increasing hollowness at the heart of the postwar consensus, I will argue, ultimately helped to contribute to its collapse.

The Search for Technical Fixes: Controlling Speculation

Any comprehensive analysis of the collapse of the Bretton Woods regime must tackle three central and intersecting pressures: the problems of liquidity, adjustment and speculation. The question of liquidity – the amount of credit available internationally – received the most direct attention at the time. The 'liquidity debate' was initiated by Robert Triffin's warning that the system was not sustainable as long as global liquidity remained dependent on the US dollar as a reserve currency: in order to create sufficient international liquidity, the US would have to run a sizeable balance of payments deficit which would ultimately erode confidence in the dollar's convertibility into gold; if, on the other hand, the US sought to reduce its deficit, it would starve the world of much needed liquidity.[49] The objective was thus to create a new source of international reserves which was not dependent on the dollar.[50] Adjustment also became a problem after the achievement of convertibility in 1958. While adequate liquidity could help to ease short-term payments imbalances, it did little to resolve the growing disequilibrium between the surplus states in Europe and the deficit states of the UK and the US. Here, the exchange rate regime was very much to blame, for it had become increasingly rigid after the sterling crisis of 1947 and was no longer capable of playing the role for which it was designed. Finally, the growing power of speculative capital movements was proving to be very difficult to manage. With the move to convertibility in 1958, capital suddenly became far more mobile. As the Euromarkets evolved, the volume of mobile capital also began to grow. Short-term capital flows increased markedly, chasing speculative profits from state to state. More often than not, these flows were disequilibrating, further undermining a country's balance of payments deficit or ballooning an already significant surplus.[51]

A single chapter cannot do justice to these many and complex factors.[52] What it can do, however, is to focus on one of the central pressures at work: the rise of speculative capital movements. While speculation was not a sufficient cause of the regime's collapse, it was certainly a necessary one: in fact, the form that the regime's collapse ultimately took was that of a series of speculative attacks on the dominant currencies of the era. Moreover the rising tide of speculative capital flows

---

49 Robert Triffin, *Gold and the Dollar Crisis* (New Haven, CT: Yale University Press, 1960).

50 A challenge, which ultimately – and belatedly – produced the agreement on Special Drawing Rights. De Vries, *The International Monetary Fund 1966–1971*, p. 205.

51 Ibid., pp. 496–98; De Vries, *The IMF in a Changing World: 1945–1985* (Washington, DC: International Monetary Fund, 1986), p. 36.

52 I have provided a more thorough account of the role of all three factors in the regime's collapse in: Best, *Uncertain Economies*, ch. 5.

greatly exacerbated the problems of liquidity and adjustment: had capital been better regulated, there would not have been the same need for what Susan Strange has called 'crisis liquidity' – large volumes of international credit required not to sustain economic growth but rather to offset debilitating capital outflows.[53] Since many of these flows worked to exacerbate existing payments disequilibria, they also made adjustment far more difficult. This was nowhere clearer than in the case of the United States whose growing payments deficit was an increasing source of global concern.

State and international leaders sought to respond to these speculative pressures through a series of different strategies. Domestically, many states adopted capital controls to combat inflationary or deflationary pressures. Internationally, various *ad hoc* measures were developed to limit or offset the destabilising effects of short-term capital flows. Yet, as I will argue below, both of these strategies were limited by their narrow conception of the source of the problem: having forgotten Keynes' insights into the intersubjective origins of speculative activity, they developed limited technical solutions to a far more complex and pervasive problem.

Domestic Responses: Capital Controls

In response to the increasing volatility of capital flows, states devised various new forms of capital controls; debtor states did so in order to protect domestic expansionary policies from capital flight, and creditor states, to buffer their economies from the potentially inflationary effects of excess capital inflows. The US was only one of many states that sought to limit the impact of capital flows on its domestic economy.[54] Yet it is a country worth focusing on since the international stakes for its success or failure were so high.

While the US balance of payments deficit was the product of a number of different factors, chief among them was the growing volume of capital outflows. Early in 1961, Kennedy established a Cabinet Committee on Balance of Payments; through this and other institutions, members of the CEA, together with Roosa from Treasury and McChesney Martin, Chair of the Federal Reserve, devised a range of different mechanisms for influencing the flow of capital in and out of the economy.[55] One of their first efforts was a strategy that came to be known as 'Operation Twist', a name that aptly evokes the technical gymnastics involved. The US government sought to manipulate the interest rate structure, using the Treasury's sales to drive up short-term rates and the Federal Reserve's open market operations to keep long-

---

53 Susan Strange, *International Economic Relations of the Western World, 1959–1971: International Monetary Relations*, vol. 2, ed. Andrew Shonfield (London: Oxford University Press, 1976), p. 294.

54 The British government, for example, retained controls over direct and portfolio investment abroad to improve its balance of payments position. On the surplus side, the German Bundesbank took measures to discourage foreign residents' purchases of German assets in order to limit upward pressure on the deutschemark. France, Italy and the Scandinavian states used capital controls to protect domestic state-led investment strategies. Eichengreen, 'Epilogue: Three Perspectives on the Bretton Woods System', p. 643; Helleiner, *States and the Reemergence of Global Finance*, p. 92.

55 Bach, *Making Monetary and Fiscal Policy*, pp. 132–3.

term rates down.[56] This policy reflected a typical neoclassical desire to reconcile the domestic priority of stimulating investment to alleviate a minor recession (through low long-term interest rates) with the external concern with keeping short-term capital in the country (through high short-term rates). In fact, the policy did succeed in closing the gap between short- and long-term rates, yet this small success was not enough to stem the tide of dollars escaping the country.[57]

In their 1965 Annual Report, the Council of Economic Advisers registered with concern the magnitude of capital outflows and noted: 'This led to the adoption of special remedial measures, notably the imposition of the Interest Equalization Tax on purchases of new and outstanding foreign securities by U.S. investors'.[58] The IET sought to limit foreign lending by taxing Americans on any income earned from foreign investments. As David Calleo notes, this tax was consistent with 'Operation Twist', since it worked to discourage American portfolio investment abroad without affecting domestic long-term interest rates.[59] Both policies were characterised by a peculiarly neoclassical sensibility: they sought to respond to international pressures without sacrificing domestic demand-management policies; they demonstrated faith in the capacity of government to intervene in financial markets with considerable technical sophistication; and yet, in spite of these Keynesian attributes, these policies also reflected a far more classical faith in the rationality of the market. As Roosa noted, the US government opted consistently for market-based mechanisms rather than using direct controls, for fear that they would 'literally congeal the bloodstream of American capitalism'.[60] In the end, none of the domestic policies adopted by the US – or, for that matter, by other states – ultimately proved capable of compensating for the effects of increasingly volatile capital movements. Thus, they turned increasingly to international forms of monetary cooperation.

International Responses: Offsetting Strategies

As financial crises escalated throughout the 1960s, states developed a series of collaborative strategies to offset disequilibrating capital flows. The first major postwar crisis struck in 1960, in response to growing concerns about the US dollar, and took the form of a rush to buy gold. The crisis was halted initially by an informal bilateral agreement between the US and Britain to jointly manage the gold market. This agreement was soon expanded and formalised as the Gold Pool, which sought to stabilise the private gold market.[61] The next major crisis to hit the international system was a run on sterling in early 1961, as investors feared that the sterling rate

---

56 *Economic Report of the President* (Washington, DC: 1964).

57 Karier, *Great Experiments*, p. 15.

58 *Economic Report of the President* (Washington, DC: The White House, 1965), pp. 72–3.

59 David Calleo, *The Imperious Economy* (Cambridge, MA: Harvard University Press, 1982), pp. 225–26.

60 Robert Roosa. Cited in Helleiner, *States and the Reemergence of Global Finance*, p. 87.

61 Strange, *International Economic Relations*, pp. 71, 77–8.

would not hold and began to shift massive volumes of capital out of the UK.[62] This time, it was the Bank for International Settlements, or BIS, which responded first. At their monthly meeting in Basle in March 1961, central bankers came to an informal agreement to compensate for such volatile capital flows. Central banks committed through the Basle Agreement to hold one another's currencies for longer periods rather than readily converting them into gold or dollars, thus stretching existing reserves further. At the same time, they would seek to 'recycle' any hot money flows in order to minimise their impact on the foreign exchange market.

While the Gold Pool and the Basle Agreement each tackled different aspects of the international monetary system, both adopted similar strategies: they were informal, *ad hoc* solutions to immediate problems which did not attempt to resolve any of the underlying causes of the instabilities that they sought to manage. While their creators recognised the destabilising impact of increased speculation in both capital and foreign exchange markets and sought to minimise its effects, they nonetheless remained content to tinker around the edges of the market. In a press statement shortly after the Basle meeting in 1961, the central bankers recognised the stop-gap nature of what they referred to as their 'so-called agreement':

> These procedures will be temporary, pending the evolution of more permanent techniques for dealing with the problems of international financial disequilibria, particularly short-term capital movement within the framework of, or through reform of, the International Monetary Fund'.[63]

The IMF's only significant response, however, was the creation of the General Agreements to Borrow (GAB) in 1962. Through the provisions of the GAB, the ten largest industrial members – soon to form the Group of Ten – agreed that they would lend the Fund $6bn if necessary in order to help its members offset capital movements. Once again, Fund members adopted what was essentially a short-term solution to the growing long-term problem of increasing capital mobility.[64]

A Neoclassical Logic at Work

What motivated this turn to temporary and limited strategies? While part of the answer no doubt lies in the expediency of such measures, it also appears that policymakers truly believed that this piecemeal approach would solve the problem.[65] The strategy of offsetting capital movements seemed to present an ideal compromise. A laissez-faire approach to capital flows was not acceptable because it would constrain domestic

---

62 Ibid., pp. 87–8; Robert Roosa, 'Assuring the Free World's Liquidity', in Herbert C. Grubel (ed.), *World Monetary Reform: Plans and Issues* (Stanford, CA: Stanford University Press, 1963), pp. 57, 74.

63 BIS press statement, 12 March 1961. Cited in J. Keith Horsefield (ed.), *The International Monetary Fund 1945–1965: Chronicle*, vol. I (Washington, DC: International Monetary Fund, 1969), p. 483.

64 J. Keith Horsefield (ed.), *The International Monetary Fund 1945–1965: Analysis*, vol. II (Washington, DC: International Monetary Fund, 1969), pp. 374–77; De Vries, IMF, p. 69.

65 Roosa, *Dollar*, pp. 134–9; *Economic Report of the President* (1965), pp. 115–19.

commitments to demand-management policies. On the other hand, a more thorough set of capital controls was not deemed necessary, since the market was viewed as essentially rational. Offsetting thus seemed like the ideal neoclassical solution to the challenges of an evolving international monetary system.

If we examine the logic behind these new policies, we find a common tendency to downplay the destabilising potential of capital movements. In a critical assessment of two of the earliest IMF policy papers on the need for systemic reform, Thomas Balogh notes that their assumptions already stray considerably from Keynes' theory. Thus a key staff report published in 1958 begins from the premise that most movements of short- and long-term capital are equilibrating.[66] In his 1967 book, *The Dollar and World Liquidity*, Robert Roosa underlined the differences between the attitude to capital movements at the Bretton Woods conference and in the 1960s, noting that there was a 'great gap left unfilled at Bretton Woods' regarding the management of free capital movements:

> For the European participants could only visualize, at best, progress toward the free convertibility of all currencies for transactions on current account. … It was indeed implied that members would, particularly in the case of large or sustained capital outflows, use controls to regulate capital movements.[67]

While Roosa remained concerned about the potentially destabilising effects of too rapid capital flows, he was nonetheless more optimistic than his postwar predecessors about the possibility of allowing for the free movement of capital. Noting that the government had been forced to place some limits on capital markets, he insisted that 'the United States was resolved that this should not last'.[68] Domestically, the Interest Equalization Tax was to play a similarly temporary role, as 'a transitional measure' designed to slow excessive capital outflows 'until the other policies already under way succeed in encouraging more balanced flows of capital'.[69] The long-term goal of the government, he argued, was 'to widen the areas of freedom for the movement of capital in response to the competitive forces of the market place'.[70] While the Fund was returning to the neoclassical assumption that capital movements are essentially equilibrating, Roosa and other state leaders began to propose a series of responses designed to build an international financial system that facilitated the free movement of capital flows. These policies were seen as a response to a limited problem – those occasional excesses in capital flows caused by interest rate differentials or exogenous political shocks – within what was deemed to be an essentially rational global financial market.[71]

---

66 Thomas Balogh, 'International Reserves and Liquidity', *World Monetary Reform: Plans and Issues* (Stanford, CA: Stanford University Press, 1963), pp. 344–5. 'International Reserves and Liquidity: A Study by the Staff of the International Monetary Fund' (16 September 1958) in Horsefield (ed.), *The International Monetary Fund 1945–1965: Documents*, pp. 349–420.

67 Roosa, *Dollar*, pp. 222–3.

68 Ibid., p. 277.

69 Roosa, 'Assuring the Free World's Liquidity', p. 141.

70 Roosa, *Dollar*, p. 138.

71 Ibid., p. 52.

This view of capital flows was notably different from that which had been held by Keynes and his peers. As Arthur Bloomfield, an economist then working for the Federal Reserve Bank of New York, noted in 1946, there had been a 'doctrinal *volte-face*' among economists on the question of the control of capital movements by the end of the Second World War: 'It is now highly respectable doctrine, in academic and banking circles alike, that a substantial measure of *direct* control over private capital movements, especially of the so-called "hot money" varieties, will be desirable for most countries not only in the year immediately ahead but also in the long run as well'.[72] Such theoretical commitments had helped to shape capital control policy in the immediate postwar era: the IMF's own articles of agreement embraced capital controls, while two key institutions in the 1940s and 50s, the Marshall Plan and the European Payments Union, adopted an open policy towards the regulation of capital accounts.[73] Moreover, more comprehensive controls, like the cooperative measures initially proposed by Keynes and Dexter-White, remained as options under the terms of the Bretton Woods Agreement.

By the mid-1960s, however, the attitude towards capital controls had begun to shift. Controls were increasingly seen as temporary responses to limited difficulties rather than longer-term solutions to more pervasive problems. By ignoring Keynes' original insight into speculative practices as a peculiarly human – and intersubjective – aspect of economic practices, these later scholars and policymakers assumed that they could find a technical fix. Speculation was seen as a natural, if perhaps excessive, expression of a healthy market economy. The trick was to keep it within certain limits in order to ensure that it didn't interfere with other state priorities. Hence the recourse to a limited strategy – a patchwork of domestic capital controls, supplemented by a series of *ad hoc* interstate agreements to provide offsetting financing for the worst capital shocks.

What if this diagnosis was wrong and Keynes' concerns about the more pervasive instability of investment behaviour proved true? Then these measures would only succeed as long as speculative forces remained below a certain threshold. Once they grew beyond that level – as confidence deteriorated and as the volume of speculative capital grew – these various offsetting measures would fail. This indeed turned out to be the case.

The first major currency crisis hit the United Kingdom in 1967, with a panicked run on the pound.[74] As the speculative attack overwhelmed attempts by the IMF and the G-10 to bolster the pound, it quickly became clear that the international system's

---

72 Arthur L. Bloomfield, 'Postwar Control of International Capital Movements', *The American Economic Review*, 36:2 (1946), p. 687. Italics in the original.

73 Louis Pauly, *Who Elected the Bankers? Surveillance and Control in the World Economy* (Ithaca, NY: Cornell University Press, 1997), pp. 93–5; Charles P. Kindleberger, 'The European Recovery Program', Marshall Plan Days (Boston, MA: Allen and Unwin, 1987), pp. 77, 79; Robert Triffin, *Europe and the Money Muddle* (New Haven, CT: Yale University Press, 1957), pp. 186–7.

74 For detailed accounts of the crises leading up to the regime's collapse, see: Strange, *International Economic Relations*, chs. 9 and 11; De Vries, *The International Monetary Fund 1966–1971*, part 5.

measures for offsetting capital movements had failed. By the end of the decade, capital speculation had broken free from international regulation and threatened to swamp what little remained of domestic controls. The offsetting strategies adopted by the G-10 and IMF had been overwhelmed by the sheer volume and volatility of speculative capital. Once these crises began they quickly became self-fulfilling, as the failure of the international financial community to come to the rescue of the pound demonstrated that no currency was safe from attack. In August 1971, the crisis reached its apex with Nixon's decision to end the US dollar's convertibility into gold. Not even the mighty dollar, it appeared, was invulnerable from international pressure. While in many ways the transition from a gold-exchange system had been under way for a considerable time, the US decision to unilaterally halt convertibility had suddenly cut out the symbolic heart of the system. By 1973, the regime was dead.

Conclusion: Hollowing out Keynesian Norms

Between 1944 and 1973, there was a significant qualitative shift in the nature of the political economic ideas and norms that characterised the Bretton Woods regime. By the 1960s, Keynes's theories had been transformed and reinterpreted, and monetarism, while gaining ground, had yet to exercise much influence over financial decision-makers. Instead, the final decade of the Bretton Woods regime is best understood as the era of the neoclassical synthesis, a theoretical framework that drew on Keynes while at the same time eroding some of his most powerful insights into the intersubjective nature of international finance. It was these hollowed-out norms that provided the intellectual and normative lenses through which policymakers sought to respond to the growing challenges of the later Bretton Woods years. While retaining their commitment to government regulation of domestic and international economic forces, US policymakers and IMF staff were increasingly drawn to narrow technical solutions to the problem of speculation.

This analysis of the hollowing out of Keynesian norms thus provides us with some clues to solving our first puzzle – why the Bretton Woods regime collapsed when it did. In this chapter, I have focused on the role that the neoclassical synthesis played in shaping policymakers' response to the challenge of speculative capital movements. Counterfactuals are always difficult to pin down in the context of complex historical events. Nonetheless, one can reasonably assume that a more robust Keynesian approach to capital regulation, which treated speculation as psychologically-driven and structurally dangerous, would have sought to more permanently contain those capital flows and to challenge the benign vision of speculation which helped to legitimise them. A more coherent approach to capital regulation would have provided much needed respite from periodic crises, allowing time for Special Drawing Rights to come into effect, easing the liquidity crisis, and reducing the disequilibrating impact of capital movements, thus lessening the pressure for adjustment. Instead, the rise of speculative activity fostered a vicious cycle in which increased speculative capital flows exacerbated the twin problems of adjustment and liquidity, encouraging fears of an imminent crisis, which only fuelled the speculative fever. By changing the terms through which financial and political leaders defined the problems at hand and devised possible solutions, the eclipse of Keynes by the neoclassical synthesis did indeed change the course of financial history, contributing to the regime's decline.

This study has contributed evidence to support the initial theoretical question of why ideas matter. In doing so, this chapter necessarily raises doubts about the explanatory power of neoliberal institutionalist and power-based analyses that neglect their central role. Economic institutionalists such as Michael Bordo and Barry Eichengreen have turned to the institutional weaknesses of the Bretton Woods regime to explain its ultimate demise. Both blame structural flaws in the exchange system, made worse by the lack of clear rules and definitions within the regime. Together, they argue, these institutional weaknesses reduced the capacity of the regime to effectively coordinate state and market action.[75] Yet, this focus on technical weaknesses only leads us to a further question: why were those institutional arrangements and policies adopted? As this study has demonstrated, in order to answer this question we must examine the influence of the economic theories of the era, which combined a classical faith in the value of market-based solutions with a Keynesian belief in the importance of government in fine-tuning such solutions.

Power-based analysts seek to provide a more robust answer to the question of why particular institutional options were pursued at this time, by focusing on the interests that informed those decisions. These analysts suggest that the Bretton Woods regime survived as long as it did, in spite of its technical weaknesses, because it was underwritten by American hegemony. A bargain of sorts was struck: the US benefited from unlimited credit, while the other major powers benefited from the increased liquidity provided by US dollars. Yet, as US economic and political power declined relative to other states and the structural imbalances grew, the agreement broke down.[76] Joanne Gowa suggests that the crucial shift in US policy occurred in the early Nixon years, when the US first ceased to actively support the regime and then closed the gold window. Yet Gowa herself admits that that the tensions in the Bretton Woods regime had begun long before Nixon came to power.[77] To understand the sources of the regime's collapse, we must therefore look further back in time, to the Kennedy and Johnson administrations. Here, we do find significant efforts towards cooperation including multilateral strategies to offset capital movements and manage the price of gold. It was only once these efforts failed, and the economic imbalances grew too large, that the US hegemonic bargain broke down.

Once again, however, we need to ask ourselves why US policymakers pursued their interests in the terms that they did. To answer that question, we need to focus on the policies that led up to the crises of the late 1960s – and the ideas that informed them. Throughout the 1960s, I have suggested, US policymakers, together with IMF staff members and others, increasingly defined their economic interests and the policies that were to achieve them through a particular set of economic ideas – those of the neoclassical synthesis. The forms of technical cooperation that the US and

---

75 Eichengreen, *Globalizing Capital*, pp. 122–3; Eichengreen, 'Epilogue', pp. 641–3.
76 See, for example, Keohane and Nye, *Power and Interdependence*.
77 Gowa, *Closing the Gold Window*, p. 176.

others pursued – an approach that Michael Webb has called 'symptom-management' – were shaped by those ideas.[78] It was the failure of those policies that ultimately set the stage for the regime's collapse.

What have we learned that might help to resolve our second, theoretical, puzzle – the apparent contradiction between two of the most persuasive accounts of the role of norms in the Bretton Woods financial system – those of John Ruggie and Eric Helleiner? Ruggie suggests that the norms that had governed the postwar embedded liberal compromise persisted well after the collapse of the formal Bretton Woods exchange rate regime. He thus describes the transition undertaken in the 1970s as an example of norm-governed change. Helleiner, on the other hand, suggests that it was the US's adoption of monetarist ideas that precipitated the breakdown in international consensus and thus contributed to the collapse of the regime. Whereas Ruggie emphasises a continuity in Keynesian norms, Helleiner points to a significant breach.

The evidence in this study suggests that there exists an interesting solution to this particular puzzle: Ruggie and Helleiner are both partly – but not entirely – correct. In the final years of the Bretton Woods regime there was neither a breach nor continuity in the norms governing international finance. There was instead a process of hollowing out. The Keynesian ideas which had informed the Bretton Woods institutions remained, but in an attenuated form as the neoclassical synthesis. The core of Keynes' insight into the intersubjective nature of international finance – and thus the need to build a system capable of managing those intersubjective dynamics – was replaced by a focus on providing functional solutions to technical problems.

Ruggie is therefore correct in emphasising the continuity in certain underlying norms – such as the attempt to reconcile domestic autonomy and an open international economy. Yet he does not examine the content of those norms sufficiently, and therefore misses a crucial shift in the ontological assumptions that underpinned them. Helleiner, on the other hand, does point to an important normative shift, but he ultimately overstates the change. While it is certainly true that monetarist ideas were on the rise – and Helleiner makes an excellent case for their influence on the US resistance to capital controls in the early 1970s – nonetheless, their role was at most a precipitating one. The damage to the system had long been done before the US change of heart, through successive attempts in the 1960s to find narrowly technical solutions to the problem of speculation. The hollowing out of the Keynesian-inspired norms fostered the collapse of the Bretton Woods regime; it was in the confusion that followed that monetarist and new-classical ideas finally came into their own, having had the ground laid for them by the advocates of the neoclassical synthesis.

I began this chapter by asking what a study of the decline of the last great financial regime might teach us about the kind of 'new financial architecture' we

---

78 Michael Webb, *The Political Economy of Policy Coordination* (Ithaca, NY: Cornell University Press, 1995). Webb does an excellent job of pointing to the limits of hegemonic stability theory in explaining the shift towards 'symptom-management' strategies such as the Gold Pool and swaps during this period. Where my analysis differs from his is in my emphasis on the importance of shifting economic ideas in shaping the form that the policy shift took – and in explaining its limits.

might build today. In fact, we might draw a number of insights – perhaps even warnings – from this historical study. If anything, the years since the collapse of the Bretton Woods regime have witnessed an increase in the belief in the sufficiency of technical solutions. Yet the past ten years of chronic financial crises suggest that Keynes' insights into the intersubjective nature of financial activity – and of the potentially destabilising effects of their force if left unchecked – are more relevant than ever before. Technique, while useful, will never be enough in a realm that will always remain resistant to complete control or understanding. Financial stability depends on confidence, and confidence is a matter of faith – not simply in the efficiency of institutions, but also in the robustness and legitimacy of the norms that inform them. If we are to take away one lesson from the failure of the Bretton Woods regime, perhaps it should be to recognise the hubris of assuming the sufficiency of technique.

PART II
Embedded Liberalism in Practice

Chapter 3

Trade Globalization, Economic Performance, and Social Protection: Nineteenth-Century British Laissez-Faire and Post-World War II U.S.-Embedded Liberalism

Salvatore Pitruzzello

How have market and state shaped the long-term evolution of economic performance and social protection during the nineteenth-century globalization associated with British laissez-faire liberalism and the post-World War II globalization associated with U.S.-embedded liberalism?

The intensification of globalization has thrust this question to the core of an emerging body of political economy research that compares the two waves of globalization to draw lessons from the nineteenth-century wave and apply those lessons to the current wave.[1] This research strongly reflects the political tensions informing recent mass demonstrations against perceived economic and social costs of unfettered globalization.[2] It also reflects two major themes voiced in the popular press by neoliberals and neointerventionists: the long-term stability and viability of post-World War II embedded liberalism in a fast globalizing world; and fears

---

1   See James 2002; Aghion and Williamson 1998; Bordo, Eichengreen, and Irwin 1999; and O'Rourke 1999.

2   See Bhagwati 2002; Broad 2002; Dollar and Kraay 2002; and Stiglitz 2002. Critiques of globalization span the ideological spectrum: (1) neoclassical economists who now believe that capitalism is subject to structural political conflicts over the requirements of global competitiveness and domestic social protection; see Stiglitz 2002; and Rodrik 1997; (2) new Keynesians reasserting that capitalism engenders periodic economic breakdowns; see Cornwall and Cornwall 2001; (3) third-way social philosophers and activists advocating political control of unfettered global markets; see Tonelson 2000; Gray 1998; and Giddens 1998; (4) disillusioned liberals criticizing the destructiveness of unregulated markets; see Soros 1998; and T. Friedman 1999; (5) communitarians advocating a world of self-sufficient closed communities; see Klein 2002; and Etzioni 1994; and (6) populists supporting protectionism as they blame globalization for long-term unemployment and increasing labor market inequalities; see Meny and Surel 2002; and P. Buchanan 1998.

of backlashes against globalization that are reminiscent of the nineteenth-century wave.[3]

Relying on neoclassical views of self-regulating economies, neoliberals privilege the intensification of unfettered globalization: they lament the inefficiency of state-steered embedded liberalism; fear politically driven protectionist backlashes against globalization; praise the efficiency of nineteenth-century laissez-faire in ensuring superior economic growth; and favor the reconstitution of market dominance as the ideal pathway to long-run growth, which best ensures full employment and social protection.[4] In contrast, neointerventionists fear the intensification of globalization: they lament the social inequalities associated with unfettered markets; denounce the social costs of nineteenth-century laissez-faire; also fear protectionist backlashes; but privilege political control of markets to ensure better economic performance – growth and employment – as well as social protection.[5]

Undoubtedly, these supposedly novel debates represent the resurgence of the interwar "ideology debate" – pitting Keynes and Polanyi versus Hayek and Von Mises – over the efficiency of market and state in shaping the long-run evolution of economic performance and social protection. The interwar debates concerned the long-term stability and viability of nineteenth-century laissez-faire and its replacement with embedded liberalism.[6] Today, after half a century of experiments with embedded liberalism, debates are about its long-term stability and viability and its replacement with novel forms of laissez-faire.[7] Nevertheless, systematic comparisons of the two regimes that satisfactorily assess the empirical adequacy of neoliberal and neointerventionist claims remain severely lacking.

The political economy research focuses on a variety of related issues: for example, properties of globalization;[8] economic and political determinants of long-run growth;[9] wage and income convergence;[10] inequality and growth;[11] and backlashes against globalization.[12] Ultimately, however, such research fails to capture how market and state have shaped the coevolution of economic performance and social protection in each of the two regimes. I argue that there is an unsettling disjunction between theoretical claims about the long-run dynamics driving the two regimes and empirical evidence derived from neoclassical theories of short-run dynamics and

---

3 See James 2002; Gilpin 2000; and Rodrik 1997.
4 See Lindsey 2002; Vasquez 2000; Lai 2000; and Micklethwait and Wooldridge 2000.
5 See Broad 2002; Gray 1998; and Greider 1997.
6 See James 2002; and Ruggie 1982.
7 See Gilpin 2000; and Ruggie 1997.
8 Baldwin and Martin 1999. Comparisons focus on globalization as an economic phenomenon: (1) nineteenth-century globalization is as encompassing; see Vasquez 2000; (2) post-World War II globalization is more encompassing; see Bordo, Eichengreen, and Irwin 1999; (3) trade and financial aggregates conceal features that render comparisons misleading; see Krugman 1995.
9 See Cornwall and Cornwall 2001; and Maddison 1995.
10 See Boyer and Drache 1996; and Williamson 1996.
11 See Aghion and Williamson 1998; and Williamson 1998.
12 See O'Rourke 1999; and Williamson 1998.

statistical methodologies – such as means, correlations, and ordinary least squares (OLS)-based regressions. At best, such theories and methods can describe short-run stationary fluctuations, not long-run dynamics.[13] The utter neglect of persistent, nonstationary, dynamics of historical processes central to the debates – for example, trade and financial flows, gross domestic product (GDP), unemployment, government spending – triggers such disjunction. It also results in spurious findings that inform erroneous inferences about the long-run stability of regimes and unwarranted policy lessons.[14]

Nonstationarity, however, suggests alternative long-run stable dynamics if the persistent processes were cointegrated, or coevolving, around common stochastic trends driving the evolution of the two regimes.[15] This chapter adopts the theoretical and methodological framework of cointegration to evaluate the rival neoliberal and neointerventionist claims about how market and state shape the long-term coevolution of economic performance and social protection in the two regimes. Cointegration allows for the investigation of three crucial dimensions of long-run dynamics: (1) common stochastic trends, which capture system stability and rigidity; (2) cointegrated equilibrium relations coevolving stably around the common trends; and (3) adjustment mechanisms that maintain the relations in long-run equilibrium.

To investigate these long-run dynamics, this article develops a core multidimensional model rooted in the constructivist approach to international political economy.[16] The model links four historical processes that are central to political economy debates on the coevolution of economic performance and social protection in the two regimes: (1) trade openness, (2) real GDP, (3) unemployment, and (4) government spending.[17] In the context of constructivism, the research design relies on the ideal-typical comparison of the normative structures of social purpose of the two regimes.[18] Empirically, the comparison focuses on the normative structures of the hegemonic powers that spearheaded and influenced the evolution of the two regimes: Great Britain for nineteenth-century laissez-faire during the 1865–1913 period; and the United States for post-World War II embedded liberalism during the 1955–2000 period.

Cointegration analyses of the long-run dynamics of the hegemons challenge core neoliberal claims. First, unit root tests shatter claims about the greater flexibility of nineteenth-century laissez-faire: all four processes in both regimes exhibit nonstationary persistence, which implies similar rigidity. Second, cointegration tests

---

13 For a discussion of such disjunction, especially in economics, see Juselius 1999; Granger 1997; and Pesaran 1997.

14 See Nelson and Plosser 1982; and Granger and Newbold 1974. I discuss stationary and nonstationary dynamics below.

15 See Johansen 1995; and Engle and Granger 1991.

16 See Ruggie 1998; Wendt 1999; and Adler 2002.

17 With regard to globalization, the analytic focus is on trade openness. Research in progress that builds on this core model investigates the coevolution of monetary regimes – the nineteenth-century gold standard and the postwar sequences of fixed, flexible exchange rates – and trade openness; see Eichengreen 1996; and Verdier 1998.

18 Weber 1949.

challenge scenarios of regime instability foreboding the implosion of globalization: the presence of one common trend driving the long-run evolution of both regimes establishes the long-run stability of the two regimes. The one common trend also challenges claims about the greater rigidity of embedded liberalism: both regimes feature similar degrees of rigidity. Third, equilibrium relations refute claims about the economic inefficiency of the state in embedded liberalism and the efficiency of laissez-faire markets: state interventions in postwar United States are associated with better economic performance and social protection. Fourth, adjustment dynamics question beliefs that markets shape the dynamics of laissez-faire liberalism whereas the state shapes the dynamics of embedded liberalism: state interventions are necessary to maintain the equilibria both of nineteenth-century British laissez-faire and of postwar-U.S.-embedded liberalism. Ultimately, these findings question the wisdom of the neoliberal political project to reconstitute market dominance: novel laissez-faire worlds may yield inferior economic performance and social protection. Rather, as neointerventionists claim, political control of markets ensures superior economic performance together with better social protection.

The first section below traces the resurgence of the "ideology debate". The second section presents the four-dimensional model rooted in the constructivist theory of regimes. The third section justifies the comparative research design. The fourth section demonstrates the ubiquity of nonstationary dynamics. The fifth section outlines the VECM cointegration model. The next three sections provide tests of regime stability and rigidity (sixth); of equilibrium relations (seventh); and of adjustment dynamics (eighth). The final section discusses the implications of the research.

The "Resurgence of the Ideology Debate": Efficiency of Market and State

The ideology debate between neoliberals and neointerventionists over the relative efficiency of market and state in shaping the coevolution of economic performance and social protection in embedded liberalism finds its roots in the highly unstable interwar period.[19] Between World War I and the Great Depression, the highly interconnected laissez-faire international regime that had been dominant in the second half of the nineteenth century imploded, and countries reverted to autarchic and near-autarchic nationalistic forms of economic management.[20] Interventionists such as Keynes and Polanyi, in contrast to economic liberals such as Von Mises and Hayek, challenged the long-run viability of nineteenth-century laissez-faire liberalism and laid the theoretical and political grounds for postwar embedded liberalism.[21]

---

19 Hoover 2003.

20 See James 2002; and Simmons 1994.

21 See Keynes 1936, 1982; Polanyi 1957; Von Mises 1977; and Hayek 1944, 1966. A rich body of recent research has retraced the theoretical and policy relevance of the interwar debates; see Hoover 2003; Cochran and Glahe 1999; Allen 1998; Shearmur 1996; Mendell and Salee 1991; and Hayek and Caldwell 1995. However, the roots of the debates extend well into nineteenth-century British liberalism; see Coats 1971. Classical liberals – Smith,

The interwar debate hinged on diametrically opposite hypotheses that are central to contemporary debates: the trade-off or complementarity between market and state and between economic efficiency and social protection. The trade-off hypothesis, dominant in nineteenth-century laissez-faire, pitted efficient markets against inefficient state, and economic efficiency against inefficient social protection. Best captured by neoclassical formulations of Walrasian equilibria, perfectly competitive and self-regulating markets converged endogenously toward intertemporal equilibria of full-employment growth.[22] State interventions in the economy and society were unnecessary and inefficient: unnecessary because markets endogenously converged toward optimal economic and welfare equilibria; inefficient because they hampered spontaneous convergence toward equilibria.

Confronting the massive economic breakdowns, social unrest, and the final implosion of the global economy, Keynes and Polanyi questioned the trade-off hypothesis in favor of the complementarity of market and state: state interventions were necessary to ensure economic stability and social protection. Far from being self-regulating, laissez-faire markets were inherently self-destructive and generated severe economic and social instabilities that sparked backlashes against unfettered globalization, finally leading to its implosion.[23] Keynes traced instabilities to the "stickiness" of goods and labor markets and to the volatility of global financial markets. Capital controls and aggregate demand policies, via government spending, would contribute to economic stability in an open world economy. Polanyi traced instabilities to the social and political responses against the unprecedented historical experiment, spearheaded by nineteenth-century Britain, of disembedding capitalist markets from social relations. Re-embedding markets – global and domestic – required governments to assume broader economic and social responsibilities.

Hayek and Von Mises, instead, reasserted the validity of the trade-off hypothesis. Beyond the negative effects of the singular event of World War I, they traced the socioeconomic instabilities and the ultimate implosion of the laissez-faire regime to inefficient positive economic and social state interventions. Such interventions, which were associated with the emergence of "collectivism", undermined the spontaneous functioning of laissez-faire markets. In particular, as later research attempted to demonstrate empirically, inefficient monetary policies were the principal cause of the Great Depression.[24] Hence, only the unfettering of markets, by means of negative state interventions that bolstered market dominance, would ensure long-run, full-employment growth and the wealth necessary for social protection.

Malthus, Ricardo, Bentham, and Mill – shared a faith in the economic and welfare efficiency of unfettered markets and rejected that the state could ameliorate socioeconomic conditions. Social liberals – Green, Hobhouse, Hobson, and Bonsaquet – advocated legislation that provided protection against market dislocations.

22 Walras 1954.

23 This "apocalyptic" view of capitalism was widely shared at the time; see Schumpeter 1928.

24 Friedman and Schwartz 1963.

By the early 1960s, the "end of ideology debate" appeared to irreversibly sanction the complementarity hypothesis. In the context of the Keynesian-based Bretton Woods multilateral system, the historical compromise informing embedded liberalism seemed to successfully ensure global growth, full employment, and social protection.[25] The "end of ideology" captured a new balance between market and state: the political left had accepted the market as a central instrument of growth; the political right, the state as an instrument of growth and redistribution.[26] Political conflict was confined to valence issues, away from the interwar fundamental clashes over the proper relations between market and state.

Instead, by the early 1980s, following the breakdown of the Bretton Woods system, stagflations, and the intensification of globalization, the "resurgence of the ideological debate" under fierce neoliberal critiques weakened the postwar consensus on the long-term viability of embedded liberalism.[27] A first wave of attacks – especially from monetarist and new classical economists, social conservatives, and the Virginia school of public choice – challenged the complementarity hypothesis in the domestic arena: the inherently inefficient positive economic and welfare interventions, best captured by the historically unprecedented growth of the public sector, hampered long-term economic growth.[28] Negative interventions, à la Hayek, were necessary to achieve market deregulation and the withdrawal of the state from the economy and society.[29] Social inequality was deemed necessary to provide incentives for economic growth.[30] A second wave of critiques challenged the complementarity hypothesis in a fast globalizing world: international markets, especially financial, inexorably weakened the ability of the state to stabilize the economy and to provide social protection;[31] the welfare state, in particular, undermined international competitiveness.[32] Neo-Hayekean evolutionary theories predicted the irreversibility of unfettered globalization as well as the inevitability of convergence toward laissez-faire.[33]

More recently, however, several countercritiques have reasserted the complementarity between market and state. Endogenous growth theories claim that selected types of government spending are economically efficient.[34] In addition to

---

25 See Marglin and Schor 1990; Ruggie 1982; and Shonfield 1969.

26 See Bell 1962; and Lipset 1960. In economics, the "end of the business cycle" captured the success; see Okun 1975.

27 See Ruggie 1982, 1997; and Keohane 1984b.

28 Monetarist and new classical critiques challenged the efficiency of economic stabilization; see J. Stein 1982; Sargent and Wallace 1975; and M. Friedman 1968. Demand-push neoconservative theorists argued that malignant interest groups formation triggered demands that overloaded the state budget; see Olson 1982; and Crozier, Watanuki, and Huntington 1975. Supply-pull public choice theorists pointed to the fiscal irresponsibility of self-regarding politicians; see Mueller 2003; and J. Buchanan 1977.

29 Campbell and Pedersen 2001.

30 Aghion, Caroli, and Garcia-Penalosa 1999.

31 See Mishra 1999; Ohmae 1990; and Strange 1996.

32 Alesina and Perotti 1998.

33 See Vasquez 2000; Hayek 1996; and Fukuyama 1993.

34 See Aghion and Howitt 1998; and Barro and Sala-i-Martin 1999.

investments on research and development, spending on human capital is particularly relevant. New political economy theories link social protection, especially reduction of poverty and inequality, to productive efficiency.[35] Claims that globalization inevitably leads to the retrenchment of the welfare state appear to be dubious, particularly in the context of postindustrialism.[36] The state continues to shape national adaptations to globalization.[37] The strategies and instruments of interventions used in embedded liberalism have changed but have not eroded the normative structure of social purpose that defines market-state-society relations.[38] These critiques have informed neointerventionist defenses of the capacity of embedded liberalism to ensure long-term economic stability and social protection.[39] Even self-professed neoclassical economists now maintain that laissez-faire liberalism is a threat to democracy and social stability: social protection is necessary to forestall backlashes against unfettered globalization.[40]

In historical context, the resurgence of the ideology debate represents a rupture with the postwar consensus on embedded liberalism. Neoliberals now explicitly admire the once discredited nineteenth-century laissez-faire and question the long-term viability of embedded liberalism established at Bretton Woods to replace the then-discredited laissez-faire liberalism.[41] Simultaneously, they praise the efficiency of nineteenth-century laissez-faire: it generated superior growth through more encompassing globalization, greater flexibility of global and domestic markets, and minimal state intervention. The policy lesson they advocate – "to go back to the future" by politically reconstituting global laissez-faire – rests on the promise that unfettered markets, as in the nineteenth century, will deliver sustained long-term growth.[42]

In contrast, mindful of Keynes's and Polanyi's critiques, neointerventionists fear the reconstitution of unfettered globalization: nineteenth-century laissez-faire might have created unprecedented wealth but the social costs associated with disembedded markets also triggered harsh backlashes against globalization.[43] Concerns about renewed backlashes against unfettered globalization inform an alternative policy lesson – "to go forward to the future" by enhancing political control over global and domestic markets to better ensure long-term economic growth, full employment, and social protection.

---

35 Aghion and Williamson 1998.

36 In "postindustrialism", structural changes in population aging, female labor participation, and skill-biased unemployment drive the growth of the public sector; see Pierson 2001; Iversen 2001; and Esping-Andersen 1999.

37 See Hirst and Thompson 1999; Weiss 1998; and Keohane and Milner 1996.

38 Ruggie aptly distinguishes between "norm transforming" and "norm governed" change; Ruggie 1998.

39 See Esping-Andersen 2002; Swank 2002; Garrett 1998; and Giddens 1998.

40 See Stiglitz 2002; and Rodrik 1997.

41 See Lai 2000; Hayek and Caldwell 1995; and Friedman and Friedman 1980.

42 The metaphor "to go back to the future" is borrowed from Bordo, Eichengreen, and Irwin 1999.

43 See Aghion and Williamson 1998; Williamson 1998; Gray 1998; and Rodrik 1997.

The Model: Centrality of Long-Run Dynamics

At the core, the ideological debate between neoliberals and neointerventionists is about the long-run dynamics – stability and viability – of the two international regimes. A model ought to capture the rival claims about long-run dynamics. The theoretical roots of such a model are best traced to constructivist theories of international regimes. A basic multidimensional model usefully captures core mechanisms through which market and state shape economic performance and social protection in the two regimes.

International Regimes: Structure and Dynamics

Tracing the model to constructivist regime theory is problematic: all major schools of international relations – realism, neoliberal institutionalism, and constructivism – disagree fundamentally on the causal relevance of regimes.[44] Realism attributes little importance to international regimes: they are instruments for hegemons to enhance their power in the anarchic international system. Neoliberal institutionalism attributes greater instrumental significance to regimes: given anarchy, they can reduce transaction costs in the interaction of states. Only in constructivism are regimes ontologically independent from configurations of interstate power and indeed can autonomously affect such power. By privileging a social ontology that rests on holism, norm-based behavior, socially constructed institutions, and historical contingency, constructivism explicitly considers how the normative structure of social purpose shapes the identity of regimes.[45] Such identity rests ultimately on authority relations defining the relationship of market and state to society and their contributions to economic performance and social protection.[46]

In the constructivist framework, international regimes emerge as stable and viable social institutions around which the long-run expectations of actors participating in the regime converge. Organizing principles of legitimate order and meaning shape the historical evolution – formation and transformation – of regimes. Market, state, and society represent three fundamental macro-structures of regimes. Authority relations define the legitimate orderings of market, state, and society. The two regimes – nineteenth-century laissez-faire and post-World War II embedded liberalism – represent distinct and historically contingent institutional configurations of authority relations.

Neoliberals and neointerventionists largely agree that diametrically opposite principles and authority relations inform the normative structures of the two regimes. Laissez-faire liberalism rests on market dominance over the state and on disembedding markets from society. Its central objective is economic growth through markets unfettered by positive state interventions. Growth determines the dynamics of unemployment. Growth also determines social protection via lower unemployment

---

44 See Simmons and Martin 2002; and Hasenclever, Mayer, and Rittberger 1997.
45 See Adler 2002; and Wendt 1999.
46 Ruggie 1982, 1998.

and higher living standards. Negative interventions of the laissez-faire state, à la Hayek, bolster market dominance. In contrast, embedded liberalism rests on the complementarity of market and state and on the social embedding of markets. Full-employment growth and social protection are both central objectives. Positive state interventions – stabilizing and welfare – in the international and domestic arenas, as in the multilateral Bretton Woods system, serve to achieve these twin objectives.

Neoliberals and neointerventionists, however, clash over how the distinctive organizing principles of the two regimes ensure their long-term stability and viability.[47] According to neoliberals, the institutional framework of laissez-faire liberalism generates stable long-run dynamics. Unfettered – that is, politically deregulated – markets endogenously adjust to shocks: they quickly clear and converge toward a long-run stable equilibrium characterized by full-employment growth. Instead, the institutions of embedded liberalism inevitably generate unstable, sticky, dynamics: inefficient state interventions in the economy and society hamper spontaneous convergence of markets toward long-run equilibrium. Mindful of Keynes, neointerventionists challenge the economic and welfare efficiency of laissez-faire liberalism: unfettered markets fail to clear and to converge toward the long-run equilibrium. Markets rather tend toward disequilibrium characterized by persistent and socially costly underemployment. Positive state interventions are necessary to ensure convergence toward full-employment growth and social protection.

The Multidimensional Model: Testable Hypotheses

Such disagreements over long-run dynamics inform the debates on the specific mechanisms by which market and state shape the long-run coevolution of economic performance and social protection in the two regimes. A simple multidimensional model, which focuses on the demand side of the economy, captures the basic relations at the core of such debates:

$$g = f_1(y, u) \qquad f_{1,y} > 0, f_{1,u} > 0 \tag{1}$$

$$y = f_2(x, g, t) \qquad f_{2,x} > 0, f_{2,g} \neq 0, f_{2,t} > 0 \tag{2}$$

$$u = f_3(x, y) \qquad f_{3,x} > 0, f_{3,y} < 0 \tag{3}$$

where g is government spending as a ratio of GDP; y is the level of real GDP; u is the unemployment rate; x, trade, describes the openness of the economy; and t is a linear time trend capturing productivity shocks.[48] The model thus links the coevolution of

47 Ruggie 1994, 1997.

48 These processes, albeit in single-equation format, are central to the research on the post-World War II era; see Swank 2002; Iversen 2001; Huber and Stephens 2001; and Garrett 1998. They are also central to research on nineteenth-century laissez-faire; see O'Rourke and Williamson 1999; and Williamson 1998. However, the single-equation modeling obscures the complexity of dynamics stemming from feedbacks traversing the three equations.

economic growth, unemployment, and government spending in the context of trade regimes. As in established research, trade is analytically exogenous to the model.[49]

Equation (1) captures the evolution of the public sector. It links the dynamics of government spending (g) to shocks in GDP and unemployment – two crucial mechanisms of social protection. The positive spending-GDP relation operates via Wagner, or wealth, redistributive effects: spending increases as a proportion of national income.[50] The positive spending-unemployment relation captures welfare interventions that protect social strata exposed to labor market shocks, especially those linked to trade.[51]

Equation (2) captures economic growth – a crucial dimension of economic performance. It links the evolution of GDP (y) to shocks in trade, spending, and productivity. The positive GDP-trade relation describes the openness-growth connection.[52] The GDP-spending relation gauges the effects of economic and social interventions on economic growth. The inequality sign $\neq$ indicates the disagreements between neoliberals and neointerventionists over the long-term efficiency of positive state interventions: the sign is positive, or growth inducing, for neointerventionists; negative, or growth dampening, for neoliberals.[53] The trend t describes technology-driven productivity shocks.[54]

Equation (3) captures a second crucial dimension of economic performance – unemployment. It links the evolution of unemployment (u) to shocks in trade and GDP. Trade, as in Heckscher-Ohlin models, induces socioeconomic dislocations best captured by unemployment.[55] GDP describes the business cycle trade-off between growth and unemployment.[56]

---

49 The dimensionality, or complexity, of the model can be increased by introducing other historical processes: for example, (1) real wage, (2) investment, and (3) political institutions such as the organizational and political power of labor and parliamentary institutions. The increased dimensionality would not change the theoretical argument and the empirical predictions of this core model.

50 In the historical context of Bismarckian Germany, Wagner's original formulation of the growth of the public sector was rooted in the requirements of statism and militarism; see Wagner 1958; and Von Mises 1969.

51 For the postwar era, several theories have linked public sector expansion to the unemployment effects of economic openness: for example, for modernization, see Cameron 1978; for political-class conflict, see Garrett 1998; Esping-Andersen 1990; and Flora and Heidenheimer 1981; for the compromise of embedded liberalism, see Ruggie 1982; for adaptive responses of small but highly open economies, see Katzenstein 1985; for deindustrialization, see Iversen 2001; Rodrik 1997; and Wood 1994.

52 The theoretical literature posits the positive trade-growth link; see Obstfeld and Rogoff 1996. New growth theories for the postwar era focus on trade-induced positive effects of R&D, increasing returns to scale, and technological spillovers; see Aghion and Howitt 1998. Research on the nineteenth century also posits the positive link; see O'Rourke 2000.

53 Abrams 1999.

54 Aghion and Howitt 1998. Productivity shocks encompass shocks in investments.

55 Greenaway and Nelson 2001.

56 Sargent 1987.

In this system, government spending plays the crucial role in determining the dynamics of the two regimes.[57] Regarding the laissez-faire regime, the model captures rival claims over the efficiency of unfettered markets in the presence of minimal state intervention. Neoliberals and neointerventionists share a basic agreement about the spending equation (*g*). Given the minimal state, small wealth and welfare effects do not engender a considerable long-run growth of government spending. Accordingly, *g* cannot shape significantly the dynamics of growth and unemployment. For neoliberals, self-regulating markets unencumbered by state interventions ensure quick convergence toward long-term full-employment equilibrium growth. Shocks are temporary, and any long-run dynamics are traceable to exogenous deterministic trends.[58] Instead, for neointerventionists, in Keynesian fashion, laissez-faire markets are sticky: they fail to clear quickly and yield suboptimal long-run equilibria characterized by long-term underunemployment. Thus, in the *y* equation, booms and busts in trade are persistent and generate long-term fluctuations in economic growth. In the *u* equation, persistent booms and busts in trade and GDP generate long-term fluctuations in unemployment.

For embedded liberalism, the model captures the sharp divisions over the efficiency of the large public sector. Here, neoliberals and neointerventionists also share a basic agreement about the g equation: significant wealth and welfare effects have contributed to the historically unprecedented long-term growth of public spending. Wealth effects point to strong mechanisms of redistribution: vis-à-vis nineteenth-century laissez-faire, a greater proportion of national income goes toward government spending. Given the centrality of social protection, unemployment also represents a major mechanism of growth for spending. For neoliberals, the trade-off hypothesis predicts that the growth of the inefficient public sector dampens long-run growth and yields persistent unemployment. For neointerventionists, given the complementarity hypothesis, spending contributes to long-term growth, lower unemployment, and social protection.

---

57 In the context of constructivism, the focus on government spending is meant to capture two main dimensions of state intervention in the economy and society: (1) economic stabilization, and (2) social security/protection; Ruggie 1982. The objective of spending aimed at macroeconomic stabilization is to bring the economy toward full employment growth – which is itself a crucial component of social protection. The *y* and, via recursive substitutions, *u* equations capture this first dimension. The objective of social spending aims at minimizing the domestic social costs of economic openness stemming from adjustments to structural change in the international division of labor. The wealth (*y*) and welfare (*u*) effects in the *g* equation capture this second dimension. A narrower focus on social and welfare spending would miss the complexity of these multiple dimensions of social protection. Moreover, new growth theory demonstrates how difficult it is to disaggregate government spending in its economic and social components – for example, investment in physical and human capital, welfare, and even military; Aghion and Howitt 1998.

58 Aghion and Howitt 1998.

Comparative Research Design: Inference from Hegemonic Powers to Regimes

How does one evaluate the empirical adequacy of the rival claims about the long-run dynamics of the two international regimes? A first crucial methodological decision concerns the appropriate research design and sample for valid inference. All theories of international political economy – realism, neoliberal institutionalism, constructivism – tend to rely on comparisons of the hegemonic powers to investigate the core properties of the two regimes.[59] A fundamental, but by no means uncontroversial, hypothesis supports the comparative design: hegemons influence the evolution – creation and maintenance – of regimes.[60] Thus, theoretical inference about the dynamics of regimes is drawn from their respective hegemons. Moreover, constructivist social theory, which in its critical version relies on Gramscian views of hegemony, suggests the comparison of the normative structures of the respective hegemons – nineteenth-century Britain and post-World War II United States. The logic of inference is that the relative dominance of market and state in the hegemonic countries influences the evolution of regimes, and that the investigation of the normative structures of hegemons provides significant insights into the dynamics of regimes.[61]

Three specific claims legitimize the constructivist comparative design. The first justifies the comparison of the normative structures of hegemons: the normative structures of the hegemons exemplify those of regimes, thereby capturing their identity. Hegemons influence the evolution of regimes through the fusion of two principles that project their authority in the international system: (1) concentration of wealth and power, and (2) normative structure of social purpose. Resource concentration, central to realism, helps explain why a hegemon creates and

---

59 See Keohane 1984a; A. Stein 1984; and Ruggie 1982. Formally, the comparison involves regimes as ideal types. More precisely, it involves the class of ideal types based on particular historical phenomena, such as "the Protestant Ethic," and "modern capitalism," which appear only in specific historical periods and in particular cultural areas; Weber 1949. The polar regimes of nineteenth-century laissez-faire and post-World War II embedded liberalism represent such types. The analytic task is to identify the core features of these two polar types, which essentially relate to the normative structure of social purpose. The empirical task is to determine whether and how the normative structures of the hegemons – nineteenth-century Britain and post-World War II United States – approximate the properties of the two types.

60 Controversies concern: (1) differences in motives ascribed to hegemons in realist, liberal, and constructivist theories; (2) whether hegemons are necessary and/or sufficient for regime formation and maintenance; and (3) whether hegemons privilege an open international economy; Hasenclever, Mayer, and Rittberger 1997.

61 In this constructivist framework, the main objective of the research is to achieve a better understanding of the normative structures and causal macro-social mechanisms of the two political economy regimes, rather than the intersubjective dimensions of human consciousness and action; see Adler 2002; Wendt 1999; Gill 1993; and Ruggie 1982, 1998. Nevertheless, the research has a strong reflexive – practical and political – component: establishing the relative empirical congruence of the rival neoliberal and neointerventionist claims has significant implications for political discourse and political action.

maintains an international order based on its self-interest while enhancing global welfare. However, resource concentration does not capture the distinctiveness of laissez-faire and embedded liberalism. The normative structure does. The authority relations defining state-market-society relations in each hegemonic provide the legitimate social purpose in pursuit of which state power is employed in both the domestic and international arenas. Hence, comparison of the normative structures of hegemons best captures how market and state shape economic performance and social protection of regimes.

The second claim justifies the sample selection: the normative structures of nineteenth-century Britain and post-World War II United States capture the distinctiveness of the regimes of laissez-faire and embedded liberalism respectively. Resource concentration remains crucial to explain British and U.S. hegemony. Britain, under the impulses of the industrial revolution, colonization, and global trade and finance, developed the largest and most open economy.[62] As the paramount military power in a system of interstate hegemony, Britain also enforced its preferred rules of free trade and the gold standard by maintaining freedom of the seas.[63] The Pax Britannica ensured an international order of relative peace and security.[64] As for the United States, its large economy drives the world economy.[65] The United States also fulfills power criteria of hegemony: for example, acting as world police; establishing the Bretton Woods regimes of trade and finance; and providing investment and aid. The Pax Americana, too – debates on the decline of hegemony notwithstanding – has ensured an international order of relative peace and security.[66]

Resource concentration alone, however, does not capture the laissez-faire identity of nineteenth-century Britain: its fusion with the normative structure that privileged self-regulating markets does. The authority relations instituted in the international regime reflected the domestic balance of British market-state relations that determined the dominance of market over society. Laissez-faire Britain privileged market forces both domestically and internationally: it limited positive state interventions in the commodity, currency, and labor markets; and it engaged in negative interventions to institute and safeguard self-regulating markets.[67] Likewise, for the United States, the fusion of resource concentration and a normative structure that privileges state steering of markets uniquely identifies embedded liberalism. The authority relations instituted in the regime reflect the domestic balance of U.S. state-society relations that rest on the dominance of state over market and on the subordination of market to society. From the New Deal to Bretton Woods and to the Great Society, the state

---

62 See Maddison 1995; Floud and McCloskey 1994; and Kindleberger 1975.

63 See Hobsbawm 1990; and De Cecco 1984.

64 Gilpin 2000.

65 Obstfeld and Rogoff 1996.

66 Gilpin 2000.

67 Three pieces of legislation institutionalized the principles of laissez-faire: (1) the Poor Law Amendment Act of 1834 facilitated the flexibility of labor markets; (2) the Peel's Bank Act of 1844 launched the gold standard monetary regime; and (3) the Anti-Corn Law Bill of 1846 and the Cobden-Chevalier Treaty of 1860 set in motion international trade; see Hobsbawm 1990; Taylor 1972; and Polanyi 1957.

has taken greater responsibilities to buffer the domestic economy and society from external shocks without sacrificing the benefits of economic openness.[68]

The third claim establishes the validity of inference from the comparison of hegemonic Britain and United States. Britain is the extreme representative of laissez-faire. This ideal status had long been noted in political economy: Britain exemplified the evolution of nineteenth-century global capitalism.[69] Other powers, such as France and Germany, differed in socioeconomic and political structures but were integrated in the global capitalism that Britain spearheaded.[70] This ideal status continues to inform the contemporary ideological debates on market and state: for neoliberals, laissez-faire Britain exemplifies the world to which to return; for Polanyi's "neointerventionist children" the world from which to escape.[71]

In contrast, vis-à-vis other industrial democracies, the United States is the weakest representative of embedded liberalism. It never had a significant socialist movement or labor party.[72] The social and economic reforms of the New Deal lacked a strong ideological basis, were modest in scope, and confronted strong opposition.[73] The Great Society saw its limitations in the small public sector and residualistic welfare state.[74] Labor markets have remained the most flexible among the advanced industrial democracies.[75] The ideological attacks on the normative structure of embedded liberalism since the early 1980s have been strongest in the United States.[76] Indeed, the weakening consensus in the United States over the future of embedded liberalism is about the new order that should replace the New Deal state domestically and the Bretton Woods system internationally.[77] Yet, despite weak representativeness, the central hypothesis – the normative structure of hegemonic United States influences the identity of embedded liberalism – holds.[78]

Historical Persistence: From Nonstationarity to Cointegration

Testing the rival neoliberal and neointerventionist claims about the long-run dynamics of the two regimes requires a second crucial methodological decision: the choice of the appropriate statistical framework. Graphical analyses and unit root tests of the four processes in the model reveal that persistence, in the form

---

68 The New Deal represented the U.S. reaction against the collapse of laissez-faire and the Great Depression; the U.S.-driven Bretton Woods regime sought to reconstruct the postwar international economic order while minimizing cost of social disruption generated by international integration; the Great Society programs added several layers of social protection; Ruggie 1982.
69 See Taylor 1972; Polanyi 1957; Keynes 1936; and Marx 1976.
70 Kindleberger 1975.
71 Lindsey 2002.
72 Lipset 1996.
73 Brinkely 1995.
74 Esping-Andersen 1990.
75 See Kitschelt, Lange, Marks, and Stephens 1999; and Crouch and Streeck 1997.
76 See Ruggie 1997; and Pierson 1994.
77 See Stiglitz 2002; and Ruggie 1997.
78 Ruggie 1998.

of nonstationary random walk dynamics, drives the evolution of both Britain and the United States. Nonstationary persistence undermines established claims about the long-run dynamics of the two regimes. It also suggests that the framework of cointegration is necessary to investigate such dynamics.

Historical Processes: I(0) Stationary and I(1) Nonstationary Dynamics

Historical persistence hinges on the concepts of stationary and nonstationary series.[79] The properties of a series, z_t, are described usefully by an autoregressive process of order one – AR(1):

$$z_t = c + \beta t + p_1 z_{t-1} + \varepsilon_t$$

where c is a constant; βt, a deterministic time trend; ρ_1, the autoregressive parameter describing persistence; ε_t, a random disturbance term. Table 3.1 summarizes the properties of stationary and nonstationary series. z_t is I(0) stationary, or integrated of order zero, if $|\rho_1| < 1$. This property establishes the time-independence of the (1) mean ($\mu = c/1 - \rho_1$), which captures the intertemporal equilibrium; (2) finite variance ($\sigma^2/(1 - \rho^2)$) describing the dispersion around the intertemporal equilibrium; and (3) quickly decaying autocovariances (γ_s) and autocorrelations (ρ_s), which reveal the memory of historical processes. Accordingly, past shocks ε_i do not cumulate historically but converge quickly toward the intertemporal equilibrium. The trend βt describes deterministic patterns of growth and decay, but its detrending yields stationary, temporary fluctuations.

Instead, z_t is a nonstationary random walk integrated of order one, or I(1), if $\rho_1 = 1$. This property establishes the time-dependence of the variance ($t\sigma^2$), which tends to infinity, and of covariances ($(t - s)\sigma^2$) and autoregressions $\rho_1 = 1$, which do not decay over the long run. With nonstationary dynamics, past shocks ε_i cumulate permanently, or integrate, in the memory of historical series. Therefore, such series cannot have an intertemporal equilibrium to which they can converge. The absence of an intertemporal equilibrium is obvious for a drift-driven random walk, which exhibits a time-varying mean ($\mu = z_0 + c_0 t$): the drift $c_0 t$ captures cumulating patterns of growth/decay from the historical origin z_0.[80] For a drift-less random walk ($c = 0$), the mean is $\mu = z_0$, which is time invariant and corresponds to its origin z_0. Thus only stochastic shocks ε_i shape the evolution of z_t, which unfolds with sticky waves around z_0. However, given stochastic waves, the mean of z_t does not describe a meaningful intertemporal equilibrium to which historical processes converge systematically and quickly.[81]

---

79 Patterson 2000.

80 The intertemporal equilibrium is mathematically undefined: given $\rho_1 = 1$, $\mu = c/(1 - \rho_1)$ yields $\mu = c/0$.

81 Such equilibrium is also mathematically undefined: given $\rho_1 = 1$, $\mu = c/(1 - \rho_1)$ yields $\mu = 0/0$.

Table 3.1   Properties of AR(1) processes

	Stationary	Nonstationary	
		Drift-driven	Drift-less
μ: mean	$\mu = c/(1 - \rho_1)$	$\mu = z_0 + c_0 t$	$\mu = z_0$
σ^2: variance	$\sigma^2/(1 - \rho^2)$	$t\sigma^2$	$t\sigma^2$
γ_{t-s}: autocovariance	γ_s	$(t - s)\sigma^2$	$(t - s)\sigma^2$
ρ_1: autocorrelation	$|\rho_1| < 1$	$\rho_1 = 1$	$\rho_1 = 1$

Note: ρ_1 = first autocorrelation. z_0 = origin of historical series. t = time index starting at z_0. $t - s$ = time lags.

Nonstationary Persistence: Britain and the United States

Nonstationary persistence suggests that neoliberals commonly rely on neoclassical equilibrium models that associate market flexibility with stationary I(0) converging processes and sticky markets with nonstationary I(1) nonconverging processes.[82] Thus, given highly flexible markets, nineteenth-century laissez-faire would be a stationary world: shocks are temporary, and historical processes quickly converge toward stable intertemporal equilibria. By contrast, given sticky markets, postwar embedded liberalism would be a nonstationary world: shocks are persistent, and sticky historical processes fail to converge quickly and systematically to equilibrium. By contrast, reliance on Keynesian disequilibrium models informs neointerventionist beliefs that markets in nineteenth-century laissez-faire are sticky and therefore generate unstable – that is, persistent, nonconverging, and hence nonstationary – dynamics.

Preliminary empirical evidence from Britain and the United States, shown in Figure 3.1, challenges any claims of converging stationary dynamics, particularly the neoliberal claims about nineteenth-century laissez-faire.[83] Simply, persistent random walk dynamics appear to be ubiquitous.

British trade exhibits long-memory stochastic waves of openness and implosion.[84] Instead, a drift, which may have fueled recent concerns about the intensification of

---

82 See Aghion and Howitt 1998; Juselius 1999; and Sargent 1987.

83 For Britain, data are for the 1865–1913 period. The onset at 1865 eliminates the confounding effects of the Crimean War while capturing the free trade drives of the 1860s. Trade and government spending are from Mitchell 1998; real GDP, from Backus and Kehoe 1992; unemployment, from Mitchell 1988. For the United States, data for 1955–99 are from *Economagic* (www.economagic.com). The start at 1955 eliminates the effects of the Korean War. Trade is exports (EXPGS) plus imports (IMPGS) as a ratio of nominal GDP (GDPN). Government spending is federal expenditures (AFEXPND) net of federal grants in aid to state and local governments (AFGL) as a percentage of GDP. Real GDP is GDPC.

84 The implosion is associated with the Great Depression of 1873–96; Floud and McCloskey 1994.

globalization, drives U.S. trade. GDP exhibits clear drift-driven growth patterns in both countries. U.S. unemployment exhibits substantial persistence, which is associated with rigid labor markets. The higher frequency fluctuations in British unemployment may suggest more flexible labor markets, as neoliberals maintain. Yet long-memory swings typical of random walks may characterize its evolution, as neointerventionists contend. Lastly, upward sloping drifts ($c_0 t > 0$) also drive the growth of government spending in both countries, albeit with different strength and from significantly different initial historical conditions (z_0).[85] For Britain, z_0 in 1865 was about 6 percent of GDP; for the United States, z_0 in 1955 was about 16 percent. Drifts indicate that for the sample period the absolute growth of British public spending was roughly about 3 percent; in the United States, spending grew by about 15 percent.

Augmented Dickey Fuller (ADF) unit root tests lend support to the qualitative insights that all four processes are long-memory random walks.[86] ADF tests take the form

$$\Delta z_t = c + \beta t + \gamma z_{t-1} + \delta_1 \Delta z_{t-1} + \delta_2 \Delta z_{t-2} + \dots + \delta_p \Delta z_{t-p} + \varepsilon_t$$

where z_t is a nonstationary I(1) process and Δz_t is its stationary I(0) change; δ_i capture higher-order correlations in lagged Δz_t that whiten ε_t; and βt describes the time trend. Given $\gamma = (\rho - 1)$, ADF tests evaluate two hypotheses: (1) the null of unit root (H_0: $\gamma = 0$), by which $\rho = 1$; and (2) the alternative of stationarity (H_1: $\gamma < 0$), by which $\rho < 1$. A random walk has a drift if $c \neq 0$, and no drift if $c = 0$. Table 3.2 shows the findings.[87] MacKinnon's critical values of the t-statistic for γ, $t(\gamma)$, fail to reject the null $\gamma = 0$: for the sample period, all four processes in both regimes appear to be I(1) random walks.

GDP is drift-driven in both countries ($c > 0$).[88] In postwar United States, trade is drift-driven, which validates concerns about the "acceleration" of globalization. In Britain, instead, trade is a pure random walk, which suggests that by the 1860s, and for the subsequent period up to World War I, trade had reached maximum expansion. In both countries, unemployment appears to exhibit drift-less random walk properties.[89] Government spending is drift driven in both countries. Both the

---

86 Dickey and Fuller 1979.

87 Phillips-Perron tests yield similar results; Phillips and Perron 1988. Tests are performed in *Eviews*.

88 Established research corroborates the validity of these findings for the United States; Fatás 2000.

89 The nonstationary persistence of unemployment, and more generally of variables defined as shares, requires a distinction between conceptual and statistical properties; Patterson 2000, 285–99. With regard to statistical properties, shocks are better described as having permanent rather than transitory effects. Conceptually, however, economic theory finds it difficult to consider unemployment as I(1) nonstationary: its "random walk" is bounded between 0 and 1 and therefore has finite variance. Indeed, historically those boundaries are not reached or even approached. Nonstationary persistence emerges as a local, or sample-specific, property reflecting the effects of a big historical shock – such as the oil shock of the 1970s – and not the global property of unemployment unfolding in infinite time. In a long sample, say 200 years, there may be no significant trace of the local shock. Thus if tests indicate that the null $\gamma = 0$ cannot be rejected over the sample period, then the series is locally but not globally I(1). Current research on unemployment reflects the tension between theoretical

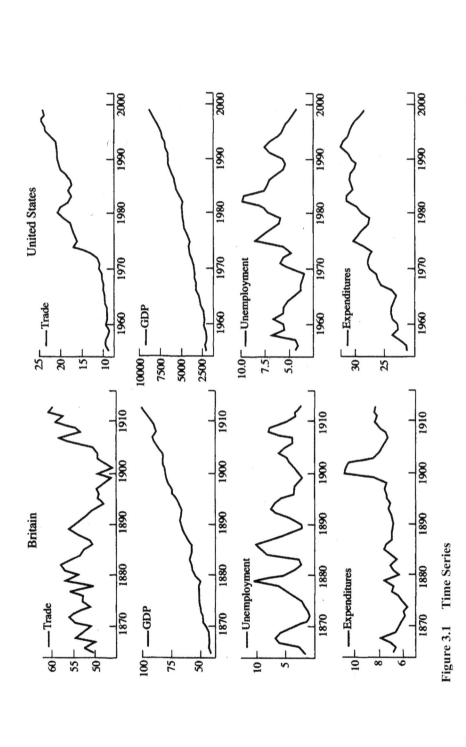

Figure 3.1   Time Series

Table 3.2 ADF Unit Roots Tests

	Nineteenth-century Britain					Post-World War II United States				
	c	β	γ	$t(\gamma)$	p	c	β	γ	$t(\gamma)$	p
Δx_t	0.0	0	0.001	0.69	2.6/1.9	0.05	0	–0.01	2.1	3.5/2.9
Δy_t	0.03	0	–0.003	0.03	3.5/2.9	0.09	0	–0.006	2.1	3.5/2.9
Δu_t	0.0	0	–0.03	0.9	2.6/1.9	0.0	0	–0.001	1.0	2.6/1.9
Δg_t	0.1	0	–0.1	2.0	3.5/2.9	0.3	0	0.03	1.4	3.5/2.9

Note: Variables are in logs. c = drift. β = deterministic time trend. t (γ) = estimated t-statistics for the null H_0: γ = 0. p = MacKinnon one-sided p-values at 1 percent and 5 percent for $N \approx 50$.
Source: MacKinnon 1996.

bigger size of government spending at the onset (z_0) and the stronger drift-driven growth (c = 0.3) for the United States seemingly provide the rationale to neoliberal claims of the economic inefficiency of the public sector. Nevertheless, despite the significant institutional differences in the normative structures of social purpose, both regimes share one common property: nonstationary dynamics drive their long-run evolution. Shocks cumulate permanently to generate persistent patterns of historical inheritance.

Implications of Nonstationarity: Disjunctions Between Theory and Evidence

Nonstationarity in Britain challenges neoliberal claims about the stability of nineteenth-century laissez-faire that rest on neoclassical models of converging stationary dynamics. Nonstationarity lends support to neointerventionist claims, inherited from Keynes, about the stickiness of laissez-faire markets. Nonstationarity in the United States, especially of unemployment and government spending, would support neoliberal claims about the instability of embedded liberalism. However, the persistence, even hysteresis, of unemployment in both countries suggests that labor markets are sticky in both regimes. Ultimately, these claims of regime instability based on the nonstationarity of individual historical processes are mistaken. Random

and statistical properties. Neoclassical theory continues to treat unemployment persistence in terms of protracted, yet converging, deviations from natural equilibrium; Pissarides 2000. Nevertheless, unit root dynamics are considered to be consistent with unemployment hysteresis, by which unemployment has a permanent component and a path-dependent natural rate; see Papell, Murray, and Ghiblawi 2000; and Blanchard and Summers 1986. In the context of cointegration, even if the roots were slightly lower than unity, the unit root model is a sound approximation because it provides a more reliable framework for statistical inference in a multivariate setting; Juselius 1999.

walks may exhibit stable long-run equilibria if, as a system, they are cointegrated – that is, coevolving historically around common stochastic trends.[90]

Nonstationarity also challenges the use of standard univariate statistics – most crucially algebraic means – to compare the levels, or magnitudes, of historical processes in the two regimes. For instance, it challenges neoliberal claims about the superiority of nineteenth-century laissez-faire such as the claim that higher levels of trade and smaller public sectors are associated with better economic performance. Means properly depict intertemporal equilibria of stationary processes; means of random walks are nonsensical.[91] Comparing means of nonstationary trade, GDP, unemployment, and government spending in the two regimes is mistaken.[92] Appropriate comparisons would focus on the historical origins z_0 and the drifts $(c_0 t)$ of series.

Lastly, nonstationarity invalidates claims of causal relations based on fashionable single-equations OLS regressions.[93] Such regressions at best would capture stationary relations. Given nonstationarity, they yield spurious findings and mistaken causal inference. While explicit comparisons of how market and state shape economic performance and social protection in the two regimes are lacking, OLS techniques dominate within-regimes research.[94] Indirect comparisons of such findings to establish the superior empirical congruence of the trade-off and complementarity hypotheses would lead to misleading inference about the long-run dynamics driving the two regimes. A cointegration model in VECM form more properly captures the complexity of persistent historical dynamics.[95]

---

90 Engle and Granger 1991.

91 Note that the mean of stationary series $\mu = c/(1 - \rho_1)$ varies with the values of ρ_1. This property cautions against the uncritical use of algebraic means even for stationary processes.

92 The use of stationary growth rates is problematic because stochastic detrending obliterates long-term persistence, which is the crucial phenomenon under investigation.

93 See King, Plosser, Stock, and Watson 1991; and Granger and Newbold 1974.

94 Dominance is clear in research on the postwar era; see Swank 2002; Huber and Stephens 2001; and Garrett 1998. It is also clear in research on the nineteenth century; see O'Rourke and Williamson 1999; Verdier 1998; and Williamson 1996.

95 Recent considerations of cointegration methods reveal the concern with historical persistence; see Iversen 2001; and Freeman et al. 1998. Otherwise, two strategies, both unsatisfactory, have been fashionable. One models the levels of variables with the inclusion of an AR(1) term controlling for persistence; see Swank 2002; and Garrett 1998. Controlling is noninformative about the properties of persistence. The other models stationary first-differences; see Alesina and Perotti 1998. Such strategy simply obliterates persistence.

The Cointegration Model in VECM Form

The standard VECM model of long-run dynamics is

$$\Delta z_t = \mu + \Pi z_{t-1} + \Psi D_t + e_t \quad e_t \sim IN(0, \Sigma)^{96}$$

where z_t is a vector of at most I(1) n variables in levels and z_{t-1} is its lagged vector; Δz_t is the vector of differenced, and hence I(0) stationary, variables in changes; and D_t is a vector of deterministic variables, such as time trends and step dummies, which capture policy interventions and regime breaks. This model captures three dimensions of long-term dynamics: (1) common trends, (2) equilibrium relations, and (3) adjustments.

Common Trends

Cointegration assumes stationarity of a set n of I(1) nonstationary variables in z_t by linear combination. The hypothesis of cointegration is formulated as a reduced rank of the Π-matrix

$$H_1(r): \Pi = \alpha\beta'.$$

α and β are $p \times r$ matrices of full rank, where r, the rank of Π, is equal to the number of independent cointegrating vectors, and p is the number of common stochastic trends. The hypothesis implies that Δz_t is stationary, z_t is I(1) nonstationary, but $\beta' z_t$ is stationary.[97]

The rank of Π suggests three main scenarios concerning system (1) stability, (2) instability, and (3) rigidity. A system is stable if Π has rank $0 < n - r < n$: the nonstationary processes are cointegrated and coevolve around one or more stochastic trends that drive the stable long-run evolution of the system. Instability occurs if Π has rank $n - r = n$: there are as many stochastic trends in the cointegration space as I(1) variables. Such trends evolve independently following unrelated historical logics, and thus fail to share a common history. Lastly, the higher the number of trends, but clearly less than n, the greater system rigidity: a system evolves historically in as many unrelated directions as there are trends.

Equilibrium Relations

The matrix $\beta' z_t$ represents up to $(n - 1)$ stationary cointegrated relations describing the stable coevolution of nonstationary variables around common trends. The series share a history precisely because they evolve around such trends. The equilibrium

---

96 Since the analytic focus is on long-run dynamics, the model omits the matrix $\Gamma_k \Delta z_{t-k}$, which describes short-run fluctuations in the changes of variables that meander around the long-run relations.

97 See Johansen 1995; and Engle and Granger 1991.

relations represent long-term stationary associations between variables. They also represent long-run steady states ($\beta' z_{t-1} = 0$) toward which variables converge when shocks push them away from equilibrium. Disequilibrium ensues when ($\beta' z_{t-1} \neq 0$).

Adjustment Dynamics

The α matrix describes the direction and speed of adjustments of variables in z_t to disequilibrium in the steady state of z_{t-1}. Relations are in equilibrium at $\beta' z_{t-1} = 0$, and in disequilibrium when $\beta' z_{t-1} \neq 0$. In the presence of disequilibrium, the variables in the system adjust to restore equilibrium in the next period such that $\beta' z_{t-1} = 0$. Larger α_{ij} indicate faster adjustments. If $\alpha_{ij} = 0$, the variables are weakly exogenous and do not adjust.

Deterministic Components

The matrix ΨD_t describes the effects of deterministic components, such as trends and level-shifts, on the equilibrium relations. Especially when level shifts are observed, prior knowledge suggests that something special has happened in a given historical period, and that it should be modeled using dummy variables.

Stability and Rigidity of Regimes: Rank of Π and Common Trends

Are the regimes of laissez-faire and embedded liberalism stable in the long run? If they are stable, which of the two regimes exhibits greater rigidity? The first question – about regime stability – concerns whether the four nonstationary processes are cointegrated, that is, stably coevolving around one or more common trends. The second question – about regime rigidity – concerns the number of trends driving the nonstationary yet stable evolution of the regimes. Determining the rank of Π helps answer both questions.

The reliance of political economy theories on neoclassical models of stationary dynamics provides little guidance in determining the rank of Π.[98] Table 3.3 proposes a strong version of neoliberal and neointerventionist hypotheses about the stability of regimes for the four-dimensional ($n = 4$) model. Neoliberals claim regime stability for the laissez-faire regime. Hence, Π has rank $0 < n - r < 4$: the random walks are cointegrated and evolve around one or more stochastic trends. In contrast, neointerventionists, mindful of Keynes's critiques, claim system instability. Hence, Π has rank $n - r = 4$: with as many trends as variables, the random walks are not cointegrated and evolve in four unrelated directions. The opposite set of hypotheses would hold for embedded liberalism.

It is difficult, however, to fathom such an unstable social system in which historical processes evolve independently of one another. Therefore, a softer set of hypotheses assumes that both regimes are stable but differ in rigidity. For neoliberals,

---

98 For a critique of the weak theoretical guidance, especially in economics, see Juselius 1999; Granger 1997; and Pesaran 1997.

Table 3.3   **Rank of Π: Hypotheses**

	Laissez-faire	Embedded liberalism
Neoliberals	$0 < n - r < 4$	$n - r = 4$
Neointerventionists	$n - r = 4$	$0 < n - r < 4$

Note: n = number of variables in the model. r = number of cointegrating vectors. $(n - r) = p$ = number of common stochastic trends.

the institutions of embedded liberalism generate greater rigidities; hence, this regime would exhibit a higher number of trends. For neointerventionists, in contrast, the stickiness of laissez-faire markets generates greater rigidity, and hence a higher number of trends.

Table 3.4 shows eingenvalue tests of the rank of II for Britain and the United States. Tests refute the strong hypotheses of regime instability. They also refute the softer hypotheses of differences in rigidity.[99]

With one root at unity ($p = 1$), the eigenvalues of the companion matrix indicate that Π has rank $r = 3$: hence, one common trend ($n - r = 1$) spans the entire history of each regime – at least for the sample period. Implicitly, three equilibrium relations coevolve around such trends. The common trends capture the nonstationary, yet stable, evolution of the two regimes. The four nonstationary series are cointegrated and share a history because they evolve around the common trend. Thus, regardless of institutional differences in the relative dominance of market and state, both regimes exhibit long-run stability and similar rigidity. Hence, the neoliberal claims of instability and greater rigidity of embedded liberalism find no support. Each regime

Table 3.4   **Rank of Π: Findings**

Modulus for Britain		Modulus for United States	
Unrestricted	Restricted	Unrestricted	Restricted
0.8869	1.0000	0.9057	1.0000
0.4366	0.6702	0.8071	0.8448
0.4336	0.6702	0.8071	0.7376

Note: "Unrestricted" = eigenvalues without initial rank restriction. "Restricted" = rank restriction with $r = 3$. Only the largest three roots are reported.

---

99 Estimation is done in *PcFiml 10.0*; Doornik and Hendry 2000. Tests reject the null of serially correlated, non-normal, heteroskedastic vector residuals. The λ_{max} and *trace* rank tests are not appropriate with dummy variables.

appears to represent a stable and viable historical experiment: one allegedly driven by unfettered markets; the other, by the complementarity of market and state.

Long-Term Equilibrium Relations (β_{ij}): Distinctiveness of Evolutionary Paths

Given regime stability, how do market and state shape the evolution of the equilibrium relations? The rank of Π suggests a four-dimensional model with three equilibrium relations that evolve around one stochastic trend. The multidimensional model cast in terms of cointegrated dynamics is[100]

$$
\begin{bmatrix} \Delta x_t \\ \Delta y_t \\ \Delta u_t \\ \Delta g_t \end{bmatrix} = \begin{bmatrix} 0 & 0 & 0 \\ \alpha_{21} & \alpha_{22} & \alpha_{23} \\ \alpha_{31} & \alpha_{32} & \alpha_{33} \\ \alpha_{41} & \alpha_{42} & \alpha_{43} \end{bmatrix} \begin{bmatrix} \beta_{11} & 1 & 0 & \beta_{14} & \beta_{15} & 0 \\ \beta_{21} & \beta_{22} & 1 & 0 & 0 & 0 \\ 0 & \beta_{32} & \beta_{33} & 1 & 0 & \beta_{36} \end{bmatrix} \begin{bmatrix} x_{t-1} \\ y_{t-1} \\ u_{t-1} \\ g_{t-1} \\ t_t \\ d_t \end{bmatrix} + \begin{bmatrix} e_{1t} \\ e_{2t} \\ e_{3t} \\ e_{4t} \end{bmatrix}
$$

The $\beta' z_t$ matrix describes the three relations theoretically normalized to capture the evolution of GDP (y_{t-1}), unemployment (u_{t-1}), and government spending (g_{t-1}).[101] The time trend t_t in the cointegration space describes the long-run growth of GDP.[102] The term d_t identifies the effects of deterministic components on spending: (1) the Boer War for Britain;[103] and (2) state retrenchment and weakening of embedded

100 This cointegration model has two dimensions: (1) that of the model, which is four-dimensional since it includes four endogenous variables ($n = 4$); and (2) that of the cointegration space, which in this model happens to have one common trend ($p = 1$) and three cointegrating vectors ($r = 3$). Had there been two common trends ($p = 2$), the four-dimensional model would have had two cointegrating vectors ($r = 2$).

101 Cointegrating vectors are normalized by theoretically setting variables to 1 to provide meaningful interpretations of vectors; Boswijk 1996. Normalization indicates that y_t, u_t, and g_t are endogenous, whereas x_t is exogenous.

102 The model contains stochastic and deterministic trends. Stochastic trends represent the contributions to the variables in the system of "unexpected" events with permanent effects, whereas deterministic trends represent "expected" events with permanent influence; see Aghion and Howitt 1998; and Engle and Granger 1991. With regard to GDP, growth theory interprets technological progress, and hence productivity shocks, as an expected, regular phenomenon with permanent contributions. That is, following "unexpected" innovations, technological change exhibits some regularity, and the deterministic trend in GDP captures this regularity. The stochastic trend, instead, captures the irregular, or unexpected, technological changes, together with other unexpected permanent changes. Thus, in the cointegrated GDP relations, the common stochastic trend is shared among the variables in that relationship, while the deterministic trend is unique to GDP, and therefore is included in the relation explicitly.

103 See Hobsbawm 1990; and Floud and McCloskey 1994. The deterministic component is described by a step dummy that takes the value of 1 for the 1900–1903 war period and of 0 before and after the war years.

liberalism since the early 1980s for the United States.[104] The α matrix captures markets adjustments via GDP (α_{2j}) and unemployment (α_{3j}), and state adjustments via government spending (α_{4j}). Trade, assumed to be weakly exogenous, does not adjust to disequilibrium in domestic variables ($\alpha_{1j} = 0$).

Table 3.5 summarizes the neoliberal and neointerventionist hypotheses of long-run dynamics for the two regimes, and Table 3.6 shows the empirical findings for Britain and the United States. The findings challenge neoliberal trade-off hypothesis of inefficient state interventions in embedded liberalism while they strongly support neointerventionist claims of the complementarity between market and state.

Spending Relations: $\beta' g$

The $\beta' g$ rows in Table 3.5 indicate that neoliberals and neointerventionists share a basic hypothesis: persistent bursts in GDP and unemployment are associated with stronger long-term spending expansions in embedded liberalism than in laissez-faire liberalism. Larger wealth ($\beta_{32.EL} > \beta_{32.LF} > 0$) and welfare ($\beta_{33.EL} > \beta_{33.LF} > 0$) effects capture the stronger associations.[105] With regard to deterministic components, for Britain d_t describes the temporary increase in spending during the Boer War ($\beta_{36.uk} > 0$). For the United States, d_t captures state retrenchment, which is characterized by a permanent new lower equilibrium in spending after 1980 ($\beta_{36.us} < 0$).

Findings in Table 3.6 challenge claims of stronger long-term wealth and welfare effects in embedded liberalism. Unemployment exhibits comparable positive associations ($\beta_{32.uk} = 0.36 \approx \beta_{32.us} = 0.30$). Shocks in GDP are more strongly associated with spending increases in Britain ($\beta_{32.uk} 0.50 > \beta_{32.us} = 0.20$). Thus, as long claimed, far from being unique to embedded liberalism, wealth and welfare effects were operative in British laissez-faire.[106] Finally, for Britain, the Boer War temporarily increased spending by about 5 percent ($\beta_{36.uk} = 0.5$). For the United States, the "Reagan-Volcker legacy" exerted a moderate permanent downward shift in the equilibrium level of spending after 1980 ($\beta_{36.us} = -0.12$). This shift is consistent with the hypothesis of neoliberal retrenchment aimed at disembedding markets and weakening social protection.

Growth Relations: $\beta' y$

The $\beta' y$ rows show a sharp disagreement over the efficiency of the state: by the trade-off hypothesis, neoliberals claim that persistent spending expansions are negatively associated with long-term growth ($\beta_{14.LF} < 0$); by the complementarity hypothesis, the association is positive or growth inducing for neointerventionists ($\beta_{14.EL} > 0$). Disagreement also involves the positive trade-GDP link: to neoliberals, persistent bursts in trade are associated with stronger economic expansions in

---

104 For the retrenchment and weakening in the United States, see Ruggie 1997; and Pierson 1994. The model tests for such events by including a step dummy that takes the value of 1 for the post-1982 period and 0 for the period before.

105 In the subscripts, LF = laissez-faire; EL = embedded liberalism.

106 Flora and Heidenheimer 1981.

Table 3.5   Normalized Equilibrium Relations: Hypotheses

Relations	Regimes		x_{t-1}	y_{t-1}	u_{t-1}	g_{t-1}	t_t	d_t
$\beta' y$	LF_y_{t-1}	=	$\beta_{11} > 0$	1	$\beta_{13} = 0$	$\beta_{14} = 0$	$\beta_{15} > 0$	$\beta_{16} = 0$
	EL_y_{t-1}	=	$\beta_{11} > 0$	1	$\beta_{13} = 0$	$\beta_{14} \neq 0$	$\beta_{15} > 0$	$\beta_{16} = 0$
$\beta' u$	LS_u_{t-1}	=	$\beta_{21} > 0$	$\beta_{22} < 0$	1	$\beta_{24} = 0$	$\beta_{25} = 0$	$\beta_{26} = 0$
	EL_u_{t-1}	=	$\beta_{21} > 0$	$\beta_{22} < 0$	1	$\beta_{24} = 0$	$\beta_{25} = 0$	$\beta_{26} = 0$
$\beta' g$	LF_g_{t-1}	=	$\beta_{31} = 0$	$\beta_{32} > 0$	$\beta_{33} > 0$	1	$\beta_{35} = 0$	$\beta_{36} > 0$
	EL_g_{t-1}	=	$\beta_{31} = 0$	$\beta_{32} > 0$	$\beta_{33} > 0$	1	$\beta_{35} = 0$	$\beta_{36} < 0$

Note: LF = laissez-faire. EL = embedded liberalism. The "1" indicates the normalized variable for the corresponding equilibrium relation. Relations are in structural form by setting normalized variables on the left side of equation. d_t = effects of the Boer War for Britain and the "Reagan-Volcker legacy" for the United States.

Table 3.6   Long-run Equilibrium Relations: Findings

Relations			x_{x-1}	y_{t-1}	u_{t-1}	g_{t-1}	t_t	$dwar_t$	$d82_t$
$\beta' y$	UK_y_{t-1}	=	+0.11	1	0	0	+1.8	0	–
			(0.07)				(0.02)		
	US_y_{t-1}	=	+0.12	1	0	+0.32	+3.0	–	0
			(0.05)			(0.11)	(0.002)		
$\beta' u$	UK_u_{t-1}	=	–4.0	0	1	0	0	0	–
			(1.5)						
	US_u_{t-1}	=	+5.4	–5.1	1	0	0	–	+1.7
			(0.5)	(0.5)					(0.2)
$\beta' g$	UK_g_{t-1}	=	0	+0.50	+0.36	1	0	+0.5	–
				(0.13)	(0.08)			(0.07)	
	US-g_{t-1}	=	0	+0.20	+0.30	1	0	–	–0.12
				(0.04)	(0.04)				(0.03)

Note: Variables are in logs. $dwar_t$ = Boer War (1900–1902). $d82_t$ = effects of the "Reagan-Volcker legacy" on the unemployment and spending relations. Standard errors are in parentheses.

laissez-faire liberalism ($\beta_{11.LF} > \beta_{11.EL} > 0$); to neointerventionists, the association is stronger in embedded liberalism ($\beta_{11.EL} > \beta_{11.LF} > 0$). With regard to productivity shocks, neoliberals maintain that trend growth is higher in laissez-faire liberalism ($\beta_{15.LF} > \beta_{15.EL} > 0$) ; to neointerventionists, trend growth is higher in embedded liberalism ($\beta_{15.EL} > \beta_{15.LF} > 0$).

Findings challenge all three core neoliberal claims. The first – economic inefficiency of state interventions – is unwarranted. Spending in British laissez-faire, unsurprisingly, appears to be unrelated to growth ($\beta_{14.uk} = 0$). Instead, in postwar United States, persistent spending increases are associated with long-term economic expansions ($\beta_{14.us}$ = 0.40). This positive relation supports the complementarity hypothesis. The second – trade globalization in nineteenth-century laissez-faire generated superior growth – is also unwarranted: both Britain and the United States exhibit small, and statistically weak, positive associations between trade and GDP ($\beta_{11.uk}$ = 0.11 $\approx$ $\beta_{11.us}$ = 0.12). The third – higher trend growth in nineteenth-century laissez-faire – is indefensible: growth is more than 1 percent higher in the United States ($\beta_{15.us}$ = 3.1 > $\beta_{15.uk}$ = 1.8).

Unemployment Relations: β'

The $\beta'u$ rows show that neoliberals and neointerventionists share a basic agreement on the trade-unemployment relations. In laissez-faire liberalism, persistent trade expansions are associated with long-term declines in unemployment ($\beta_{21.ak}$ < 0). In contrast, given hypotheses of socioeconomic structural changes – whether due to processes of modernization, or postindustrialism, or deindustrialization – in embedded liberalism, persistent trade expansions are associated with long-term increases in unemployment ($\beta_{21.us}$ > 0). The negative GDP-unemployment relations suggest another agreement concerning long-run business cycles: persistent economic expansions are associated with long-term declines in unemployment (β_{22} < 0). However, the greater flexibility of labor markets in the laissez-faire regime yields stronger associations ($\beta_{22.uk}$ < $\beta_{22.us}$ < 0).

Findings lend partial support to these claims. The negative trade-unemployment relation finds significant support in laissez-faire Britain: labor markets appear to be synchronized with long-term trade fluctuations, whereby persistent trade expansions are associated strongly with long-term declines in unemployment ($\beta_{21.uk}$ – 4.0). The positive trade-unemployment relation also finds significant support in U.S.-embedded liberalism: trade expansions are associated, also strongly, with long-term unemployment increases ($\beta_{21.us}$ = +5.4). In contrast, the hypotheses of long-term domestic business cycles find support only in the United States: persistent economic expansions are strongly associated with long-term declines in unemployment ($\beta_{22.us}$ = –5.1). Laissez-faire Britain seems not to exhibit such a link ($\beta_{22.uk}$ = 0).[107] This finding about Britain is consistent with the form of imperial industry based on imports of raw materials and export of finished goods, with growth depending more on foreign markets than on domestic consumption.[108] The two relations – trade-unemployment and trade-GDP – indicate the high dependence of the British economy on foreign markets. Finally, the "Reagan-Volcker legacy" since the early 1980s permanently shifted the equilibrium level of unemployment upward by a sizeable 1.7 percent ($\beta_{26.us}$ = +1.7).[109] This shift, together with the downward shift in the spending relation, provides further evidence of neoliberal retrenchment: the significant increase in unemployment is accompanied by a contraction of government spending.

---

107 Tests could not reject the null of no long-term association.

108 See Floud and McCloskey 1994; and Hobsbawm 1990.

109 Tests rejected the null of no shift in the unemployment relation since the early 1980s.

Distinctiveness of Adjustment Dynamics to Disequilibrium: α_{ij}

Lastly, how do market and state adjust to maintain the three cointegrated relations in long-run equilibrium? Neoliberals and neointerventionists largely share the belief that market adjustments dominate in laissez-faire liberalism whereas state adjustments dominate in embedded liberalism. Table 3.7 summarizes the hypotheses and Table 3.8 shows the empirical findings. The findings lend no support to beliefs that market adjustments dominate in laissez-faire liberalism and state adjustments dominate in embedded liberalism. Crucially, the state plays a crucial role in both regimes.[110]

State Adjustments (g_t)

The g_t row in Table 3.7 captures the absence of the state in maintaining the long-run equilibria in laissez-faire liberalism ($\alpha_{4j.LF} = 0$). Government spending is weakly exogenous to the GDP, unemployment, and spending relations. Only markets, via y_t and u_t, adjust to disequilibrium in the relations. In contrast, spending plays a crucial role in maintaining equilibria in embedded liberalism. Congruent with Wagner's wealth effects, the state absorbs disequilibrium growth in GDP ($\beta'y_{t-1} > 0$) via spending expansions ($\alpha_{41.EL} > 0$). Congruent with welfare effects, disequilibrium growth in unemployment ($\beta'u_{t-1} > 0$) also triggers spending expansions ($\alpha_{42.EL} > 0$). Lastly, disequilibrium growth in spending ($\beta'g_{t-1} > 0$) is offset by endogenous mechanisms that curb spending ($\alpha_{43.EL} < 0$).

Findings in the last row of Table 3.8 refute beliefs in the absence of the state in nineteenth-century laissez-faire: government spending plays a crucial role in maintaining the long-run equilibria of both nineteenth-century Britain and postwar United States. First, supporting Wagner's wealth effects, disequilibrium growth in GDP triggers spending increases in both regimes. Indeed, state adjustments are significantly faster in Britain ($\alpha_{41.uk} = 1.0 > \alpha_{41.us} > 0.4$): government spending absorbs 100 percent of disequilibrium within one year; postwar United States absorb about 40 percent.[111] Second, contradicting the welfare effects hypothesis, excess unemployment triggers slow gradual declines in spending: the state confronts increases in unemployment with fiscal contractions, not expansions. Adjustments, while slow, are faster in Britain ($\alpha_{42.uk} = -0.10 > \alpha_{42.us} = -0.02$). Third, disequilibrium growth in spending is followed by comparable moderate gradual declines in spending ($\alpha_{43.uk} - \alpha_{43.us} = -0.3$): both Britain and the United States absorb 30 percent of disequilibrium after one year. Clearly, the state was not absent from the evolution of

---

110 Three main types of dynamics are of interest: (1) $\alpha_{ij} < |1|$ indicates either gradual or oscillatory convergence; (2) $\alpha_{ij} = |1|$ suggests that 100 percent convergence is achieved very fast within one year; (3) $\alpha_{ij} > |1|$ (implies overreaction, or overshooting, which is followed by stable convergence since none of the roots lies outside the unit circle.

111 With $\alpha_{41.us} = 0.4$, 40 percent of disequilibrium is absorbed in the first year, 20 percent in the second year, and so on in geometric progression. With $\alpha_{41.uk} = 1.0$, all (100 percent) disequilibrium would be eliminated within one year. In reality, the dynamics of other variables do not allow the stochastic equilibrium to be actually restored.

Table 3.7   Adjustment Dynamics: Hypotheses

	$\beta'y > 0$		$\beta'u > 0$		$\beta'g > 0$	
α	*LF*	*EL*	*LF*	*EL*	*LF*	*EL*
$\mathbf{x_t}$	$\alpha_{11}=0$	$\alpha_{11}=0$	$\alpha_{12}=0$	$\alpha_{12}=0$	$\alpha_{13}=0$	$\alpha_{13}=0$
$\mathbf{y_t}$	$\alpha_{21}<0$	$\alpha_{21}<0$	$\alpha_{22}>0$	$\alpha_{22}>0$	$\alpha_{23}=0$	$\alpha_{23}\neq 0$
$\mathbf{u_t}$	$\alpha_{31}>0$	$\alpha_{31}<0$	$\alpha_{32}<0$	$\alpha_{32}<0$	$\alpha_{33}=0$	$\alpha_{33}\neq 0$
$\mathbf{g_t}$	$\alpha_{41}=0$	$\alpha_{41}>0$	$\alpha_{42}=0$	$\alpha_{42}>0$	$\alpha_{43}=0$	$\alpha_{43}<0$

Note: LF = laissez-faire. EL = embedded liberalism. $\beta'y$, $\beta'u$, and $\beta'g$ are the equilibrium relations for GDP, unemployment, and government spending for each regime described in Tables 3.5 and 3.6. α_{ij} coefficients are set to zero on the assumption that trade is weakly exogenous.

Table 3.8   Adjustment Dynamics: Findings

	$\beta'y > 0$		$\beta'u > 0$		$\beta'g > 0$	
α	Britain	U.S.	Britain	U. S.	Britain	U.S.
$\mathbf{x_t}$	$\alpha_{11}=0$	$\alpha_{11}=0$	$\alpha_{12}=0$	$\alpha_{12}=0.05$ (0.01)	$\alpha_{13}=0$	$\alpha_{13}=0$
$\mathbf{y_t}$	$\alpha_{21}=-1.0$ (0.15)	$\alpha_{21}=0$	$\alpha_{22}=-0.03$ (0.005)	$\alpha_{22}=0.03$ (0.005)	$\alpha_{23}=0$	$\alpha_{23}=0$
$\mathbf{u_t}$	$\alpha_{31}=+8.4$ (2.0)	$\alpha_{31}=0$	$\alpha_{32}=0$	$\alpha_{32}=-0.20$ (0.04)	$\alpha_{33}=0$	$\alpha_{33}=-0.5$ (0.14)
$\mathbf{g_t}$	$\alpha_{41}=+1.0$ (0.3)	$\alpha_{41}=+0.4$ (0.06)	$\alpha_{42}=-0.10$ (0.02)	$\alpha_{42}=-0.02$ (0.006)	$\alpha_{43}=-0.3$ (0.03)	$\alpha_{43}=-0.3$ (0.07)

Note: α_{ij} = speed of adjustment parameter. Larger α_{ij} indicate faster response to disequilibrium. $\alpha_{ij}=0$ imply that variables do not contribute to reestablishing equilibrium. Standard errors are in parentheses.

nineteenth-century laissez-faire. It contributed to maintain market-driven equilibria in Britain and state-steered equilibria in the United States.

Market Adjustments (y_t, u_t)[112]

$\beta'y_{t-1} > 0$ Disequilibrium growth in GDP is followed by economic contractions ($\alpha_{21}<0$) and by concurrent increasing unemployment ($\alpha_{31}>0$) to restore equilibrium. Given the high flexibility of laissez-faire markets, GDP contracts faster ($\alpha_{21,LF} <$

---

112 As with equilibrium relations, trade is exogenous to domestic variables – GDP, unemployment spending ($\alpha_{ij}=0$).

$\alpha_{21.EL}$ < 0) and unemployment increases faster ($\alpha_{31.LF}$ > $\alpha_{31.EL}$ > 0). Findings support the hypotheses for Britain. Excess GDP triggers very quick GDP contractions (α_{21} = −1.0) and unemployment increases (α_{31} = 8.4).[113] The United States exhibits no significant adjustments in y_t and u_t. Only government spending appears to restore equilibrium GDP in the United States.

$\beta'u_{t-1}$ > 0 Excess unemployment is offset by higher economic growth (α_{22} > 0) and by declining unemployment (α_{32} < 0). Given the flexibility of laissez-faire markets, GDP expands faster ($\alpha_{22.LF}$ > $\alpha_{22.EL}$ > 0) and unemployment declines faster ($\alpha_{32.LF}$ < $\alpha_{32.EL}$ < 0). Findings support this stabilization pattern only for the United States: GDP increases, albeit very slowly (α_{22} = 0.03), and unemployment declines slowly (α_{32} = −0.20). In Britain, excess unemployment seemingly foreshadows recessions that result in very slow GDP contractions (α_{22} = −0.03).[114] The small adjustment coefficients provide further evidence of the stickiness of unemployment in both regimes: any deviations of unemployment from equilibrium persist for a relatively long time.

$\beta'g_{t-1}$ > 0 Neoliberals and neointerventionists largely agree on the adjustment dynamics to the disequilibrium growth in government spending in the laissez-faire regime: by the trade-off hypothesis, neither GDP nor unemployment adjusts ($\alpha_{23.LF} - \alpha_{33.us}$ = 0). The "no-effect" outcome would be congruent with the equilibrium relations where spending does not enter the GDP and unemployment relations. Thus, spending itself would bear the burden of reestablishing its own equilibrium ($\alpha_{43.LF}$ < 0). Indeed, findings show that both GDP and unemployment in Britain are unresponsive to deviations in government spending, and that contractions in spending itself reestablish equilibrium ($\alpha_{43.uk}$ = 0.3).

In contrast, disagreement is sharp with regard to public spending in embedded liberalism. For neoliberals, the growth of inherently inefficient spending results in economic slowdown ($\alpha_{23.EL}$ < 0) and increasing unemployment ($\alpha_{33.EL}$ > 0). For neointerventionists, the growth of spending results in stabilization patterns of higher growth ($\alpha_{23.EL}$ > 0) and declining unemployment ($\alpha_{33.EL}$ < 0). Findings for the United States provide partial support to claims of complementarity: growth in public spending eliminates half of disequilibrium unemployment within one year ($\alpha_{33.us}$ = −0.5).

Conclusions

These results yield seven major conclusions.

1. *Dynamics of nineteenth-century laissez-faire.* Reliance on neoclassical models of short-run equilibrium leads neoliberals to claim stationary dynamics:

---

113 For $\alpha_{31.uk}$ = 8.4, it is possible to interpret only the sign. Interpretation of the size/speed would require the renormalization of the $\beta'y$ vector to u, which is not possible because u has a zero coefficient in $\beta'y$.

114 Tests fail to reject the hypotheses of exogeneity of trade for the United States. Trade adjusts slowly ($\alpha_{12.us}$ = 0.05), which indicates that U.S. trade is not exogenous to the large domestic economy; see Ruggie 1982; and Keohane 1984a.

shocks have transitory effects and fluctuations quickly converge toward stable intertemporal equilibria. The nonstationary persistence of historical processes in Britain shatters claims of stationary dynamics while lending implicit support to Keynesian claims about the "stickiness" of laissez-faire markets. In the univariate domain, no significant differences distinguish the two regimes. If nonstationarity of single variables – hysteretic unemployment, "unsustainable" growth of government spending, acceleration of globalization – justifies claims of regime instability, then both regimes would be unstable.

2. *Regime stability.* By relying on persistent, and allegedly unstable, dynamics of single historical processes, neoliberals and neointerventionists alike fear the disintegration of embedded liberalism – as happened for nineteenth-century laissez-faire. Cointegrated dynamics refute the simplistic derivation of regime instability and disintegration from the nonstationarity of single variables. The common stochastic trend driving the evolution of both regimes captures their long-run stability – at least for the sample periods.

3. *Regime rigidity.* Neoliberals associate the institutions of embedded liberalism with market rigidities and "stickiness" of government spending, whereas neointerventionists point to the "stickiness" of laissez-faire markets. The one trend spanning the history of each regime challenges neoliberal claims of greater rigidity of embedded liberalism as well as neointerventionist claims of greater rigidity of laissez-faire liberalism. Despite differences in the normative structure defining the relative dominance of market and state, the two regimes exhibit comparable rigidities.

4. *Efficiency of market and state.* The equilibrium relations challenge neoliberal beliefs in the ineluctable trade-off between market and state, lending support instead to neointerventionist claims of complementarity. Market dominance in laissez-faire Britain is associated with lower growth and weaker social protection – as captured by weaker public spending and persistent unemployment. Complementarity of market and state in U.S.-embedded liberalism is associated with superior growth and stronger social protection – the persistence of unemployment notwithstanding. Neoliberal beliefs in efficient markets and inefficient state appear to be a myth.

5. *Trade openness and economic performance.* For nineteenth-century Britain, the association of trade with weak economic expansions and significant declines in unemployment lends partial support to neoliberal claims about the benefits of trade openness in laissez-faire regimes. However, it also feeds neointerventionist concerns that unemployment bears the burden of stabilization during economic downturns. In postwar United States, the association of trade with weak economic expansions and significant increases in long-term unemployment provide fertile ground for contention. Neoliberals blame persistent unemployment on labor market rigidities, and hence they call for deregulation. Neointerventionists blame deregulation, lack of global labor standards, and the asymmetric North-South trade relations, and hence they call for a stronger embedding of markets and for global labor standards.[115]

---

115 See Dollar and Kraay 2002; Rodrik 1997; and Wood 1994.

These rival interpretations require additional investigations of the supply side of the economy – specifically, of how the evolution of labor market institutions affects the persistence of unemployment.[116]

6. *Adjustment dynamics*. Such dynamics challenge the core neoliberal beliefs that markets provide the key mechanisms to reestablish equilibria in nineteenth-century laissez-faire whereas state interventions do so in embedded liberalism. State adjustments are ubiquitous, yet play distinctive roles. For nineteenth-century Britain, they contribute to maintain market-driven equilibria, whereas for postwar United States, they maintain the equilibria stemming from the complementarity of market and state. The belief in the absence of the state from the long-run evolution of nineteenth-century laissez-faire appears to be a myth. The belief that the state in embedded liberalism undermines convergence toward long-run stable equilibria also appears to be false.

7. *Policy lesson*. Equilibrium relations suggest that the political project "to go back to the future" – by politically reengineering novel forms of laissez-faire – would mean a reversion to a highly globalized world, albeit one with lower long-run growth, persistent unemployment, and weak social protection. Moreover, the adjustment dynamics reveal that such a laissez-faire world would still require state interventions to maintain market-driven equilibria. Instead, the neointerventionist project "to go forward to the future" – by enhancing political control of domestic and global markets – seems to promise superior growth and social protection. Persistent unemployment remains as puzzling for embedded liberalism as for laissez-faire liberalism.

Beyond these conclusions, cointegration analyses of the two regimes make significant contributions to several debates in political economy.

Theoretical contributions principally regard historical dynamics. Cointegrated dynamics challenge the reliance of political economy on neoclassical models of short-run dynamics. The fundamental dynamics are long term. The persistent dynamics of the trade-unemployment relation in nineteenth-century Britain contradict neoliberal claims of temporary unemployment in laissez-faire regimes. Keynes may have been correct about the "stickiness" of markets in nineteenth-century laissez-faire. In addition, persistent dynamics in the spending-GDP relation for embedded liberalism challenge neoliberal claims of policy ineffectiveness and inefficiency. Government spending has long-term positive effects on the real economy – growth and employment. Rather, cointegrated dynamics are congruent with endogenous growth theory, which allows for the stable coevolution of persistent historical processes.[117] Moreover, such dynamics lend validity to the emerging research in historical institutionalism and historical evolution, which acknowledges historical persistence.[118] This chapter simply demonstrates that the fundamental

---

116 Established political economy research addressing these issues remains dubious because of its reliance on stationary theories and methods that are inappropriate for nonstationary processes.

117 Aghion and Howitt 1998.

118 See Büthe 2002; and Pierson 2001.

macro-historical dynamics driving the evolution of global capitalism belong to the family of cointegrated processes.

Methodological contributions concern the significance of the cointegration framework for the investigation of long-term historical dynamics. Analyses of the long-run evolution of the two regimes lend strong support to recent critiques of the disjunction between theoretical claims about persistent, nonstationary dynamics and theoretical models and statistical methodologies that at best capture temporary fluctuations.[119] Comparisons of the long-run evolution of the two regimes are best accomplished within the cointegration framework. Reliance on means and variances in the univariate domain and on correlations and single-equation OLS-based regressions in the multivariate domain simply fails to capture historical persistence and its complexity. Worse, it results in model misspecification and spurious findings that ultimately inform mistaken inference and unwarranted policy solutions. The multidimensional VECM best captures the complexity of persistent historical dynamics stemming from feedbacks – multiple trends, equilibrium relations, and adjustment mechanisms.

Substantive contributions concern debates specific to embedded liberalism. Cointegration analyses demonstrate the analytic usefulness of constructivist social theory for investigating how the normative structures of social purpose shape the relative dominance of market and state in the two regimes as well as their relevance for the coevolution of economic performance and social protection. Specifically, equilibrium relations unfolding around the common trend reveal that market dominance in nineteenth-century Britain and complementarity of market and state in postwar United States differentiate sharply between the laissez-faire and embedded liberal regimes. Similarly, adjustment dynamics show the uniqueness of equilibrium mechanisms in each regime. Cointegration analyses also provide novel insights into the long-term stability and viability of embedded liberalism. The unfolding of the equilibrium relations around a common trend that spans the entire post-World War II era does not suggest a rupture in the normative structure.[120] The breaks at the onset of the 1980s indicate that shifts in the unemployment and spending relations have contributed to disembed labor markets and to decommodify social life but have not yet changed fundamentally the normative structure.

Policy contributions mainly concern fears of backlashes against the intensification of unfettered globalization in embedded liberalism, and even the possibility of its disintegration – as allegedly happened in the first wave of globalization.[121] Such fears – best captured by the query: "Has globalization gone too far?"[122] – seem to stem from the interaction of two phenomena associated with the acceleration of trade openness: weak growth and persistent unemployment; and reduction of public spending for social protection in the name of international competitiveness. The complementarity of market and state, which is associated with superior economic growth and social protection in post-World War II embedded liberalism, may best

---

119 See Juselius 1999; Granger 1997; and Pesaran 1997.

120 Ruggie 1998.

121 See Williamson 1998; and Aghion and Williamson 1998.

122 Rodrik 1997.

preempt feared backlashes against globalization. Nevertheless, reconstituting politically novel laissez-faire worlds, akin to nineteenth-century liberalism, may represent a viable and stable, but seemingly inferior, historical alternative.

References

Abrams, Burton. 1999. The Effects of Government Size on the Unemployment Rate. *Public Choice* 99 (3–4):395–401.

Adler, Emanuel. 2002. Constructivism and International Relations. In *Handbook of International Relations,* edited by Walter Carlsnaes, Thomas Risse, and Beth Simmons, 95–118. Thousand Oaks, Calif.: Sage Publications.

Aghion, Philippe, Eve Caroli, and Cecilia Garcia-Penalosa. 1999. Inequality and Economic Growth: The Perspective of the New Growth Theories. *Journal of Economic Literature* 37 (4):1615–60.

Aghion, Philippe, and Peter Howitt. 1998. *Endogenous Growth Theory.* Cambridge, Mass.: MIT Press.

Aghion, Philippe, and Jeffrey Williamson. 1998. *Growth, Inequality, and Globalization: Theory, History, and Policy.* Cambridge: Cambridge University Press.

Alesina, Alberto, and Roberto Perotti. 1998. The Welfare State and Competitiveness. *American Economic Review* 87 (5):921–39.

Allen, Richard. 1998. *Beyond Liberalism: The Political Thought of F. A. Hayek & Michael Polanyi.* New York: Transaction Publishers.

Backus, David, and Patrick Kehoe. 1992. International Evidence on the Historical Properties of Business Cycles. *American Economic Review* 82 (4):864–88.

Baldwin, Richard, and Philippe Martin. 1999. Two Waves of Globalization: Superficial Similarities, Fundamental Differences. Working Paper 6904. Cambridge, Mass.: National Bureau of Economic Research.

Barro, Robert, and Xavier Sala-i-Martin. 1999. *Economic Growth.* Cambridge, Mass.: MIT Press.

Bell, Daniel. 1962. *The End of Ideology: On the Exhaustion of Political Ideas in the Fifties.* London: Collier Macmillan.

Bhagwati, Jagdish. 2002. Coping with Antiglobalization. *Foreign Affairs* 81 (1): 2–7.

Blanchard, Olivier, and Lawrence Summers. 1986. Hysteresis and the European Unemployment Problem. *NBER Macroeconomics Annual* 1:15–78.

Bordo, Michael, Barry Eichengreen, and Douglas Irwin. 1999. Is Globalization Today Really Different than Globalization a Hundred Years Ago? Working Paper 7195. Cambridge, Mass.: National Bureau of Economic Research.

Boswijk, H. Peter. 1996. Testing Identifiability of Cointegrating Vectors. *Journal of Business and Economic Statistics* 14 (2):153–60.

Boyer, Robert, and Daniel Drache, eds. 1996. *States Against Markets: The Limits of Globalization.* London: Routledge.

Brinkley, Alan. 1995. *The End of Reform: New Deal Liberalism in Recession and War.* New York: Knopf.

Broad, Robin, ed. 2002. *Global Backlash: Citizen Initiatives for a Just World Economy.* Lanham, Md.: Rowman.

Buchanan, James. 1977. *Democracy in Deficit: The Political Legacy of Lord Keynes.* New York: Academic Press.

Buchanan, Patrick. 1998. *The Great Betrayal: How American Sovereignty and Social Justice Are Being Sacrificed to the Gods of the Global Economy.* Boston: Little Brown.

Büthe, Tim. 2002. Taking Temporality Seriously: Modeling History and the Use of Narratives as Evidence. *American Political Science Review* 96 (3):481–93.

Cameron, David. 1978. The Expansion of the Public Economy: A Comparative Analysis. *American Political Science Review* 72 (4):1243–61.

Campbell, John, and Ove Pedersen, eds. 2001. *The Rise of Neoliberalism and Institutional Analysis.* Princeton, N.J.: Princeton University Press.

Coats, Alfred, ed. 1971. *The Classical Economists and Economic Policy.* London: Methuen.

Cochran, John, and Fred Glahe. 1999. *The Hayek-Keynes Debate.* Lewiston, N.Y.: Edwin Mellen Press.

Cornwall, John, and Wendy Cornwall. 2001. *Capitalist Development in the Twentieth Century: An Evolutionary-Keynesian Analysis.* Cambridge: Cambridge University Press.

Crouch, Colin, and Wolfgang Streeck, eds. 1997. *Political Economy of Modern Capitalism: Mapping Convergence and Diversity.* Thousand Oaks, Calif.: Sage.

Crozier, Michel, Joji Watanuki, and Samuel Huntington. 1975. *The Crisis of Democracy.* New York: New York University Press.

De Cecco, Marcello. 1984. *The International Gold Standard: Money and Empire.* New York: St. Martin's Press.

Dickey, David, and Wayne Fuller. 1979. Distribution of the Estimators for Autoregressive Time-Series with a Unit Root. *Journal of the American Statistical Association* 74 (366):427–31.

Dollar, David, and Aart Kraay. 2002. Spreading the Wealth. *Foreign Affairs* 81 (1):120–33.

Doornik, Jurgen, and David Hendry. 2000. *Modelling Dynamic Systems Using PcFiml 10.0.* London: International Thompson Business Press.

Eichengreen, Barry. 1996. *Globalizing Capital: A History of the International Monetary System.* Princeton, N.J.: Princeton University Press.

Engle, Robert, and Clive Granger. 1991. *Long-Run Economic Relationships: Readings in Cointegration.* New York: Oxford University Press.

Esping-Andersen, Gøsta. 1990. *The Three Worlds of Welfare Capitalism.* Cambridge: Polity Press.

———. 1999. *The Social Foundations of Postindustrial Economies.* Oxford: Oxford University Press.

———. 2002. *Why We Need a New Welfare State.* Oxford: Oxford University Press.

Etzioni, Amitai. 1994. *The Spirit of Community: Rights, Responsibilities, and the Communitarian Agenda.* New York: Simon and Schuster.

Eviews. 2003. Quantitative Micro Software. Irvine, Calif.

Fatás, Antonio. 2000. Do Business Cycles Cast Long Shadows? Short-Run Persistence and Economic Growth. *Journal of Economic Growth* 5 (2):147–62.

Flora, Peter, and Arnold Heidenheimer, eds. 1981. *The Development of Welfare States in Europe and America.* New Brunswick, N.J.: Transaction Books.

Floud, Roderick, and Deirdre McCloskey, eds. 1994. *The Economic History of Britain since 1700.* 2nd ed. Cambridge: Cambridge University Press.

Freeman, John, Daniel Houser, Paul Kellstedt, and John Williams. 1998. Long-Memoried Processes, Unit Roots, and Causal Inference in Political Science. *American Journal of Political Science* 42 (4):1289–327.

Friedman, Milton. 1968. The Role of Monetary Policy. *American Economic Review* 58 (1):1–17.

Friedman, Milton, and Rose Friedman. 1980. *Free to Choose.* New York: Harcourt.

Friedman, Milton, and Anna Schwartz. 1963. *A Monetary History of the United States 1867–1960.* Princeton, N.J.: Princeton University Press.

Friedman, Thomas. 1999. *The Lexus and the Olive Tree.* New York: Farrar Strauss & Girroux.

Fukuyama, Francis. 1993. *The End of History and the Last Man.* New York: Avon Books.

Garrett, Geoffrey. 1998. *Partisan Politics in the Global Economy.* Cambridge: Cambridge University Press.

Giddens, Anthony. 1998. *The Third Way: The Renewal of Social Democracy.* Cambridge: Polity Press.

Gill, Stephen. 1993. *Gramsci, Historical Materialism, and International Relations.* Cambridge: Cambridge University Press.

Gilpin, Robert. 2000. *The Challenge of Global Capitalism.* Princeton, N.J.: Princeton University Press.

Granger, Clive. 1997. On Modelling the Long Run in Applied Economics. *Economic Journal* 107 (1):169–77.

Granger, Clive, and Paul Newbold. 1974. Spurious Regression in Econometrics. *Journal of Econometrics* 2:111–20.

Gray, John. 1998. *False Dawn: The Delusions of Global Capitalism.* New York: New Press.

Greenaway, David, and Douglas Nelson, eds. 2001. *Globalization and Labour Markets.* Cheltenham, England: Edward Elgar.

Greider, William. 1997. *One World, Ready or Not.* New York: Simon and Schuster.

Hasenclever, Andreas, Peter Mayer, and Volker Rittberger. 1997. *Theories of International Regimes.* Cambridge: Cambridge University Press.

Hayek, Friedrich. 1944. *The Road to Serfdom.* London: Routledge.

———. 1966. *Monetary Theory and the Trade Cycle.* Clifton, N.J.: Augustus M. Kelley.

———. 1996. *Individualism and Economic Order.* Chicago: University of Chicago Press.

Hayek, Friedrich, and Bruce Caldwell. 1995. *Contra Keynes and Cambridge.* Chicago: University of Chicago Press.

Hirst, Paul, and Grahame Thompson, eds. 1999. *Globalization in Question.* 2nd ed. Cambridge: Polity Press.

Hobsbawm, Eric. 1990. *Industry and Empire: From 1750 to the Present Day.* Harmondsworth, England: Penguin.

Hooks, Gregory. 1991. *Forging the Military-Industrial Complex.* Urbana: University of Illinois Press.

Hoover, Kenneth. 2003. *Economics as Ideology: Keynes, Laski, Hayek, and the Creation of Contemporary Politics.* Lanham, Md.: Rowman & Littlefield.

Huber, Evelyne, and John Stephens. 2001. *Development and Crisis of the Welfare State.* Chicago: University of Chicago Press.

Iversen, Torben. 2001. The Dynamics of Welfare State Expansion: Trade Openness, De-industrialization, and Partisan Politics. In *The New Politics of the Welfare State,* edited by Paul Pierson, 45–79. Oxford: Oxford University Press.

James, Harold. 2002. *The End of Globalization: Lessons from the Great Depression.* Cambridge, Mass.: Harvard University Press.

Johansen, Soren. 1995. *Likelihood-Based Inference in Cointegrated Vector Autoregressive Models.* Oxford: Oxford University Press.

Juselius, Katarina. 1999. Models and Relations in Economics and Econometrics. *Journal of Economic Methodology* 6 (2):259–90.

Katzenstein, Peter. 1985. *Small States in World Markets: Industrial Policy in Europe.* Ithaca, N.Y.: Cornell University Press.

Keohane, Robert. 1984a. *After Hegemony: Cooperation and Discord in the World Political Economy.* Princeton, N.J.: Princeton University Press.

———. 1984b. The World Political Economy and the Crisis of Embedded Liberalism. In *Order and Conflict in Contemporary Capitalism,* edited by John Goldthorpe, 15–38. Oxford: Oxford University Press.

Keohane, Robert, and Helen Milner, eds. 1996. *Internationalization and Domestic Politics.* Cambridge: Cambridge University Press.

Keynes, John Maynard. 1936. *The General Theory of Employment, Interest, and Money.* London: Macmillan.

———. 1982. National Self-Sufficiency. In *Collected Writings of John Maynard Keynes,* Vol. 21. London: Macmillan.

Kindleberger, Charles. 1975. The Rise of Free Trade in Western Europe, 1820–1875. *Journal of Economic History* 35 (1):20–55.

King, Robert, Charles Plosser, James Stock, and Mark Watson. 1991. Stochastic Trends and Economic Fluctuations. *American Economic Review* 81 (1):819–40.

Kitschelt, Herbert, et al. 1999. *Continuity and Change in Contemporary Capitalism.* New York: Cambridge University Press.

Klein, Naomi. 2002. *No Logo: No Space, No Choice, No Jobs.* New York: Picador.

Krugman, Paul. 1995. Growing World Trade: Causes and Consequences. *Brookings Papers on Economic Activity* 1:327–62.

Lai, Deepak. 2000. The Challenge of Globalization: There Is No Third Way. In *Global Fortune,* edited by Ian Vásquez, 29–42. Washington, D.C.: Cato Institute.

Lindert, Peter. 2004. *The Story: Social Spending and Economic Growth since the Eighteenth Century.* In *Growing Public,* Vol. 1. Cambridge: Cambridge University Press.

Lindsey, Brink. 2002. *Against the Dead Hand: The Uncertain Struggle for Global Capitalism.* New York: John Wiley.

Lipset, Seymour Martin. 1960. *Political Man: The Social Bases of Politics.* Garden City, N.Y.: Doubleday.

——. 1996. *American Exceptionalism: A Double-Edged Sword.* New York: Norton.

MacKinnon, James. 1996. Numerical Distribution Functions for Unit Root and Cointegration Tests. *Journal of Applied Econometrics* 11:601–18.

Maddison, Angus. 1995. *Monitoring the World Economy, 1820–1992.* Paris: Organization for Economic Co-operation and Development.

Marglin, Stephen, and Juliet Schor. 1990. *The Golden Age of Capitalism.* Oxford: Clarendon Press.

Marx, Karl. 1976. *Capital, Vol. 1.* Translated by Ben Fowkes. New York: Vintage.

Mendell, Marguerite, and Daniel Salee, eds. 1991. *The Legacy of Karl Polanyi.* New York: Palgrave.

Meny, Yves, and Yves Surel, eds. 2002. *Democracies and the Populist Challenge.* New York: Palgrave.

Micklethwait, John, and Adrian Wooldridge. 2000. *A Future Perfect: The Challenge and Hidden Promise of Globalization.* New York: Crown Publishers.

Mishra, Ramesh. 1999. *Globalization and the Welfare State.* Cheltenham, England: Edward Elgar.

Mitchell, Brian. 1988. *British Historical Statistics.* Cambridge, Mass.: Cambridge University Press.

——. 1998. *International Historical Statistics: Europe 1750–1993.* 4th ed. London: MacMillan.

Mueller, Dennis. 2003. *Public Choice III.* New York: Cambridge University Press.

Nelson, Charles, and Charles Plosser. 1982. Trends and Random Walks in Macroeconomic Time Series: Some Evidence and Implications. *Journal of Monetary Economics* 10 (2):139–62.

Obstfeld, Maurice, and Kenneth Rogoff. 1996. *Foundations of International Macroeconomics.* Cambridge, Mass.: MIT Press.

Ohmae, Kenichi. 1990. *The Borderless World: Power and Strategy in the Interlinked Economy.* New York: Harper and Collins.

Okun, Arthur. 1975. *Equality and Efficiency: The Big Trade-Off.* Washington: Brookings Institution.

Olson, Mancur. 1982. *The Rise and Decline of Nations.* New Haven, Conn.: Yale University Press.

O'Rourke, Kevin. 2000. Tariffs and Growth in the Late 19th Century. *Economic Journal* 110 (463): 456–83.

——. 1999. Globalization in Historical Perspective. Working Paper 99/17. Dublin, Ireland: University College Dublin, Centre for Economic Research.

O'Rourke, Kevin, and Jeffrey Williamson. 1999. *Globalization and History: The Evolution of a Nineteenth-Century Atlantic Economy.* Cambridge, Mass.: MIT Press.

Papell, David, Christian Murray, and Hala Ghiblawi. 2000. The Structure of Unemployment. *Review of Economics and Statistics* 82 (2):309–15.

Patterson, Kerry. 2000. *An Introduction to Applied Econometrics: A Time Series Approach.* New York: St. Martin's Press.

Pesaran, M. Hashem. 1997. The Role of Economic Theory in Modelling the Long Run. *Economic Journal* 107 (440):178–91.

Phillips, Peter, and Pierre Perron. 1988. Testing for Unit Root in Time Series Regression. *Biometrika* 75 (2):335–46.

Pierson, Paul. 1994. *Dismantling the Welfare State?* Cambridge: Cambridge University Press.

———. 2000. Increasing Returns, Path Dependence, and the Study of Politics. *American Political Science Review* 94 (2):251–67.

———. ed. 2001. *The New Politics of the Welfare State.* Oxford: Oxford University Press.

Pissarides, Christopher. 2000. *Equilibrium Unemployment Theory.* Cambridge, Mass.: MIT Press.

Polanyi, Karl. 1957. *The Great Transformation.* Boston: Beacon Press.

Rodrik, Dani. 1997. *Has Globalization Gone too Far?* Washington, D.C.: Institute for International Economics.

Ruggie, John. 1982. International Regimes, Transactions, and Change: Embedded Liberalism in the Post-War Economic Order. *International Organization* 36 (2):379–415.

———. 1994. Trade, Protectionism, and the Future of Welfare Capitalism. *Journal of International Affairs* 48 (1):1–11.

———. 1997. Globalization and the Embedded Liberalism Compromise: The End of an Era? Working Paper 97/1. Bonn, Germany: Max-Planck-Institut.

———. 1998. *Constructing the World Polity.* London: Routledge.

Sargent, Thomas. 1987. *Macroeconomic Theory.* 2nd ed. Boston: Academic Press.

Sargent, Thomas, and Neil Wallace. 1975. "Rational" Expectations, the Optimal Monetary Instrument, and the Optimal Money Supply Rule. *Journal of Political Economy* 83 (2):241–54.

Schumpeter, Joseph. 1928. The Instability of Capitalism. *Economic Journal* 38 (151):361–86.

Shearmur, Jeremy. 1996. *Hayek and After: Hayekian Realism as a Research Programme.* New York: Routledge.

Shonfield, Andrew. 1969. *Modern Capitalism: The Changing Balance of Public and Private Power.* London: Oxford University Press.

Simmons, Beth. 1994. *Who Adjusts? Domestic Sources of Foreign Economic Policy during the Interwar Years.* Princeton, N.J.: Princeton University Press.

Simmons, Beth, and Lisa Martin. 2002. International Organizations and Institutions. In *Handbook of International Relations,* edited by Walter Carlsnaes, Thomas Risse, and Beth Simmons, 192–211. Thousand Oaks, Calif.: Sage Publications.

Soros, George. 1998. *The Crisis of Global Capitalism.* New York: Public Affairs.

Stein, Arthur. 1984. The Hegemon's Dilemma: Great Britain, the United States, and the International Economic Order. *International Organization* 38 (2):355–86.

Stein, Jerome. 1982. *Monetarist, Keynesian, and New Classical Economics.* Oxford: Blackwell.

Stiglitz, Joseph. 2002. *Globalization and Its Discontent.* New York: Norton.

Strange, Susan. 1996. *The Retreat of the State.* Cambridge: Cambridge University Press.

Swank, Duane. 2002. *Global Capital, Political Institutions, and Policy Changes in Developed Welfare States.* Cambridge: Cambridge University Press.

Tanzi, Vito, and Ludger Schuknecht. 2000. *Public Spending in the 20th Century.* Cambridge: Cambridge University Press.

Taylor, Arthur. 1972. *Laissez Faire and State Intervention in Nineteenth-Century Britain.* London: Macmillan.

Tonelson, Alan. 2000. *Race to the Bottom.* Boulder, Colo.: Westview Press.

Vásquez, Ian. 2000. The Return to a Global Economy. In *Global Fortune: The Stumble and Rise of Global Capitalism,* edited by Ian Vásquez, 1–14. Washington, D.C.: Cato Institute.

Verdier, Daniel. 1998. Domestic Responses to Capital Market Internationalization under the Gold Standard, 1870–1914. *International Organization* 52 (1):1–34.

Von Mises, Ludwig. 1977. *A Critique of Interventionism.* New Rochelle, N.Y.: Arlington House.

———. 1969. *Omnipotent Government: The Rise of the Total State and Total War.* New Rochelle, NY: Arlington House.

Wagner, Adolph. 1883. Three Extracts on Public Finance. In *Classics in the Theory of Public Finance,* edited by Richard. A. Musgrave and Alan T. Peacock, 1–15. London: Macmillan.

Walras, Leon. 1954. *Elements of Pure Economics; The Theory of Social Wealth.* New York: Allen and Unwin.

Weber, Max. 1949. *The Methodology of the Social Sciences.* Translated and edited by Edward A. Shils and Henry A. Finch. New York: Free Press.

Weiss, Linda. 1998. *The Myth of the Powerless State.* Ithaca, N.Y.: Cornell University Press.

Wendt, Alexander. 1999. *Social Theory of International Politics.* Cambridge: Cambridge University Press.

Williamson, Jeffrey. 1996. Globalization, Convergence, and History. *Journal of Economic History* 56 (2):277–306.

———. 1998. Globalization, Labor Markets, and Policy Backlash in the Past. *Journal of Economic Perspectives* 12 (4):51–72.

Wood, Adrian. 1994. *North-South Trade, Employment, and Inequality.* Oxford: Clarendon Press.

Chapter 4

Why Do More Open Economies Have Bigger Governments?

Dani Rodrik

I. Introduction

This chapter documents a little-known empirical regularity and provides a plausible explanation for it. The regularity consists of a robust association between an economy's exposure to foreign trade and the size of its government. The explanation is that government expenditures are used to provide social insurance against external risk.

The claim that there is a *positive* association between trade exposure and the scope of government is surprising at first sight. It is widely presumed that the effectiveness of government intervention is lower in economies that are highly integrated with the world economy. This would suggest a negative correlation between the volume of trade and the scope of government. Yet the small, highly open economies of central and northern Europe (e.g., Austria, Netherlands, and Norway) have some of the world's highest shares of government spending in gross domestic product.

The evidence presented in this chapter suggests that the European pattern is not an exception. There is a positive and robust partial correlation between openness, as measured by the share of trade in GDP, and the scope of government, as measured by the share of government expenditure in GDP. The correlation is robust in the sense that (*a*) it is unaffected by the inclusion of other control variables, (*b*) it exists for measures of government spending drawn from all available data sets, (*c*) it prevails for both low- and high-income countries, and (*d*) it is not an artefact created by outliers. In addition, openness in the early 1960s is a statistically significant predictor of the *expansion* of government consumption over the subsequent three decades.

The explanation that best fits the evidence is one that focuses on the role of external risk. Societies seem to demand (and receive) an expanded government role as the price for accepting larger doses of external risk. In other words, government spending appears to provide social insurance in economies subject to external shocks. The central evidence in favor of this explanation comes from regressions in which openness is interacted with two measures of external risk, volatility of the terms of trade and the product concentration of exports. In each case, the interaction term is strongly significant (and the fit of the regression improves), whereas the coefficient on openness *per se* becomes insignificant or negative. The same result is confirmed in panel regressions with fixed effects for time periods and countries. Hence, unlike other explanations for the correlation between openness and government size, this one receives considerable support.

If the key argument advanced in this chapter is valid, a number of ancillary hypotheses follow. First, increases in external risk must lead to greater volatility in domestic income and consumption. Second, a larger share in GDP of government purchases of goods and services must reduce income volatility. Third, the risk-mitigating role of government spending should be displayed most prominently in social security and welfare spending, particularly in the advanced countries that possess the requisite administrative capability to manage social welfare systems. Fourth, causality should run from exposure to external risk to government spending. I provide evidence in favor of each of these propositions. I also provide a simple general equilibrium model that clarifies how government consumption can alleviate exposure to external risk under certain plausible conditions.

An important precursor to this chapter is a study by David Cameron (1978). In that study, he showed that the best single predictor of the increase in an OECD government's tax revenue (as a share of GDP) between 1960 and 1975 was the economy's openness in 1960 (exports plus imports divided by GDP), with a correlation coefficient of .78. By way of explanation, Cameron argued that more open economies have higher rates of industrial concentration, which tend to foster higher unionization, greater scope for collective bargaining, and stronger labor confederations. These in turn result in larger demands for government transfers – social security, pensions, unemployment insurance, job training, and so forth – which mitigate external risk.

Cameron's study was limited to 18 OECD countries, and his explanation for the finding is probably too specific to be relevant to my 100-plus country sample. In particular, it may not be plausible to attach such importance to the role of labor organizations in most developing countries. Further, the empirical relationship between openness and government spending holds for government *consumption* as well, and not just for transfers on which Cameron based his argument. Nonetheless, the hypothesis advanced here is consistent with the idea, considered also by Cameron, that public spending is a risk-reducing instrument on which there is greater reliance in more open economies (see also Bates, Brock, and Tiefenthaler 1991).

The chapter is organized as follows. Section II demonstrates the close association between openness and various measures of government spending. Focusing on government consumption, Section III analyzes the robustness of the association as well as tests for (and dismisses) some alternative explanations for the association. Section IV discusses the analytics of the central hypothesis of the chapter and provides evidence on both the central and ancillary hypotheses mentioned above. Section V presents concluding comments.

II. The Evidence

Figure 4.1 shows the simple relationship between openness and government spending in a sample of 23 OECD countries. The vertical axis represents government spending as a share of GDP, excluding interest payments, averaged over the 1990–92 period. Along the horizontal axis is shown the share of exports plus imports in GDP, averaged over the decade 1980–89. Data are taken from the World Bank's *World Data 1995* for government spending and from Penn world tables 5.6 for openness.

The figure reveals an unmistakable positive association between openness and size of government. A semilogarithmic regression equation fits the data extremely well, explaining 44 percent of the cross-country variance in government expenditures. The United States and Japan are at one end of the distribution with the lowest trade shares in GDP and (along with Turkey and Canada) the lowest shares of government spending. Luxembourg, Belgium, and the Netherlands are at the other end with very high degrees of openness and large government. Aside from Cameron (1978), earlier studies that have found a correlation between openness and the size of the public sector for the OECD countries include Schmidt (1983) and Saunders and Klau (1985). Figure 4.1 shows that the correlation continued to hold as of the early 1990s.

Could the association between openness and the scope of government be a spurious one? The OECD evidence is in fact fragile against alternative hypotheses, such as the following: (*a*) small countries have larger government shares and are at the same time more open or (*b*) European countries have large government sectors (for social and cultural reasons) and are also more open because of the presence of a common market among members of the European Union. The small size of the OECD sample rules out testing these various hypotheses meaningfully against each other. When population and a dummy for European countries are added to the regression for the OECD sample, the coefficient on openness remains significant only at the 90 percent level.

I now turn to a broader sample of countries, for which the sample size should be less constraining. My preferred measure of government for the larger sample is real

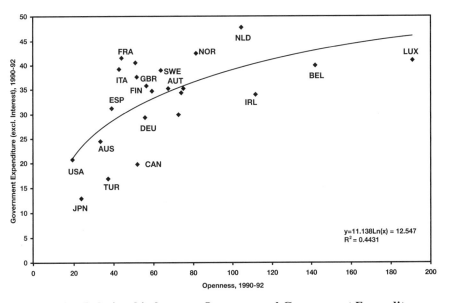

Figure 4.1   Relationship between Openness and Government Expenditures

government *consumption* from the Penn world tables. These data have a couple of advantages. They are available for a much larger group of countries than contained in the World Bank data. In addition, they are free of biases arising from cross-country differences in the relative price of government purchases. Two countries with identical levels of *real* government purchases will appear to have very different shares of government in GDP if the price index for such purchases relative to the GDP deflator differs. The disadvantage is that this measure of government includes only consumption and excludes income transfers and public investment.[1] I show results for public investment as well in passing, for comparison purposes. Results for more disaggregated levels of government spending will be shown later.

Previous studies on the determinants of government spending in large cross sections of countries have focused on a number of explanatory variables. According to Wagner's law, for example, the demand for government services is income elastic, so that the share of government consumption in GDP is expected to rise with income. Other variables typically considered are demographic and structural indicators (see, e.g., Tait and Heller 1982; Ram 1987; Heller and Diamond 1990). In light of these studies, my benchmark regression includes the following explanatory variables in addition to openness: per capita GDP (GDPSH5xx), the dependency ratio in the population (DEPEND90), the urbanization rate (URBAN90), a dummy for socialist countries (SOC), a dummy for OECD members (OECD), and dummies for geographical regions (LAAM, ASIAE, and SAFRICA for Latin America, East Asia, and sub-Saharan Africa, respectively). These variables were selected after some experimentation to achieve the best overall fit for the regression (but without regard for the significance of the coefficient on openness), within the constraints of data availability. In addition to the variables just discussed, the regressions also include a measure of openness (OPENAVGxxyy), which is the ratio of trade (sum of imports and exports) to GDP, averaged over the prior decade. Aside from the Penn world tables, Barro and Lee (1994) and the World Bank's *World Data 1995* are the main sources for the data. More detail on the sources is provided in the Appendix.

The dependent variable in most of these regressions is a 3- or 5-year average of real government consumption (as a share of GDP) expressed in international prices (CGAVGxxyy). The sample consists of all countries included in the Penn world tables (version 5.6a) for which the requisite data exist. I have excluded observations for which the openness ratio exceeds 200 percent. This cutoff has very little significance for the actual results since it leads to the exclusion of only one observation, that for Hong Kong in the 1990–92 regressions.

Table 4.1 displays the benchmark results. Columns 1 and 2 relate shares of government consumption in GDP to the previous decade's openness during the two

---

1   Government consumption is defined in the U.N. System of National Accounts as "expenditure, including imputed expenditure, incurred by general government on both individual consumption goods and services and collective consumption services" (United Nations 1993, p. 516). In view of the difficulty of valuing government services, in practice this item is measured as the *cost* to the government of the services it provides, including most significantly the wage bill. Some of its main subcategories are public administration, public order, national defense, health, and education.

periods 1990–92 and 1985–89. I present results for the 1985–89 period alongside those for 1990–92 because the sample size is larger than in the later period (125 vs. 103 countries). The fit of the regressions is generally good, with an adjusted R^2 of .43–.46. Contrary to Wagner's law, per capita income enters with a negative sign as a determinant of government consumption in both periods but is statistically significant at the 90 percent level only for 1985–89. The dependency ratio enters positively and is statistically significant at the 99 percent level for both periods. Urbanization enters negatively and is significant at the 95 percent level in 1990–92 and at the 90 percent level in 1985–89. The dummy for socialist countries has a positive coefficient but is not significant at conventional levels. Neither is the dummy for OECD countries. The regional dummies are all statistically significant at the 95 percent level in 1985–89, but not in 1990–92.

I am mainly interested in the estimated coefficient on openness. This coefficient turns out to be positive and highly significant in both cases – at the 99.9 percent level of confidence. The estimated elasticity is a bit larger than 0.2, implying that a share of total trade (exports *plus* imports) in GDP that is larger by 10 percent is associated with a share of government consumption in GDP that is higher by 2 percent. Perhaps a better sense of the quantitative significance of this elasticity can be obtained from the following calculation. The median shares of government consumption and openness in the sample are around 18 percent and 60 percent, respectively. A country whose openness is 80 percent (a difference of 33.3 percent from the median, corresponding to an increase in the share of imports by 10 percent of GDP) would be expected to have a level of government consumption that is larger than the median by 1.2 percent of GDP ($0.333 \times 0.2 \times 0.18$) – an increase from 18 to 19.2 percent of GDP. Whether this is a large or modest effect can be debated, but it is relatively tightly estimated. A 95 percent confidence interval from the 1990–92 regression would place the "true" elasticity between 0.095 and 0.351.

Columns 3 and 4 show regressions in which the dependent variable is now government investment (as a share of GDP). The same set of independent variables as before is used, and results are reported for both 1990–92 and 1985–89. The data, which come from the *World Data 1995* of the World Bank, are available for a smaller group of countries and have the relative price problem noted before. Nonetheless the results are interesting and provide a useful complement to those for government consumption. The estimated coefficients on openness are positive and statistically significant as before. Moreover, they are quite a bit larger in magnitude: 0.53 and 0.83, respectively.

In column 5 of Table 4.1 we can see that openness during the early 1960s can also explain the subsequent *increase* in government consumption. The dependent variable here is the ratio of the government consumption share in GDP in 1990–92 to that in 1960–64. For most countries, this ratio is greater than one, indicating an expansion of government in the last three decades. The independent variables include the initial share of government consumption as well as initial openness (in 1960–64). The adjusted R^2 of the regression is quite respectable at .66. The estimated coefficient on initial government is strongly negative, implying a (conditional) convergence effect on government spending. More important from my perspective, the estimated coefficient on initial openness is positive and significant at the 99 percent level.

Table 4.1   Openness and Government Spending

	Dependent Variable					
Independent Variable	Log CGAVG9092 (1)	Log CGAVG8589 (2)	Log GIAVG9092 (3)	Log GIAVG8589 (4)	DGOV6092 (5)	DOPEN6092 (6)
Constant	3.289* (.536)	3.786* (.383)	−1.778*** (.990)	−4.708 (2.872)	6.426 (.936)	4.439 (.852)
Log GDP per capita	−.030 (.084)	−.105*** (.063)	−.413* (.143)	−.013 (.448)	−.151 (.133)	−.194 (.121)
Log dependency ratio	.642* (.241)	.630* (.193)	.372 (.499)	−.304 (1.457)	.387 (.388)	.146 (.353)
Log urbanization	−.203** (.093)	−.136*** (.075)	−.006 (.185)	−.556 (.537)	−.381* (.123)	.080 (.112)
Socialist	.169 (.130)	.092 (.100)	−.559 (.413)	−1.631*** (.909)	.924* (.227)	.260 (.207)
OECD	−.007 (.144)	−.014 (.122)	−.051 (.246)	−.080 (.851)	.040 (.254)	.384 (.231)
Latin America	−.171 (.113)	−.218** (.094)	−.564** (.221)	.122 (.661)	−.072 (.191)	−.041 (.174)
East Asia	−.206 (.140)	−.338** (.130)	−.193 (.267)	−.206 (.913)	−.693 (.228)	.836 (.208)
Sub-Saharan Africa	−.107 (.118)	−.239** (.101)	−.161 (.232)	.002 (.732)	−.100 (.194)	.041 (.177)
Log CGAVG6064					−1.308* (.119)	−.019 (.108)
Log OPENAVG8089	.223* (.064)		.534* (.134)			

Log OPENAVG7584		.205* (.057)		.835** (.401)		
Log OPENAVG6064					.272* (.094)	-.510* (.086)
Adjusted R^2	.428	.458	.456	.013	.664	.360
Standard error	.317	.313	.558	1.931	.512	.466
Observations	103	125	75	98	99	99

* Significant at the 99 percent level.

** Significant at the 95 percent level.

*** Significant at the 90 percent level.

Hence, not only is openness an important determinant of government consumption levels across countries, but openness in the early 1960s turns out to be a significant predictor of the *expansion* of government consumption in the subsequent three decades.

Column 6 of Table 4.1 repeats the previous regression, replacing the increase in government consumption with the increase in openness as the dependent variable. The point of this exercise is to check whether the previous regressions may have been capturing the effect of government spending on openness rather than vice versa. However, it turns out that the level of government consumption in 1960–64 has no predictive power for the increase in openness over the following three decades. The estimated coefficient on government consumption in 1960–64 is actually negative (but far from significant). It seems that it is openness early on that determines the subsequent size of government, not the other way around.

Using World Bank data, Table 4.2 shows the relationship between openness and disaggregated categories of government spending. The evidence shows that openness has a statistically significant association with most types of government spending, including general public services, education, health, housing and community amenities, and economic affairs and services. The estimated coefficients are generally significant at the 99 percent level of confidence. Openness does not enter significantly in the 1985–89 regression for social security and welfare spending, but it does so in the 1990–92 regression (not shown). The only major spending item that does not exhibit a statistically significant correlation with openness in either period is interest payments on the public debt. More detail on the disaggregated data is provided in Rodrik (1997a).

Finally, note that the association between openness and government size apparently exists in all available data sets. These include the Penn world tables and the World Bank's *World Data 1995*, as noted above. In addition, data on government spending on education from the United Nations Educational, Scientific, and Cultural Organization exhibit a strong positive correlation with openness. The same is true for data on government *revenue* from the International Monetary Fund as well: more open economies have larger tax/GDP ratios, with other characteristics held constant (see also Tanzi 1992). Government *employment* (as a share of the labor force) is also positively correlated with openness. See Rodrik (1997a, 1997b) for studies that cover these additional data sources.

III. Probing Deeper: Some Hypotheses and Checks of Robustness

One aspect of robustness has already been discussed: the correlation between exposure to trade and scope of government spans a wide range of data sets and exists for different measures of government size. In this section I shall experiment with various versions of the benchmark regressions reported in Table 4.1 and in doing so also check for the validity of some possible explanations for the association.

Table 4.3 reports the results of various experiments with the benchmark specification. I use the 1985–89 equation for government consumption since this covers the largest number of countries (125). Column 1 of Table 4.3 reproduces

Table 4.2   Openness and Government Expenditures by Functional Category (1985–89)

| | Dependent Variable (as a Percentage of GDP) | | | | | | | | | |
Independent Variable	All Government Spending (Excluding "Other")	Public Services	Defense	Education	Health	Social Security and Welfare	Housing	Culture etc.	Economic Affairs and Services	Other (Including Interest Payments)
Log OPENAVG7584	.300*	.397*	.267***	.532*	.349**	.273	.616*	.618*	.496*	.097
	(.091)	(.145)	(.154)	(.142)	(.174)	(.292)	(.225)	(.240)	(.111)	(.184)
Observations	81	83	82	84	84	78	81	81	83	81
Adjusted R^2	.244	.132	.154	.085	.099	.322	.127	.079	.333	.120

Note: Other regressors not shown in the table: constant, log GDPSH5A5, log DEPEND90, log URBAN90, SOC, OECD, LAAM, ASIAE, and SAFRICA.

 * Significant at the 99 percent level.
 ** Significant at the 95 percent level.
 *** Significant at the 90 percent level.

Table 4.3   Checking for Robustness and Alternative Explanations (Dependent Variable: Log CGAVG8589)

Independent Variable	Benchmark (1)	Splitting the Sample by Income		Controlling For:										
		< $25,000 (2)	> $25,000 (3)	Country Size		External Borrowing (6)	Inflation (7)	Trade Taxes		Sales Taxes and VAT		Export Revenue from Primary Exports	
				(4)	(5)			(8)	(9)	(10)	(11)	(12)	(13)
Log OPENAVG7584	.205* (.057)	.266* (.081)	.230* (.083)	.345* (.068)	.221** (.087)	.229* (.070)	.214* (.065)	.385* (.080)	.355* (.067)	.296* (.079)	.315* (.068)	.248* (.060)	.209* (.058)
Log AREA				.065* (.019)									
Log POP85					.005 (.030)								
Log DETGNP85						088*** (.053)							
Log inflation rate (1975–90)							.015 (.041)						
Log INTL8688								−.098*** (.057)					
INTL8688/ TOTAL8688									−.617* (.227)				
Log GSVAT8688										.027 (.038)			
GSVAT8688/ TOTAL8688											.194 (.286)		
Log PRIMSHR85												.134** (.056)	
OIL													.049 (.117)
Adjusted R^2	.458	.273	.447	.547	.483	.429	.440	.491	.521	.475	.472	.460	.455
Observations	125	61	61	115	120	89	113	79	79	64	79	107	125

Note: Same as Table 4.2.

the coefficient estimate on the openness variable from column 2 of Table 4.1, for purposes of comparison with later columns. Note that these regressions include the complete set of independent variables considered in Table 4.1, but the estimated coefficients for the other independent variables are not shown in the table to avoid clutter.

Columns 2 and 3 of the table show the results of splitting the sample into two subsamples of roughly equal size according to level of income, using $2,500 in 1985 dollars as the cutoff. The coefficient on openness is virtually identical for the two income groups, and it remains statistically significant at the 99 percent level for both subsamples. Hence the relationship between openness and government consumption exists for both the lower- and higher-income halves of the sample.

The remaining columns check whether the coefficient on openness remains stable and statistically significant when additional candidate explanatory variables are included in the regression. Let us first consider the possible influence of country size. Columns 4 and 5 experiment with two different measures of country size: land area (AREA) and population (POP85). (Note that since all variables are included in logs and per capita income is already a regressor, including total GDP is redundant once population has already been added.) The idea behind including these variables is to test whether the observed correlation between openness and government size is due to the following possibility: Assume that the provision of public services is subject to significant indivisibilities; for example, every country, regardless of size, needs one parliament. Then government size as a share of GDP will be negatively correlated with country size (see, e.g., Alesina and Wacziarg 1997) . Since openness is negatively correlated with country size as well, the observed association between openness and government spending could be spurious and could arise from the omission of a size variable. However, there is no evidence that something like this is at work here. Both of the size variables enter with a *positive* sign, and the estimated coefficient on land area is actually highly significant. But in both cases the coefficient on openness remains statistically significant. With land area included, the openness coefficient actually increases significantly in magnitude (to 0.34).

Column 6 checks for the possibility that openness increases government spending by enhancing the economy's ability to borrow from external sources. If the penalty to be suffered by a sovereign debtor (from trade sanctions, say) increases with the economy's dependence on trade, which seems plausible, external credit rationing will tend to be less binding in more open economies. In such economies, the government can borrow more and spend more, if it views spending as inherently desirable. To control for this possibility, the debt/gross national product ratio is included as an independent variable (DETGNP85). The estimated coefficient on the debt/GNP ratio is positive and significant at the 90 percent level, so there is some support for the theoretical prediction. However, the coefficient on openness remains unchanged and highly significant.

Another hypothesis is that more open economies have lower inflation and, because of that, a larger tax base. Under high inflation conditions, the government's tax base erodes both as a result of delays in tax payments in unindexed systems (the Olivera-Tanzi effect) and as a consequence of the shrinkage of the formal sector at the expense of the informal sector. The regression in column 7 includes the average inflation rate during 1975–90 on the right-hand side to check for this possibility. The estimated coefficient on inflation turns out to be insignificant, whereas the coefficient on openness remains unaffected.

Next consider that trade itself may be a convenient tax handle for governments in poor countries that have difficulty raising taxes from other sources. Openness may then allow for higher levels of government spending by allowing a higher level of tax revenues. Restricting the sample now to developing countries, for which the hypothesis is primarily relevant, let us check whether openness exerts an effect on government consumption once the level of trade taxes is controlled for. Column 8 shows the result of including trade tax revenues (as a share of GDP) as an additional independent variable (INTL8688). This variable covers all revenue from trade source, including import duties and export taxes. The estimated coefficient on it turns out to be negative (and statistically significant at the 90 percent confidence level). The coefficient on openness increases in magnitude and remains highly significant. While the sign on trade taxes may be surprising, what seems to be going on is the following: governments that raise a lot of revenue from trade (even after one controls for per capita income) tend to have very few other tax handles, and therefore their ability to spend tends to be severely restricted. Further evidence for this interpretation comes from column 9, which includes the share of trade taxes in all tax revenues on the right-hand side (INTL8688/TOTAL8688). The estimated coefficient on this variable is negative and significant at the 99 percent level. Including this particular variable in the regression also result in raising the *t*-statistic on the openness elasticity to above 5!

A related version of the previous argument is that large trade volumes may help governments collect higher revenues from indirect taxes such as sales taxes and value-added taxes (VAT). In many poor countries, such taxes are collected disproportionately at the border.[2] To check for this possibility, I control for indirect tax revenues including VAT (both as a share of GDP and as a share of total tax revenues) in columns 10 and 11. The estimated coefficient on openness remains unaffected.

I also check for the possibility that the correlation is due to resource rents or other revenue derived by the government from export activities. Columns 12 and 13 introduce the share of primary products in total exports (PRIMSHR85) and a dummy for oil-exporting countries (OIL), and in neither case is the coefficient on openness affected. I have also used a direct measure of export tax revenues (not shown), with similar results.

Finally, what about the possibility of outliers? Figure 4.2 displays the partial relationship between openness and government consumption – partial in the sense that other determinants of government consumption are controlled for – generated by the regression in column 4 of Table 4.3. There are 115 countries in this figure, and some of them have been identified by country codes to give the reader a sense of where different countries stand. The figure is a good way of summing up what we have learned so far: there is a tight and robust empirical association between

---

2   I am grateful to a referee for making this point.

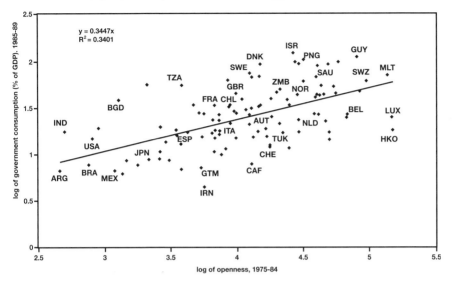

Figure 4.2 Partial Relationship between Openness and Government Consumption (when one controls for per capita income, urbanization, dependency ratio, area, and regional dummies)

openness to trade and government consumption (as a share of GDP) in a large cross section of countries. Further, the figure makes clear that the result is not driven by the presence of outliers: the 115-country sample covers practically the full range of my measures of openness and government consumption.

IV. A Possible Explanation: Social Insurance against External Risk

Hence the statistical association between openness and government spending appears to be a robust one. It is not a spurious relationship generated by omitted variables. Nor is it an artefact of the sample of countries selected or of a specific data source. The question is why this relationship exists.

One plausible answer, which I shall show below is consistent with the evidence, is the following. More open economies have greater exposure to the risks emanating from turbulence in world markets. One can view larger government spending in such economies as performing an insulation function, insofar as the government sector is the "safe" sector (in terms of employment and purchases from the rest of the economy) relative to other activities, and especially compared to tradables. Hence in countries significantly affected by external shocks, the government can mitigate risk by taking command of a larger share of the economy's resources.

To fix ideas, consider the following framework. Divide the economy into three sectors: private tradables, private nontradables, and the government sector. Think of a representative extended household in this economy as having claims on income streams from each of these three types of activities. The larger the share of government consumption in the economy, the larger the share of the household's total income that derives from the government sector. Can a (permanently) higher share of government consumption mitigate the representative household's exposure to external risk in such an economy? And when will it be optimal for the government to reduce risk in this fashion?

Assume that the government sector is the "safe" sector in a sense that will be made more precise empirically later on. Suppose, in the extreme, that employment and incomes in the government sector are stable and uncorrelated with any of the shocks to which the economy is subjected. Under these circumstances, some of the riskiness in the household's income due to external shocks can be mitigated by having a larger government sector. And if the government acts as the agent of households that dislike risk, it will choose to consume a greater share of the society's resources in economies that are subject to greater amounts of external risk. I shall illustrate this argument with a simple model below.

In principle, external risk should be diversifiable for small countries through participation in international capital markets. In practice, this does not appear to be the case. Lewis (1995, p. 1914) summarizes the literature on international portfolio diversification thus: "recent evidence shows that domestic investors continue to hold almost all of their wealth in domestic assets." For the majority of the countries in the sample, the reason may be that full capital market openness conflicts with other objectives of government policy, or that incentive and sovereign risk problems restrict the range and extent of financial instruments available to them. For others, the apparent incompleteness of international portfolio diversification remains a puzzle – indeed a central puzzle in the theory of international finance (Lewis 1995). The empirical implications of perfect international consumption risk sharing – that consumption growth rates should be unaffected by country-specific shocks – are usually rejected by the data even for the advanced industrial countries with completely liberalized financial markets (Lewis 1995; Obstfeld 1995).

One might also object that the government's risk-reducing role would be best played through the establishment of a safety net, in which case it would show up mainly in government spending on social security and welfare, and not in government *consumption*. I shall show below that this prediction is borne out in the case of the more advanced countries, which do have the administrative capacity to manage social welfare systems. In these countries, government consumption is uncorrelated with exposure to external risk, whereas spending on social security and welfare is strongly correlated. But governments in the developing countries that predominate in the cross section appear to rely on a broader set of instrumentalities – including, notably, public employment – to achieve risk reduction.

Even if one accepts that full diversification through participation in international capital markets is realistically not possible, the story outlined above makes two leaps of faith. One is that economies subject to greater amounts of *external* risk necessarily experience more risk in total income as well, the latter being what really matters to the representative household. The second is that the government sector is "safe" in the sense that an expansion in it would reduce aggregate income risk. Neither of these propositions is obvious, but I shall present evidence below that suggests that they are both empirically valid.

A. A Simple Model

Consider an economy that has a fixed supply x of an export good and produces two additional goods: a publicly provided good and a private good. The economy also has a labor endowment normalized to unity, with λ employed in the public sector and $1 - \lambda$ in the private sector. Let π denote the (stochastic) price of the export good in terms of the import good (i.e., the terms of trade). Assume that the export good is not consumed at home and that the import good is not produced domestically. Trade is balanced continuously, so the home economy purchases a quantity πx of imports.

Let us treat imports as intermediate goods and assume that they increase the productivity of private production domestically. The production function for the private good is taken to be linear in labor and can be written as $\pi x (1 - \lambda)$. Note that by making domestic productivity a function of the level of imports, we have captured one plausible channel through which trade risk spills over to the domestic economy. There is strong evidence of such spillovers in the data, as we shall see later (subsection D). (Expressing private production as a linearly homogeneous production function $f(\pi x, 1 - \lambda)$ would not alter any of the qualitative results below, but would add several terms to the algebra.) Finally, the supply of the publicly provided good is given by $h(\lambda)$, with $h' > 0$ and $h'' < 0$.

The government determines the size of the public sector (λ) before the specific realization of π is known. We can view this as the optimal determination of the size of the public sector in view of the underlying variability of the terms of trade. For simplicity, let the publicly provided good and the private good be perfect substitutes in consumption. The government's problem is

$$\max_{\lambda} V(\lambda) \equiv E[u(h(\lambda) + \pi (1 - \lambda))],$$

where $u(\cdot)$ stands for the utility function of the representative household, with $u'(\cdot) > 0$ and $u''(\cdot) < 0$. Let π be distributed with mean π_m and variance σ^2. Taking a second-order Taylor approximation to $u(h(\lambda) + \pi x(1 - \lambda))$ around π_m and taking expectations, we can express $V(\lambda)$ as

$$V(\lambda) \approx u(h(\lambda) + \pi_m x(1 - \lambda)) + \frac{1}{2} u''(h(\lambda)$$
$$+ \pi_m x(1 - \lambda))(1 - \lambda)^2 x^2 \sigma^2.$$

Expected utility is decreasing in the variance of the terms of trade. Define $R = x\sigma$ as our measure of exposure to external risk. The associated first-order condition is

$$\left[u'(\cdot) + \frac{1}{2} u''''(\cdot)(1 - \lambda)^2 R^2 \right] \left[h'(\lambda) - \pi_m x \right] - \frac{1}{2} u''(\cdot) R^2 = 0.$$

A sufficient condition for the first term in brackets to be positive is that the representative household exhibit "prudence" in consumption (i.e., that $u'''(\cdot) > 0$), which we assume. A direct implication is that as a result of exposure to external risk ($R > 0$), the optimal level of λ is *larger*.

Hence consider two economies A and B, with $R_A = 0$ and $R_B > 0$, but identical in all other respects. The first-order condition for the A economy simplifies to $h'(\lambda_A) = \pi_m x$. For the B economy, $h'(\lambda_B) < \pi_m x$. Since $h''(\cdot) < 0$, we have $\lambda_B > \lambda_A$.

Standard portfolio arguments suggest that an increase in the riskiness of exports calls for a reallocation of the economy's resources toward the safe activity (government), even when the return to government activities lies below the (mean) return to other activities.[3] I have shown this result in a model with a *fixed* supply of exports. In a model in which export supply is variable and exports compete for resources with the government sector, the risk-reducing effect of government consumption would be even more direct and immediate.

B. Empirical Tests of the Central Hypothesis

A test of the central hypothesis can be carried out by checking whether the relationship between openness and government consumption is stronger in economies that are exposed to greater amounts of external risk. For this we need empirical proxies for exposure to external risk. There are two such measures that I use here.

One is *terms-of-trade* risk, which is the measure used in the model above. In an economy with no market imperfections, a measure of the volatility of the streams of income associated with fluctuations in the external terms of trade not only would be the theoretically appropriate measure of external risk, but would be the *only* relevant measure of such risk. More formally, let x, m, and y stand for volumes of exports, imports, and GDP, respectively. Let π be the natural logarithm of the price of exports relative to imports (the terms of trade). Let the log of the terms of trade follow a random walk, possibly with drift (a hypothesis that cannot be rejected for most countries). The unanticipated component of the income effects of a terms-of-trade change can then be expressed (as a percentage of GDP) as $\frac{1}{2}[(x + m)/y]\,(d\pi - \alpha)$, where α is the trend growth rate in the terms of trade. The standard deviation of this is $\frac{1}{2}[(x + m)/y] \times$ st.dev. $(d\pi)$. Hence, interacting the measure of openness ($[x + m]/y$) with the standard deviation of the first (log) differences in the terms of trade gives us (twice) the appropriate measure of external risk.

The second measure I use is a quantity-based measure, and it is an index of the *product concentration of exports*. More specifically, it is a Gini-Hirschman index of concentration defined over 239 three-digit standard international trade classification categories of exports, as calculated by the United Nations Conference on Trade and Development. Countries that export only a few commodities are presumably more exposed to external risk than countries with a diversified set of exports, in a way that need not necessarily show in fluctuations in the terms of trade. So the second measure of external risk is generated by interacting openness with this concentration index. In practice, however, the two measures turn out to be very closely related (with a correlation coefficient close to .8).

---

3   The presence of a complete set of state-contingent markets at home would not affect this conclusion as long as the technology employed in government production was not available to the private sector. The reason is that external risk is not diversifiable domestically.

The basic strategy in the next set of regressions, then, is to interact with openness (*a*) the terms-of-trade variability and (*b*) the product concentration of exports to see whether the inclusion of these additional variables results in statistically significant coefficients and improves the fit of the regressions. Table 4.4 shows the results for the 1990–92 sample. Column 1 displays the benchmark regression for government consumption, to facilitate comparison with the new regressions in the rest of the table. (Note that OPENAVG8089 is not in logs in this version of the benchmark, to allow for the inclusion of the new variables both on their own and in interaction with openness.)

Column 2 of the table displays the results when the export concentration index (CI90) is added to the regression, both individually and interacted with openness. Note that the adjusted R^2 rises somewhat, and as predicted by the risk-mitigating hypothesis, the coefficient on the interaction term is positive and statistically significant at the 95 percent confidence level. Equally important, the coefficient on openness (entered alone) has now become completely insignificant. Hence we have rather clear confirmation that the effect of openness on government consumption is strongest in countries with more concentrated exports.

The results with terms-of-trade risk (TOTDLOGSTD) are even more striking (col. 3). When this variable is included, the improvement in the fit of the regression is sizable (with the adjusted R^2 rising from .395 to .445). The interaction term is significant at the 99 percent level, and the estimated coefficient on openness now turns negative. These results are particularly encouraging in light of the fact that, as discussed above, this particular interaction term is the theoretically appropriate measure of external risk for an open economy. In fact when the terms-of-trade and export concentration measures of risk are included simultaneously in the regression (col. 4), it is terms-of-trade risk that does all the work, despite the high correlation between the two. Results using the 1985–89 sample (not shown) are, if anything, stronger: both measures of external risk are statistically significant at the 99 percent level, and once again there is a strong indication that it is terms-of-trade risk that is the operative channel.

Columns 5 and 6 of Table 4.4 check for the possibility that the measures of external risk may be proxying for low income or for greater revenue extraction when exports are made up of predominantly primary resources. Terms-of-trade instability and export concentration are negatively correlated with per capita income and positively correlated with the primary commodity share of exports. The interaction terms could be capturing a nonlinearity in income or rent extraction by the government from primary exports (through marketing boards, government ownership, and other controls on exports). However, when per capita income is interacted with openness and included in the regressions, the results reported above do not change (col. 5). Neither is there a change when the primary share of exports (interacted with openness) is included (col. 6). The coefficients on the external risk variables are robust to the addition of these new terms. Moreover, the findings are

Table 4.4 The Importance of External Risk

Independent Variable	Dependent Variable: Log of Real Government Consumption as a Percentage of GDP (Log CGAVG9092)					
	(1)	(2)	(3)	(4)	(5)	(6)
OPENAVG8089	.003**	.000	−.003	−.004	−.005	−.004
	(.001)	(.002)	(.002)	(.003)	(.003)	(.003)
C190		−.661		.429		
		(.366)		(.594)		
OPENAVG8089 × C190		**.011****		**−.004**		
		(.005)		**(.008)**		
TOTDLOGSTD			−3.053*	−4.155**	−3.284*	−2.640**
			(1.087)	(1.833)	(1.122)	(1.118)
OPENAVG8089 × TOTDLOGSTD			**.053***	**.064****	**.058***	**.043****
			(.017)	(.027)	(.018)	(.020)
OPENAVG8089 × GDPSH589					2.27E-07	
					(2.68E-07)	
OPENAVG8089 × PRIMSHR90						.003
						(.003)
Observations	103	94	97	92	97	96
Adjusted R^2	.397	.417	.438	.436	.437	.446

Note: Same as Table 4.2.

unaffected by the inclusion in the regression of *all* the other variables considered previously in Table 4.3 (results not shown).[4]

Table 4.5 replicates the results in a panel setting: it shows that past exposure to external risk is a statistically significant determinant. of government consumption, *even after a full set of period and country fixed effects is introduced.* For the purposes of this estimation, I have divided the period from 1960 to 1992 into seven subperiods and calculated averages of government consumption, openness, and terms-of-trade risk for each of these subperiods. The panel regressions are run using both fixed and random effects, as well as first differences. The coefficient on lagged external risk is positive and statistically significant in all specifications but one (where it is borderline insignificant). The results indicate that the association between exposure to external risk and government size is not a purely cross-sectional one; it exists also in the time series for individual countries.

One way to summarize what has been learned from these exercises is to use the estimated coefficients to ask how much openness matters to government consumption in countries at different points along the distribution of terms-of-trade instability. Consider a country with the mean level of government consumption in the sample (which is around 20 percent). Estimates in column 3 of Table 4.4 suggest that an increase in the share of total trade (exports plus imports) in GDP of 10 percentage points would increase government consumption by 0.8 percentage points of GDP if that country is located at the mean of the cross-country distribution of terms-of-trade instability. The same increase in openness would lead to an increase in government consumption of 1.7 percentage points of GDP if that country experiences terms-of-trade instability one standard deviation above the mean. For a country with terms-of-trade instability one standard deviation *below* the mean, the impact on government consumption would be virtually nil.

Hence, we can conclude that openness matters to the scope of government because of the role played by external risk. Governments consume a larger share of domestic output in economies subject to greater amounts of external risk. Once external risk is controlled for, openness does not seem to exert an independent effect on government consumption. Put differently, openness appears to work purely through its consequence of exposing the economy to greater amounts of external risk.

C. The Role of Social Security and Welfare Spending

If government spending played a risk-mitigating role, we would expect to see this primarily reflected in income transfer programs and in social security and welfare spending. In most developing countries, income transfer schemes tend to be rudimentary for reasons of administrative capacity. Consequently, their governments tend to rely on public employment, in-kind transfers, and public-works programs – all of which show up in government consumption – in order to broaden safety

---

4   The results on the importance of exposure to external risk in determining government consumption levels have also been confirmed in a subsequent paper by Commander, Davoodi, and Lee (1996), which uses a somewhat different data set and econometric specification.

Table 4.5   Panel Estimation

	Dependent Variable				
	Log of Real Government Consumption (Percentage of GDP)				Δ Real Government Consumption (Percentage of GDP)
	Fixed Effects	Random Effects	Fixed Effects	Random Effects	
GDP per capita	6.17E-06	−1.48E-05*	−2.83E-05*	−3.60E-05*	−8.90E-05***
	(7.60E-06)	(5.56E-06)	(7.83E-06)	(5.50E-06)	(4.63E-05)
Openness$_{-1}$	.0018**	.0011***	−.0012	−.0007	
	(.0008)	(.0006)	(.0008)	(.0006)	
Terms-of-trade variability$_{-1}$	.2321	.1539	−.2481	−.2985	
	(.2423)	(.2266)	(.2252)	(.2193)	
Openness$_{-1}$ × terms-of-trade variability$_{-1}$	**.0061**	**.0087****	**.0081****	**.0097***	
	(.0038)	**(.0036)**	**(.0034)**	**(.0033)**	
Δ openness					−.0172
					(.0161)
Δ terms-of-trade variability					−5.1396***
					(3.0161)
Δ (openness × terms-of-trade variability)					**.0997****
					(.0482)
Period dummies	no	no	yes	yes	yes
F	11.76		20.34		50.11
Prob > F	.00		.00		.00
χ²		56.30		217.20	
Prob > χ²		.00		.00	.00
Observations	662	662	662	662	472

Note: Data are period averages for 1960–64, 1965–69, 1970–74, 1975–79, 1980–84, 1985–89, and 1990–92 (except for GDP per capita, which pertains to the beginning of each period).

nets. But in advanced countries with social welfare programs in place, it should be primarily spending on social security and welfare that is correlated with exposure to external risk, not government consumption. That is indeed what we find.

Table 4.6 displays a set of regressions for three separate groups of countries: (i) members of the OECD, (ii) countries with 1985 GDP per capita greater than $4,500, and (iii) all countries. For each set of countries, I have run two regressions, one with social security and welfare spending as the dependent variable and the other with government consumption. To make the estimated coefficients comparable across the two specifications, I restrict the sample to countries for which I have data for both types of government spending. (This explains the sample size of 68 in the regressions for "all countries".)

The results are interesting. For each of the three groups of countries, the estimated coefficient on external risk is considerably larger in the social security and welfare regression than in the government consumption regression. This indicates that spending on social security and welfare is significantly more sensitive to exposure to external risk than government consumption, which is consistent with our theory.[5] Note, however, that this coefficient becomes smaller as one moves from the high-income to the broader sample of countries, and the precision with which it is estimated becomes lower. This is also plausible since it reflects both the greater difficulty of administering income transfer programs in low-income countries and the greater measurement error. Note finally that exposure to external risk does not have a statistically significant impact on government consumption *in the OECD or high-income samples.* In these samples, it is spending on social security and welfare that correlates with external risk, and not government consumption. Once again, this bears out the theory.

D. Does Exposure to External Risk Increase Aggregate Risk?

Let us now return to one of the doubts raised above about the relevance of the hypothesis advanced here. The idea that greater exposure to external risk increases the *total* risk to which residents of a country are exposed should raise some eyebrows. It is certainly the case that the world economy as a whole is *less* volatile than the economy of any single country. We can expect the world market to be less risky than any of its constituent parts, thanks to the law of large numbers. Hence it is entirely possible that greater exposure to external risk is accompanied by reduced exposure to domestic sources of risk and that the balance works out in favor of lower risk in aggregate. What goes against this is that openness to trade generally implies *specialization* in production through the forces of comparative advantage. All else equal, one would expect the production structure to be less diversified in more open economies. In an economy that cannot purchase insurance from the rest of the world, what matters is not the stability of the world economy as a whole, but the stability of the stream of earnings from *domestic* production. Consequently, whether greater

---

5 Removing the OECD countries from the "all countries" sample does not affect the estimated coefficient on external risk (or its level of statistical significance) in col. 5 of Table 4.6.

Table 4.6   Effect of External Risk on Social Security and Welfare Expenditures, by Income Groups

| | Dependent Variable: Log of Government Expenditure (by Type) as a Percentage of GDP | | | | | |
| | OECD Countries ($N = 19$) | | Countries with 1985 per Capita GDP > \$4,500 ($N = 25$) | | All Countries ($N = 68$) | |
Independent Variable	Social Security and Welfare (1)	Government Consumption (2)	Social Security and Welfare (3)	Government Consumption (4)	Social Security and Welfare (5)	Government Consumption (6)
OPENAVG7584	−.170*	−.005	−.043***	.006	−.018	−.002
	(.043)	(.010)	(.021)	(.005)	(.013)	(.003)
TOTDLOGSTD	−134.088*	−9.371***	−35.010**	1.057	−16.484*	−2.953**
	(22.147)	(5.198)	(12.418)	(2.732)	(5.665)	(1.391)
OPENAVG7584 × TOTDLOGSTD	1.869*	.069	.438**	−.039	.183***	.048**
	(.431)	(.101)	(.210)	(.046)	(.096)	(.023)
Adjusted R^2	.75	.35	.23	.05	.48	.50

Note: See App. table A1 for variable definitions. Regressions in cols. 5 and 6 include other regressors in the benchmark specification, whose coefficients are not shown.

exposure to external risk is accompanied by higher or lower amounts of risk in total is an empirical matter.

Table 4.7 provides the relevant evidence. I regressed income volatility on the measure of external risk to see whether countries with greater exposure to external risk also tend to experience greater volatility in income. I used three measures of income: (*a*) real GDP adjusted for changes in the terms of trade, which gets closest to a measure of real national income; (*b*) real GDP; and (*c*) real GDP net of government consumption (which I call "private" GDP). The measure of volatility is the standard deviation of the first (log) differences of these series over the 1960–90 period. External risk is captured, as before, by multiplying openness with the standard deviation of the first (log) differences of the terms of trade.

The results indicate that external risk is positively (and significantly) associated with income volatility for all three measures of income. The estimated coefficients indicate (after suitable transformation) that a 10 percent increase in external risk is accompanied by a 1.0–1.6 percent increase in income risk. This finding is least

Table 4.7   Impact of External Risk on Volatility of Income and Consumption ($N = 104$)

Independent Variable	Real GDP Adusted for the Terms of Trade (1)	Real GDP (2)	Real "Private" GDP (3)	Real Consumption (4)
	Dependent Variable: Standard Deviation of Growth Rates of:			
Constant	.026*	.026*	.025*	.027*
	(.003)	(.003)	(.003)	(.004)
GDPSH575	–4.22E-07	–3.40E-07	–1.42E-07	–7.53E-07
	(3.97E-07)	(3.64E-07)	(3.91E-07)	(7.37E-07)
SOC	.001	.001	.004	.006
	(.006)	(.005)	(.006)	(.005)
OECD	–.012*	–.012*	–.013*	–.013***
	(.004)	(.004)	(.004)	(.007)
LAAM	–.006	–.005	–.005	–.005
	(.004)	(.003)	(.004)	(.004)
ASIAE	–.012*	–.011*	–.011*	–.016*
	(.003)	(.003)	(.003)	(.006)
SAFRICA	.001	.002	.004	.006
	(.004)	(.004)	(.004)	(.004)
OPENAVG6092	**.0007***	**.0004****	**.0006***	**.0012***
× TOTDLOGSTD	**(.0002)**	**(.0002)**	**(.0002)**	**(.0003)**
Adjusted R^2	.39	.36	.36	.48

surprising for the terms-of-trade adjusted GDP; after all, fluctuations in the terms of trade enter this measure of income directly. But GDP and private GDP are not influenced by the terms of trade directly, so these results have real economic content. In particular, they provide justification for a key feature of the model used above, namely that external risk spills over to domestic production (see Gavin and Hausmann (1996) for similar results). It is also interesting to note that private GDP appears to be more responsive to external risk than aggregate GDP, if one judges by both the estimated coefficients and their significance levels.

Column 4 of Table 4.7 shows that external risk is a significant determinant of the volatility of private *consumption* as well. In fact, the estimated coefficient on external risk is largest by far in the regression for consumption volatility, as is the R^2. This can be read as strong evidence against the presence of consumption smoothing through participation in international capital markets.[6]

E. Can a Higher Level of Government Consumption Stabilize Income?

Let us next turn to another question raised about the central hypothesis: Can a higher level of government consumption really help stabilize income?[7] A critical feature of the model discussed previously is that the technologies for private and public production are different. I assumed in particular that the government sector is the safe sector, in which production and incomes are nonstochastic.[8] In practice, however, government consumption is unstable as well, and it will generally covary with all sources of risk including the terms of trade. Whether public production exhibits stochastic properties different from those of private production is ultimately a question that can be settled only empirically.

A paper by Galí (1994) has documented a robust negative correlation between government size and GDP volatility in the OECD countries. This result is informative for the purposes of this paper but falls short in one respect: Under the maintained hypothesis that government consumption tends to be systematically higher in economies subjected to greater shocks, a cross-country regression that regresses income volatility on the share of government consumption in GDP (as in Galís paper) is misspecified. In particular, the coefficient on government consumption in such a regression would be biased downward. So I take a different approach here, one that is more consistent with the framework of this chapter and relies on

---

6　Note also that the results reported in Table 4.7 are unchanged when exposure to external risk is instrumented in the fashion described in subsection *F* below.

7　Note that the relevant question is not whether countercyclical fiscal policy can stabilize income in Keynesian fashion. It is whether a *permanently* higher level of government consumption can do so.

8　This difference can derive in practice from the distinct nature of the goods that are typically considered to be public goods: public administration, law and order, and national defense. It can also result from the divergent incentive and governance structures that characterize production in the two. For example, there is a large literature on government employment practices that suggests that earnings and employment levels in the public sector tend to be either relatively immune to business cycle conditions or purposefully countercyclical (see Kraay and van Rijckeghem 1995; Agenor 1996; Lindauer and Nunberg 1996).

the variance-covariance structure of the components of GDP for each individual country.

I begin with some notation. Let $Y_p = C + I + (X - M)$ stand for private GDP, $\Pi = p/p^*$ for the external terms of trade, α for openness (the share of imports in absorption or, equivalently with balanced trade, the share of exports in GDP), GDP for $Y_p + G$, and λ for G/GDP (the share of government consumption in GDP). In the absence of net factor payments from abroad, real income can be expressed as

$$Y = \Pi^\alpha (Y_p + G)$$

and in natural logarithms (with lowercase letters denoting natural logs) as

$$y = \alpha\pi + (1 - \lambda) y_p + \lambda g.$$

The growth rate of real income is in turn

$$dy = \alpha d\pi + (1 - \lambda) dy_p + \lambda dg.$$

Let σ_y^2 stand for the variance of the growth rate of real income, which is the measure of income volatility and risk. This can be expressed as

$$\sigma_y^2 = \alpha^2 \sigma_\pi^2 + (1-\lambda)^2 \sigma_{y_p}^2 + \lambda^2 \sigma_g^2 + 2\alpha(1-\lambda)\mathrm{cov}(d\pi, dy_p)$$

$$+ 2\alpha\lambda \, \mathrm{cov}(d\pi, dg) + 2(1-\lambda)\lambda \, \mathrm{cov}(dy_p, dg),$$

where $\sigma_{y_p}^2$, σ_g^2, and σ_g^2. are the variances of the growth rates of private income, government consumption, and the terms of trade, respectively, and the other terms have the obvious interpretations. Now one could ask how income volatility would respond to a small increase in the share of government consumption, with the variance-covariance structure held constant. If the previous expression is differentiated with respect to λ,

$$\frac{1}{2}\frac{d\sigma_y^2}{d\lambda} = \left[\lambda\sigma_g^2 - (1-\lambda)\sigma_{y_p}^2\right] + \alpha\left[\mathrm{cov}(d\pi, dg) - \mathrm{cov}(d\pi, dy_p)\right]$$

$$+ (1 - 2\lambda) \, \mathrm{cov}(dg, dy_p). \tag{1}$$

This result states that the consequence depends on the pattern of variances and covariances of the different income streams, as well as on the prevailing α and λ. When government consumption is nonstochastic, equation (1) reduces to

$$\frac{1}{2}\frac{d\sigma_y^2}{d\lambda} = -(1-\lambda)\sigma_{y_p}^2 - \alpha \, \mathrm{cov}(d\pi, dy_p),$$

which is unambiguously negative provided that cov $(d\pi, dy_p)$ is positive, as strongly suggested by the results in Table 4.6. Even when government consumption is stochastic, an increase in λ will reduce income volatility provided that λ, σ_g^2 and cov $(d\pi, dy_p)$ are sufficiently small.

One can actually use the observed pattern of variances and covariances in the sample to calculate for each country the magnitude and sign of the expression in (1). In other words, one can rely on the historical pattern of shocks experienced by each country to form an idea about how a small increase in the share of government consumption in GDP is likely to affect the volatility of real income in that country. For this purpose, I have calculated the relevant variances and covariances over the 1971–90 period (the period for which terms-of-trade data are available in the World Bank's *World Data 1995*) for each country with the requisite data. Plugging this data into equation (1) gives a distribution of $d\sigma_y^2 / d\lambda$ for a total of 147 countries. The result is quite striking: *a small (permanent) increase in government consumption (as a share of GDP) would result in more stable incomes in the overwhelming majority of countries: 119 out of 147.* All advanced industrial countries, without exception, have $d\sigma_y^2 / d\lambda < 0$.

A couple of caveats may be in order. First, the calculation is obviously valid only for small changes in λ. Second, this approach assumes that the pattern of variances and covariances would remain unaffected following an increase in government consumption. This may be defensible for a small enough increase in λ. Third, there is an endogeneity problem here as well, in that governments that choose the level of λ to minimize income risk would set $d\sigma_y^2 / d\lambda = 0$, confounding the effect we are looking for. However, this last problem is not severe since governments have many other objectives besides minimizing risk.

Consider, for example, a formulation of the government's planning problem that is more general (but is also more heuristic) than the one laid out above. Suppose that the government cares about both risk and economic activity, γ. Let us write its objective function as $v(\gamma, \sigma_y^2)$, with $\partial v / \partial \gamma > 0$ and $\partial v / \partial \sigma_y^2 < 0$. The first-order condition for maximizing $v(\times)$ is

$$\left(\frac{\partial v}{\partial \gamma}\right)\left(\frac{d\gamma}{d\lambda}\right) + \left(\frac{\partial v}{\partial \sigma_y^2}\right)\left(\frac{d\sigma_y^2}{d\lambda}\right) = 0.$$

Assume that increasing government size is costly to real activity either because it has to be financed by distortionary (and growth-impeding) taxes or because government production is less efficient; that is, $d\gamma/d\lambda < 0$. Then an interior solution will be found at a level of λ such that $d\sigma_y^2 / d\lambda < 0$. Intuitively, governments will never push the risk-minimizing motive to its maximum limit as long as increasing government size has some cost (see Cashin (1995) and Slemrod (1995) for reviews of the evidence on these costs). Hence in practice we can expect to observe levels of government consumption that fall well short of the point at which no further reductions in income volatility could be achieved.

F. Causality Issues

Countries differ in their exposure to trade for a number of reasons. One set of reasons has to do with geography: countries that are large and distant from their trade partners will naturally tend to be more self-sufficient and have lower ratios of trade to GDP. But, in addition, exposure to trade is also a function of government policy: countries with high tariff and nontariff barriers to trade will have lower exposure to trade, with all else held constant. The measure of openness, which is the ratio of trade to GDP, conflates these two sets of determinants. One potential problem this raises is that of endogeneity. Could causality be running from government size to external risk exposure rather than the other way around? (While I have used lagged measures of openness in the regressions, this obviously does not fully get around the endogeneity problem.)

I try three related approaches to demonstrating causality, all of which rely on extracting the exogenous component of trade shares. I first create a measure of "natural" openness for each country (NATLOPEN) by regressing the log of OPENAVG7584 on the logs of distance from major trade partners (DIST) and population (POP85), plus a set of country-grouping dummies (SOC, OECD, LAAM, ASIAE, and SAFRICA). This regression has an R^2 of .71 and yields the expected signs on the coefficients (negative and significant on both DIST and POP85). The predicted values from this regression tell how open a country is expected to be on the basis of geographic and other exogenous determinants alone. I call this predicted value NATLOPEN. Using NATLOPEN in lieu of OPENAVGxxyy is one way of eliminating potential simultaneous-equation bias. Column 1 of Table 4.8 displays the results. Because of the availability of DIST for a smaller number of countries, the sample size is now reduced to 82. Nonetheless, the fit of the regression is not much affected. More important, the coefficient on the interaction term (NATLOPEN × TOTDLOGSTD) is positive and statistically significant (at the 95 percent level) as before.

Second, I use a measure developed by Frankel and Romer (1996) that is available for a larger set of countries. This is an instrument for trade shares based on geographical determinants similar to those employed here. The major difference is that their instrument is constructed using *bilateral* trade data and a gravity-like estimating framework. Column 2 of Table 4.8 shows the results using the Frankel-Romer instrument for openness. The coefficient on external risk remains statistically significant (but at the 90 percent level).

Finally, an explicit instrumental variables approach using population and distance as instruments (in addition to the other exogenous variables in the benchmark specification) yields the results in column 3. The estimated coefficient on external risk is now larger and significant at the 99 percent level. Note that the set of instruments (distance and population) is as close to being exogenous as one can hope for in cross-country regressions. The validity of this instrument set is easily confirmed using standard tests for overidentifying restrictions.

Hence, the results using the *exogenous component* of openness are quite similar to those obtained earlier. They confirm the theory about the importance of external risk in determining the size of government consumption.

V. Concluding Comments

The correlation between openness and government size has a number of implications. For one thing, it makes it more difficult to disentangle the relationship between

Table 4.8   Exogenous Measures of Exposure to External Risk (Dependent Variable: Log CGAVG8589)

	Estimation Method		
Independent Variable	OLS NATLOPEN Used for Openness (1)	OLS Frankel-Romer Measure Used for Openness (2)	Instrumental Variables (3)
Openness	−.005	−.001	−.006**
	(.004)	(.004)	(.003)
TOTDLOGSTD	−2.899**	−.886	−4.360**
	(1.373)	(.722)	(1.102)
Openness ×	.058**	.043***	.076*
TOTDLOGSTD	(.027)	(.025)	(.018)
Observations	82	116	82
Adjusted R^2	.46	.42	.60

Note: Coefficients on other included regressors are not shown. Col. 3 uses log population (POP85), log distance (DIST), and the exogenous variables in the benchmark specification (alone and interacted with TOTDLOGSTD) as instruments for openness and openness × TOTDLOGSTD.

government size and openness, on the one hand, and economic growth, on the other. If one assumes, for example, that openness exerts an independent effect on growth, the typical regression in which growth is regressed on government size would yield a biased coefficient. A similar bias would exist in a regression of growth on trade, if government size has an independent effect on growth.

But there are broader implications as well, with regard to the relationship between markets and governments. These two are often viewed as substitutes. Most types of government intervention, except those related to the provision of public goods, law and order, and property rights, are viewed as inimical to the operation of markets. The international integration of markets is often perceived as undercutting the effectiveness of governmental action at the national level. The findings presented in this paper provide a different perspective, suggesting that there may be a degree of complementarity between markets and governments. The scope of government has been larger, not smaller, in economies taking greater advantage of world markets. Indeed, governments have expanded fastest in the most open economies.

The evidence considered here suggests that the reasons have to do with the provision of social insurance. Openness exerts the strongest influence on government consumption in economies that are subject to the greatest amounts of external risk. Governments appear to have sought to mitigate the exposure to risk by increasing the share of domestic output they consume.

This chapter has focused on the cross-country statistical evidence. But there also exist a number of country studies, mostly undertaken by political scientists, that discuss how governments in different parts of the world have responded to the insecurities generated by trade by expanding government programs. Katzenstein (1984, 1985), for example, has documented in detail how the small European states such as Sweden, Austria, and the Netherlands "complement[ed] their pursuit of liberalism in the international economy with a strategy of domestic compensation" (1985, p. 47), entailing, among other policies, investment programs, incomes policies, industrial subsidies, and income transfers. The experience of Spain prior to its accession to the European Union in 1986 is also instructive: public expenditure on transfers, social programs, and compensatory programs aimed at regional inequalities expanded greatly prior to the mid-1980s, partially in anticipation of the eventual impact of membership in the European Union (see Maravall (1993) for an account). In Chile, which had become increasingly open to trade under the Pinochet regime, the first priority of the incoming democratically elected government in 1990 was "the restoration of benefits for low- and middle-income groups ... and the development of new social programs targeted at high-risk groups" (Marcel and Solimano 1994, p. 228).

There are few natural experiments in the social sciences, but the experiences of Spain and Chile perhaps come close. The expansion of social welfare spending in both cases – one of them following the death of a dictator and in anticipation of accession to the European Union, the other in the immediate aftermath of transition to democracy following a period of extensive opening up to trade – is illustrative of the hypothesis discussed in this paper. Another case in point, smaller in scope, is the use of trade adjustment assistance programs in the United States. These programs cover extended unemployment benefits and training and relocation subsidies for workers displaced by imports. They have been used (originally in the context of multilateral liberalization in the General Agreement on Tariffs and Trade and more recently in the North American Free Trade Agreement) as an explicit quid pro quo for labor's acquiescence in trade liberalization.

International trade has expanded significantly during the post-war period. Despite some reversals since the 1980s, so has the scope of government activity in most countries of the world. The findings presented in this chapter suggest that this was perhaps no coincidence.[9] For the future, they also suggest that scaling governments down without paying attention to the economic insecurities generated by globalization may actually harm the prospects of maintaining free trade.

---

9   See Ruggie (1982) for a very useful discussion on this point. Ruggie argues that the international economic liberalism of the postwar period, far from shunting aside the role of government policy, gave it a central role. He calls this "the compromise of embedded liberalism": "The task of postwar institutional reconstruction ... was to ... devise a framework which would safeguard and even aid the quest for domestic stability without, at the same time, triggering the mutually destructive external consequences that had plagued the interwar period. This was the essence of the embedded liberalism compromise: unlike the economic nationalism of the thirties, it would be multilateral in character; unlike the liberalism of the gold standard and free trade, *its multilateralism would be predicated upon domestic interventionism*" (p. 893; emphasis added). According to Ruggie, the objective of stabilizing domestic employment and output was never meant to be sacrificed at the altar of free trade. Such arguments are reminiscent of Polanyi's (1944) classic book, which argued that unfettered free trade is fundamentally incompatible with social order and stability.

Appendix

Table A1   List of Variables and Sources

Variable	Definition	Source
AREA	Land area	Barro and Lee (1994)
ASIAE	Dummy for East Asian countries	Barro and Lee (1994)
CIxx	Export concentration index	UNCTAD
GIAVGxxyy	Government capital expenditures	WD
CGAVGxxyy	Real government consumption as a percentage of GDP	PWT 5.6
DEPENDxx	Dependency ratio	WD
DETGNP85	Debt/GNP ratio, 1985	WD
DGOV6092	CGAVG9092/CGAVG6064	PWT 5.6
DIST	Geographical distance from 20 major world exporters	Barro and Lee (1994)
DOPEN6092	OPENAVG9092/OPENAVG6064	PWT 5.6
GDPSH5xx	Real per capita GDP	Barro and Lee (1994)
GSVAT8688	Indirect tax revenues on goods and services and VAT	FAD
INTL8688	Taxes on international trade	FAD
LAAM	Dummy for Latin American countries	Barro and Lee (1994)
NATLOPEN	"Natural" openness: exogenous component of OPENAVG7584	Computed from Barro and Lee (1994) and WD
OECD	Dummy for OECD countries	
OIL	Dummy for oil exporters	
OPENAVGxxyy	Exports plus imports divided by GDP	PWT 5.6
POPxx	Population	WD
PRIMSHRxx	Share of primary exports in total exports	WD
SAFRICA	Dummy for sub-Saharan African countries	Barro and Lee (1994)
SOC	Dummy for socialist countries	Sach and Warner (1995)
TOTAL8688	Total tax revenue as a share of GDP, 1986–88 average	FAD
TOTDLOGSTD	Standard deviation of log differences in terms of trade, 1971–90	WD
URBANxx	Urbanization rate	WD

Note: xx refers to year 19xx, and xxyy refers to an average during 19xx–19yy (unless specified otherwise). All government expenditure and revenue data are expressed as a percentage of GDP or GNP. PWT 5.6 stands for Penn world tables 5.6; WD for *World Data 1995* (World Bank); FAD for the Fiscal Affairs Department of the International Monetary Fund; UNCTAD for *Handbook of International Trade and Development Statistics of UNCTAD*, various issues.

References

Agenor, Pierre-Richard. "The Labor Market and Economic Adjustment." *IMF Staff Papers 43* (June 1996): 261–335.

Alesina, Alberto, and Wacziarg, Romain. "Openness, Country Size, and the Government." Working Paper no. 6024. Cambridge, Mass.: NBER, May 1997.

Barro, Robert J., and Lee, Jong-Wha. "Data Set for a Panel of 138 Countries." Manuscript. Cambridge, Mass.: Harvard Univ., January 1994.

Bates, Robert H.; Brock, Philip L.; and Tiefenthaler, Jill. "Risk and Trade Regimes: Another Exploration." *Internat. Organization* 45 (Winter 1991): 1–18.

Cameron, David R. "The Expansion of the Public Economy: A Comparative Analysis." *American Polit. Sci. Rev.* 72 (December 1978): 1243–61.

Cashin, Paul. "Government Spending, Taxes, and Economic Growth." *IMF Staff Papers* 42 (June 1995): 237–69.

Commander, Simon; Davoodi, Hamid; and Lee, Una J. "The Causes and Consequences of Government for Growth and Well-Being." Manuscript. Washington: World Bank, December 1996.

Frankel, Jeffrey A., and Romer, David. "Trade and Growth: An Empirical Investigation." Working Paper no. 5476. Cambridge, Mass.: NBER, March 1996.

Galí, Jordi. "Government Size and Macroeconomic Stability." *European Econ. Rev.* 38 (January 1994): 117–32.

Gavin, Michael, and Hausmann, Ricardo. "Sources of Macroeconomic Volatility in Developing Economies." Manuscript. Washington: Inter-American Development Bank, February 1996.

Heller, Peter S., and Diamond, Jack. *International Comparisons of Government Expenditure Revisited: The Developing Countries, 1975–86.* Occasional Paper no. 69. Washington: Internat. Monetary Fund, April 1990.

Katzenstein, Peter J. *Corporatism and Change: Austria, Switzerland, and the Politics of Industry.* Ithaca, N.Y.: Cornell Univ. Press, 1984.

——. *Small States in World Markets: Industrial Policy in Europe.* Ithaca, N.Y: Cornell Univ. Press, 1985.

Kraay, Aart, and van Rijckeghem, Caroline. "Employment and Wages in the Public Sector – a Cross-Country Study." Working paper. Washington: Internat. Monetary Fund, July 1995.

Lewis, Karen K. "Puzzles in International Financial Markets." In *Handbook of International Economics*, vol. 3, edited by Gene Grossman and Kenneth Rogoff. Amsterdam: North-Holland, 1995.

Lindauer, David, and Nunberg, Barbara. *Rehabilitating Government: Pay and Employment Reform in Africa.* Avebury, U.K.: Aldershot, 1996.

Maravall, José Maria. "Politics and Policy: Economic Reforms in Southern Europe." In *Economic Reforms in New Democracies: A Social-Democratic Approach*, edited by Luiz Carlos Bresser Pereira, José Maria Maravall, and Adam Przeworski. New York: Cambridge Univ. Press, 1993.

Marcel, Mario, and Solimano, Andres. "The Distribution of Income and Economic Adjustment." In *The Chilean Economy: Policy Lessons and Challenges*, edited by Barry Bosworth, Rudiger Dornbusch, and Raul Laban. Washington: Brookings Inst., 1994.

Obstfeld, Maurice. "International Capital Mobility in the 1990s." In *Understanding Interdependence. The Macroeconomics of the Open Economy*, edited by Peter B. Kenen. Princeton, N .J.: Princeton Univ. Press, 1995.

Polanyi, Karl. *The Great Transformation*. Boston: Beacon, 1944.

Ram, Rati. "Wagner's Hypothesis in Time-Series and Cross-Section Perspectives: Evidence from 'Real' Data for 115 Countries." *Rev. Econ. and Statis.* 69 (May 1987): 194–204.

Rodrik, Dani. "International Trade and Big Government." In *International Trade and Finance: New Frontiers for Research: Essays in Honor of Peter B. Kenen*, edited by Benjamin J. Cohen. New York: Cambridge Univ. Press, 1997. (*a*)

———. "What Drives Public Employment?" Working Paper no. 6141. Cambridge, Mass.: NBER, August 1997. (*b*)

Ruggie, John Gerard. "International Regimes, Transactions, and Change: Embedded Liberalism in the Postwar Economic Order." *Internat. Organization* 36 (Spring 1982): 379–415.

Sach, Jeffrey, and Warner, Andrew M. "Economic Reform and the Process of Global Integration." *Brookings Papers Econ. Activity*, no. 1 (1995), pp. 1–95.

Saunders, Peter, and Klau, Friedrich. "The Role of the Public Sector: Causes and Consequences of the Growth of Government." *OECD Econ. Studies*, no. 4 (Spring 1985), pp. 5–239.

Schmidt, Manfred G. "The Growth of the Tax State: The Industrial Democracies, 1950–1978." In *Why Governments Grow: Measuring Public Sector Size*, edited by Charles Lewis Taylor. Beverly Hills, Calif.: Sage, 1983.

Slemrod, Joel. "What Do Cross-Country Studies Teach about Government Involvement, Prosperity and Economic Growth?" *Brookings Papers Econ. Activity*, no. 2 (1995), pp. 373–415.

Tait, Alan A., and Heller, Peter S. *International Comparisons of Government Expenditure*. Occasional Paper no. 10. Washington: Internat. Monetary Fund, April 1982.

Tanzi, Vito. "Structural Factors and Tax Revenue in Developing Countries: A Decade of Evidence." In *Open Economies: Structural Adjustment and Agriculture*, edited by Ian Goldin and L. Alan Winters. Cambridge: Cambridge Univ. Press, 1992.

United Nations. *System of National Accounts, 1993*. New York: United Nations, 1993.

Chapter 5

Government Spending and Public Support for Trade in the OECD: An Empirical Test of the Embedded Liberalism Thesis

Jude C. Hays, Sean D. Ehrlich, and Clint Peinhardt

According to Ruggie, the international community learned two important lessons from the collapse of the gold standard and interwar global economy. First, the international economy would break down if states pursued unilateral, beggar-thy-neighbor trade policies. As a result, postwar governments around the Organization for Economic Cooperation and Development (OECD), by and large, have committed themselves to pursuing free trade through multilateralism. Second, governments could not ignore the internal costs of adjusting to external economic shocks. Because trade causes economic dislocations and exposes workers to greater risk, it generates political opposition that democratically elected leaders ignore at their peril. Thus, one important implication of the commitment to free trade is that political leaders have had to be aware of and actively manage public support for economic openness. To do this, governments have exchanged welfare state policies that cushion their citizens from the vagaries of the international economy in return for public support for openness.

Ruggie has termed this exchange the bargain of embedded liberalism.[1] According to this story of postwar reconstruction, a link between trade and welfare state spending was established soon after World War II ended. Of course, the specific form this bargain takes is both geographically and historically contingent. The Keynesianism that emerged in the United States, for example, differed from the social democratic corporatism that developed in Sweden and Austria, and the demand management policies of the Bretton Woods era have given way to the active (supply-side) labor market policies of the so-called Third Way. But the idea

Earlier versions of this chapter were presented at the Midwest Political Science Association's 2002 Meeting and at the University of Illinois during summer 2003. We thank the respective panel and seminar participants for their feedback. In addition, we want to acknowledge valuable comments from William Bernhard, Rebecca Blank, Kerwin Charles, Alan Deardorff, John DiNardo, John Freeman, Brian Gaines. Jim Granato, Nathan Jensen, William Keech, Layna Mosley, Robert Pahre, Ken Scheve, Marina Whitman, two anonymous reviewers, and Lisa Martin. They, of course, are not responsible for any errors.

1 Ruggie 1982, 1994, 1997, and 2003.

that there is a more or less universal expectation held by citizens in the developed democracies that their governments will limit the costs and distribute the benefits of open markets through some kind of government intervention and spending, and that public support for liberalism depends on the willingness and ability of governments to do this successfully, is the core of the embedded liberalism thesis. This is what distinguishes the embedded liberalism of the postwar period from the ideology of pure laissez-faire that guided economic policy under the gold standard.[2]

Recently, the argument that trade and government spending go hand in hand because governments have to compensate market losers has come under attack. Several studies claim that the relationship between trade and spending is weak at best and largely attributable to omitted variable bias. We have three criticisms of this research, which has focused almost entirely on the macro-level (country) empirical relationship. First, this research rarely distinguishes between imports and exports. Most studies use the summed value of imports and exports as a percentage of gross domestic product (GDP) – trade openness – as an independent variable in their respective regression analyses. This constrains the effects of imports and exports on government spending to have the same sign. We suspect these flows should have opposite signs. Second, it fails to consider the varying degrees of labor market exposure to international trade. We argue the postindustrial shift in production from tradables to nontradables should reduce the effect that trade has on government spending, because it reduces the number of workers employed in import-competing sectors of the economy.

Our final and most important criticism is that no one has tested the micro-foundations of the embedded liberalism thesis. The key assumption is that government policies can build public support for trade. We believe macro-empirical studies that put spending on the left-hand-side of regression models will always be vulnerable to claims of omitted variable bias and that to make a convincing empirical case for the free trade-welfare state linkage, it is necessary to examine data at a lower level of aggregation. In this chapter, we provide a micro-level test of the embedded liberalism thesis. Our results have important and testable implications for the relationship between aggregate trade and government spending.

The chapter is organized as follows. In the first section, we briefly review and critique the literature on trade and government spending. In the second section, we present an empirical examination of the determinants of individual support for protectionism. Our results show that individuals employed in import competing industries are the strongest opponents of trade, but unemployment insurance and active labor market programs can moderate their opposition. Based on these findings we argue that (1) politicians respond to surges in imports and not necessarily to expanding trade if it is balanced, and (2) the extent to which politicians respond to rising imports will be a function of how many workers are employed in tradable

---

2   See Blyth 2002. Blyth argues that liberal capitalism has become less embedded since the Ronald Reagan and Margaret Thatcher period, but the changes, in his view, do not amount to a return to pre-World War I policies. Others argue that the significance of the Reagan and Thatcher "revolutions" has been exaggerated – for example, Pierson 1994.

industries. We test these two macro-level hypotheses in the third section of the chapter as a way to check the significance of our micro-level results for the trade-welfare state debate. We conclude in the final section.

Trade and Government Spending in the Developed Democracies

It is well known that countries with open economies have bigger governments.[3] It is also true that OECD countries have increased both their levels of trade and government spending during the post-World War II period. However, the debate remains unresolved as to whether these strong cross-national and over-time correlations reflect a causal relationship between trade and government spending, a politically conditioned relationship, or a completely spurious one. In addition to Ruggie, those who have argued government policies, by neutralizing the negative effects of trade, can deliver protrade majorities are Rodrik, Adserà and Boix, Swank, and Mares.[4] These scholars argue there is a short-term causal relationship between trade and government spending.[5]

This position has been challenged in two ways. First, Garrett and Mitchell argue the relationship between trade and welfare state effort is long term and historically contingent.[6] For the small economies of Western Europe, trade dependence facilitated unionization, which, in turn, created strong social democratic parties that built large welfare states when they came to power. They distinguish this argument from Ruggie's:

> With respect to trade, for example, Cameron (1978) and Katzenstein (1985) both argue that there is a historical relationship between trade and welfare state effort. ... This is a very different argument from another perspective with which it is often conflated – Ruggie's (1983) notion of embedded liberalism. For Ruggie, the American welfare state expanded immediately after World War II because the government chose to liberalize trade, and realized they had to compensate market losers directly for the dislocations liberalization generated.[7]

Garrett and Mitchell contend that when country dummies (fixed-country effects) are added to regression models, the analyst can distinguish between the long-term historical argument of Cameron and Katzenstein and Ruggie's notion of embedded liberalism. In Garrett and Mitchell's analysis, the positive relationship between trade openness and government spending disappears.[8]

---

3   See, for example, Cameron 1978; Katzenstein 1985; and Rodrik 1998.

4   Rodrik 1997, 1998; Adserà and Boix 2002; Swank 2002a; and Mares 2004.

5   By short-term we mean changes in trade at time $t - 1$ have a discernible effect on government spending at time t.

6   Garrett and Mitchell 2001.

7   Ibid., 163. We believe both short-term and long-term historical forces are operating. Our empirical analysis bears this out.

8   In fact, they find that the relationship is negative and statistically significant.

The strongest challenge to the embedded liberalism thesis, however, has come from Iversen and Cusak, who argue the post-World War II growth of the welfare state is a product of deindustrialization not globalization.[9] They posit that workers who move from manufacturing and agriculture to services cross significant skill boundaries that make the transition difficult and uncertain. These problems, in turn, create demands for government spending. Iversen and Cusak show that the relationship between trade and spending is either statistically or substantively insignificant after controlling for deindustrialization. Moreover, they claim that deindustrialization and globalization are largely independent processes.

Garrett and Mitchell and Iversen and Cusak raise serious questions about the validity of the embedded liberalism thesis. Thus the causal mechanisms identified by Ruggie and others deserve closer empirical scrutiny. We believe it is difficult to do this effectively by working only with data at the country level, and so in the next section, we test the microfoundations of the embedded liberalism argument using survey data. However, before moving on, we note two important criticisms of the research described in this section.

First, the research fails to adequately distinguish between imports and exports. Most studies use trade openness – the summed value of exports and imports as a percentage of GDP – as the key independent variable.[10] This variable constrains the effect of imports and exports on government spending to have the same sign. Yet theory tells us increasing imports and exports should have opposite effects on government spending.[11] Rising imports create losers – displaced workers in import competing industries – that may have to be compensated, rising exports do not. Similarly, falling exports are harmful to domestic employment in a way that declining imports are not.

Second, the research also fails to recognize that the impact of trade flows on government spending depends on the underlying structure of the economy, in particular how many workers are employed in vulnerable traded industries. Because democratically elected governments are sensitive to numbers of votes, ceteris paribus, their response will be conditioned by the scope of threatened industries. If imports displace a large number of workers/voters, governments will have little choice but to provide compensation. If a small number of workers are displaced, politicians will face less pressure to respond.[12]

---

9   Iversen and Cusak 2000.

10   In addition to trade openness, Garrett and Mitchell, 169–70, include the value of imports from low-wage countries in their analysis. They find these imports are weakly positively correlated with higher government spending and transfers. They do not examine the effects of total imports on spending and transfers.

11   This is true unless one is interested in measuring a country's exposure to external risk. To do this, one would interact a country's trade openness – a measure of how exposed it is to the international economy – with a measure of external risk like its terms of trade volatility. See Rodrik 1997, 1998. By itself, trade openness is not a good measure of risk.

12   The ceteris paribus condition is important. We are assuming that the ability of those employed in traded industries to organize remains constant. Because small groups may find it easier to engage in collective action, they are often able to exert political influence that is

In the next section, we test whether government policies can build support for economic openness among groups that oppose it. If government spending on programs such as unemployment insurance and active labor market programs successfully reduces the level of opposition, there is micro-level evidence that the embedded liberalism compromise is a viable solution to the political problems faced by democratically elected leaders who commit their countries to free trade.

Unemployment Benefits and Individual Attitudes Toward Trade

A flurry of research on the determinants of individual support for trade has been published in the last couple of years. Most of it, drawing on international trade theory, focuses on how skill level and sector of employment determine an individual's support for protectionism. Examples include studies by Scheve and Slaughter, O'Rourke and Sinnot, and Mayda and Rodrik.[13] The main conclusion of this research is that groups adversely affected by international economic competition are less likely to support policies of free trade. If government spending is driven partly by the need to generate public support for economic openness, this micro-level research has significant implications for the macro debate over trade and government spending. Yet none of these studies examine the impact of government programs on support for trade. It is surprising that few scholars have tried to bridge the micro-macro divide.

The exception is new work being done by Aldrich, Lange, and others at Duke University, who, picking up where the economists leave off, show that objective conditions of vulnerability translate into subjective feelings of insecurity and strong policy preferences that then determine an individual's party identification and ideology, variables that significantly affect vote choice.[14] In other words, if it is true that globalization produces economic losers and anxiety, citizens will demand insurance and/or compensation and vote for politicians who are likely to provide these policies. In democracies, this situation should pressure politicians to respond. While this important research looks at the relationship between globalization and government spending, it focuses almost entirely on the "demand side" of the political bargain.

We focus much more on the "supply side" of the welfare state/trade openness nexus. We suspect that those adversely affected by trade are more likely to demand tariff protection than welfare state compensation. Governments that want to maintain free trade policies supply compensation as a compromise solution. Our "supply side" focus leads us to ask: If governments provide compensation in the form of unemployment insurance or active labor market programs, will it effectively

---

disproportionate to their numbers. For a discussion of the importance of collective action issues in trade policy politics, see Alt and Gilligan 1994.

13 See Scheve and Slaughter 2001; O'Rourke and Sinnot 2002; and Mayda and Rodrik 2002.

14 For a summary of this research, see Aldrich *et al.* 2002. One of the underlying motivations behind this project is that the macro-level literature on globalization rests on simple micro-level assumptions that have not been tested.

build support for free trade among those who are likely to oppose it otherwise? This relationship between government spending and support for trade is essential to the embedded liberalism thesis, and it has yet to be tested directly.

Before turning to our empirical analysis, we note another strength of the Duke project – its attention to the role of institutions in shaping individual policy preferences. Drawing on important insights from the varieties of capitalism literature, the Duke project examines the effects of different national production regimes on policy attitudes.[15] Because these regimes determine the underlying nature of an economy's factor markets, they shape the political cleavages over trade, determine how vulnerable workers are to economic downturns, and influence whether or not firms will support or oppose welfare state policies. For example, coordinated market economies rely more heavily on labor with sector-specific skills. Skill specificity makes workers more vulnerable to unemployment during economic downturns increasing political pressure for social insurance. In general, firms tend to be more supportive of welfare state policies in the coordinated economies as well. Moreover, because of the low levels of intersectoral mobility, trade politics is likely to divide along sector lines. In these ways, national production regimes affect how individuals perceive globalization.

We do not doubt that a country's institutional structure plays an important role in shaping individual attitudes toward trade, but we believe there are more general forces at work as well. We begin with these and leave the effects of production regimes and other important national differences (beyond welfare state policies) for future research. Institutions also constrain how governments respond to changes in the policy preferences of organized interests and voters. We return to this topic in our conclusion.

Data and Methods

The data we use is from the International Social Survey Program's (ISSP) 1995 survey on national identity. This data set, used by both Mayda and Rodrik and O'Rourke and Sinnot, provides information about individuals' attitudes toward free trade. The countries in our sample are Australia, Germany, the United Kingdom, the United States, Austria, Hungary, Norway, Sweden, the Czech Republic, Poland, New Zealand, Canada, and Spain.[16] The dependent variable (FREETRADE) is constructed from respondents' answers to the following question asked in the survey:

How much do you agree or disagree with the following statement: (Respondent's Country) should limit the import of foreign products in order to protect its national economy.

---

15 See Hall and Soskice 2001 for an exposition of the varieties of capitalism argument.

16 We included all countries reporting occupational categories that allowed us to determine a respondent's industry of employment.

1. Agree strongly
2. Agree
3. Neither agree nor disagree
4. Disagree
5. Disagree strongly

We assigned a value of 1 to respondents who answered, "agree strongly", a 2 to those who answered, "agree", etc. Thus, high values of FREETRADE reflect protrade attitudes whereas low values reflect support for protectionism.

Our baseline regression is grounded in trade theory.[17] The specific factors (Ricardo-Viner) model from international economics identifies sector of employment as crucial to determining an individual's attitudes toward trade. Individuals employed in export industries are likely to benefit from trade whereas individuals employed in import industries are likely harmed. This contrasts with the mobile factors (Stolper-Samuelson) model, which highlights the importance of one's factor endowment. Regardless of their industry of employment, the owners of relatively abundant factors of production benefit from trade. For the countries in our sample, the abundant factors are highly skilled labor and capital.[18]

In our analysis, we use an income dummy variable as a proxy for one's capital endowment. We gave everyone in our sample whose annual family income was greater than $35,000 a score of one and everyone else a score of zero.[19] Following Mayda and Rodrik and Scheve and Slaughter, we use one's level of education as a proxy for skill endowment. We identify a respondent's (or spouse's) industry of employment by their occupation using the reported four-digit code from the International Labor Organization's *International Standard Classification of Occupations*. We created a dummy variable indicating whether the respondent or respondent's spouse was employed in one of fourteen tradable industries identified in the OECD's Industry Structural Analysis (STAN) database.[20] We then used the STAN database to create an

---

17 See Alt and Gilligan 1994; and Hiscox 2002.

18 These models tell us the direct effect of trade on income earned from employing different factors of production. It is also possible that trade affects the wealth and (unearned) income of asset owners. For example, Scheve and Slaughter 2001 find that home owners who live in import competing regions of the United States are, ceteris paribus, more likely to oppose trade than renters. Unfortunately, the data that we would need to test this and similar hypotheses on a cross-national basis is not readily available.

19 Local currencies were converted into dollars using the appropriate exchange rate: monthly income was converted to annual income when necessary. This is the same income measure used by Hiscox and Burgoon 2003.

20 The industries are (1) agriculture, hunting, forestry, and fishing; (2) mining and quarrying; (3) food products, beverages, and tobacco; (4) textiles, textile products, leather, and footwear; (5) wood and products of wood and cork; (6) paper and paper products; (7) publishing, printing, and reproduction of recorded media; (8) chemical, rubber, plastics, and fuel products; (9) other nonmetallic mineral products; (10) basic metals; (11) fabricated metal products, except machinery and equipment; (12) machinery and equipment; (13) transport equipment; and (14) manufacturing not elsewhere classified.

export and import variable using each industry's ratio of exports and imports to value added. The export variable ranges from a low of zero for nontraded industries to a high of 3.28 for the transportation equipment industry in Austria. The denominator in this ratio, value added, represents each sector's contribution to the country's GDP. The ratio can be greater than one for industries with costly inputs. The import variable ranges from zero for all nontraded industries to 7.47 for the textile industry in Norway.

To this list we add several demographic and ideological variables used by Hiscox and Burgoon.[21] They identify gender, age, employment status, and marital status as important determinants of trade preferences. They also focus on an individual's political ideology and whether or not the respondent self-identifies with a particular religious faith. For ideology we use a five-point party affiliation scale provided in the ISSP data set that ranges from far left (1) to far right (5). For our religion variable, we use a dummy that takes a value of one for individuals who self-identify with a religious denomination and zero for everyone else. We also include whether one holds nationalist attitudes, which was found by both Mayda and Rodrik and O'Rourke and Sinnott to be an important determinant of trade policy preferences. In their analysis, Mayda and Rodrik use four separate questions that gauge whether one holds patriotic, nationalistic, and/or chauvinistic attitudes. Using factor analysis, we extract a single component from the answers to these four questions that measures the degree to which an individual holds nationalist attitudes.

Finally, we include three policy variables in our analysis. Two of the three variables are objective measures of government policy: the net replacement rate for unemployment insurance (NRR) and the amount of government spending on active labor market programs per unemployed worker (ALM). The former measure varies across individuals within countries while the latter does not. We also include a subjective evaluation of the social security system (SOCIAL SECURITY). This variable is based on a question that asks respondents how proud they are of the social security system in their country. Respondents can answer "very proud", "somewhat proud", "not very proud", or "not proud at all". We scored these responses from 1 to 4, giving those who were not proud at all a 1 and those who were very proud a 4. We included a subjective measure out of concern that respondents might not be aware of the details of the unemployment insurance and active labor market policies in their countries. We assume that respondents who are "very proud" of their social security system feel that they are well protected by it, and those who are "not proud at all" feel that they are not.[22]

Turning to the objective measures, we calculated each country's spending on active labor market programs per unemployed worker (ALM) using data from the OECD's Social Spending and Labor Force databases. These active labor market programs, which are designed to improve job seekers' prospects of finding employment and

---

21 Hiscox and Burgoon 2003.

22 We realize that this measure has its limitations. Political conservatives, for example, might not say they are proud of their country's social security system even if it offers generous proiection. However, if conservatives are more supportive of trade, this will bias against finding a positive relationship between this subjective evaluation and support for free trade.

increase the earning potential of workers, include spending on public employment, labor market training, and other policies intended to promote employment among the unemployed. We include the net replacement rate of each respondent's government-provided unemployment benefits (NRR). The 1998 OECD's *Benefit Systems and Work Incentives* calculates net replacement rates for four family types at two income levels.[23] The family types are single, married couple, couple with two children, and lone parent with two children. The income levels are average and two-thirds the average income level. This gives up to eight different net replacement rates for each country in the sample.

We used SINGLE, NUMBER OF PERSONS IN HOUSEHOLD, and the HOUSEHOLD CYCLE variables from the ISSP data set (v202, v293, and v294 respectively) as well as the family income dummy variable (INCOME) to identify each survey respondent's net replacement rate. The HOUSEHOLD CYCLE variable indicates whether there are children in the household. There are no problems identifying singles and married couples without children. In many instances it is not difficult to identify lone parents and married couples with children because these family types are included in the HOUSEHOLD CYCLE variable. The difficult cases arise when singles live in households with more than one adult and couples live in households with more than two adults. In these cases, parental status is unknown. We gave all identified married respondents with children the married two-child net replacement rate. Similarly, we gave all lone parents the lone parent two-child net replacement rate. When we could not identify parental status, we gave the respondent the average value of their no dependent and two-child net replacement rate.

The HOUSEHOLD CYCLE variable was not available for the United Kingdom, Austria, the Czech Republic, and Poland. For the respondents in these countries, we used the NUMBER OF PERSONS IN HOUSEHOLD variable to identify cases where there are no children living in the household (for example, a single respondent living in a household with only one person). When we could not determine whether or not children were living in the household, we used an average net replacement rate. In most countries net replacement rates are higher for low-income individuals. We used our existing income dummy variable (INCOME) to assign average income and below average net replacement rates. The main advantage of our NRR variable is that, with eight replacement rates, it provides substantial within country variation in unemployment insurance coverage.[24] (See the Appendix Tables 5.A1 and 5.A2 for summary statistics.)

We estimate ordered probits because the dependent variable, FREETRADE, is ordinal. Ordinal dependent variables can create problems for linear models because these models assume that the intervals between adjacent categories are equal. If this assumption does not hold, the estimated coefficients will be biased and misleading.[25]

---

23 OECD 1998. See tab. 3.1, 30, for these net replacement rates.

24 In terms of research design, this variable is an improvement over countrywide measures of unemployment protection because it allows the analyst to incorporate fixed country effects into the regressions. The fixed-effects model allows us to control for unobservable or otherwise omitted country-level factors that correlate with a country's average net replacement rate.

25 McKelvey and Zavoina 1975.

Also, because many individuals in each country are exposed to the same "treatment" (for example, the same active labor market programs) and cannot be considered independent trials, we have to be careful estimating the standard errors for our regression coefficients.[26] We reported robust "clustered" standard errors as a way to address the "duplication" problem.[27]

Results

The regression results are presented in Table 5.1.[28] Model 1 includes the baseline controls and the respondent's net replacement rate variable (NRR). All of the variables are correctly signed and statistically significant. Individuals employed in either import industries are more likely to support tariffs to protect the economy than individuals who are employed in either high export or nontradable industries. Moreover, individuals with high levels of education (skills) and income (capital) are less likely to support protectionism. Finally, the higher an individual's net replacement rate the less likely they are to support protectionism. This confirms an important element of the embedded liberalism argument: government policies that remedy the negative effects of trade increase support for economic openness. In the second regression (Model 2), we include each country's active labor market spending per unemployed worker. Again, the coefficient is correctly signed and statistically significant. Next, we add the demographic and ideological variables to the net replacement model rate (Model 3). The coefficient on NRR remains positive and statistically significant. Then we add fixed-country effects (Model 4) – that is, we include country dummies in the regression. This allows us to control for any omitted or unobservable variables at the national level that are correlated with the generosity of a country's unemployment insurance benefits. The results do not change.[29] In Model 5 we switch the variable NRR for the subjective measure of an individual's satisfaction with the variable SOCIAL SECURITY. Again, the results are consistent with our expectations. In Model 6 we include active labor market spending in a model with the full set of individual-level controls.[30] The coefficient on the variable ALM is statistically significant and correctly signed.

In order to demonstrate the size of the effects that the key variables have on individual support for free trade, we conduct several counter factual experiments

---

26 Moulton 1990.

27 Fur a discussion of this problem, see Steenbergen and Jones 2002, 219–20. In calculating our standard errors, we assume respondents are clustered by country.

28 The cut-point estimates are omitted from the table to save space.

29 We get similar results when we interact our measures of trade exposure with the social protection variables. For example, in Model 4, if we make the effect of trade exposure on support for trade dependent on the level of social protection, we continue to find that employment in import competing sectors of the economy has a large negative impact. The size of this effect declines, however, as the level of social protection rises.

30 Because this variable is constant across individuals within countries, we cannot include it in a model with fixed country effects.

using simulation methods.[31] The results are reported in terms of predicted probabilities and changes in predicted probabilities in Table 5.2. As our benchmark, we use an individual with median scores on all of the variables included in the analysis. This individual is not employed in a tradable sector of the economy, comes from a family with a combined annual income of less than $35,000, has the equivalent of a high school education, and supports protectionism as a means to bolster the domestic economy with an approximate probability of 0.60. This representative respondent opposes protection with an approximate probability of 0.20. If this respondent were employed in an export-oriented sector of the economy, the probability of support for protectionism would be similar. In our counterfactual, where the sector's exports are about 118 percent of value added, we cannot reject the hypothesis of no change. If this respondent were employed in an import-competing sector of the economy, the probability of supporting protection rises by about 0.13 from 0.60 to 0.73.[32] If the respondent had a college degree instead of a high school diploma, support for protectionism would drop by approximately 0.11. Increasing this respondent's unemployment insurance from the median net replacement rate of 72 percent to 88 percent would lower the probability of supporting protection by 0.05 and raise the probability of opposing it by 0.04. Finally, raising the level of active labor market spending from the median of $4,180 to $12,730 would decrease support for protectionism by 0.14.

Overall, our results are very supportive of the embedded liberalism thesis. The strongest opposition to trade comes from individuals employed in sectors of the economy that have the highest levels of imports. Yet, these results demonstrate that politicians can, in fact, build support for trade, even among these sectors. Politically feasible policy reforms can offset declines caused by increased exposure to international competition.

Imports and Government Spending in Postindustrial Economies

Our micro results confirm the significance of the tradable/nontradable and import/export distinctions. Politicians who want to maintain support for trade will have to respond to surges in imports. This is particularly true if there are a large number of individuals employed in tradable sectors of the economy. However, as individuals move out of tradable industries it becomes less important for politicians to respond to increased imports. Thus, our micro results suggest that the movement of workers from tradable to nontradable sectors will increase support for trade. Therefore, globalization and deindustrialization should have interdependent effects

---

31 These experiments were conducted using the software developed by Tomz, Wittenberg, and King 1999.

32 This number is calculated by totaling the first two columns of Table 5.2. In our experiment, we define import competing as a sector with imports worth 184 percent of value added. The two percentages – 118 percent (exports) and 184 percent (imports) – are at the 95th percentile in our sample. Note that this percentile is for our entire sample and most respondents are employed in nontraded industries. These numbers are more representative for the subsample of respondents employed in tradable industries.

Table 5.1   Models of Individual Support for Trade

Variables	Model 1	Model 2	Model 3	Model 4	Model 5	Model 6
TRADABLE	-.281***	-.239***	-.233***	-.248**	-.241***	-.220***
	(.080)	(.081)	(.085)	(.097)	(.080)	(.082)
EXPORTS	.234***	.211**	.248***	.171***	.174***	.236***
	(.087)	(.087)	(.049)	(.052)	(.050)	(.050)
IMPORTS	-.052*	-.049*	-.067***	-.030**	-.027**	-.063***
	(.029)	(.028)	(.024)	(.014)	(.012)	(.022)
EDUCATION	.145***	.160***	.117***	.142***	.150***	.138***
	(.032)	(.030)	(.025)	(.021)	(.023)	(.026)
INCOME	.282***	.138***	.367***	.231***	.165***	.177***
	(.047)	(.042)	(.057)	(.037)	(.038)	(.045)
MALE	—	—	.284***	.268***	.246***	.250***
			(.048)	(.049)	(.046)	(.045)
AGE	—	—	-.002*	-.002	-.002	-.002*
			(.001)	(.001)	(.001)	(.001)
SINGLE	—	—	.152***	.081**	.031	.039
			(.058)	(.036)	(.040)	(.028)
UNEMPLOYED	—	—	-.226**	-.198**	-.201**	-.240***
			(.096)	(.091)	(.079)	(.078)
IDEOLOGY	—	—	.045	.072**	.085***	.072**
			(.031)	(.030)	(.025)	(.032)
RELIGIOUS	—	—	-.024	-.130**	-.139**	-.095
			(.079)	(.066)	(.062)	(.069)
NATIONALISM	—	—	-.279***	-.260***	.277***	-.291***
			(.050)	(.035)	(.033)	(.040)
NRR	.768**	—	.871**	.597***	—	—
	(.361)		(.367)	(.186)		

ALM	—	.043*** (.009)	—	—	—	.046*** (.008)
SOCIAL SECURITY	—	—	—	—	.097*** (.023)	—
Fixed-country effects	no	no	no	yes	yes	no
Observations	8768	9780	4975	4975	5619	5772
Log likelihood	−12469.4	−13759.0	−6724.8	−6595.0	−7397.8	−7683.5
Pseudo R^2	.029	0.034	.059	.078	.077	.066

Note: Robust standard errors are in parentheses. Respondents are clustered by country. ALM = active labor market; NRR = net replacement rate. *** significant at 1%; ** significant at 5%; * significant at 10%.

Table 5.2 Simulated Effects of Key Variables on Individual Support for Free Trade

	Pr(freetrade=1) (support protection)	Pr(freetrade=2)	Pr(freetrade=3) (indifferent)	Pr(freetrade=4)	Pr(freetrade=5) (oppose protection)
Benchmark (predicted probability)	.218	.377	.203	.163	.038
	(.033)	(.022)	(.027)	(.022)	(.010)
1. Impact of changing from nontradable to export industry	-.000	.002	-.000	-.011	-.001
	(.023)	(.008)	(.008)	(.016)	(.007)
2. Impact of changing from nontradable to import industry	.126**	.007	-.047**	-.065**	-.021**
	(.043)	(.019)	(.016)	(.016)	(.006)
3. Impact of changing from high school to college graduate	-.073**	-.040**	.022**	.060**	.031**
	(.012)	(.018)	(.006)	(.015)	(.012)
4. Impact of changing from low income to high	-.072**	-.038**	.023**	.058**	.029**
	(.010)	(.014)	(.006)	(.012)	(.007)
5. Impact of raising NRR front 72% to 88%	-.032**	-.015**	.011**	.025**	.012**
	(.013)	(.011)	(.004)	(.012)	(.008)
6. Impart of raising ALM from $4,180 to $12,730	-.091**	-.051**	.030**	.074**	.038**
	(.019)	(.014)	(.009)	(.015)	(.009)

Note: Standard errors are in parentheses. For each experiment, we report the change in predicted probabilities.
** significant at 5% (based on simulated 95% confidence interval using Model 1 except for the sixth counterfactual that uses Model 2). ALM = active labor market; NRR = net replacement rate; Pr = probability.

on government spending.[33] In postindustrial economies, the effect of imports on spending should be smaller in magnitude. We test this hypothesis below.

Data and Methods

Our sample, which spans from 1960 to 2000, includes seventeen OECD countries: Australia, Austria, Belgium, Canada, Denmark, Finland, France, Germany, Ireland, Italy, Japan, the Netherlands, New Zealand, Norway, Sweden, the United Kingdom, and the United States. The key independent variable is the natural log of imports measured in millions of 1995 U.S. dollars.[34] The size of the effect that imports will have on spending depends on how many workers are employed in tradable industries. We use Iversen and Cusak's measure of deindustrialization as a measure of the number of workers exposed to import competition.[35]

We include three separate dependent variables in our analysis. The first two are common in the literature: government consumption as a percentage of GDP (GOVCON) and social benefits as a percentage of GDP (SOCBEN).[36] The third is based on the NRR measure from our micro analysis. We use spending on unemployment insurance per unemployed worker divided by the average level of compensation per employee as a proxy for each country's NRR.[37] The first two measures are less specific to the causal argument being made – we might expect changes in these variables to be driven by a number of other factors – but there is almost twenty additional years of data available for them. Moreover, it is possible that the NRR measure is too limited in its scope. Constrained governments might respond in less direct ways to demands for insurance. For example, in the United States, much of the insecurity associated with losing one's job comes from the fear of losing one's health insurance. In theory, the U.S. government could respond to globalization pressures by providing better health care for its poorest citizens, and this would not show up in the NRR measure.

---

33 Many believe that globalization and deindustrialization are interdependent processes in the sense that expanding trade explains the decline of manufacturing among the OECD economies. Iversen and Cusak reject this argument. See Iversen and Cusak 2000, 339–45. We are not arguing that trade causes deindustrialization but rather deindustrialization conditions the effect of trade on government spending. A similar argument is made by Mares 2004.

34 OECD's Economic Outlook Database. See OECD 2003b.

35 Their measure is 100 minus the workers employed in manufacturing and agriculture as a percentage of the working age population.

36 This data is from OECD's Economic Outlook Database. See OECD 2003b.

37 The variables used to construct NRR are from the OECD's Social Spending, Labor Force, and Economic Outlook Databases. See OECD 2001, 2003a, and 2003b. For a critique of the research using government consumption and social benefits as dependent variables, see Burgoon 2001; and Mares 2004. Mares argues that all expenditure-based measures are problematic because they do not reflect politically salient aspects of policy design. We disagree because expenditures are directly related to the generosity of benefit payments, and the generosity of benefits is as politically salient as (if not more salient than) any other feature of welfare state policy.

We add five control variables to our analysis: GDP per capita; the percentage of the population above the age of sixty-five; the percentage of cabinet seats held by left-wing parties; union density; and exports.[38] The first variable controls for Wagner's law, which predicts that governments will spend a higher proportion of GDP as per-capita real income rises. Pierson and others have identified an aging population as the key demographic change driving government spending in the OECD today.[39] (For the NRR variable, by contrast, we would expect a negative relationship because retired individuals do not benefit from unemployment insurance.) One would expect government spending to be higher where the political left and/or organized labor is strong. Because imports and exports are highly correlated, the log of exports is also included as a control variable. We expect the coefficients on imports and exports to have opposite signs. (See the Appendix for summary statistics.)

We estimate six panel regressions, two for each of our dependent variables. One model includes the controls; the other does not. As do many political scientists, we include the lag of the dependent variable and country dummies in all of our models to control for persistence and unit heterogeneity respectively. In other words, we estimate a dynamic panel model using the least squares with dummy variables (LSDV) estimator.[40] For this purpose, the LSDV estimator performs well against some of the more sophisticated alternatives.[41] All of our right-hand-side variables are lagged one period to address potential problems of endogeneity.

Results

The regression estimates are reported in Table 5.3. In short, we find that the effect of imports on a country's level of government spending depends on how exposed the domestic labor market is to trade.[42] The estimated coefficients on the imports and deindustrialization interaction variables are correctly signed in all six of the regressions.[43] An increase in a country's imports is associated with an increase in government spending. This effect is magnified when a large portion of the working-age population is employed in tradable industries. As for the controls, real GDP per capita is correctly signed and statistically significant in all three regressions. The coefficients on union density in the government consumption and social benefits

---

38 The sources are OECD 2003b; Franzese 2002, and Swank 2002b.

39 See, for example, Pierson 2001.

40 For a good introduction to the LSDV estimator, see Hsiao 2003, chap. 3.

41 Judson and Owen 1999.

42 This is similar to Mares's finding for the interwar period that both terms-of-trade and unemployment volatility have a larger impact on the coverage of unemployment insurance when the percentage of the workforce employed in manufacturing is high. See Mares 2004.

43 We do not include deindustrialization as a stand-alone regressor in Model 5 because it is highly collinear with the interaction term and we have a small sample. Our estimates of the other coefficients are much more precise when deindustrialization is omitted from the model. We feel comfortable dropping the variable because its coefficient is not statistically significant. In other words, we cannot reject the hypothesis that deindustrialization does not have a direct effect on net replacement rates. Excluding deindustrialization as a stand-alone regressor does not change the results in a qualitative sense though it does make them stronger.

regressions are correctly signed and statistically significant. The coefficient on the percentage of the population over sixty-five years of age is correctly signed and statistically significant in the net replacement rate regression: the greater the percentage of retirees, the lower the benefits for unemployed individuals.

To demonstrate the implications of the regressions, we conduct a set of counterfactual experiments that compare the effects of increasing imports on government spending in a hypothetical industrial and postindustrial economy.[44] To do this, we extend the first difference procedure described in King, Tomz, and Wittenberg.[45] The change in government spending caused by a simulated increase in imports is called the first difference. We simulate the effects of an increase in imports for both types of economy. Thus we record two first differences for each trial in our experiments.[46] Because we are interested in whether the responses (that is, first differences) differ systematically across our two hypothetical economies, we also record the difference in the size of the changes across our two cases. This comparison is the difference in the first differences, which we record for each trial. We can then use this distribution to put a confidence interval around the mean difference in expected changes in government spending for our industrial and postindustrial economies.

We set the deindustrialization variable to its sample values at the 10th (62.32) and 90th percentiles (80.32) to simulate our industrial and postindustrial economies respectively. In each experiment we increase the logged level of imports from $9.111 to $9.551. This is the size of the import surge New Zealand experienced between 1973 and 1974.[47] All other variables are held at the sample median. We conducted one thousand trials for each experiment.

The results, which are reported in Table 5.4, are similar for all three types of government spending. The short-term effect of increasing a country's imports is larger for industrial than postindustrial economies. The difference in first differences is statistically and politically significant for each measure of government spending. The short-term effect of an import surge on government consumption is 0.100 higher for our hypothetical industrial economy when compared to its postindustrial counterpart. If the increase in imports were sustained, after three years the gap would increase to 0.287 (0.679–0.392). The differences for social benefits and net replacement rates are 0.155 and 0.328 respectively. Again, these differences would grow over time with a sustained increase in imports.

Our macro results demonstrate the significance of our individual-level findings for the trade/welfare state debate. Previous research has concluded that the short-term

---

44 For the experiments, we use regressions 1, 3, and 5.

45 King, Tomz, and Wittenberg 2000.

46 Each trial involves drawing a new vector of parameters from the multivariate sampling distribution defined by the coefficient estimates and the estimated variance-covariance matrix.

47 This is the largest one-period increase in imports experienced by a country in our sample. We prefer to use this within country change rather than, for example, the difference from the 25th to 75th percentile, which is a much larger difference but one that is only observed across countries in our sample.

Table 5.3 Imports, Deindustrialization, and Government Spending

Variables	GOVCON			SOCBEN	NRR	
	Model 1	Model 2	Model 3	Model 4	Model 5	Model 6
LAGGED DV	.954***	.914***	.972***	.940***	.781***	.669***
	(.030)	(.029)	(.034)	(.034)	(.063)	(.068)
IMPORTS	1.329***	2.106***	1.772***	2.560***	8.566***	28.927*
	(.372)	(.487)	(.638)	(.667)	(1.708)	(15.266)
DEINDUSTRIALIZATION	.084*	.066	.168**	.131*	–	3.711
	(.046)	(.053)	(.084)	(.078)		(2.219)
imports × DEINDUSTRIALIZATION	-.013***	-.011**	-.019**	-.015**	-.041***	-.387*
	(.004)	(.004)	(.008)	(.007)	(.013)	(.203)
EXPORTS	–	-1.747***	–	-1.760***	–	.172
		(.372)		(.466)		(2.984)
RGDP PER CAPITA	–	2.272***	–	1.238***	–	21.763***
		(.465)		(.375)		(6.472)
OLD AGE	–	-.054	–	.052	–	-.813**
		(.035)		(.035)		(.390)
LEFT GOVERNMENT	–	.001	–	-.000	–	.017
		(.001)		(.001)		(.012)
UNION DENSITY	–	.016***	–	.013**	–	.047
		(.005)		(.007)		(.158)
R^2	.976	.979	.982	.984	.962	.966
Joint Wald test	17.77***	33.46***	12.35***	31.00***	25.70***	11.23**
Observations	639	599	575	535	280	262
Number of countries	17	17	17	17	17	17

Note: Panel-corrected standard errors are in parentheses. GOVCON = government consumption; NRR = net replacement rate; RGDP = real gross domestic product; SOCBEN = social benefits. *** significant at 1%; ** significant at 5%; * significant at 10%.

Table 5.4   Effect of Increasing Imports on Government Spending

	Government consumption	Social benefits	Net replacement rate (unemployment insurance)
High exposure (industrial economy)	0.237**	0.252**	2.636**
first difference standard deviation	(.068)	(.088)	(.542)
95% confidence interval	[.104, .383]	[.076, .416]	[1.661, 3.709]
Low exposure (postindustrial)	0.137**	0.097	2.308**
first difference standard deviation	(.054)	(.058)	(.510)
95% confidence interval	[.028, .247]	[−.014, .212]	[1.347, 3.318]
Difference in difference	0.100**	0.155**	0.328**
standard deviation	(.032)	(.059)	(.100)
95% confidence interval	[.037, .163]	[.041, .263]	[.126, .532]

Note: ** Significant at 5% (based on a simulated 95% confidence interval using the robust Beck-Katz variance-covariance matrix. All values held at the sample median unless noted otherwise).

relationship between trade and government spending is an artefact (caused by omitted variable bias) that disappears when fixed-country effects and deindustrialization are taken into account. Our results show that this is not the case. The relationship between trade and government spending is robust when imports and exports are distinguished and the interactive effects of trade and deindustrialization are recognized.

Conclusion

Ruggie's embedded liberalism involves a political compromise in which leaders commit their countries to freer trade while managing the dislocations that follow. Our empirical tests – the first of the microfoundations of this theory – demonstrate that this compromise is a politically feasible one. Citizens' attitudes toward trade are malleable and well informed by their self-interest according to the predictions of trade theory. Workers who compete against imports tend to oppose free trade, but their opposition can be reduced with policies designed to protect them like unemployment insurance and active labor market programs.

We suspect many readers will be persuaded by our statistical results. Others will be skeptical because our results do not square with their previous beliefs about the importance of trade in determining government spending. If it is such a good idea politically to compensate those who lose from trade, why does it not happen more often? We have three responses to this query. First, it happens more often than many realize. The bargain of embedded liberalism is alive and well even in countries where we might not expect to find it. In the United States, for example, the Bush administration and free trade proponents in the Congress recently bought off opposition to Trade Promotion Authority by increasing the size of trade adjustment assistance and providing wage insurance for older workers displaced by trade.

Second, our results suggest that governments are less responsive to imports today than in the past. As OECD countries have moved more toward service economies, the effect of import surges on spending has declined because fewer citizens work in import-competing sectors. Having made this point, we want to stress that this situation is unlikely to persist. There is every reason to believe those employed in services sectors of the economy will become increasingly exposed to international competition over time, especially if trade in services is effectively incorporated into the General Agreement on Tariffs and Trade (GATT) and the World Trade Organization (WTO). Some of the recent U.S. backlash against Indian phone centers, for instance, shows that service industries are increasingly competitive across borders. Therefore, it is likely that the bargain of embedded liberalism will remain politically significant well into the twenty-first century.

Finally, even though our analysis in this chapter largely avoids institutions, we believe national institutions play an important role in determining if, when, and how the bargain of embedded liberalism is implemented in different countries. Cross-national variation in a number of political and economic institutions ranging from national production regimes to electoral systems is likely to be important. Welfare state policies are likely to be more attractive to politicians in coordinated market economies and majoritarian political institutions can insulate politicians from the pressures of trade losers. Future research should focus on how these and other institutions shape individual attitudes toward trade and constrain policy responses to economic globalization.

Appendix

Table 5.A1   Summary Statistics for Micro-level Data

Variable	Observations	Mean	Standard deviation	Median	Minimum	Maximum
FREETRADE	16,222	2.418	1.150	2	1	5
TRADABLE	11,476	0.2390	0.427	0	0	1
EXPORTS	11,476	0.176	0.431	0	0	3.282
IMPORTS	11,476	0.283	0.815	0	0	7.472
EDUCATION	17,007	4.604	1.401	5	1	7
INCOME	14,873	0.348	0.476	0	0	1
MALE	16,991	0.479	0.500	0	0	1
AGE	16,881	45.618	16.868	44	14	98
SINGLE	16,897	0.371	0.483	0	0	1
UNEMPLOYED	16,699	0.051	0.220	0	0	1
IDEOLOGY	13,119	2.861	0.936	3	1	5
RELIGIOUS	16,356	0.781	0.414	1	0	1
NATIONALISM	13,242	0.085	0.985	0.127	−3.315	1.759
SOCIAL SECURITY	16,070	2.516	0.920	3	1	4
NRR	13,503	0.693	0.099	0.72	0.37	0.88
ALM	17,103	4.707	3.960	4.18	0.49	12.73

Note: ALM = active labor market; NRR = net replacement rate.

Table 5.A2   Summary Statistics for Macro-level Data

Variable	Observations	Mean	Standard deviation	Median	Minimum	Maximum
GOVCON	681	19.143	4.104	18.905	9.838	31.329
SOCBEN	615	12.496	4.490	12.568	2.681	23.890
NRR	299	37.130	23.181	30.546	7.111	133.582
IMPORTS	667	11.250	1.167	11.189	8.591	13.965
DEIND	662	71.902	7.044	72.255	48.31	84.53
EXPORTS	667	11.260	1.193	11.201	8.431	13.743
RGDPPC	675	9.634	0.326	9.684	8.469	10.368
OLD AGE	680	12.368	2.609	12.374	5.970	18.282
LEFIC	680	31.176	38.193	0	0	100
UNDENS	632	43.987	17.189	42.782	9.867	85.483

Note: DEIND = deindustrialization; GOVCON = government consumption; LEFTC = left-wing government; NRR = net replacement rate: RDGPPC = real gross domestic product per capita: SOCBEN = social benefits; UNDENS = union density.

References

Adserà, Alicia, and Carles Boix. 2002. Trade, Democracy, and the Size of the Public Sector: The Political Underpinnings of Openness. *International Organization* 56 (2): 229–62.

Aldrich, John H., Claire Kramer, Peter Lange, Renan Levine, Jennifer Merolla, Laura Stephenson, and Elizabeth Zechmeister. 2002. In Pursuit of the Missing Link: Do Voters Make the Connection Between Macroeconomic Change and Welfare State Growth? Paper presented at the 98th Annual Meeting of the American Political Science Association, August–September, Boston.

Alt, James, and Michael Gilligan. 1994. The Political Economy of Trading States: Factor Specificity, Collective Action Problems and Domestic Political Institutions. *Journal of Political Philosophy* 2 (2): 165–92.

Blyth, Mark. 2002. *Great Transformations: Economic Ideas and Institutional Change in the Twentieth Century*. Cambridge: Cambridge University Press.

Burgoon, Brian. 2001. Globalization and Welfare Compensation: Disentangling the Ties that Bind. *International Organization* 55 (3):509–51.

Cameron, David. 1978. The Expansion of the Public Economy: A Comparative Analysis. *American Political Science Review* 72 (4): 1243–61.

Franzese, Robert J. 2002. *Macroeconomic Policies of Developed Democracies*. Cambridge: Cambridge University Press.

Garrett, Geoffrey, and Deborah Mitchell. 2001. Globalization, Government Spending and Taxation in the OECD. *European Journal of Political Research* 39 (2): 145–78.

Hall, Peter, and David Soskice. eds. 2001. *Varieties of Capitalism: The Institutional Foundations of Comparative Advantage*. New York: Oxford University Press.

Hiscox, Michael. 2002. *International Trade and Political Conflict: Commerce, Coalitions, and Mobility*. Princeton. NJ.: Princeton University Press.

Hiscox, Michael, and Brian Burgoon. 2003. Trade Openness and Political Compensation: Explaining Labor Demands for Adjustment Assistance. Unpublished manuscript. Cambridge. Mass.: Harvard University.

Hsiao, Cheng. 2003. *Analysis of Panel Data*. 2nd ed. Cambridge: Cambridge University Press.

Iversen, Torben, and Thomas R. Cusack. 2000. The Causes of Welfare State Expansion: Deindustrialization or Globalization? *World Politics* 52 (3): 313–49.

Judson, Ruth A., and Ann L. Owen. 1999. Estimating Dynamic Panel Data Models: A Guide for Macroeconomists. *Economic Letters* 65 (7): 9–15.

Katzenstein, Peter. 1985. *Small States in World Markets: Industrial Policy in Europe*. Ithaca. N.Y.: Cornell University Press.

King, Gary, Michael Tomz, and Jason Wittenberg. 2000. Making the Most of Statistical Analyses: Improving Interpretation and Presentation. *American Journal of Political Science* 44 (2): 347–61.

Mares, Isabela. 2004. Economic Insecurity and Social Policy Expansion: Evidence from Interwar Europe. *International Organization* 58 (4).

Mayda, Anna M., and Dani Rodrik. 2002. Why Are Some People (and Countries) More Protectionist than Others? Unpublished manuscript. Cambridge, Mass: Harvard University.

McKelvey, Richard, and William Zavoina. 1975. A Statistical-Model for Analysis of Ordinal Level Dependent Variables. *Journal of Mathematical Sociology* 4 (1): 103–20.

Moulton, Brent R. 1990. An Illustration of a Pitfall in Estimating the Effects of Aggregate Variables on Micro Units. *Review of Economics and Statistics* 72 (2): 334–38.

Organization for Economic Cooperation and Development (OECD). 1998. *Benefit Systems and Work Incentives*. Paris: OECD.

——. 2001. Social Spending Database. Paris: OECD.

——. 2003a. Labor Force Database. Paris: OECD.

——. 2003b. Economic Outlook Database. Paris: OECD.

O'Rourke, Kevin H., and Richard Sinnott. 2002. The Determinants of Individual Trade Policy Preferences: International Survey Evidence. In *Brookings Trade Forum: 2001*, edited by Susan M. Collins and Dani Rodrik, 157–206. Washington, D.C.: Brookings Institution.

Pierson, Paul. 1994. *Dismantling the Welfare State? Reagan, Thatcher, and the Politics of Retrenchment*. Cambridge: Cambridge University Press.

——. 2001. The Dynamics of Welfare State Expansion: Trade Openness. De-industrialization, and Partisan Politics, in *The New Politics of the Welfare State*, edited by Paul Pierson. 80–104. New York: Oxford University Press.

Rodrik, Dani. 1997. *Has Globalization Gone Too Far?* Washington, D.C.: Institute for International Economics.

——. 1998. Why Do More Open Economies Have Bigger Governments? *Journal of Political Economy* 106 (5): 997–1032.

Ruggie, John G. 1982. International Regimes, Transactions, and Change: Embedded Liberalism in the Postwar Economic Order. *International Organization* 36 (2): 195–231.

——. 1994. Trade, Protectionism, and the Future of Welfare Capitalism. *Journal of International Affairs* 48 (1): 1–11.

——. 1997. Globalization and the Embedded Liberalism Compromise: The End of an Era? Working Paper 97/1. Cologne. Germany: Max Planck Institut für Gesellschaftsforschung.

——. 2003. Taking Embedded Liberalism Global: the Corporate Connection. In *Taming Globalization: Frontiers of Governance*, edited by David Held and Mathias Koenig-Archibugi, 93–129. Oxford: Polity Press.

Scheve, Kenneth, and Matthew Slaughter. 2001. *Globalization and the Perceptions of American Workers*. Washington, D.C.: Institute for International Economics.

Steenbergen, Marco R., and Bradford S. Jones. 2002. Modeling Multilevel Data Structures. *American Journal of Political Science* 46 (1): 218–37.

Swank, Duane. 2002a. *Global Capital, Political Institutions, and Policy Change in Developed Welfare States*. Cambridge, UK: Cambridge University Press.

——. 2002b. 21-Nation Pooled Time-Series Data Set, 1950–1999: Political Strength of Political Parties by Ideological Group in Capitalist Democracies.

Milwaukee, Wis.: Marquette University. Available at (www.marquette.edu/polisci/Swankpart5099.xls). Accessed January 18, 2005.

Tomz, Michael, Jason Wittenberg, and Gary King. 1999. *Clarify: Software for Interpreting and Presenting Statistical Results*. Version 1.2.1. Cambridge, Mass: Harvard University. Updated version 2.1 (produced 5 January 2003). Available at (http://gking.harvard.edu/stats.html). Accessed January 18, 2005.

Chapter 6

Globalization and the Decline of the Welfare State in Less-Developed Countries

Nita Rudra

Is the welfare state withering away, or will it survive current globalization trends?[1] Recent literature framing this academic debate has extolled the resilience of this institution, despite the pressures of international market integration.[2] These studies have reversed doomsday scenarios from the 1980s and 1990s that contemplated the ultimate demise of the welfare state.[3] Yet trends in welfare spending in developed and developing countries have diverged. During the past quarter century, globalization penetrated both groups. However, while the more developed countries were expanding resources devoted to this form of safety net, the average share of gross domestic product (GDP) allocated in a sample of fifty-three less-developed countries (LDCs) began much lower and fell lower still (see Figure 6.1). My analysis goes beyond existing studies by providing an original model of the determinants of welfare spending in LDCs.[4] I focus on how globalization can affect rich and

For help with various aspects of this chapter, I am grateful to Barry Ames, Mithun Dutt, Gary Dymski, Stephan Haggard, Nora Hamilton, Robert Kaufman, James Robinson, Peter Rosendorff, Samira Salem, Ravi Sundaram, Krish Sundaram, Cassandra Thomas, Quang Vuong, Leslie Wirpsa, Adrian Wood, and the editors and anonymous reviewers at *IO*. I am especially indebted to Hayward Alker and John Odell for their detailed and extremely helpful comments. I would also like to gratefully acknowledge the assistance of the Center for International Studies at the University of Southern California.

    1   Economic globalization is operationalized by the level of international trade and the level of capital flows as a share of GDP.

    2   See Bernauer and Achini 2000; Iversen and Cusack 2000; Hicks 1999; Rieger and Leibfried 1998; Garrett 1998; Garrett and Mitchell 1996; Rodrik 1998; Quinn 1997; Pierson 1996.

    3   See Tyrell 1977; Brown 1988; Morris 1988; Sherer 1987; Ruggles and O'Higgins 1987; and Wicks 1987.

    4   Bernauer and Achini 2000; Garrett 2001; Rodrik 1998 and 1997b; and Quinn 1997 are exceptions in two very important ways: (1) LDCs are treated as conceptually distinct from developed countries; and (2) important institutional variables expected to affect welfare expenditures, such as labor power, are included. Note that after this chapter was accepted for publication; Kaufman and Segura (2001) published an analysis of the effects of globalization on Social Spending in Latin America.

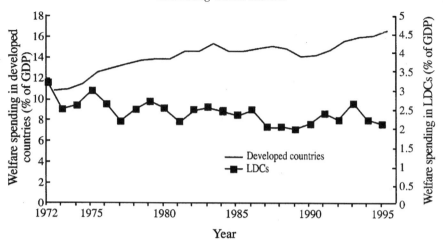

**Figure 6.1   The Contrast in Government Welfare Spending between
Developed and Developing Countries, 1972–95**

Sources: IMF, *International Finance Statistics and Government Finance Statistics*, various
years.

Notes: Data for the following countries was included in all the figures and regressions. *Less-
developed countries*: Argentina, Bangladesh, Bolivia, Botswana, Brazil, Cameroon, Chile,
Colombia, Costa Rica, Cyprus, Dominican Republic, Ecuador, Egypt Arab Rep., El Salvador,
Fiji, Ghana, Greece, Guatemala, Guyana, Honduras, India, Indonesia, Iran, Israel, Jordan,
Kenya, Korea Rep., Kuwait, Lesotho, Liberia, Malawi, Malaysia, Mali, Mauritius, Mexico,
Morocco, Nepal, Nicaragua, Pakistan, Panama, Paraguay, Philippines, Singapore, Sri Lanka,
Syria, Tanzania, Thailand, Trinidad and Tobago, Tunisia, Turkey, Uruguay, Venezuela, and
Zimbabwe. *Developed countries* (the fourteen OECD nations analyzed by Garrett 1998):
Austria, Belgium, Canada, Denmark, Finland, France, Germany, Italy, Japan, Netherlands,
Norway, Sweden, United Kingdom, and United States. The welfare trend was calculated using
King *et al.*'s (2001) multiple imputation model for missing data. According to King *et al.*,
most methodologists and statisticians agree that multiple imputation is a "superior approach"
to the problem of missing data.

poor countries differently and present a model that includes a new measure of labor
strength. I show that in the face of globalization labor in LDCs has been unable to
prevent the dismantling of the welfare state, quite unlike labor in the more developed
countries.

   A long tradition in political science puts labor at the center of studies pertaining
to welfare state outcomes.[5] Focusing primarily on the historical experience of the
developed countries of Western Europe, these scholars maintain that the growth of
a welfare state depends on a well-organized labor movement.[6] More recently, the
debate has centered on whether the increasing integration of international markets

---

   5   See Korpi 1983; O'Connor and Olsen 1998; Esping-Andersen 1990; Hicks 1999; and
Garrett 1998.
   6   See, for example, Garrett 1998; Hicks 1999; Korpi 1983; and Esping-Andersen
1990.

has become the most powerful force affecting the ability of governments to uphold their welfare commitments. Several scholars have convincingly shown that strong labor movements, such as those in European social democracies, can discourage governments from reducing welfare spending during globalization.[7] I challenge the generalizability of these findings using an analysis of the political power of labor in LDCs. The Stolper-Samuelson theorem implies that the most abundant factors of production will gain from increased openness. In LDCs, low-skilled labor is highly abundant, yet persistent collective-action problems accompanying globalization undermine labor's political clout in LDCs. I assess these two opposing effects by introducing a new indicator of labor power (potential labor power, PLP). My results clearly indicate that the collective-action problems of labor in countries with large pools of low-skilled and surplus workers tend to offset labor's potential political gains from globalization.

This study is the first large-*n* cross-national time-series study of LDC welfare programs that focuses on globalization and the political strength of labor in LDCs as two of the main forces driving government social spending. Conventional analyses that impose models insensitive to the political and economic conditions prevailing in LDCs have biased our understanding of the sustainability of welfare spending in this era of globalization. I use empirical work based on the politics of social spending in developed countries as a starting point for building a model more suitable for developing countries.[8] To mitigate the disadvantages of making broad generalizations about many different LDCs, I obtained estimates using panel data (unbalanced) and the fixed-effects method. I find that in response to globalization pressures, governments' commitments to welfare spending ultimately depend on strong labor-market institutions like those that exist in developed countries.

My analysis proceeds as follows. I first evaluate the literature on globalization and social spending in developed countries with an eye toward building a theory of domestic and international determinants of government welfare expenditures in LDCs. I then compare trends in capital flows, trade, and welfare spending in LDCs with those in developed countries. In the third section I provide evidence in support of my primary argument by establishing the premise of a globalization–welfare model specific to LDCs and then testing it by way of panel regressions. In the final section I discuss the implications of the econometric results for LDCs.

Existing Literature on Welfare States in this Era of Globalization

The literature on the politics of welfare-state spending does not sufficiently explain how or why long-run trends in welfare spending in LDCs differ from those in developed countries. The conventional wisdom is that expanding international markets and prioritizing efficiency and national competitiveness concerns will undermine the welfare state. Geoffrey Garrett and several other theorists, however, have refuted such claims, but only for countries within the Organization for Economic

---

7   See Garrett 1998; 1996; Hicks 1999; and Cameron 1978.

8   Garrett 1998; and Garrett and Mitchell 1996.

Cooperation and Development (OECD).[9] Are LDCs similarly defying such doomsday predictions in the age of globalization? Although some scholars, albeit vaguely, do question the sustainability of welfare programs in LDCs, systematic explorations of government social spending in LDCs have yet to be undertaken.[10]

Conventional wisdom suggests that all states, regardless of their partisan compositions and national differences, would embrace neoliberal policies in order to maintain international competitiveness in a globalizing world.[11] Consequently, the demise of the welfare state is expected for two reasons. First, generous welfare benefits are not regarded as good market-disciplining devices on labor. Both the resulting upward pressures on labor costs and the dampening effects on work incentives are claimed to adversely affect export competitiveness. Second, globalization discourages governments from raising revenue. "Footloose capital", or the capacity to withdraw and shift both productive and financial capital with greater ease, has made it increasingly difficult for governments to generate revenues through taxation.[12] This "race to the neoliberal bottom" in tax rates is compounded by governments' lowering taxes to compete with other states for international investors and to prevent capital flight. By the same token, state borrowing, which leads to higher debt and interest rates, also deters investment. The last two decades have thus become witness to the reification of Charles Lindblom's "markets as prisons" idea.[13] With increasing global competition, governments supposedly find it more difficult to protect citizens from market-generated risks and inequalities.

By analyzing fourteen OECD countries, Geoffrey Garrett presents the most recent and convincing challenge to the notion that welfare states are crumbling under these pressures.[14] Garrett's analysis extends the globalization–welfare debate initiated by Karl Polanyi, John Gerard Ruggie, and Peter J. Katzenstein.[15] He demonstrates that international market exposure actually induces greater government spending on redistribution programs that compensate for market-generated inequalities. Key to Garrett's analysis is the ability of labor-market institutions to effectively negotiate

---

9   See Garrrett 1998; and Garrett and Mitchell 1996. Others who challenge the conventional wisdom are Hicks 1999; Hicks and Swank 1992; Cameron 1978; and Katzenstein 1995.

10 For more general analyses on LDC welfare states, see, for example, Heredia 1997; Hurrell and Woods 1995; Schmidt 1995; Tang 1996; Esping-Andersen 1996; Mesa-Lago 1994; Usui 1994; Ahmad and Hussain 1991; Midgley 1984; and Wahl 1994.

11 See Drunberg 1998; Strange 1997; Gray 1998; Greider 1998; Cerny 1995; Ruggie 1994; Evans 1997; and Gill 1995.

12 For a critique of this idea, see Swank 1998.

13 Maxfield 1998.

14 Garrett 1998.

15 The theoretical basis for this debate was laid by Karl Polanyi and advanced by John Ruggie with his concept of "embedded liberalism." See Polanyi 1944; and Ruggie 1982. These authors separately conjecture that the state must make a broader commitment to social welfare in order to temper the "pernicious effects" of international markets. See also Cameron 1978; Rodrik 1998; and Katzenstein 1995, who demonstrate that there has been a positive relationship between trade exposure and government social spending throughout much of the twentieth century.

between government and labor. He convincingly argues that if labor markets are highly centralized and well developed, then labor and government can effectively coordinate economic performance with redistribution policies. He concludes that globalization has in fact strengthened left-labor movements, and, consequently, cross-national partisan differences in the developed world have been sustained.

Several theorists have provided alternative institutional explanations for the resilience of the welfare state in developed countries.[16] Specifically, Paul Pierson's widely cited study maintains that relatively new cross-class coalitions have resisted the dismantling of the contemporary welfare state.[17] He rebukes advocates of the conventional thesis for overlooking the crucial importance of the well-developed interest group environment in industrialized nations. Consumers of welfare benefits (such as the elderly and the disabled), he argues, have successfully mobilized to prevent a sharp deceleration of social spending.[18] Significantly, this research de-emphasizes the role that well-organized labor groups might currently play in the continuation of government welfare spending in developed countries.

Both arguments imply that social spending under globalization depends on liberal democratic organizations and their derivative institutions. Arguably such assets are not readily available for citizens of a majority of nations. In LDCs, those most disadvantaged by globalization do not have the formal democratic means by which to negotiate with governments.[19] Most developing countries lack both favorable institutional arrangements for establishing cross-class coalitions and strong labor market institutions (as defined by Garrett).

Thus, the situation of contemporary LDC welfare states, where labor is the primary pressure group, remains unexplained. Compared with other societal forces in LDCs, labor groups have historically been the most well-organized (though not in all cases).[20] Therefore, an LDC model that effectively captures the globalization–welfare nexus must account for labor's role in the existence of the welfare state.[21] Such an analysis draws from power resource theories that suggest that the success of welfare states depends on a well-organized labor movement.[22] The question remains whether labor in LDCs has the same wherewithal to withstand the pressures of globalization that it does in Garrett's sample of fourteen OECD countries.

---

16 See Hicks 1999; Pierson 1996; and Hicks and Swank 1992.

17 Pierson 1996. See also Clayton and Pontusson 1998, who challenge some of the tenets of this thesis and move forward with a critique of Pierson 1996.

18 Pierson 1996.

19 Statistical data in Keith Jaggers and Ted Robert Gurr's *Polity III* (1994) on democracy ratings make valid this comparison between developed and developing countries. For an index on democracy for 132 developing countries in 1988, see Hadenius 1992. Note, in particular, the low ratings of LDCs in organizational freedoms and effective and correct elections. For more theoretical discussions on the limitations of democracies in developing countries, see Rueschemeyer *et al.* 1992; and Crisp 1994.

20 See Midgley 1984; and Schmidt 1995.

21 Unless otherwise specified, "labor" refers to both low-skilled and skilled workers.

22 See O'Connor and Olsen 1998; Esping-Andersen 1990; and Korpi 1983.

Trade, Capital Flows, and Government Welfare Spending: The Contrast Between Developed and Developing Countries

From 1972 to 1995, globalization increased in both developed and developing countries, yet trends in government spending for social welfare diverged during this period: spending rose in rich countries and slightly declined in LDCs. The historical relationship between globalization and the welfare state in developed countries makes it all the more intriguing why this same relationship does not seem to be materializing in LDCs. Social-welfare programs are not a new phenomenon in LDCs; they were implemented as early as 1924, beginning with Chile, and have since spread to over seventy developing countries.

Trade and capital flows are two common indicators of globalization.[23] Trade is measured here as imports plus exports as a percentage of GDP, and capital mobility is represented by the sum of capital inflows and outflows as a percentage of GDP. The concept of the "LDC welfare state" is adopted from Alfred Phaller, Ian Gough, and Goran Therborn and refers to "the use of state power and responsibility towards the ends of protecting citizens against economic adversities and ensuring a certain standard of prosperity to all."[24] The figures on welfare pertain primarily to central government expenditures on social security and welfare services (as a percentage of GDP). Some provincial and municipal spending is thus not captured.

OECD countries expanded their spending from an average of 12 percent of GDP in 1972 to 16 percent in 1995. Meanwhile, LDCs spent an average of 3.2 percent in 1972–74 and 2.5 percent in 1994–95. Figures 6.2 and 6.3 illustrate the striking contrast between these two groups of nations.[25]

The LDC sample in this analysis includes all those for which I could obtain comparable data on welfare spending. The fifty-three countries in the sample are low, middle, and high-income non-OECD countries as categorized in the World Bank's 1997 *World Development Indicators.*[26] This data set is regionally diverse, covering twenty Latin American and Caribbean countries, twelve African countries, eight Middle Eastern countries, ten Asian countries, and three European countries. Of these, the majority are low and middle income countries (sixteen and thirty-two, respectively), and five are high-income non-OECD countries. Thus the sample is biased in the sense that it excludes Eastern European countries[27] and several newly

---

23 See Garrett 1998; Garrett and Mitchell 1996; Rodrik 1997b; and Bernauer and Achini 2000.

24 Pfaller *et al.* 1991.

25 See Figure 6.1 for the list of countries included and Appendix A for a more detailed description of how trade and gross capital flows are calculated.

26 Although Greece, Turkey, Mexico, and Korea are currently OECD members, they were included in the LDC sample because of the lower income levels that characterized them at the beginning of this study (1970s). To determine whether they were outliers, regressions were run with each country alternatively excluded and then with the group as a whole excluded. The estimates were not affected by their exclusion.

27 Eastern European countries were intentionally excluded from this data set because their historical circumstances (particularly regarding state social spending) are distinct from the majority of non-OECD developing countries. These countries are not readily comparable

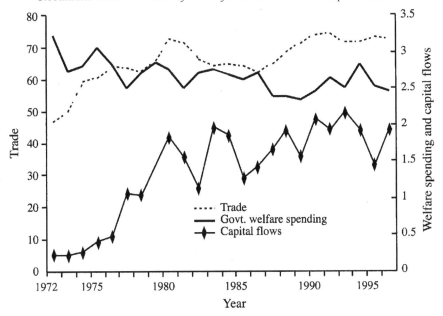

Figure 6.2   Trade, Capital Flows, and Welfare Spending in Fifty-three LDCs
Sources: IMF, *International Finance Statistics* and *Government Finance Statistics*, various years.

industrialized countries. Fast-emerging international market participants, such as China and Taiwan, were among those excluded because of the lack of data.[28]

The Theory

Globalization is likely to adversely affect government commitments to social welfare in nations highly endowed with low-skilled labor. This theory challenges the view that labor in LDCs will experience both economic and political gains with globalization; following such logic, if exposure to international markets is increasing, abundant labor should be in a better political position to demand greater government social-welfare spending. I suggest, however, that labor in LDCs is in a weak bargaining position because the sizeable population of low-skilled workers

to other LDCs because they are undergoing a unique historical experience with respect to their market transitions, have comparatively different functions for the state and welfare, and on average, maintain much higher levels of spending on welfare relative to GDP. Therefore, inclusion of these countries would skew the data and bias the results.

28 It is likely, however, that such an omission creates a more homogenous sample of developing countries, since these missing countries tend to have exceptionally high levels of globalization and would thus skew the data. Compared to the average LDC, integration into the world economy for the NICs has been occurring at an exceptionally rapid pace. See Griffith-Jones and Stallings 1995.

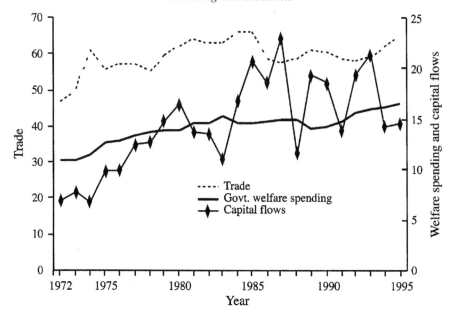

Figure 6.3   Trade, Capital Flows, and Welfare Spending in Fourteen OECD Countries

Sources: IMF, *Government Finance Statistics* and *Balance of Payments Statistics*, various years; World Bank, *World Development Indicators*, various years.

faces collective-action problems that are exacerbated by large pools of surplus labor. Labor in LDCs, unlike in developed countries, does not generally have national labor-market institutions that can help mitigate these problems and strengthen workers' bargaining power. Thus globalization in LDCs will lead to less, not more, social-welfare spending.

The theory I propose is based on specific assumptions regarding the different motivations behind welfare spending. First, the theory assumes that workers desire greater welfare benefits, and owners of capital prefer lower welfare spending. Owners' predisposition is based on a preference for paying lower taxes, receiving higher investment returns, and encountering less overall government interference. Second, it assumes that governments are primarily concerned with promoting the aggregate level of economic performance and, at the same time, arbitrating between the political demands of societal groups commanding power resources.

The importance of factor endowments in determining who gains and who loses with globalization stems from the Hecksher-Ohlin model and the related Stolper-Samuelson theorem. These suggest that with increased exposure to international markets, low-skilled labor in LDCs should experience higher wages and employment, whereas in the more developed countries, high-skilled labor and capital should gain. This logic could also be applied to capital flows. Both productive and financial capital flows will increase in nations that are more efficiently utilizing their most abundant factor. Thus, in LDCs rich in low-skilled labor and poor in capital and high-skilled labor, globalization should improve the economic conditions of low-skilled labor.

Ronald Rogowski combines the above theorem with a model of politics to show that owners of locally abundant factors will consequently expand their political power.[29] His analysis suggests that low-skilled labor in LDCs will have a stronger bargaining position because of the greater wealth that accompanies openness.[30] Conversely, capitalists and skilled workers will be better able to influence government policies in the more developed countries. Yet the implicit assumption in Rogowski's model that the organizing potential of labor is strong is inappropriate for LDCs. Labor groups in LDCs have serious collective-action problems and, therefore, have difficulty advancing their common political interests, despite the economic gains they might reap from globalization.

Low-skilled workers are initially difficult to mobilize because they have little education, work erratic hours, and a growing percentage of them are women, who, according to the literature, are exceptionally hard to organize.[31] In addition, this group is large in LDCs and growing with globalization. This situation results in collective-action problems because, according to Mancur Olson, the larger the group, the greater the propensity for the free-rider problem to occur, and the less likely that the collective good (welfare benefits, for instance) will be supplied.[32]

The crux of the problem lies in the existence of the surplus labor population in most LDCs. Large numbers of surplus workers alter the cost–benefit ratio of organizing and for two reasons reduce the incentives for low-skilled labor to mobilize. First, in an era of heightened global competition, large enterprises profit from the existence of surplus labor pools because they help minimize labor costs, are unprotected, and increase flexibility. To participate in this highly competitive environment, low-skilled workers are thus unlikely to unionize. Second, the presence of surplus labor makes it impossible to offer "selective incentives", as Olson suggests, to help labor overcome its collective-action problems.[33] For example, surplus labor makes it extremely difficult for union organizers to offer secure employment for union members.[34] Because so many low-skilled workers are without work, they focus on gaining employment rather than on lobbying for social-welfare benefits.

Skilled-labor groups in LDCs, on the other hand, are better able to surmount their collective-action problems. These groups are generally smaller in size, less

---

29 Rogowski 1989.

30 Note that Rogowski does not make the distinction between skilled and low-skilled labor with respect to factor endowments. This distinction was emphasized by Wood. See Wood 1997, 1995, and 1994; and Wood and Mayer 1998. Wood defines skilled workers as those with more than a basic general education, for example, professional and technical workers, managers, and craftsmen. Wood 1994, 6. Thus, skilled workers are generally employed in high-skilled intensive manufacturing. Low-skilled labor refers to workers who have limited or no education (referring to both Wood's BAS-EDs and NO-EDs, respectively).

31 For more detailed hypotheses on why low-skilled labor groups in LDCs are difficult to organize, see Deyo 1989, chap. 6; Gereffi 1995; Lok 1993; and Ingersen 1984.

32 Olson 1971.

33 Ibid.

34 Note that while LDCs with state-corporatist systems might offer some of these incentives, it has been argued that the objective is to control and weaken labor. Thus, the reference here is to independent unions.

threatened by a surplus labor population, and more likely to lobby for welfare benefits.[35] In fact, the skilled industries (such as heavy industry and the white-collar professions) have historically been the recruiting grounds for labor organizations in LDCs. Not surprisingly, therefore, skilled-labor groups tend to comprise the bulk of welfare beneficiaries in LDCs.[36]

Given this logic, an increase in the number of skilled workers relative to low-skilled workers would help labor as a whole to overcome its collective-action problems and advance low-skilled workers' political interests, provided that the level of surplus labor is not too high. The higher the ratio of skilled to low-skilled labor and the lower the surplus in a country, the greater the likelihood that labor will form coalitions and be able to defend welfare spending.

In sum, globalization leads to lower social-welfare spending in labor-rich LDCs because low-skilled workers have limited political leverage. In LDCs, labor's political power and interests are the opposite of what existing political and economic theories predict. In most developed countries, however, labor groups have the institutional clout to ensure that they do not lose political power with globalization and can successfully demand compensation in the form of social-welfare spending.

The Evidence

To test the theory, I first provide comparative data on labor skills and labor surpluses in developed and developing countries. I then present a model of the globalization–welfare nexus in LDCs and conduct a more thorough empirical test of the theory using multivariate panel regressions.

Increased Global Supply of Goods Produced by Low-Skilled Workers

Globalization is generating greater competition among countries with similar factor endowments. In several empirical studies, Adrian Wood convincingly shows that nations with large numbers of low-skilled workers follow the principles of comparative advantage and place more emphasis on labor-intensive manufactured goods.[37] As Table 6.1 clearly shows, and in line with the Stolper-Samuelson theorem, labor-intensive exports have grown faster than other exports in countries known to have large pools of low-skilled workers. As I argued earlier, trade in goods and services and in capital flows has driven this growth.

---

35 See Mesa-Lago 1994 and 1991; Midgeley 1984; and Esping-Andersen 1996.

36 See Manning 1998; Shafer 1994; and Deyo 1989 and 1991.

37 Wood emphasizes the importance of this distinction between low-skilled and skilled labor. See Wood 1997, 1995, 1994; Wood and Berge 1997. He claims that trade is based on the availability of skills, not capital. Wood defines skilled workers as those with more than a basic general education, for example, professional and technical workers, managers, and craftsmen; Wood 1994, 6. Thus skilled workers are generally employed in high-skilled intensive manufacturing. Low-skilled labor refers to workers who have limited or no education (referring to both Wood's BAS-EDs and NO-EDs, respectively).

Table 6.1　　**The Growth and Share of Labor-intensive Manufacturing Exports**

	Growth 1992–96	Share of exports (1996)
Low income countries		
Primary products	12.7	60.1
Natural-intensive manufacturing	12.6	13.4
Labor-intensive manufacturing	18.9	14.6
Technology-intensive manufacturing	13.2	3.6
Human capital-intensive manufacturing	14.7	2.8
Low-middle-income countries		
Primary products	9.4	56.6
Natural-intensive manufacturing	7.6	4.6
Labor-intensive manufacturing	14.8	20.8
Technology-intensive manufacturing	21.2	11.3
Human capital-intensive manufacturing	11.6	6.0
High-middle-income countries		
Primary products	9.0	49.23
Natural-intensive manufacturing	18.8	7.23
Labor-intensive manufacturing	10.5	13.46
Technology-intensive manufacturing	13.3	15.54
Human capital-intensive manufacturing	9.8	12.00
High-income OECD countries		
Primary products	8.07	23.86
Natural-intensive manufacturing	10.21	4.79
Labor-intensive manufacturing	8.57	9.07
Technology-intensive manufacturing	12.14	35.47
Human capital-intensive manufacturing	9.50	23.43

Source: UN ITC InfoBase: National Trade Performances by Country 1999.

Yet whether the increasing number of low-skilled workers in LDCs relative to skilled workers implies positive political advantages for labor depends on the size of the surplus labor pool. Figure 6.4 shows that surplus labor in LDCs has indeed declined slightly over time, suggesting that labor power in LDCs may have improved. Yet it cannot be overlooked that by the mid-1990s, the average level of surplus labor in LDCs was as high as 19 percent of the working-age population, whereas in OECD countries it was only 6 percent. Moreover, since then surplus labor in LDCs has declined, on average, by only fifteen percentage points. In sharp contrast, surplus labor in the OECD countries Garrett sampled fell by almost 60 percent. A recent UN report confirmed that employment growth has failed to significantly reduce the vast amount of surplus labor that exists in LDCs.[38]

38　UN 1992–93.

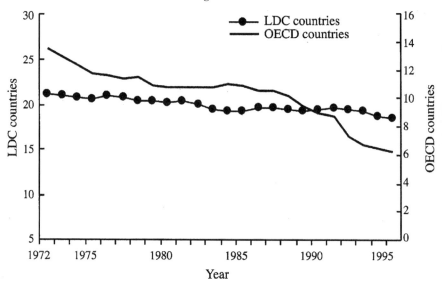

Figure 6.4   Surplus Labor in LDCs and Developed Countries from 1972 to 1995 (as % of Economically Active Population)

Sources: World Bank 1999, World Development Indicators; and USA. D. Global Education Database, 1999.

Note: Surplus labor is calculated as the (working age population minus students enrolled in secondary education minus students enrolled in 'post-secondary' education) minus (labor force/the working age population). I am grateful to Hayward Alker for helping me derive this measure.

Given that since the 1980s the number of low-skilled workers has been steadily increasing in LDCs and that the surplus labor population is still relatively high, the logic of Olson's theory suggests that labor will be unable to overcome its collective-action problems with globalization. An econometric test is needed to more precisely analyze labor's ability to mediate between the forces of globalization and pressures for welfare retrenchment.

Model Specification

I assess the LDC globalization–welfare nexus in two stages. First, I develop an LDC model to examine the influence of both domestic- and international-level variables on government welfare spending. To check the robustness of the findings, I reevaluate the globalization results for the globalization-labor variable using alternative indicators of government commitment to welfare. Second, I apply the model to Garrett's sample of OECD countries to assess whether or not the labor power variable drives the different outcomes in welfare spending in LDCs and developed countries.[39]

---

39 Garrett 1998.

The LDC Model

$$\text{WELF}_{it} = \beta_1 \text{WELF}_{it-1} + \beta_2 \text{TRADE}_{it-1} + \beta_3 \text{KFLOW}_{it-1} + \beta_4 \text{PLP}_{it}$$
$$+ \beta_5 \text{TRADE}_{it-1} * \text{PLP}_{it} + \beta_6 \text{KFLOW}_{it-1} * \text{PLP}_{it} + \Sigma(\beta_j X_{jit-1})$$
$$+ \Sigma(\beta_k \text{COUNTRY}_{ki}) + \Sigma(\beta_l \text{YEAR}_{lt}) \mu_{it} \tag{1}$$

where WELF is the government welfare-spending variable; TRADE and KFLOW, or capital flows, are the globalization variables; and Potential Labor Power (PLP) is the labor power variable. The β's are parameter estimates; β_1 is the coefficient of the lagged rate of welfare spending, incorporated to alleviate problems of serial correlation across error terms; i and t are the country and year of the observations, respectively; and μ is an error term. ΣX represents the vector of control variables. The globalization variables are lagged to account for the period of "adjustments".[40] Also, note that logarithms are taken of all the primary variables.[41] This type of relationship assumes the property of constant elasticities between the variables. (For a detailed description of all the variables, see Appendix A.)

Like Rodrik and Garrett, I use pooling cross-section and time-series data to estimate the model.[42] This procedure has two benefits. First, the use of the fixed-effects model allows me to control for unobservable country-specific differences, eliminating much of the omitted variable bias of cross-section data.[43] Second, I can assess important changes that have occurred in a country over time. The use of panel data (unbalanced) ultimately combines the benefits of an increased number of observations with the ability to eliminate country-specific fixed effects.

To disentangle the causal relationship between the globalization variables and PLP I rely on a two-stage least-squares estimate for the statistical analysis. Recall that globalization is likely to further enhance collective-action problems in LDCs by adding larger numbers of low-skilled workers to the workforce. The conventional method for coping with this endogeneity issue and mitigating bias of the regression estimates is to use the instrumental variable approach; however, the difficulty is to find outside data (or instruments) that are not correlated with the error of the equation yet highly correlated with the explanatory variables. Therefore, instead of using conventional variables as instruments in this model, I employ the Lewbel procedure of using higher moments of the labor power variable as the instrument.[44]

---

40 It is theoretically more sensible to anticipate a lagged effect because international market occurrences take time to affect policy outcomes. See, for example, Rodrik 1997b, who uses lagged measures of openness.

41 Because there is very little dispersion in the urbanization and democracy variables, these values have not been logged.

42 See Rodrik 1997b and 1998; and Garrett 1998.

43 The country-specific fixed effects most relevant to this model are culture and history. Informal systems of support for the elderly (such as extended families) are common methods of providing social security in many parts of Africa and Asia. See *World Bank Policy Research Report* 1994. Such variables are more significant in some countries than in others. Fixed effects allow us to control for the influence of such idiosyncratic differences between countries without our having to model them explicitly.

44 Lewbel 1997.

Embedding Global Markets

The Variables

Dependent variable: Social security and welfare. Most globalization studies have focused on total government spending, rather than welfare spending, as the dependent variable, but doing so can be misleading.[45] Central government spending (or, according to Rodrik, government consumption[46]) is a poor indicator of actual welfare outcomes or government commitment to welfare. Indeed, since total government spending includes a broad range of items – such as defense and nondefense spending, capital and current spending, industrial subsidies, and wages and salaries – it can no doubt increase without welfare's share going up. Rather than cushioning market dislocations, higher proportions of the government budget may be allocated toward funding more "competitive" ventures[47] or national security projects.[48] The estimated covariance between total government spending and spending on social security and welfare in LDCs is close to zero (at a mere – 0.00004; see Appendix B).

The more narrow variable used here more precisely captures welfare effort. The ratio of social spending to GDP is a direct indicator of the amount of national resources a country has committed to social welfare in relation to its total resources. Thus investigating government social security and welfare spending is one sure method of assessing government priorities in the era of globalization.

Nonetheless, one caveat might be that measuring welfare-state commitments in relation to GDP, while assuring compatibility across countries, could also be misleading. Rapid GDP growth could cause the indicator to shift downward. As a check against this possibility, welfare spending as a share of total government spending and social-welfare spending per capita are used as alternative dependent variables.[49]

Primary causal variables: The interaction of economic globalization and potential labor power in LDCs. I use both capital and trade flows to operationalize globalization in order to replicate the most sophisticated empirical works on globalization and welfare state expansionism,[50] as well as to incorporate the two primary international forces said to affect contemporary social policies.[51] Several

---

45 A few scholars take a brief look at social insurance and welfare spending as the variable to be explained. See, for example, Bernauer and Achini 2000; Rodrik 1997b; and Garrett 1998. However, most IPE scholars – including those just mentioned – use government spending as their central dependent variable.

46 Rodrik 1998.

47 Drunberg 1998 suggests that with globalization, public authorities in LDCs have greater incentives to help firms compete internationally by raising industrial subsidies.

48 Looney 1993.

49 For another example of a study that uses per capita social expenditures as a third dependent variable, see Kaufman and Segura-Ubiergo 2001.

50 See Garrett 1998; and Garrett and Mitchell 1996.

51 Rodrik argues that capital mobility and trade have differential effects on social policies. See Rodrik 1997b and 1998.

empirical studies have declared LDCs as *de facto* open in capital and trade markets.[52] I incorporate the conventional measure of openness, exports plus imports relative to GDP, in this LDC model. I measure capital mobility in LDCs using capital inflows plus outflows, in contrast to Garrett and Rodrik's use of capital controls to measure capital mobility in OECD countries. Gross flows are an exogenously-determined measure of capital mobility, whereas capital controls are not, and annual data are available.[53]

At the heart of my theory is the idea that the effect of globalization on welfare spending depends on labor's influence in the political economy in LDCs. The most common indicator of this is unionization rates.[54] However, a fundamental problem with this indicator is that, unlike the situation in developed countries, union density (percentage of the working population who are unionized) is not comparable across LDCs. Many LDC governments mandate compulsory membership in corporatist unions and impose constraints on labor's demand making, leadership, and internal governance.[55] China, for example, has the highest union density in the developing world, yet labor has very little bargaining power.[56] In general, unionization rates exaggerate labor's independent political strength in LDCs.[57] Moreover, there are no standardized cross-country time-series measures for many LDCs. PLP, an indirect measure of labor power, captures the dynamic nature of labor's influence and is comparable across LDCs. Assuming there is always some surplus labor and some low-skilled labor, PLP is measured here by the following ratio:

$$PLP = \left(\frac{\text{Number of skilled workers}}{\text{Number of low-skilled workers}} \right)$$

$$\times \left(\frac{1}{\text{Surplus labor as \% of working-age population}} \right)$$

PLP decreases as the number of low-skilled workers increases relative to skilled workers, and as surplus labor expands. To the extent that the surplus labor pool shrinks and labor markets become tighter, PLP increasingly depends on the ratio of skilled to low-skilled workers.

This assessment of PLP is limited to the manufacturing sector, since data are not available for most countries outside this sector. Significantly, however, research has shown that most labor-organizing activities occur in this sector. Figure 6.5 gives

---

52 See Montiel 1994; Amirahmadi and Wu 1993; Dean 1995; and Mamingi 1997.

53 For a discussion on gross capital flows as one of the four different ways of measuring capital mobility, and their pros and cons, see Montiel 1994; and Agenor and Montiel 1996. For other economists implementing this proxy of capital flows, see Taylor and Sarno 1997; and Chuhan, Claessens, and Mamingi 1993.

54 See Devarajan *et al.* 1997; Galenson 1962.

55 Collier and Collier 1991.

56 Chan and Senser 1997.

57 See, for example, Valenzuela 1989, 449; and Banuri and Amadeo 1991, 175. McGuire 1997 adds that unreliability of union data can result in huge discrepancies in existing cross-country compilations of union-density estimates.

	High	Low
	Skilled labor/low-skilled labor	Skilled labor/low-skilled labor
High Surplus labor	(+) Moderate PLP (Chile, Venezuela, Egypt)	(−) Low PLP (Guatemala, Pakistan, Honduras)
Low Surplus labor	(+) High PLP (Singapore, Korea, Turkey)	(+) Moderate PLP (Uruguay, Indonesia)

Figure 6.5   Labor Power in LDCs

Note: These are averaged low and high PLP values, ranked according to the 25th and 75th percentiles, respectively. Signs in parentheses represent the expected direction of the relationship of potential labor power to welfare.

examples of how countries are ranked on the two components of PLP. Table 6.2 shows PLP values in countries selected from the larger sample. Country scores above and below the mean represent "high" and "low" values for skill levels and surplus labor.

The advantage of using this proxy is that it can capture variations in labor strength irrespective of the type of state–labor relations. It abstracts from the historical complexities behind the political relationship between LDC governments and labor, a relationship that ranges widely from state control of labor or corporatism (such as in Brazil, Mexico, Egypt, Ghana, and Tanzania), state repression of labor (such as in Korea, Zambia, Taiwan, and Singapore), to relative autonomy of labor (such as in India and Nigeria[58]). PLP thus provides an indication of labor's underlying capacity to form alliances and influence government fiscal decisions in both state corporatist and noncorporatist systems. Appendix C shows that PLP aligns well with other qualitative rankings of labor power that have been applied to a few select LDCs.

It is also important that the labor power indicator can capture changes over time. For example, a close look at the data shows that PLP in South Korea has moved successfully from the low PLP quadrant to the high PLP quadrant in Figure 6.5. This indicator should nevertheless be applied with caution. Significant externalities (such as highly repressive regimes) may undermine labor's actual political strength. Singapore is a good case in point.

The primary explanatory variables are the interactive effects of globalization and labor power. These interactive variables, by design, replicate Garrett's model of the relationship between globalization and spending in the developed economies.[59] Both trade and capital mobility are combined with PLP in order to assess labor's ability to moderate the relationship between globalization and welfare spending in LDCs.

---

58 This refers mainly to the relatively independent and effective labor movement in Nigeria during the 1970s and early 1980s, headed by the Nigeria Labour Congress (NLC). For details, see Van Hear 1988.

59 Garrett 1998.

Table 6.2   Country Skill Ratios and Percentages of Surplus Labor

Country	Skilled labor/ low-skilled labor		Surplus labor		Total PLP
	High	Low	High	Low	
Singapore	1.0			0.17	6
Korea	0.59			0.14	4
Turkey	0.42			0.15	2.8
Venezuela	0.36		0.28		1.3
Chile	0.36		0.31		1.2
Egypt	0.35		0.25		1.4
Uruguay		0.28		0.19	1.5
Indonesia		0.24		0.19	1.3
Pakistan		0.29	0.28		1.0
Guatemala		0.28	0.30		0.9
Honduras		0.11	0.26		0.4

Notes: The mean value for skilled labor/low-skilled labor is 0.30. The mean value for percentage of surplus labor is 0.20.

If the interactive effects are negative, then it can be determined that the combined effects of weak labor and of increased exposure to higher levels of trade and capital flows result in lower government welfare commitments.

Control variables.   Several control variables will help isolate this main relationship and check for other influences on welfare spending. Given that most nations in this sample are considerably underdeveloped, supplementary political and economic variables are included in order to tailor the model to the LDC cases.[60] LDC welfare spending is expected to increase with the number of young and elderly dependents,[61] the level of urbanization,[62] both GDP per capita and growth,[63] low debt, lower levels of privatization,[64] and democracy,[65] which are the control variables used in this analysis. Unemployment figures, frequently linked to higher welfare spending in

---

60 Statistical tests determined that significant multicolinearity did not exist between the control variables.

61 See World Bank Policy Research Report 1994; Esping-Andersen 1990; Tang 1996; and Schmidt 1995.

62 Tang 1996.

63 See Brown and Hunter 1999; Usui 1994, Rodrik 1996; and Tang 1996.

64 Privatization can potentially affect state budgets in multiple ways. However, for the purposes of clarity and the goals of this article, the focus will be on the revenue effects (either positive or negative) of privatizing state-owned enterprises (SOE).

65 Brown and Hunter 1999; Eichengreen 1996; and Hicks and Swank 1992.

developed countries, are excluded because of the unreliability of such figures in underdeveloped nations.[66]

All of the control variables are lagged to ensure that the direction of causality occurs from the exogenous variables to the dependent variable.

The Results

Equation (1) was estimated for fifty-three LDCs, from the years 1972 through 1995, using the fixed-effects procedure. To summarize the results, LDC welfare spending was quite sensitive to variations in international-level variables. Most significantly, interaction effects of PLP and globalization were highly significant and negative in a model specific to LDCs. When all relevant domestic variables were controlled for, globalization combined with weak labor power has clearly had an adverse effect on welfare spending in LDCs. Conversely, the interactive globalization/PLP variable had a positive impact on spending when applied to Garrett's sample of OECD countries.

The LDC globalization/welfare model.   Table 6.3 reports the results conditioned on both international and domestic effects. I conducted numerous tests to confirm the stability of the results.[67] To check for robustness, I reestimate Model (1) using different dependent variables: welfare as a percentage of total government spending and per capita welfare spending, Models (2) and (3) respectively. After testing the baseline regressions containing all of the predictors under consideration, I reestimated the models by dropping one insignificant variable at a time.[68] If the fit statistics improved and the null restriction could not be rejected using the *F* test, I permanently dropped the predictor from the model.[69] I placed the greatest weight on the models reported below because they had the best fit overall, and the results are likely to be less biased. The *F* test (not shown here) confirmed that the final model was better than the full model.

All the measures except capital and trade flows had the anticipated signs. According to Model (1), uninteracted effects of capital flows tend to increase welfare spending, supporting the arguments of recent proponents of globalization

---

66 Agenor and Montiel 1996.

67 These results are robust to several different estimation techniques. First, results running the regressions with and without missing data, based on the multiple interpolation technique in King *et al.* 2001, had minimal effect on the key variables. Varying the lag structure also had little impact on the results.

68 The privatization variable could not be included in the full model because this data was severely limited. Regressions including this variable were run separately using five-year averages. The coeffucient for privatization did not come out as significant.

69 More specifically, in addition to comparing adjusted *R* squares, smaller values of Akaike's Information Criterion (AIC) and of Bayesian Information Criterion (BIC) indicate better fits of the covariance structure. In addition, we can test whether the reduced parameters significantly improve the model using the *F* test. See, for example, Intriligator, Bodkin, and Hsiao 1996, 107.

Table 6.3   Fixed-effects Regression Estimates: The Relationship between Globalization and Welfare Spending in LDCs

Independent variable	Model 1	Model 2	Model 3
	Dependent variable: welfare as % of GDP	Dependent variable: welfare as % of total gov. spending	Dependent variable: per capita welfare expenditures
Lagged dependent variable	0.649***	0.805***	0.704***
	(0.065)	(0.049)	(0.063)
TRADE * PLP (*interactive variable*)	–0.163*	–0.159*	–0.160*
	(0.099)	(0.097)	(0.098)
KFLOW * PLP (*interactive variable*)	–0.053*	–0.040**	–0.051**
	(0.032)	(0.019)	(0.026)
Potential labor power (PLP)	1.31**	1.28**	1.16**
	(0.509)	(0.570)	(0.571)
KFLOW	0.274*		
	(0.157)		
TRADE	0.787		0.150**
	(0.484)		(0.067)
DEMOC	0.023**	0.039	0.017**
	(0.011)	(0.031)	(0.008)
Urbanization	–0.005	0.001	0.007
	(0.006)	(0.004)	(0.005)
Growth	0.489		1.76
	(0.820)		(1.08)
GDP per capita			0.0004***
			(0.0008)
N	794	820	768
AIC (smaller is better)	*1.14*	*1.75*	*0.956*
BIC (smaller is better)	*–3992*	*–3675*	*–3973*
Adjusted R^2	*.930*	*.897*	*.973*

Notes: Standard errors, corrected for general forms of heteroskedasticity, are in parentheses. Estimates in italics represent the fit statistics.
***$p < .01$.
**$p < .05$.
*$p < .10$.

who challenge the conventional wisdom that international market exposure leads to higher social spending.[70] Similarly, increasing trade openness had a positive effect on welfare spending per capita. However, the direct effect of potential labor power (when trade and capital flows are zero) was associated with higher levels of welfare in all three models, strongly supporting power resource theories and indicating that some proxy of labor institutions should be taken into account. These results call into question studies that altogether exclude political institutional variables in their investigations of the domestic effects of international market integration.[71]

Most relevant to the purposes of this analysis is that social spending responds negatively to the combined effects of globalization and PLP. Table 6.3 reveals that although potential labor power has had a positive and independent effect on welfare spending, it has been ineffective in doing so when combined with international market pressures. The negative coefficients of the globalization interactive terms confirm that LDC welfare spending is indeed a function of high levels of exposure to global market activity and relatively weak labor power. These results cast doubt on previous analyses of LDC welfare spending that have focused on domestic variables and downplayed the importance of international-level variables in their analyses.[72]

The pattern of coefficients for the globalization/labor power interactive variables was consistent across the three models, suggesting that these findings are quite robust. Once the appropriate control variables are used, the trade/labor power and capital flows/labor power interactions are negative and significant at the 90 percent level and above.

The effect of labor power on welfare spending decreases as exposure to international markets increases; the best way to understand this at various levels of globalization is to refer back to Equation (1). Using Model (1) as an example, the estimated equation has the form

$$
\begin{aligned}
\text{WELF} = {}&0.649\text{WELF}(\textit{lagged}) \\
&+ 1.31\text{PLP} - 0.163\text{TRADE}_{it-1} * \text{PLP} - 0.053\text{KFLOW}_{it-1} * \text{PLP} \\
&+ 0.274\text{KFLOW} + 0.023\text{DEMOC}
\end{aligned} \tag{2}
$$

The effect of PLP on welfare, $\partial\text{WELF}/\partial\text{PLP} = \beta_4 + \beta_5\,\text{TRADE}_{it-1} + \beta_6\,\text{KFLOW}_{it-1}$, depends on the levels of trade and capital flows.

$$
\partial\text{WELF}/\partial\text{PLP} = 1.31 - 0.163\,\text{TRADE}_{it-1} - 0.053\,\text{KFLOW}_{it-1} \tag{3}
$$

We can see the declining impact of labor power if we segregate the data into three sets, having low, medium, and high values of globalization, and then compute the

---

70 Since the model includes interactive effects, the more precise interpretation is that the effect of capital flows is positive when labor power is zero.

71 See Rodrik 1997a and 1998; and Cameron 1978.

72 See, for example, Schmidt 1995; Tang 1996; Midgley 1984; Wahl 1994; and Atkinson and Hills 1991.

effect of PLP on welfare for each set.[73] See Table 6.4 for estimates of the effects of PLP on welfare spending at different levels of globalization (based on Equation [3]).

Thus the effects of potential labor power on welfare depend on the level of globalization and exhibit diminishing returns. A 1 percent increase in labor power at low levels of openness leads to a 1.3 percent increase in welfare spending. Its impact on spending falls to 1.2 percent at median levels of globalization and even lower, to 1.1 percent, at high levels. The data thus supports the existence of a relationship between globalization, potential labor power, and welfare spending.

The findings regarding the impact of the labor power and democracy variables reveal the importance of domestic political variables, while controlling for international effects. Results on democracy were robust and had a positive, independent effect on welfare in both Models (1) and (3). This study is consistent with many analyses arguing that the more democratic a nation is, the more responsive the government will be to social well-being.[74] It is certainly more likely that institutions (autonomous unions, for example) will arise to solve the collective-action problems of labor in democratic LDCs than in authoritarian ones.

The F test revealed that year effects were significant in two out of the three models of welfare spending – Models (1) and (3). This suggests that, overall, global shocks and recessions have some effect on social spending in nations that spend a relatively small percentage of their GDP on welfare. The mixed results on GDP per capita and growth were, at first, surprising. Based on existing literature, it was expected that these variables would be positive and robust across dependent variables. However, on closer inspection of the data, many of the wealthier countries, such as Singapore and Korea, exhibit some of the lowest levels of spending in the sample. Coefficients on several of the remaining control variables (urbanization, age dependency, debt, and privatization variables) were also insignificant.[75]

Table 6.4   Elasticity of Welfare Spending with Respect to Labor Power

Globalization	Level of trade (as % of GDP)	Level of capital flows (as % of GDP)	Elasticity of PLP on welfare spending
Low	14%	1%	1.3%
Medium	68%	11%	1.2%
High	122%	21%	1.1%

73 The classification of "high" and "low" is based on LDC trade and capital flow values one standard deviation above and below the mean, respectively. The medium value is represented by the mean.

74 See Lake and Baum forthcoming; Brown and Hunter 1999; Atkinson and Hills 1991; and Hicks and Swank 1992.

75 It was rather surprising that the debt variable was not significant. See, for example, Brown and Hunter 1999. Also note that data on debt and age dependency was sparse and involved some interpolation. Thus the coefficients of these variables must be interpreted with caution. The insignificant coefficient on urbanization also seems counterintuitive and

Finally, the *F* test allows us to reject the null hypothesis that country differences are not important. This suggests that country-specific differences persist over time.[76] Yet it is rather telling that even though historical differences account for much of the variations in welfare expenditures, the globalization and labor variables still maintain high statistical significance. Additionally, jack-knife diagnostics reveal that the results were not sensitive to outliers.[77] The remaining impacts of globalization and labor power can, therefore, be regarded with confidence.

To summarize, the data on LDCs support the conventional wisdom and refute the revisionist perspective. The combined effects of globalization and weaker labor power in LDCs dampen welfare spending. As predicted, their product terms are negative and significant in developing economies. The positive and significant coefficient of democracy in models 1 and 3 adds evidence that regime type is another important political determinant of welfare spending in LDCs.

The comparison between LDCs and OECD countries. Estimating a globalization-welfare model for OECD countries emphasizes the importance of differences in overall labor strength. Findings in this section confirm that workers in the more developed countries, unlike their counterparts in the developing world, are strong enough politically to encourage welfare-state expansionism alongside globalization. This contrast between the two sets of countries is observed by adopting Garrett's[78] globalization-welfare model for OECD nations and substituting the PLP variable for his labor variable, and then comparing the results with the LDCs. These final regressions have two important implications. First, since the results using the PLP variable in OECD countries are similar to Garrett's results using his indicator of left-labor power (LLP) in the developed countries, these regressions considerably increase our confidence in the reliability of the PLP variable.[79] Second, a positive coefficient for the globalization-labor interactive variables confirms the disparity in bargaining power held by labor in the two sets of countries. These findings confirm that the contrasting effects of globalization on welfare states in developed and developing countries are rooted in overall differences in labor power.

It is expected that the interactive globalization-PLP variable will be positive in developed countries because richer nations not only face relatively less severe collective-action problems but also have institutions in place to help surmount them.[80] Surplus labor problems are simply not as acute in the more developed countries. Labor markets in these countries tend to be much tighter. In addition, the proportion

---

stands contrary to the positive and significant effects found by Tang 1996. Results from this model suggest that in the event of rapid urbanization, other political and economic variables outweigh its effect on government welfare spending.

76 Refer to footnote 43.

77 This method involves reestimating the regression fifty-three times, leaving out one of the countries each time.

78 Garrett 1998.

79 See Campbell's (1988) tests for evaluating the validity of variables measuring a concept.

80 Garrett 1998, 8–9.

of low-skilled workers in OECD countries has been steadily declining (see Figure 6.4), suggesting that in these countries labor can more easily overcome its collective-action problems. Finally, these are countries with long-standing liberal democratic traditions. Other welfare beneficiaries (such as the elderly and the disabled) can also form strong interest groups and make it increasingly difficult for the government to roll back welfare spending.

Table 6.5 reports Garrett's findings on the determinants of OECD income transfers alongside the new estimations substituting the PLP variable for his measure of LLP.[81] The globalization variables are not necessarily lagged in Garrett's model because his more direct measure of labor power does not call for a time lapse between globalization and changes in LLP. It is reasonable to assume that the effects of the LLP-globalization interaction variables on welfare can occur within the same year. Additional control variables used in Garrett's analysis are GDP growth, proportion of the population over sixty-five years old (ELDERLY), and unemployment.[82]

This final set of regressions appreciably strengthens the conclusions I present here. Contrary to the findings for LDCs, the product terms of globalization and PLP tend to be positive in nations exporting relatively more skill-intensive goods.[83] As predicted, workers in OECD countries do not face the same collective-action problems as those in developing countries. Comparing results from the LDCs suggests that developed countries have stronger institutions and the appropriate political apparatus to protect their citizens from the adverse effects of globalization. In addition, in agreement with Pierson, the significance of the elderly population and unemployment variables indicates that labor is only one of several welfare beneficiaries that can successfully resist government penchants for welfare-state retrenchment.[84]

These findings also more fully expose the explanatory power of the determining variable, that is, PLP. Expectations about the appropriateness of applying this new measure of labor strength to assess changes in government welfare expenditures in this era of globalization have been confirmed. The results are consistent with Garrett's fully specified model, which demonstrates the positive effects of globalization in countries that do not enjoy a comparative advantage in labor. Thus the statistical evidence presented here supports the theory that the political-structural differences between rich and poor countries drive different domestic outcomes in the contemporary era of globalization.

Significantly, year effects mattered for welfare expenditures in OECDs, just as they did in LDCs. This challenges the credibility of the conjecture that the more a nation spends on welfare as a percentage of GDP, the more susceptible its social

---

81 Garrett captures labor power in the developed world by constructing a composite measure for the political power of the left and the strength of national labor market institutions (labor encompassment) . Note that Garrett's results for income transfers are reported, instead of his primary dependent variable, government spending. Government income transfers is a better match for social security and welfare spending used in this analysis.

82 Interestingly, GDP growth was not significant in any of the LDC models.

83 Both the globalization variables (trade*left-labor power and capital mobility*left-labor power) were positive and significant in Garrett's central model of total government spending.

84 Pierson 1996.

Table 6.5   The Effects of Globalization on Welfare Spending in OECD Countries

	Dependent variable: Social security and welfare	
Independent variable	Results using left-labor index[a]	Results using PLP
Lagged dependent variable	0.86***	0.599***
	(0.03)	(0.04)
TRADE * LLP	0.007	
	(0.0019)	
TRADE * PLP (interactive variable)		−0.036
		(0.072)
KFLOW * LLP	0.066**	
	(0.027)	
KFLOW * PLP (interactive variable)		0.232**
		(0.115)
KFLOW	−0.19	0.002
	(0.15)	(0.013)
TRADE	−0.0084	−0.132***
	(0.0123)	(0.037)
GDP growth	−0.168**	0.014**
	(0.014)	(0.007)
PLP/left-labor power	0.068	1.03**
	(0.093)	(0.476)
Elderly population	0.134***	0.427***
	(0.052)	(0.112)
Unemployment	0.068***	0.067***
	(0.019)	(0.016)
Adjusted R^2	.986	.981
N	350	322

Note: Fixed-effects regression estimates. Figures in parentheses are standard errors.
[a]The left-labor index is Garrett's measure of left-labor power (LLP) in OECD countries. Garrett, 1998.
***$p < .01$.
**$p < .05$.
*$p < .10$.

programs will be to global economic shocks. Developed countries spend a high average of 15 percent of their GDP on welfare expenditures – almost five times the average spent in LDCs.

One rival explanation of my findings might be that the need for social-welfare expenditures in LDCs is declining with international market exposure. It might be thought that globalization is improving employment and incomes, and thus there should be less demand for government welfare protection. Yet it is fairly well-established in the literature that high levels of inequality and social deprivation continue to persist in most of these countries.[85] Besides, it would be difficult to conclude that welfare-state expansionism in developed countries means that citizens of these countries are in greater need of social protection than the citizens of LDCs.

Implications

Does the conventional wisdom that globalization adversely affects welfare spending hold true in LDCs? This investigation of fifty-three LDCs from 1972 to 1995 shows that welfare spending in these countries does indeed respond to greater trade flows and capital mobility. These findings challenge others who do not show that globalization affects welfare spending in developed and developing nations differently. Growing numbers of low-skilled workers relative to skilled workers, coupled with large surplus-labor populations, exacerbate the collective-action problems of labor in LDCs and make it increasingly difficult for them to organize. When confronted with the pressures of globalization, workers in LDCs are less capable of defending their welfare benefits than workers in OECD countries, where the organizing potential of labor is relatively strong and existing institutions can help workers overcome their collective-action problems. Thus, the findings suggest that the difference in welfare-state outcomes is due to a wide disparity in the bargaining power of labor in developed and developing countries. Workers' potential political gains from expanded trade and investment are ultimately outweighed in LDCs by their inability to collectively pressure the government for social programs in their favor.

In an era when many analysts are prodding LDCs to follow the path of newly industrialized countries, the findings here suggest an important cautionary note. Much of a country's successful development depends on a nation's ability to utilize its labor capacity, upgrade the skills of its workforce, and foster the development of strong political institutions. Currently, industrializing LDCs that maintain large surplus labor forces, are less democratic, and have an abundance of low-skilled workers may be reluctant to move up the technological ladder. Unless measures are taken to address these factors, it is possible that, given the competitive conditions of today's world economy, political and social development for these cheap-labor countries will proceed relatively slowly.

Yet it is not too soon to apply to the developing world optimistic visions that "in the global economy ... citizens still have a real choice to make about how to govern the market."[86] Interestingly, my analysis shows that there are political factors (such as strong labor power and democracy) that can positively affect welfare spending in this era of globalization. By recognizing that politics and institutions do matter, I have shown that welfare-state retrenchment is a consequence of the failure of politics to intervene in the economy. Minimizing the trade-off between thriving capitalism and social welfare in developing economies can be accomplished through greater political and institutional development. Labor's political influence ultimately depends

---

85 See, for example, Aghion and Williamson 1998; Quinn 1997; and Wood 1997.
86 Garrett 1998.

on workers' ability to organize and capacity to affect electoral outcomes. Thus an important challenge facing LDCs today is to reconcile international competitiveness with a democratic environment that allows autonomous labor market institutions to flourish.

This chapter represents the first attempt to explain both the political and international economic constraints on social spending in developing countries. A next step would be to investigate how other facets of social spending (health, education, and housing, for instance) might be reacting to globalization. Will spending on social ventures that contribute more directly to competitiveness increase with globalization? What are the various types of domestic political institutions that can successfully protect citizens of LDCs from the volatility of international markets? There are substantial payoffs both for identifying the most suitable social programs for developing countries in this era of globalization and for understanding the political environment in which they will prosper.

Appendix A: Data Sources, Measurements, and Definitions

Table 6.A1   Data Sources and Definitions

Concepts[a]	Measurements	Definition
Government welfare expenditures [WELF]	Social security and welfare as a percentage of GDP (dependent variable) Social security and welfare as a percentage of total government spending (second dependent variable) Special welfare expenditures per capita	"Social security" consists of income transfers and providing benefits in cash or in kind for old age, invalidity, or death, and for survivors , sickness and maternity, work injury, unemployment, family allowance, and health care. "Welfare affairs and services" is defined as assistance delivered to clients or groups of clients with special needs, such as the young, the old, or the disabled.
Globalization [TRADE] (–) [KFLOW] (–) Potential labor power [PLP] (–)	Amount of total trade (exports + imports/GDP); and gross capital flows as a percentage of GDP (Ratio of the numbers employed in skill-intensive manufacturing industries	Gross capital flows is the sum of all inflows and outflows, using the finest classifications to avoid netting "Low-skilled" refers to those who have no more than

Table 6.A1 continued

Concepts[a]	Measurements	Definition
	relative to numbers employed in low-skill manufacturing industries)* (1 divided by the number of surplus laborers in the economy)	primary or secondary education and are likely to be employed in labor-intensive manufacturing industries. "Skilled" refers to those with more than a basic general education and usually employed in heavy and high-skill manufacturing industries. "Surplus labor" is the total working-age population (between 15 and 65 years of age) minus the total labor force minus students enrolled in secondary and post-secondary education. This total is taken as a percentage of the economically active population.
Demographic variables [DEPEN] (+) [URBAN] (+)	Age-dependency ratio; urban population as a percentage of total population	"Age dependency ratio" is the number of persons over 60 years old divided by number of persons aged 20 to 59. "Urbanization" is the midyear population of areas defined as urban in each country and is measured as the percentage of the total population.
Economic development [GDP] (+) [SOE] (+) [DEBT] (−)	GDP per capita [GDP]; revenue of state-owned enterprises [SOE]; total debt service [DEBT].	"GDP" is the total GDP of a country divided by population, measured in 1995 constant U.S. dollars. "SOE" economic activity is the value added of state enterprises, estimated as their sales revenue minus the cost of their

Table 6.A1 continues overleaf

Table 6.A1 continued

Concepts[a]	Measurements	Definition
		intermediate inputs. Total "debt" service is the sum of principal repayments and interest paid in foreign currency, goods, or services on long-term debt and interest payments only on short-term debt.
Political development [DEMOC] (+)	Indicator of democracy	Using scale of 0 to 10, with 10 representing strong democracy; indicator is derived from the codings of the competitiveness of political participation, the openness and com-petitiveness of executive recruitment, and constraints on the chief executive.

[a]The expected direction of the relationship (either positive or negative) is shown in parentheses.

Data Sources for Variables

DEMOC: Jaggers and Gurr 1994.

KFLOW: IMF, Balance of Payments Statistics, various years. These include direct investment abroad, direct investment in country, portfolio investment and other investments (including trade credits, loans, currency, and deposits). Early editions (early 1970s) include some counting of nonproduced, nonfinancial assets in estimations of the financial account.

SKILL: Classification scheme developed by Wood and Mayer 1998. Their export product classifications are based on the Standard International Trade Classification (SITC, rev. 2). The following list shows which International Standard Industrial Classification (ISIC) codes correspond to the SITC codes (also supplied by Wood and Mayer 1998). The employment statistics for each manufacturing sector came from *UNIDO Database of Industrial Statistics*. The final value of SKILL is based on the total number of workers employed in high-skilled manufacturing production/ low-skilled manufacturing production.

SURP, DEPEN, GDP, SOE, DEBT: World Bank, *World Development Indicators*, various years.

TRADE: World Bank, *World Development Indicators*, various years.

WELF: IMF, *Government Finance Statistics* and *International Finance Statistics*, various years.

Table 6.A2   Manufactured Exports

	SITC2 categories	Translated to manufactured production	ISIC1 categories
Low-skill manufactures		*Low-skill manufacturing production*	
1. Leather and rubber products	61–62	1. Leather and rubber products	323, 355
2. Wood and paper products	63–64	2. Wood products, except furniture; paper and paper products	331, 341
3. Textiles, clothing, footwear, and travel goods	65, 83–85	3. Textiles; leather products; wearing apparel, except footwear; footwear, except rubber or plastic	321, 323, 322, 324
4. Nonmetallic mineral products	(66 less 667)	4. Other nonmetallic mineral products; glass and products; pottery, china, and earthenware	369, 362, 361
5. Iron and steel and metal products	67, 69	5. Iron and steel; fabricated metal products	371, 381
6. Furniture and plumbing equipment	81–82	6. Furniture, except metal	332
7. Ships, bicycles, and trains	78 (less 781–784), 79 (less 792)	—	
8. Miscellaneous	89, 9 (less 941, 971)	8. Plastic products; other manufactured products	356, 390
High-skill manufactures		*High-skill manufacturing production*	
9. Chemicals	5 (less 522.24, 522.56, 524)	9. Industrial chemicals; other chemicals; misc. petroleum and coal products; plastic products	351, 352, 354, 356
10. Cut diamonds	667.29	—	

Table 6.A2 continues overleaf

Table 6.A2 continued

	SITC2 categories	Translated to manufactured production	ISIC1 categories
11. Nonelectrical machinery	71–74	11. Fabricated metal products; machinery, except electrical; machinery, electrical	382, 383, 384
12. Computers and office equipment	75		
13. Communication equipment	76		
14. Electrical machinery	77		
15. Motor vehicles and aircraft	781–784, 792	—	
16. Scientific instruments, watches, and cameras	87, 88	—	

Note: The SITC 5–8 categories allocated to primary rather than manufactured exports are phosphorus pentoxide and phosphoric acids (522.24); aluminum hydroxide (522.56); radioactive material (524); pearls and precious stones, except cut diamonds (667 except 667.29); and nonferrous metals (68).

Appendix B

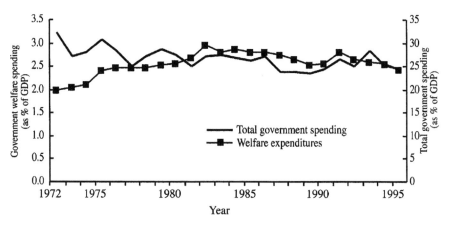

Figure 6.B1   The Difference between Total Government Spending and Welfare Spending

Sources: IMF, *International Finance Statistics* and *Government Finance Statistics*, various years.

Appendix C: Comparisons of PLP with Other Indicators

Few efforts have been made to measure and compare labor power across countries. Union density is most commonly used in cross-national comparisons of labor power, sometimes also in combination with measures of union centralization and unity. As noted earlier, union density is more appropriately applied in the developed world than in LDCs. The normal factors granting unions bargaining power in the developed economies (such as tight labor markets, stable economic growth, freedom from government control, organizational density and strength, and financial resources) are conspicuously absent in the developing world.

It is of no surprise, therefore, that the correlation between PLP and union-density levels is very low (0.04).[87] Most LDCs are still far from attaining strong and independent unions such as those that commonly exist in the developed world. Collective-action problems continue to exist in countries with high union density where labor is rife with internal divisions and still subject to many governmental controls.[88] In contrast, as skill levels increase and surplus labor is slowly absorbed, the labor movement may organize underground and reach beyond state-controlled unions to ally with other members of the working class (as has occurred in Brazil and Korea).[89]

Comparing PLP indicators to other qualitative assessments of labor power is a more precise method for assessing the usefulness of this new indicator. Most of this literature is dominated by historical-interpretative approaches to assess labor strength. Table 6.C1 lists a few rare studies that, to my knowledge, have attempted to assess the magnitude of labor power and compare it with other countries, albeit mostly in the same region – Latin America. These comparative analyses of labor use multiple indicators of labor's strength, such as the extent of state control over labor, party affiliation, and level of decentralization.

The rankings in Table 6.C1 should be interpreted with some caution. The primary problem with comparing these qualitative indicators to PLP is that the indicators are static measures of labor strength. In addition, note that in Collier and Collier's and Valenzuela's studies, the rankings were not indexed and, thus, are subject to some interpretation by the authors. The PLP indicator was ranked high, medium, or low according to the 75th, 50th, and 25th percentiles, respectively.

Table 6.C1 serves to increase confidence in the reliability of PLP as a measure of labor power. None of the qualitative rankings differ by more than one grade from the PLP rankings. The Philippine case shows the most contrast, but even Valenzuela acknowledges the complexity of classifying the Philippine labor movement because of labor's links to a broader social base.[90]

---

87 Note that these correlations are based on very few observations. Union-density data exists only for 1985 and 1995, and even then a large number of data points are missing. Correlations with McGuire's (1999) Labor Strength Index (based only on 1995 union data) are also low for the same reasons.

88 See Drake 1996; and Banuri and Amadeo 1991.

89 See, for example, Fields 1994; Drake 1996; and Kim 1997.

90 Valenzuela 1989, 455.

Table 6.C1   Comparative Assessments of Labor Strength

Country	PLP	Collier and Collier (1979)*	Valenzuela (1989)*	Cook (1998)
Argentina				
1970s	High	Strong	Strong	
1980s	High		Strong	
1990–95	High			
Overall	High			Strong
Brazil				
1970s	Medium	Moderate-weak	Weak	
1980s	Medium		Weak	
1990–95	High			
Overall	Medium			Medium
Chile				
1970s	Medium	Moderate-strong		
1980s	Low			
1990–95	Medium			
Overall	Medium			Low
Colombia				
1970s	Low			
1980s	Medium			
1990–95	High			
Overall	Medium			Low
Dominican Republic				
1970s	Low		Weak	
1980s	Medium		Weak	
1990–95				
Overall	Medium			
Ecuador				
1970s	Low		Weak	
1980s	Medium		Weak	
1990–95	Medium			
Overall	Medium			
Mexico				
1970s	Medium	Moderate-strong		
1980s	High			
1990–95	High			
Overall	High			Medium
Philippines				
1970s	High		Weak	
1980s	Medium		Weak	
1990–95	High			
Overall	Medium			
Venezuela				
1970s	Medium			
1980s	Medium			
1990–95	Medium			
Overall	Medium			Medium

Note: Neither Collier and Collier nor Valenzuela specify the exact years for their labor-strength ratings. Cook's more recent analysis does not mention dates of coverage.

Ultimately, using labor power in empirical analyses demands accurate measurement. The indicator proposed in this study, PLP, offers three advantages of a new variable: (1) it corresponds to conditions specific to labor in developing countries, (2) it is comparable across LDCs, and (3) it has a temporal component. The first advantage privileges PLP as an indicator of labor strength because it has its origins in the political and economic situation of labor in LDCs. The desirability of the second two characteristics is more obvious. A standardized measure available over time and across countries greatly reduces the biases that can affect empirical analyses.

References

Agenor, Pierre Richard, and Peter J. Montiel. 1996. *Development Macroeconomics*. Princeton, N.J.: Princeton University Press.

Aghion, Philippe, and Jeffrey G. Williamson. 1998. *Growth, Inequality, and Globalization*. New York: Cambridge University Press.

Ahmad, Ehtisham, and Athar Hussain. 1991. Social Security in China. In *Social Security in Developing Countries*, edited by Ehtisham Ahmad and Athar Hussain, 247–304. Oxford: Clarendon Press.

Amirahmadi, Hooshang, and Weiping Wu. 1993. Private Capital Flows and Developing Countries. *Journal of Third World Studies* 10 (1):327–57.

Atkinson, A. B., and John Hills. 1991. Social Security in Developed Countries: Are There Lessons For Developing Countries? In *Social Security in Developing Countries*, edited by Ehtisham Ahmad and Athar Hussain, 81–111. Oxford: Clarendon Press.

Banuri, Tariq, and Edward Amadeo. 1991. Worlds Within the Third World: Labour Market Institutions in Asia and Latin America. In *Economic Liberalization: No Panacea*, edited by Tariq Banuri, 171–200. Oxford: Clarendon Press.

Bernauer, Thomas, and Christoph Achini. 2000. From "Real" to "Virtual" States? Integration of the World Economy and Its Effects on Government Activity. *European Journal of International Relations* 6 (2):223–76.

Brown, David, and Wendy Hunter. 1999. Democracy and Social Spending in Latin America, 1980 –92. *American Political Science Review* 93 (4):779 –90.

Brown, Michael, ed. 1988. *Remaking the Welfare State*. Philadelphia, Pa: Temple University Press.

Cameron, David. 1978. The Expansion of the Public Sector: A Comparative Analysis. *American Political Science Review* 72 (4):1243–61.

Campbell, Donald. 1988. *Methodology and Epistemology for Social Science*. Chicago: University of Chicago Press.

Cerny, Philip. 1995. Globalization and the Changing Logic of Collective Action. *International Organization* 49 (4):595– 625.

Chan, Anita, and Robert Senser. 1997. China's Troubled Workers. *Foreign Affairs* 76(2):104 –17.

Chuhan, Punam, Stijn Claessens, and Nlandu Mamingi. 1993. Equity and Bond Flows to Latin America and Asia: The Role of Global and Country Factors.

World Bank Policy Research Working Paper 1160. Washington, D.C.: World Bank.

Clayton, Richard, and Jonas Pontusson. 1998. Welfare State Retrenchment Revisited. *World Politics* 51(1):67–98.

Collier, Ruth B., and David Collier. 1979. Inducements Versus Constraints: Disaggregating "Corporatism." *American Political Science Review* 73 (4):967–86.

———. 1991. *Shaping the Political Arena: Critical Junctures, Labor Movement, and Regime Dynamics in Latin America*. Princeton, N.J.: Princeton University Press.

Cook, Maria L. 1998. Toward Flexible Industrial Relations? Neo-liberalism, Democracy, and Labor Reform in Latin America. *Industrial Relations* 37 (3):311–36.

Crisp, Brian. 1994. Limitations to Democracy in Developing Capitalist Societies: The Case of Venezuela. *World Development* 22 (10):1491–1509.

Dean, Judith M. 1995. From Protectionism to Free Trade Fever? Recent Reforms in Developing Countries. *Open Economies Review* 6 (4):369–85.

Devarajam, S., Hafez Ghanem, and Karen Thierfelder. 1997. Economic Reforms and Labor Unions: A General Equilibrium Analysis Applied to Bangladesh & Indonesia. World Bank Economic Review 11 (1): 145–170.

Deyo, Frederic C. 1989. *Beneath the Miracle: Labor Subordination in the New Asian Industrialism*. Berkeley: University of California Press.

———. 1991. Export Manufacturing and Labor: The Asian Case. In *Labor in the Capitalist World Economy*, edited by Charles Bergquist. London: Sage Publications.

Drake, Paul L. 1996. *Labor Movements and Dictatorships: The Southern Cone in Comparative Perspective*. Baltimore, Md.: John Hopkins University Press.

Drunberg, Isabelle. 1998. Double Jeopardy, Globalization, Liberalization, and the Fiscal Squeeze. *World Development* 26 (4):591– 605.

Eichengreen, Barry. 1996. *Globalizing Capital*. Princeton, N.J.: Princeton University Press.

Esping-Andersen, Gosta. 1990. *The Three Worlds of Welfare Capitalism*. Princeton, N.J.: Princeton University Press.

———, ed. 1996. *Welfare States in Transition*. London: Sage Publications.

Evans, Peter. 1997. The Eclipse of the State? Reflections on Stateness in an Era of Globalization. *World Politics* 50 (1):62–87.

Fields, Gary. 1994. Changing Labor Market Conditions and Economic Development in Hong Kong, the Republic of Korea, Singapore, and Taiwan, China. *World Bank Economic Review* 8 (3):395– 414.

Galenson, Walter. 1962. Introduction. In *Labor in Developing Economies*, edited by Walter Galenson. Berkeley: University of California Press.

———. 1994. Trade Union Growth and Decline: An International Study. Praeger, Westport, CT.

Garrett, Geoffrey. 1998. *Partisan Politics in the Global Economy*. Cambridge: Cambridge University Press.

———. 2001. Globalization and Government Spending Around the World. *Studies in Comparative International Development* 35 (4):3–29.

Garrett, Geoffrey, and D. Mitchell. 1996. Globalization and the Welfare State: Income Transfers in the Industrial Democracies, 1966–90. Paper presented at the Center for International Studies, University of Southern California, Los Angeles, California.

Gereffi, Gary. 1995. Global Production Systems and Third World Development . In *Global Change, Regional Response*, edited by Barbara Stallings, 100–42. New York: Cambridge University Press.

Gill, Stephen. 1995. Globalization, Market Civilization, and Disciplinary Neoliberalism. Millenium: *Journal of International Studies* 24 (3):399–423.

Gray, John. 1998. *False Dawn: The Delusions of Global Capitalism*. New York: The New Press.

Greider, William. 1998. *One World, Ready or Not*. New York: Simon and Schuster.

Griffith-Jones, Stephany, and Barbara Stallings. 1995. New Global Financial Trends: Implications for Development. In *Global Change, Regional Response*, edited by Barbara Stallings, 143–73. New York: Cambridge University Press.

Hadenius, Axel. 1992. *Democracy and Development*. Cambridge: Cambridge University Press.

Heredia, Blanca. 1997. Prosper or Perish? Development in the Age of Global Capital. *Current History* 96 (613):383–88.

Hicks, Alexander. 1999. *Social Democracy and Welfare Capitalism*. Ithaca, N.Y.: Cornell University Press.

Hicks, Alexander M., and Duane H. Swank 1992. Politics, Institutions, and Welfare Spending in Industrialized Democracies, 1960–1982. *American Political Science Review* 86 (3):658 –74.

Hurrell, Audrey, and Nancy Woods. 1995. Globalization and Inequality. Millenium: *Journal of International Studies* 24 (3):447–70.

Ingerson, Alice. 1984. The Textile Industry and Working Class Culture. In *Labor in the Capitalist World Economy*, edited by Charles Bergquist, 217–42. London: Sage Publications.

Iversen, Torben, and Thomas R. Cusack. 2000. The Causes of Welfare State Expansion: Deindustrialization or Globalization? *World Politics* 52 (April):313–49.

International Monetary Fund (IMF). Various years. *Balance of Payments Statistics Yearbook*. Washington, D.C.: IMF.

———. Various years. *Government Finance Statistics Yearbook*. Washington, D.C.: IMF.

———. Various years. *International Financial Statistics*. Washington, D.C.: IMF.

Intriligator, Michael, Ronald Bodkin, and Cheng Hsiao. 1996. *Econometric Models, Techniques, and Applications*. 2nd ed. Upper Saddle River, N.J.: Prentice Hall.

Jaggers, Keith, and Ted Robert Gurr. 1994. *Polity III: Regime Type and Political Authority 1800–1994*. Ann Arbor, Mich: Inter-University Consortium for Political and Social Research.

Katzenstein, Peter J. 1995. *Small States in World Markets: Industrial Policy in Europe*. Ithaca, N.Y.: Cornell University Press.

Kaufman, Robert, and Alex Segura-Ubiergo. 2001. Globalization, Domestic Politics, and Social Spending in Latin America: A Time-Series Cross-Section Analysis, 1973–1997. *World Politics* 53 (4):553–587.

Kim, Eun Mee. 1997. *Big Business, Strong State: Collusion and Conflict in South Korean Development, 1960–1990*. Albany, N.Y.: SUNY Press.

King, Gary, J. Honaker, A. Joseph, and Ken Scheve. 2001. Analyzing Incomplete Political Science Data: An Alternative Algorithm for Multiple Imputation. *American Political Science Review* 95 (1):49 –70.

Korpi, Walter. 1983. *The Democratic Class Struggle*. London: Routledge and Kegan Paul.

Lake, David A., and Matthew Baum. Forthcoming. The Invisible Hand of Democracy: Political Control and the Provision of Public Services. *Comparative Political Studies*.

Lewbel, Arthur. 1997. Constructing Instruments for Regressions with Measurement Error when No Additional Data Are Available, with an Application to Patents and R&D. *Econometrica* 65 (5):1201–13.

Lok, H. P. 1993. Labour in the Garment Industry: An Employer's Perspective. In *Indonesia Assessment*, edited by Chris Manning and Joan Hardjono, 155–72. Canberra: Australian National University.

Looney, Robert. 1993. Government Expenditures and Third World Economic Growth in the 1980s: The Impact of Defense Expenditures. *Canadian Journal of Development Studies* 14 (1):23– 42.

Mamingi, Nlandu. 1997. Saving–Investment Correlations and Capital Mobility: The Experience of Developing Countries. *Journal of Policy Modeling* 19 (6):605–26.

Manning, Chris. 1998. Does Globalization Undermine Labor Standards? Lessons from East Asia. *Australian Journal of International Affairs* 52 (2):133– 47.

Maxfield, Sylvia. 1998. Understanding the Political Implications of Financial Internationalization in Emerging-Market Countries. *World Development* 26 (7):1201–19.

McGuire, James W. 1997. *Peronism Without Peron: Unions, Parties, and Democracy in Argentina*. Stanford, Calif.: Stanford University Press.

——. 1999. Labor Union Strength and Human Development in East Asia and Latin America. *Studies in Comparative International Development* 33 (4):3–34.

Mesa-Lago, Carmelo. 1991. Latin America and the Caribbean. In *Social Security in Developing Countries*, edited by Ehtifham Ahmad, Jean Dreze, Amartya Fen, and John Hills 356–94. Oxford: Oxford University Press.

——. 1994. *Changing Social Security in Latin America*. Boulder, Colo.: Lynne Rienner.

Midgley, James. 1984. *Social Security, Inequality, and the Third World*. New York: John Wiley and Sons.

Montiel, Peter. 1994. Capital Mobility in Developing Countries: Some Measurement Issues and Empirical Estimates. *World Bank Economic Review* 8 (3):311–50.

Morris, Robert. 1988. *Testing the Limits of Social Welfare*. London: Brandeis University Press.

O'Connor, Julia, and Gregg Olsen. 1998. *Power Resources Theory and the Welfare State*. Toronto: University of Toronto Press.

Olson, Mancur. 1971. *The Logic of Collective Action*. Cambridge, Mass.: Harvard University Press.

Pfaller, Alfred, Ian Gough, and Goran Therborn. 1991. *Can the Welfare State Compete? A Comparative Study of Five Advanced Capitalist Countries*. Houndmills, U.K.: Macmillan.

Pierson, Paul. 1996. The New Politics of the Welfare State. *World Politics* 48 (2):143–79.

Polanyi, Karl. 1944. *The Great Transformation*. New York: Farrar & Reinhart.

Quinn, Dennis. 1997. The Correlates of Change in International Financial Regulation. *American Political Science Review* 91 (3):531–51.

Rieger, Elmar, and S. Leibfried. 1998. Welfare State Limits to Globalization. *Politics and Society* 26 (3):363–90.

Rodrik, Dani. 1997a. Sense and Nonsense in the Globalization Debate. *Foreign Policy* 107 (summer):19–37.

Rodrik, Dani. 1997b. *Has Globalization Gone Too Far?* Washington, D.C.: Institute for International Economics.

Rodrik, Dani. 1998. Why Do More Open Economies Have Bigger Governments? *Journal of Political Economy* 106 (5):997–1033.

Rogowski, Ronald. 1989. *Commerce and Coalitions*. Princeton, N.J.: Princeton University Press.

Rueschemeyer, Dietrich, Evelyne H. Stephens, and John D. Stephens. 1992. *Capitalist Development and Democracy*. Chicago: University of Chicago Press.

Ruggie, John Gerard. 1982. International Regimes, Transactions, and Change: Embedded Liberalism in Postwar Economic Order. *International Organization* 36 (2):379–415.

———. 1994. At Home Abroad, Abroad at Home: International Liberalization and Domestic Stability in the New World Economy. *Millenium: Journal of International Studies* 24 (3):507–26.

Ruggles, Patricia, and Michael O'Higgins. 1987. Retrenchment and the New Right: A Comparative Analysis of the Impacts of the Thatcher and Reagan Administrations. In *Stagnation and Renewal in Social Policy: The Rise and Fall of Policy Regimes*, edited by Martin Rein, Gosta Esping-Andersen, and Lee Rainwater, 160–190. New York: M. E. Sharpe.

Schmidt, Sonke. 1995. Social Security in Developing Countries: Basic Tenets and Fields of State Intervention. *International Social Work* 38 (1):7–26.

Shafer, D. Michael. 1994. *Winners and Losers*. Ithaca, N.Y.: Cornell University Press.

Sherer, M. 1987. Welfare States: An Overview of Problems and Prospects. In *Modern Welfare States: A Comparative View of Trends and Prospects*, edited by Robert R. Friedmann, Neil Gilbert, Moshe Sherer, 290–98. New York: New York University Press.

Strange, Susan. 1997. The Erosion of the State. *Current History* 96 (613):365–69.

Swank, Duane. 1998. Funding the Welfare State: Globalization and the Taxation of Business in Advanced Market Economics. *Political Studies* 46 (4):671–92.

Tang, Kwong-Leung. 1996. The Determinants of Social Security in Developing Countries: A Comparative Analysis. *International Social Work* 39 (4):377–93.

Taylor, Mark, and Lucio Sarno. 1997. Capital Flows to Developing Countries: Long- and Short-Term Determinants. *The World Bank Economic Review* 11 (3):451–70.

Tyrell, Jr., Emmett. 1977. *The Future That Doesn't Work: Social Democracy's Failures in Britain.* New York: Doubleday.

United Nations. Various years. *UNIDO Database of Industrial Statistics.* Vienna: United Nations Industrial Development Organization.

———. 1992–93. *UN Industry and Development Report.* Vienna: UN Industrial Development Organization.

US Agency for International Development (US AID) 1999. Global Education Database. Center for Human Capacity Development. Washington, DC.

Usui, Chikako. 1994. Welfare State Development in a World System Context: Event History Analysis of First Historical Social Insurance Legislation Among 60 Countries, 1880–1960. In *The Comparative Political Economy of the Welfare State*, edited by Thomas Janoski and A. Hicks, 254–77. Cambridge: Cambridge University Press.

Valenzuela, Samuel. 1989. Labor Movements in Transitions to Democracy. *Comparative Politics* 21(4):445–72.

Van Hear, Nicholas. 1988. Recession, Retrenchment, and Military Rule: Nigerian Labor in the 1980s. In *Trade Unions and the New Industrialization of the Third World*, edited by Roger Southall, 144–63. Pittsburgh, Pa.: University of Pittsburgh Press.

Wahl, Ana-Maria. 1994. Economic Development and Social Security in Mexico, 1945–1985. *International Journal of Contemporary Sociology* 35:59–81.

Wicks, Malcolm. 1987. *A Future for All: Do We Need A Welfare State?* New York: Viking Penguin.

Wood, Adrian. 1994. *North–South Trade, Employment, and Inequality.* New York: Oxford University Press.

———. 1995. How Trade Hurt Unskilled Workers. *Perspectives* 9(3): 57–80.

———. 1997. Openness and Wage Inequality in Developing Countries: The Latin American Challenge to East Asian Conventional Wisdom. *World Bank Economic Review* 11 (1):33–57.

Wood, Adrian, and K. Berge. 1997. Exporting Manufactures: Human Resources, Natural Resources, and Trade Policy. *The Journal of Development Studies* 34 (1):35–59.

Wood, Adrian, and Jorg Mayer. 1998. Africa's Export Structure in a Comparative Perspective. In *UN Conference on Trade and Development, African Development in a Comparative Perspective*, study no. 4. Geneva: United Nations. Available at (www.ids.ac.uk/ids/global/pdfs/afex.pdf).

World Bank. Various years. *World Development Indicators.* Washington, D.C.: World Bank.

World Bank Policy Research Report. 1994. *Averting the Old Age Crisis.* Oxford: Oxford University Press.

PART III
A Global Civic Order?

Chapter 7

Values and Interests in Attitudes toward Trade and Globalization: The Continuing Compromise of Embedded Liberalism

Robert Wolfe and Matthew Mendelsohn

The "compromise of embedded liberalism" is one of the most powerful metaphors in the international relations literature, offering a compelling story about the political foundations of international organization in the second half of the twentieth century. The compromise was not a grand decision sealed by a treaty, but rather an ongoing process first evident in the actions of state officials during the 1940s. The metaphor is based on the work of Karl Polanyi, who described the emerging postwar order of the 1940s as a "great transformation" because of the reassertion of social control over the market. Polanyi observed that every economy is socially embedded. When the attempt was made under nineteenth-century laissez-faire to allow the market to be self-regulating, or "disembedded," society protected itself in a "double movement" in which the expansion of the market was countered by society (Polanyi, 1944: 131). In John Ruggie's extension of Polanyi's idea, the essence of the postwar system was that "unlike the economic nationalism of the 1930s, it would be multilateral in character; unlike the liberalism of the gold standard and free trade, its multilateralism would be predicated on domestic interventionism" (1982: 209). In this compromise between international openness and the domestic welfare state, liberalism continued, but it was "embedded" in the domestic social order.

Many scholars now worry that this compromise between the expansion of the global market and domestic autonomy is unsustainable in the era of globalization, citing as evidence both political resistance to trade liberalization and fiscal constraints on social spending. It is the political rather than the fiscal argument that interests us in this chapter. We address the issue of public support towards embedded liberalism as the basis for multilateral order; we do not discuss the debates in the comparative politics literature on globalization (Blyth, 2002) dealing with the state, social policy and economic adjustment. Explanations for the political threat to embedded liberalism are often based on an analysis of the material factors or interests driving individual and collective preferences, but we think that the nature of the compromise requires us to look first at the values, ideologies and normative commitments held by citizens. Embedded liberalism is a constitutive rule for a compromise between the needs for universality on which a strong order must rest, and the needs for particularity that are inevitable in a plural world order. Ruggie (1982) argued that the international order of embedded liberalism depended on a particular constellation of material power and "legitimate social purpose". In this argument, if social purposes remain constant, then material change associated with globalization would not be expected to undermine the existing international order. Citizens in industrial democracies accepted the constraints of multilateralism in the 1940s in return for a more prosperous and peaceful world. Are citizens still prepared to make this compromise?

The novelty of this chapter lies in our attempt to use the methodology of opinion research to examine individuals' attitudes in one country for evidence of a proposition about international order. Our analysis contributes to how political scientists understand public attitudes and how policy makers understand the way citizens of different countries see their relations with each other as mediated through the institutions of global governance. The legitimacy of global governance will ultimately rest on the decisions of individuals. Although we make no claim that individual attitudes are transformed directly into policy at home or abroad, public opinion is relevant for international relations and influences the climate in which policy decisions are made.[1] The literature on public opinion also suggests that citizens' beliefs about foreign policy, including trade policy, do not float freely, with no connection to their wider values.[2] Mass opinion on issues such as a new trade agreement is formed by latent opinion – that is, by underlying preferences and values – not by transient responses to ephemeral events in the media. Although the public often lacks detailed knowledge of policy proposals, it does have clear policy goals. Studying individual attitudes in the aggregate will help us to understand the political basis of global governance.

Scholars know a great deal from the public opinion literature about the factors that shape Europeans' support for European integration (Gabel, 1998b), and we have begun to learn something about North Americans' support for trade liberalization,[3]

---

1   Mass opinion is generally thought to bear some relation to policy outputs (see Page and Shapiro, 1992), and although this is not always the case (see Monroe, 1998), voter preferences do constrain policy making, even on trade, by placing limits on decision makers (see Rowe, 1995; Verdier, 1994).

2   To the extent that opinion about trade policy is an aspect of opinion about foreign policy, our expectations are consistent with those of scholars who argue that mass opinion on foreign policy is stable and well-structured, rather than ill-informed and subject to rapid "mood" swings (see Holsti, 1996; Martin and Fortmann, 1995; Martin and Fortmann, 2001). American elite attitudes to international security have been shown to be consistent through time and through policy space (see Murray and Cowden, 1999). Other scholars have found a strong relationship between foreign policy orientations and preferences on both economic and social/value domestic policy issues (see Holsti and Rosenau, 1999).

3   Although the Program on International Policy Attitudes (PIPA) consistently reports attitudes to trade (see Reilly, 1999), the first comprehensive study that we know of tracking American opinion data on trade since Bauer, Pool and Dexter, 1963 is Scheve and Slaughter, 2001a. Canadian attitudes to trade liberalization have been extensively studied (see Dasko, 1988; Gidengil, 1995; Johnston *et al.*, 1992; Johnston and Percy, 1980; LeDuc and Murray, 1984; Nadeau and Guay, 1990; Sigler and Goresky, 1974).

both apparently influenced by an individual's ability to compete in a more open market. Emerging debates around globalization, however, are about more than liberalization. Many analysts study the empirical basis of the underlying social and economic claims, seeking answers to questions such as: When did globalization begin? How extensive is it? Does it really limit policy autonomy? What we try to do in this chapter is understand how citizens respond to the discourse about globalization, defined as greater economic linkages among states. This chapter shows that economic, interest-based accounts are insufficient for trying to understand the trade-off that citizens face between the efficiency of open markets and the security of the welfare state. Instead, analysts must also look at values and world views in order to understand why citizens support "trade liberalization", always a central feature of the compromise, but are not as supportive of "globalization", because it seems to undermine local distinctiveness, the welfare state and values that they cherish. These conclusions are based on the results of a Canadian public opinion survey that we designed to test our propositions.

In the first section of this chapter, we discuss our questionnaire and survey design (our case study). In the second section, we review the literature on public opinion on trade liberalization and integration, explain our motivation for asking our two core questions, and report the results. In the third section we explain the motivation for our explanatory question and then use regression techniques to explain how citizens' attitudes with respect to globalization are more influenced by their core values than by their interests, and in the process identify the mental maps citizens use to make sense of emerging debates on globalization. The fourth section presents our conclusions. We argue that understanding the way citizens use their values and ideologies to construct their responses to the greater linkages with the world implied by globalization will be essential to understanding the political basis of global governance. If citizens are hostile to all forms of international liberalization and to a strong role for the state, and also resist a multilateral solution to this paradox, then we might infer that something has happened to embedded liberalism.

1. The Canadian Case, Our Data and Methodology

We conducted a survey of public opinion in Canada in order to test our proposition about the relationship between values and interests in shaping attitudes toward trade and globalization. It is harder to ask questions about something that people may not think about every day, like trade agreements, than to ask about vote intentions in an election campaign. Our strategy, therefore, was to ask two core questions and then a series of explanatory questions designed to allow us to analyze the differing answers to the core questions. Our survey instrument was administered by telephone to a random, probabilistic sample of 1298 Canadians between February 21 and March 13, 2001. The survey was conducted by le Centre de recherche en opinion publique (CROP), a major commercial polling firm. The Centre for Research and Information on Canada, a research think tank, commissioned the survey; the authors collaborated on the questionnaire design. Up to 12 call-backs were conducted and the response rate was 62 per cent.[4]

Our data are distinguished from previous data in their depth of coverage and comprehensiveness on a variety of issues. Although the pooled Eurobarometer data used by many scholars have greater coverage over time and across countries, and have a higher number of respondents, they do not feature a large number of items on issues related to trade, integration, liberalization and globalization. The fact that our data come from one country alone can be taken as a caveat, but not a serious shortcoming. Although national political culture does have an impact on whether a country is supportive of integration, as do political institutions that can either facilitate or thwart integration, the structure of opinion does not seem to differ much from one country to another. By this, we mean that in advanced industrial democracies, the variables which make individuals more or less likely to support trade are the same from one country to another. For example, Eichenberg and Dalton find that the basic factors at work affecting changing levels of support for the EU over time are fairly consistent from one country to another: "Although citizens of the United Kingdom, Denmark, and the Netherlands support the EC at far different levels because of differing historical and foreign policy traditions ... this variation is caused by a similar economic and political dynamic" (1993: 530).

Some readers might worry that data from spring 2001 may have gone stale, especially since our survey was conducted before the attacks of September 11, 2001, which might have made Canadians more wary about the world. We are confident, however, that new data would not show a significantly different pattern. We were not probing ephemeral opinion on daily events but rather the structure of underlying attitudes and their relations to each other. Such structures do not change quickly, a reality confirmed by the responses to an annual tracking question in a poll commissioned by the federal government: Canadian support for trade agreements was slightly higher in May 2003 than it had been in May 2001 (EKOS, 2003).

2. The Core Questions on Trade and Globalization

We seek to explain individuals' attitudes, not observable actions such as tariff levels or election outcomes. These attitudes, we contend, are relevant for understanding the political response to globalization. In order to identify the mental maps citizens use, we must frame survey questions in a discourse that makes sense to respondents. Scholars have looked at a great many questions on trade, but these questions are conceptually problematic for our purposes. Some conflate protectionism with "job protection", as if the two are the same thing. For example, some scholars have used this question from the US National Election Study of 1992: "*Some people have suggested placing new limits on foreign imports in order to protect American jobs. Others say that such limits would raise consumer prices and hurt American exports. Do you favor or oppose placing new limits on imports, or haven't you thought much*

---

4   Data for replication purposes are available through the Canadian Opinion Research Archive at Queen's University, at the website http://www.queensu.ca/cora/; site last accessed September 7, 2004.

about this?" (Scheve and Slaughter, 2001b: 275). For other studies, the dependent variable is a question from the 1995 International Social Survey Program that asks respondents to agree or disagree with the statement that *"[respondent's country] should limit the import of foreign products in order to protect its national economy"* (Mayda and Rodrik, 2002). The World Values Survey is also often used, which asks respondents to choose between *"let goods be imported if people want to buy them"* or *"imposing restrictions to protect jobs"*. The problem with all these questions is that they imply that limiting imports protects the economy or jobs. People consistently opt to protect jobs ahead of enhancing consumer choice (Scheve and Slaughter, 2001a: 23), which may simply indicate that people are choosing the promised outcome (jobs), rather than making a judgement about the policy instrument (protectionism). Not surprisingly, answers to these questions correlate with an individual's vulnerability in the labour market.

The problem is complicated by one consequence of globalization: as the focus of trade policy shifts from measures at the border (such as tariffs and quotas that affect prices directly) to domestic governance issues like social regulations (such as food safety or environmental standards), policy debates engage individuals as citizens, not only as workers, producers and consumers. As trade barriers continue to fall, for example, domestic institutional structures – including the nature of the labour market, labour standards, social policies and environmental regulations – come to be seen as impediments to trade, bringing efficiency arguments into social domains. Developments in the nature of issues brought to the trade regime and the way contested issues are adjudicated may undermine popular support for the compromise of embedded liberalism if the new trade regime challenges the domestic administrative state (Howse and Nicolaidis, 2003).

What questions, then, should we ask? "Trade" is a constructed category, as is "globalization". Their ontological status is ambiguous and their epistemological status is opaque. Traded services, for example, are famously things that you can buy and sell but cannot drop on your foot, which means they exist only as expert abstractions and can be seen only in measurements of transaction flows. To ask about the rules currently governing international trade would be even more ambiguous. We chose, therefore, to ask a question about support for "new trade agreements" generally. Because Canadians have lived with the FTA and NAFTA, this question should measure general attitudes toward the expansion of trade and trade liberalization. Our choice was influenced by our previous analysis of twenty years of questions on Canadian surveys about trade (Mendelsohn and Wolfe, 2001).

The absence of questions on globalization in other surveys made it harder to design our second core question. The concept "globalization" can mean different things to activists, business people and governments (of north and south). Globalization is usually understood by economic analysts to mean the increasing integration of factor markets, often through the actions of multinational corporations (MNCs) (Prakash, 2001), while for political analysts, it "designates a growth of connections between people across the planet" (Scholte, 2002: 286).We evoke these diverse meanings of "globalization" in our survey question, but by avoiding undue detail, technical definitions or argumentative prose (such as is found in some of the other survey questions discussed above), we are then able through our regression analysis to identify how citizens understand and make sense of emerging debates on "globalization". Table 7.1 reports the results for our core questions (Q1–Q2 – all question wording and variable operationalizations are found in the Appendix).

Canadian mass opinion became broadly supportive of free trade agreements during the 1990s (Mendelsohn and Wolfe, 2001), and it is therefore not surprising that about two-thirds of respondents said they supported the negotiation of new trade agreements, while only about one in ten said they were opposed. Yet fewer than half supported "globalization". and over a third were uncertain. The answers to both questions are interesting, as is the difference between the two, which suggests that citizens do not see "globalization" as merely the same as trade liberalization. The core of our analysis is not the frequency results on these two questions, but the relationship between explanatory variables and these two questions. Our analysis focuses on citizens' values and interests, and is designed to explain why many citizens answer the core questions (our dependent variables) differently. Through this analysis, we are able to elaborate a model of how citizens understand "globalization" and whether the compromise of embedded liberalism is sustainable.

3. Explanatory Questions about Interests and Values

When responding to questions about trade or globalization, citizens may be evaluating liberalized trade in general, the actual content of particular agreements, the emerging institutions of global governance, or such attributes of globalization as the Internet, the spread of disease and increased travel. Some analysts use questions on trade, tariffs or integration and take respondents' answers as transparent indicators of citizens' real preferences.We do not use this implicit referendum approach. Rather,

Table 7.1   Contrasting Support for Trade Agreements and Globalization

	Support	Uncertain	Oppose
New trade agreements	65%	23%	11%
Globalization	45%	38%	17%

Q1. This next section of the survey is about international trade agreements. By international trade agreements I mean things like the Canada-US free trade agreement, the North American free trade agreement (NAFTA), and the other international trade agreements that cover Canada and the over 140 other members of the World Trade Organization (the WTO). Do you strongly support, support, oppose, or strongly oppose Canada negotiating new trade agreements with other countries, or do you have no opinion on this question?

Q2. Many people say we are presently experiencing a process of globalization, which means that the economies of all of the countries of the world are becoming more and more linked. Do you strongly support, somewhat support, somewhat oppose, or strongly oppose Canada encouraging more rapid globalization, or do you have no opinion on this?

consistent with the methodological conventions of research on mass opinion, we assume that questions can mean different things to respondents, and different things than the researcher intended. Barring follow-up qualitative interviewing with respondents, the only way for a researcher to understand what the question meant to a respondent is to see how they answered other questions, and to see which ones are correlated with answers to the initial question.

Through regression analysis, we examine which values, attitudes and interests shape individuals' judgments about trade liberalization and globalization. We hypothesize that understanding the mental maps citizens use to make sense of trade and globalization requires an understanding of their values and attitudes toward politics, society and the economy generally, but standard explanations of trade policy preferences are based on the assumption best stated by Kenneth Scheve and Matthew Slaughter (2001a: 47, 48), that "individuals evaluate policies on the basis of individual welfare not aggregate national welfare – that is, of self-interest" and that "individuals know with certainty the effects policies have or will have on their incomes" (for an economist's critique of the strong version of the assumption, see Nelson, 2002: 168.) The further assumption is that "free trade" will be sought by the winners from openness, while "protection" will be sought by the losers, an assumption for which good evidence exists (Rogowski, 1989: 5). Because liberalization alters the risks and rewards to more or less mobile factors, studies find that attitudes toward liberalization are a product of an individual's material interests and place in the labour market (Rodrik, 1997; Scheve and Slaughter, 2001a).

Any model that seeks to put economic self-interest to an empirical test must have quite sophisticated measures of how individuals will be affected by integration. The two competing models of disaggregating society on the basis of interests assume that individuals will be motivated either by their factor ownership (a skills/education-based approach), or by the industry in which they are employed (an economic sector-based approach).[5] Operationalizing economic class is notoriously difficult (Butler and Stokes, 1969: chapter 4; Nie *et al.*, 1979; Wright, 1997). Gabel developed sophisticated measures of relative wages and relative human capital (Gabel, 1998a). Scheve and Slaughter used education and income as shorthand measures to capture a great deal about how well individuals will fare in less protected markets. They also experimented with various sectoral measures, but found them to be non-significant (Scheve and Slaughter, 2001a: 64). They make a persuasive case that the growing complexity of the labour market implies that a general measure of human capital, like education, is the best indicator. Anna Mayda and Dani Rodrik (2002) also found that the human capital approach is the best predictor of trade policy preferences. In our demographic questions, therefore, we replicate their use of *education* as the best measure to capture skills, and also include *income*, expecting that respondents with

---

5   On the difference between so-called Hecksher-Olin (or Stolper-Samuelson) and Ricardo-Viner models, see Hiscox, 2001: 3–4; and Scheve and Slaughter, 2001a: 48–50. The former tests opinion by different type of worker, regardless of industry, while the latter tests by type of industry, regardless of worker characteristics.

more education and income will be most supportive of integration because they are more able to compete in more open markets.[6]

The material self-interest assumption, however, ignores the consistent findings that conditions in the macroeconomy have a strong influence on voting (Norpoth *et al.*, 1991), and should influence peoples' judgments about liberalization. Strong evidence exists that general economic downturns tend to produce more caution in voters (Bowler and Donovan, 1998). Macroeconomic conditions played a role in the referendums on European integration, with those citizens more pessimistic about the national economy more likely to vote against the Amsterdam Treaty (Jenssen *et al.*, 1998). Furthermore, with issues related to trade liberalization, citizens are able to make judgments regarding the success of previous agreements on the country, and these retrospective assessments are likely to have an impact on how they evaluate new proposed agreements. We therefore include macroeconomic assessments (Q3) and retrospective assessments of previous trade agreements (Q4) in our model.

We agree that structural factors in the economy, and individual experience of those structural factors, influence American opinion on trade liberalization and have an impact on Europeans' views on European integration. However, individuals are not just factor owners, or workers in a particular sector or consumers, useful as these simplifying assumptions may be; they are also members of families, of communities, of churches. We disagree, therefore, with Matthew Gabel, who dismisses explanations other than utilitarian self-interest as "dubious" (1998a: 12), but nonetheless presents evidence (that he chooses to ignore) that alternative explanations produce robust and highly significant relationships, even when controlling for the full range of variables measuring material self-interest (1998a: Table 19). As citizens, individuals are concerned not only about the effects of commercial exchanges on their livelihood but also about the effects of new agreements on the ability of the government to pursue valued policy objectives.

Although the politics of trade policy has often been understood as a traditional left versus right struggle over policies that either strengthen the market or redistribute the risks and rewards of openness (Garrett, 1998), there are other axes of political conflict which also structure political choices, such as clashes over which cultural values should be encouraged by the state (Clarke *et al.*, 1999; Davis and Davenport, 1999; Inglehart and Abramson, 1999; Kitschelt, 1994). For example, in Canada, the economic advantages of access to a large market competed with individuals' concerns about the loss of sovereignty and maintenance of distinctive social programs during the 1988 election campaign, fought almost exclusively on the issue of the Free Trade Agreement (FTA) (Johnston *et al.*, 1992). Elizabeth Gidengel found that the significant gender gap on the FTA was not explained by different material circumstances between men and women, but by different values, with men

---

6   To ensure that we are capturing as much of the skills differential as possible, an earlier version of this chapter undertook additional specifications controlling for sector of employment (public vs. private), job classification and union membership. These variables turned out to be non-significant, although union members may have been marginally more opposed to both globalization and trade. The other coefficients in the model remained stable and the explanatory power of the model did not improve, so these variables have been excluded.

relying more heavily on economic considerations, such as their belief in the market, and women on social ones, such as their commitment to the welfare state (Gidengil, 1995).

Values will be even more important for globalization because they imply social and political integration and hence call to mind the need to protect one's community before one's job prospects. Once a certain material level of comfort has been attained in more economically advanced countries, individuals seek to protect and advance their values and symbolic interests beyond the material (Inglehart, 1990). A variety of studies suggest that people do not evaluate increased contact with the outside world through the lens of economic self-interest alone. Richard Herrmann and his colleagues find that normative considerations regarding social justice impinge on material considerations and that Americans' mental maps take into consideration a variety of values beyond the simple exploitation of American economic power (Herrmann *et al.*, 2001; see also Citrin *et al.*, 1994). Joel Fetzer concludes that citizens' opinions about immigration are influenced by the perceived threat to the majority's cultural values, not concerns about job loss (2000: 107). In their explanation of support for European integration, Richard Eichenberg and Russell Dalton conclude that it is "more than simply [a matter of] economics," because dummy variables for the UK, Denmark and Italy were by far more important than the economic variables (1993: 530). As Ronald Rogowski notes, "culture", "religion" and "ancient loyalties" partially explain views on liberalization (1989: 20), concepts interlaced with values. Dennis Chong (2000: 19–20) points out that norms (i.e., "symbolic values") can act as a protective device through which individuals evaluate new or disturbing information. Chong's work is particularly relevant because he readily concedes an important role for self-interest in decision-making, but demonstrates that preferring policies that protect one's cultural values and normative commitments is consistent with defending one's self-interest: having one's values defended by the state is psychologically satisfying.

The literature highlights the important role for values and the narrowness of the economic self-interest explanation, but which values should we include in our analysis? Leading scholars of political values have identified three (Deth and Scarbrough, 1995: 8–14). The first salient dimension structuring contemporary political conflict is economic ideology, such as general orientations towards state intervention (Q5). Second, a cultural conflict over authoritarian values and social tolerance exists in many industrial societies, with attitudes toward immigration and minorities being the most salient issues (Q6) (see Kitschelt, 1994 on these two dimensions). Third, political conflict is also dominated by an ideological clash over elitism and public participation, with some citizens deferring to elites and others demanding greater public say in decisions. Many scholars note a rise in the number of "dissatisfied democrats", citizens with high internal efficacy who are critical of current elitist democratic practices, and who demonstrate low external political efficacy, that is, not trusting government to be responsive to the public (Q7) (Norris, 1999: 3). This factor should also be relevant to citizens' views regarding globalization, as citizens with less trust in government are more likely to be protectionist (Mayda and Rodrik, 2002).

Group identifications and cues (Q8–Q11) represent a critical factor in determining how people perceive the political world (Brady and Sniderman, 1985). On an issue like globalization, which combines complexity and abstractness with an increasingly high media profile charged with emotional arguments, individuals are likely to use their values to make sense of the issues (Lupia and McCubbins, 1998; Popkin, 1991). Mythologies about multinational corporations, organized labour, foreigners and environmentalists may be called upon as shortcuts to make sense of what is a highly complex phenomenon with a variety of unknown consequences (Jenssen *et al.*, 1998).

Citizens' patterns of national and international attachments might be another factor affecting views of globalization (Q12). Some citizens may simply be more cosmopolitan and feel a greater sense of international citizenship (Q13) (Norris, 2000: 156). Mayda and Rodrik (2002), who test what they call non-economic determinants of opinion in the form of values and identities, found that people with strong local and national attachments are more likely to be protectionist. O'Rourke and Sinnott (2001) demonstrate that those countries with higher levels of chauvinistic nationalism are far more likely to oppose trade liberalization.

Finally, to citizens outside the USA, globalization might be understood as integration to an American political, cultural and economic model. Integration to an American model means not only a loss of favoured instruments of the administrative state, but perhaps the loss of that broader purpose to which those instruments were put. We therefore also examine whether attitudes toward the world's leading power, the US, and concerns about "Americanization" are important to helping citizens make sense of global integration (Q14). Such attitudes vary according to the skill level of the respondent.

In sum, we settled on a number of different clusters of considerations that could help citizens make sense of the process known as globalization: first, material self-interest as measured by education and income; second, confidence in the macroeconomy and retrospective judgments about previous agreements; third, confidence in various groups involved in debates about globalization; and fourth, values and attitudes. With reference to these values and attitudes, we have chosen one variable to measure each of the concepts of economic liberalism, cultural conservatism, political efficacy, national and international attachments, and anti-Americanism.

Regression Results

In order to better understand why respondents react differently to our two dependent variables, we conducted OLS regression analysis using the independent variables described in the previous section, and including standard controls for age and gender.[7] Before discussing the results in Tables 7.2 and 7.3 in detail, we want to

---

7   Some suggest using ordered probit analysis when dependent variables are ordinal, such as ours (see Aldrich and Nelson, 1984). We tested our models using ordered probit, but the relative size of the MLE coefficients was virtually indistinguishable from the OLS estimates; we therefore report OLS coefficients. For work highlighting the robustness of OLS, see Borgatta and Bohrnstedt, 1980.

highlight four broad conclusions emerging from the data. First, values play an important role in influencing opinion on both globalization and trade, particularly values related to attitudes toward the USA, internationalism, the welfare state and feelings about multinational corporations. Second, when skills variables are included in our models, the significance of values remains robust, demonstrating that values are not merely surrogates for interests, and that they have an independent impact on opinion on globalization across individuals with different skill levels and interests. Third, education and income do play an important role with regard to opinion on trade agreements, but do not have a comparable impact on views on globalization, highlighting that attitudes toward globalization are influenced by factors other than one's ability to compete in a more open market, whereas opinion on trade liberalization is more tightly tied to individual interests. And fourth, retrospective evaluations of the impact of previous trade agreements are more influential in shaping individual opinions on trade than on globalization, again highlighting that globalization is understood by citizens to be about far more than trade liberalization.

The first columns of Tables 7.2 and 7.3 show that values and other attitudinal variables are strongly related to opinion on both trade and globalization. The second and third columns constitute the core of our empirical test regarding the impact of skills versus values and attitudes, where we add first education, then, separately, income, to our equations. As predicted by trade economists, and as seen in Table 7.2,

Table 7.2   Explaining Support for Trade Agreements

Welfare state	.12(.04)[a]	.13(.04)[a]	.10(.04)[a]	.07(.04)
Immigration	.03(.02)	.01(.02)	.04(.02)	.03(.03)
Internationalism	.09(.03)[a]	.09(.03)[a]	.10(.03)[a]	.06(.03)[c]
Government doesn't care	−.13(.03)[a]	−.12(.03)[a]	−.11(.04)[a]	−.06(.03)[c]
Closer US ties	.22(.04)[a]	.24(.04)[a]	.21(.04)[a]	.17(.04)[a]
Attachment to Canada	−.03(.04)	−.03(.04)	−.04(.04)	−.04(.04)
Canadian businesses	.14(.05)[a]	.13(.05)[b]	.13(.05)[b]	.06(.05)
Unions	−.13(.04)[a]	−.12(.04)[a]	−.16(.04)[a]	−.15(.04)[a]
Environmental groups	−.06(.04)	−.01(.04)	.01(.04)	.00(.04)
MNCs	.11(.04)[a]	.12(.04)[b]	.11(.04)[b]	.07(.04)
Age	−.01(.01)[c]	−.01(.00)[c]	−.00(.00)[c]	−.01(.00)
Male	.02(.01)	.02(.01)	.03(.02)	.02(.02)
Education		.08(.03)[a]		.07(.03)[b]
Income			.07(.03)[b]	.04(.02)[c]
Macroeconomy				.02(.03)
Retrospective: free trade				.40(.02)[a]
Constant	.76(.08)	.71(.08)	.73(.08)	.96(.09)
Adj R square	.14	.15	.15	.23
N	1091	1091	1091	1091

OLS coefficients reported, standard errors in parentheses.
[a]$p < .001$; [b]$p < .01$; [c]$p < .05$

Table 7.3   Explaining Support for Globalization

Welfare state	.15(.04)[a]	.15(.04)[a]	.15(.04)[a]	.12(.04)[a]
Immigration	.06(.02)[b]	.06(.02)[c]	.06(.03)[c]	.06(.02)[b]
Internationalism	.14(.03)[a]	.14(.03)[a]	.15(.03)[a]	.13(.03)[a]
Government doesn't care	−.05(.03)	−.05(.03)	−.04(.03)	−.00(.03)
Closer US ties	.19(.04)[a]	.20(.04)[a]	.23(.04)[a]	.19(.04)[a]
Attachment to Canada	.05(.04)	−.03(.04)	−.08(.04)	.07(.04)
Canadian businesses	.07(.05)	.06(.04)	.05(.05)	.00(.05)
Unions	−.12(.04)[a]	−.12(.04)[a]	−.13(.04)[a]	−.13(.04)[a]
Environmental groups	.00(.04)	−.00(.04)	.00(.04)	.01(.04)
MNCs	.22(.04)[a]	.22(.04)[a]	.20(.04)[a]	.16(.04)[a]
Age	−.00(.00)	−.00(.00)	−.00(.00)	−.00(.00)
Male	.00(.01)	.00(.01)	.00(.01)	.00(.01)
Education		.02(.03)		.01(.03)
Income			.04(.03)	.03(.03)
Macroeconomy				.02(.04)
Retrospective: free trade				.30(.05)[a]
Constant	.39(.08)	.37(.08)	.38(.08)	.58(.09)
Adj R square	.16	.16	.16	.20
N	1091	1091	1091	1091

OLS coefficients reported, standard errors in parentheses.
[a]$p < .001$; [b]$p < .01$; [c]$p < .05$

both skills variables have an impact on attitudes toward trade. Respondents with more education are significantly more supportive of new trade agreements, and those with higher incomes are somewhat more supportive. Note, however, that the inclusion of these variables has little impact on the relative size of the coefficients on the initial attitudinal variables, highlighting that while skills explain some opinion formation on trade, values also play a role. If our strong initial correlations between our values variables and our dependent variable were spurious, and merely measuring the fact that respondents with higher education held different values than respondents with lower education, the size of the coefficients should have declined substantially when controlling for skills. This decline did not happen.

On the other hand, in Table 7.3, education and income have no impact on opinions on globalization, and they have no impact on the significance of the original attitudinal variables. While opinion about trade is influenced by skills and values, opinion about globalization is influenced only by values. Respondents with high and low levels of education are equally likely to support or oppose "globalization", whatever they think the concept represents. Regardless of education levels, citizens hold different values and attach different levels of importance to societal goals, and they believe these values and goals are affected by globalization.

Which values and attitudes matter? Which mental maps do citizens use to make sense of trade and globalization? Respondents who oppose globalization are more likely to support a robust welfare state, oppose Canada taking a more active role in world affairs,[8] and have less sympathy for the United States. For Canadians, globalization may imply integration towards an American model, and attitudes toward the USA are therefore important predictors of individual attitudes toward globalization. As well, respondents who support increased immigration are more likely to support globalization, a surprising finding to analysts who observe public protests, during which global social justice is often invoked as an important argument *against* globalization. We infer that most citizens do see globalization as breaking down previous national cultural barriers between societies, and those supportive of immigration as a means of achieving cultural diversity are in fact more supportive of globalization.

Although the considerations citizens use to make sense of trade are largely similar to those applied to globalization, some of the variables that structure opinion on globalization are not related to attitudes toward trade. Canadians who are more supportive of immigration are more likely to support globalization, but attitudes toward immigration are not related to attitudes toward trade. Respondents who say they have more attachment to their country are more opposed to globalization, but national attachment has no relationship to trade liberalization. Also, citizens who think the government cares about what citizens think (i.e., those with high political efficacy) are more likely to support new trade agreements, but this consideration has no impact on attitudes toward globalization.[9]

When it comes to using groups as cues to make sense of trade and globalization, we find that feelings about unions are highly important for both of our dependent variables, with those who have confidence in unions more opposed to trade and globalization. An individual's level of trust in MNCs also played an important role in influencing opinion on globalization, but had a much smaller impact on trade agreements. Confidence in Canadian businesses, on the other hand, had some impact on trade agreements, but none on globalization. In our view, this highlights the difference in citizens' reasoning: trade liberalization is about the perceived impact on Canadian businesses, while globalization has less to do with domestic economic impact and much more to do with feelings and values regarding the market and multinational corporations. Confidence in environmental groups is not related to either of our dependent variables, which might at first be surprising because some activists argue that environmental degradation might be an effect of globalization,

---

8   The question asking whether respondents thought that Canada should be more involved in world affairs came before any questions about trade or globalization in order to prevent contamination. This ordering ensures that we really measured attitudes towards Canada's involvement in the world and that individuals were not responding to the general question having been primed by earlier questions to think about it in terms of trade or globalization.

9   We constructed a variable that we called "disaffected democrats" by adding internal and external efficacy scores (those who did not trust government but thought that politics was not too complicated for them to understand were defined as "disaffected democrats"). This variable was consistently not significant in all specifications. Although citizens involved in public protests may be likely to be "disaffected democrats", respondents who share these views in the mass public are not more likely to oppose trade liberalization or globalization.

but in fact members of the general public more supportive of environmental groups differ on whether globalization helps or harms the environment.

Column 4 adds to the equation retrospective assessments of macroeconomic performance and retrospective evaluations of the impact of liberalized trade on Canada. The macroeconomic variable was not significant, but respondents who retrospectively judged the effect of previous trade agreements to have had a positive effect on Canada were much more likely to support new agreements and globalization. Nonetheless, these retrospective considerations are significantly more important to judgments about trade than to globalization. That is, respondents who have more favourable retrospective assessments about the known property of trade agreements are much more positive about extending these agreements, but some of these individuals who are generally positive about past trade agreements are nonetheless reticent about globalization.

5. Conclusion: The Continuing Compromise of Embedded Liberalism

We think the compromise of embedded liberalism remains a compelling metaphor, one that helps scholars interpret the paradoxes inherent in how citizens use their values to construct their understanding of the relationships between their communities and the world. We stress that the compromise is not a causal factor in world affairs. As a constitutive rule it can shape how citizens understand the limits of legitimacy without being something that any actor could articulate explicitly. Embedded liberalism is part of the "why" and "how" of collective life, not an explanation of a particular outcome (Kratochwil, 2000: 78; Ruggie, 1998: 869). We found that this compromise is reproduced in the values and ideologies of citizens, and it is these, more than their material interests, that allow them to make sense of what globalization represents.

As a final test of our conclusions about Canadian attitudes toward embedded liberalism, we conducted a second wave of the survey, in which we asked about global governance directly. We asked respondents whether the Canadian government or international actors should be making decisions in seven key areas. The results are reported and analyzed in more detail elsewhere (Wolfe and Mendelsohn, 2004), but we should highlight that the overwhelming majority of Canadians are willing to say there should be more international cooperation on every issue, indicating the continued strong internationalism of Canadians (Munton and Keating, 2001; Noel, Therien and Dallaire, 2004). We also found relatively high levels of support for national governments jointly making decisions at international meetings where the Canadian government is present – and even support for international institutions making decisions – so long as the issues being dealt with are "international managerial issues", such as preventing climate change and curtailing the spread of disease. There is also very strong support for collaborative international decision-making on the issue of promoting human rights. However, on domestic political issues, such as establishing standards for social programs and for the workplace, Canadians are deeply resistant to the idea that international meetings or international institutions should make decisions. We think that the pattern of responses is entirely consistent with embedded liberalism.

Canadians have been quite supportive of trade liberalization, and continue to be comfortable with even greater forms of integration, as long as the welfare objectives of the administrative state are maintained, and as long as globalization is not perceived to threaten valued objectives and Canadians' social values (Mendelsohn and Wolfe, 2001). Embedded liberalism is a compromise between self and other, or home and away, a precarious balance on which multilateralism and international organization rests. If globalization washes away the capacity of the administrative state that allows states to be different, then the legitimacy of the international organizations that allow them to work together will also be undermined, because governments will no longer be able to act in a way consistent with the compromise. This erosion of legitimacy has not yet happened in Canada, or so we infer from the fact that a large plurality of Canadians currently support both globalization and further trade agreements. If, however, Canadians became convinced that globalization represented a threat to their ability to maintain their own unique identity, particularly in the face of the USA, support could weaken. This is because Canadian and American values have diverged over the past decade and Canadians have become more self-conscious regarding their own unique set of values (Adams, 2003; Mendelsohn, 2002).

We do not challenge the work of other scholars who have found that a relationship exists between interests and attitudes to trade liberalization, but we add a number of correctives. First, the relationship between skills and attitudes toward trade liberalization is more limited than the relationship between values and attitudes to trade liberalization, and second, the relationship is much more limited when examining attitudes toward globalization. Third, while individuals do, to some extent, assess trade agreements with reference to their own economic position, we find that retrospective evaluations of previous agreements are even more important. This mode of evaluation is a form of "self-interest", but it is quite different from the notion of skills-based, individual self-interest favoured by other scholars. What these results tell us is that supporters of trade liberalization believe that previous agreements have not hurt the economy and have not hurt them personally. This support is a form of output legitimacy – that is, a conclusion that agreements have been good for the individual and national economy – rather than support based on the details of the agreements (Mendelsohn *et al.*, 2002). And finally, the material self-interest-based approach to understanding support for trade liberalization may say more about the preoccupations of American scholars or the dynamics of American politics than it does about Canadians. Assessing whether citizens in countries other than Canada use their attitudes toward the USA to shape their judgments about globalization would be an appropriate next step in the analysis.

We found that education and income (as well union membership and sector of employment) prove to be fairly poor predictors of opinion on globalization. The impact of skills and rational economic self-interest in individual calculations is virtually irrelevant when it comes to citizens' understanding of globalization. Furthermore, retrospective evaluations are less important for opinion on globalization than they were with respect to opinion on trade. This difference arises because references to earlier examples of globalization are a far more difficult calculation for citizens to use. While this calculation might be a simple mental shortcut regarding trade – How has trade affected my country up to now? – it is not nearly as simple for citizens with respect to globalization. They must therefore look to their values.

Opponents of globalization are primarily concerned that it will damage cherished symbolic goods. Debates about globalization activate them not only as workers and consumers but also as citizens. The mental maps Canadians bring to their assessments of globalization include core values, ideology, and the kind of society in which they want to live. Some of the considerations they use to make sense of globalization may not be entirely surprising to scholars who have carefully studied concepts of globalization, but many of the patterns are not necessarily intuitive. Citizens who support a larger welfare state are more likely to oppose globalization, as are those who are more culturally conservative, as measured by their opposition to immigration. Similarly, Canadians who are less cosmopolitan, as measured by their opposition to the country taking a more active role in the world, are also more opposed to globalization. Interestingly, attitudes toward the USA are in part surrogates for attitudes toward globalization, with Canadians who want closer ties to the USA also showing more support for globalization. Some of these values are correlated with education, yet even controlling for skills measures, these values have a strong impact on attitudes toward globalization. Moreover, many of these variables are not correlated with skills variables at all, so they cannot be interpreted as merely surrogates for economic interests. We conclude that if we know someone's values, we have a good idea where they will stand on globalization, but if we know their level of skills and their material self-interest, we can say little about their views. We could also say about globalization that if we know someone's values, we will not be surprised by how they understand their interests (widely defined), but the reverse is not true.

Support for the international organization of the postwar era remains strong, especially when multilateralism is framed as a force for enhancing social values. That is, the compromise between domestic autonomy and global collective action described as embedded liberalism remains legitimate. How people understand the world is constructed by embedded liberalism. Letting the market run things, which is what complete liberalization implies, or allowing global governance to displace community governance, as implied by increased linkages, would be inconsistent with what Canadians believe to be the legitimate social purposes of their governing institutions. Embedded liberalism as a constitutive rule seems likely to continue shaping attitudes to global governance. As Polanyi (1944) showed, however, the continuing social response to the sort of market expansion associated with globalization can as easily lead to war as to enhanced international organizations. Whether the international order of embedded liberalism can be sustained is therefore a separate question, but we suggest that Canadians are still willing to make the necessary compromises.

Appendix

Q1 and Q2 see Table 7.1 for question wording. Variables coded: strongly support (1), somewhat support (.75), somewhat oppose (.25), strongly oppose (0), no opinion (.5).

Q3 Macroeconomic performance: Would you say that in the last few years the Canadian economy has been very strong (1), strong (.75), weak (.25), very weak (0), or neither strong nor weak (.5)?

Q4 Retrospective free trade: Can you tell me whether you think Canada has benefited a great deal (1), benefited a little (.75), has been harmed a little (.25), has been harmed a great deal (0), or has not been affected either way by international trade agreements (.5)?

Q5 Welfare state: Do you think it should be a high priority (1) for Canada, a medium priority (.66), a low priority (.33), or should it not be a priority at all (0): Having a more generous system of social programs? Having a government that interferes as little as possible with the free market? (Reverse coding undertaken for "free market", the two variables were then added together, and the result divided by 2).

Q6 Immigration: Do you think Canada should accept more immigrants (1), fewer immigrants (0), or about the same number of immigrants (.5) as we accept now?

Q7 Government doesn't care: Do you strongly agree (1), somewhat agree (.66), somewhat disagree (.33), or strongly disagree (0) with the following statements: I don't think that governments care very much what people like me think.

Q8 Canadian businesses: Can you tell me if you have a great deal of confidence (1), some (.66), not very much (.33), or no confidence at all (0) in each of the following groups: Canadian businesses?

Q9–Q11 Unions/environmental groups/multinational corporations (wording and coding as for Q8).

Q12 Attachment to Canada: Could you tell me whether you feel very attached (1), somewhat (.66), not very (.33), or not at all attached (0) to Canada?

Q13 Internationalism: Do you think that Canada should be more involved in world affairs than it is now (1), less involved (0), or about as involved as it is now (.5)?

Q14 Closer US ties: Do you think Canada should have much closer ties to the US (1), somewhat closer (.75), about the same as now (.5), somewhat more distant (.25), or much more distant (0) ties to the US than it has now?

Education: Eight categories, ranging from "primary or less" (0) to completion of a professional or graduate degree (1).

Income: Six categories, ranging from "under $20,000 per year" (0) to "over $100,000 per year" (1).

Age: 18–90.

Male: Male (1) Female (0).

References

Adams, Michael. 2003. *Fire and Ice: Canada, the United States, and the Myth of Converging Values*. Toronto: Penguin.

Aldrich, John H. and Forrest D. Nelson. 1984. *Linear Probability, Logit, and Probit Models*. Beverly Hills: Sage.

Bauer, Raymond A., Ithiel de Sola Pool and Lewis Anthony Dexter. 1963. *American Business and Public Policy: The Politics of Foreign Trade*. New York: Atherton Press.

Blyth, Mark. 2002. *Great Transformations: Economic Ideas and Institutional Change in the Twentieth Century*. New York: Cambridge University Press.

Borgatta, E.F. and G.M. Bohrnstedt. 1980. "Level of Measurement: Once over Again." *Sociological Methods and Research* 9: 147–60.

Bowler, Shaun and Todd Donovan. 1998. *Demanding Choices: Opinion and Voting in Direct Democracy*. Ann Arbor: University of Michigan Press.

Brady, Henry E. and Paul M. Sniderman. 1985. "Attitude Attribution: A Group Basis for Political Reasoning." *American Political Science Review* 79: 1061–78.

Butler, David and Donald Stokes. 1969. *Political Change in Britain: Forces Shaping Electoral Choice*. London: Macmillan.

Chong, Dennis. 2000. *Rational Lives: Norms and Values in Politics and Society*. Chicago, Ill.: University of Chicago Press.

Citrin, Jack, Ernst B. Haas, Christopher Muste and Beth Reingold. 1994. "Is American Nationalism Changing? Implications for Foreign Policy." *International Studies Quarterly* 38: 1–31.

Clarke, Harold D., Allan Kornberg, Chris McIntyre, Petra Bauer-Kaase and Max Kaase. 1999. "The Impact of Economic Priorities on the Measurement of Value Change: New Experimental Evidence." *American Political Science Review* 93: 637–647.

Dasko, Donna. 1988. "The Canadian Public and Free Trade." In *The Free Trade Deal*, ed. Duncan Cameron. Toronto: James Lorimer & Company, pp. 246–54.

Davis, Darren W. and Christian Davenport. 1999. "Assessing the Validity of the Postmaterialism Index." *American Political Science Review* 93: 649–664.

Deth, Jan W. and Elinor Scarbrough, eds. 1995. *The Impact of Values*. Oxford: Oxford University Press.

Eichenberg, Richard C. and Russell J. Dalton. 1993. "Europeans and the European Community: The Dynamics of Public Support for European Integration." *International Organization* 47: 507–534.

EKOS. 2003. "Canadian Attitudes to International Trade: Survey Findings." Available at the Canadian Opinion Research Archive, at the Web site http://www.queensu.ca/cora/polls/2003/May6-DFAIT-International_Trade.pdf, site last accessed January 21, 2004.

Fetzer, Joel S. 2000. *Public Attitudes toward Immigration in the United States, France, and Germany*. Cambridge: Cambridge University Press.

Gabel, Matthew. 1998a. "Economic Integration and Mass Politics: Market Liberalization and Public Attitudes in the European Union." *American Journal of Political Science* 42: 936–53.

Gabel, Matthew J. 1998b. *Interests and Integration: Market Liberalization, Public Opinion, and European Union*. Ann Arbor: University of Michigan Press.

Garrett, Geoffrey. 1998. *Partisan Politics in the Global Economy*. Cambridge: Cambridge University Press.

Gidengil, Elisabeth. 1995. "Economic Man – Social Woman? The Case of the Gender Gap in Support for the Canada-United States Free Trade Agreement." *Comparative Political Studies* 28: 384–408.

Herrmann, Richard K., Philip E. Tetlock and Matthew N. Diascro. 2001. "How Americans Think About Trade: Reconciling Conflicts among Money, Power, and Principles." *International Studies Quarterly* 45: 191–218.

Hiscox, Michael J. 2001. "Class Versus Industry Cleavages: Inter-Industry Factor Mobility and the Politics of Trade." *International Organization* 55: 1–46.

Holsti, O.R. and J.N. Roseneau. 1999. "The Political Foundations of Elites' Domestic and Foreign-Policy Beliefs." In *Domestic Sources of American Foreign Policy*, eds. E.R. Wittkopf and J.M. McCormick. Lanham, MD: Rowman & Littlefield, pp. 33–50.

Holsti, Ole R. 1996. *Public Opinion and American Foreign Policy*. Ann Arbor, Michigan: The University of Michigan Press.

Howse, Robert and Kalypso Nicolaidis. 2003. "Enhancing WTO Legitimacy: Constitutionalization or Global Subsidiarity?" *Governance* 16: 73–94.

Inglehart, Ronald. 1990. *Culture Shift in Advanced Industrial Society*. Princeton: Princeton University Press.

Inglehart, Ronald and Paul R. Abramson. 1999. "Measuring Postmaterialism." *American Political Science Review* 93: 665–677.

Jenssen, Anders Todal, Pertti Pesonen and Mikael Gilljam, eds. 1998. *To Join or Not to Join: Three Nordic Referendums on Membership in the European Union*. Oslo: Scandinavian University Press.

Johnston, Richard, André Blais, Henry E. Brady and Jean Crête. 1992. *Letting the People Decide: Dynamics of a Canadian Election*. Montreal and Kingston: McGill-Queen's University Press.

Johnston, Richard and Michael B. Percy. 1980. "Reciprocity, Imperial Sentiment, and Party Politics in the 1911 Election." *Canadian Journal of Political Science* 13: 711–29.

Kitschelt, Herbert. 1994. *The Transformation of European Social Democracy*. Cambridge; New York: Cambridge University Press.

Kratochwil, Friedrich. 2000. "Constructing a New Orthodoxy? Wendt's 'Social Theory of International Politics' and the Constructivist Challenge." *Millennium* 29: 73–101.

LeDuc, Lawrence and J. Alex Murray. 1984. "Public Opinion and North American Integration: Pragmatic Nationalism." In *The Integration Question: Political Economy and Public Policy in Canada and North America*, eds. Jon H. Pammett and BrianW. Tomlin. Don Mills, Ontario: Addison-Wesley Publishers.

Lupia, Arthur and Mathew D. McCubbins. 1998. *The Democratic Dilemma: Can Citizens Learn What They Need to Know?* New York: Cambridge University Press.

Martin, Pierre and Michel Fortmann. 1995. "Canadian Public Opinion and Peacekeeping in a Turbulent World." *International Journal* 50:2 370–400.

Martin, Pierre and Michel Fortmann. 2001. "Public Opinion: Obstacle, Partner or Scapegoat?" *Policy Options* 22: 66–72.

Mayda, Anna Maria and Dani Rodrik. 2002. "Why Are Some People (and Countries) More Protectionist Than Others?" Harvard University: January 2002. (http://ksghome.harvard.edu/~drodrik/TradePref.PDF accessed September 19, 2004).

Mendelsohn, Matthew. 2002. "Canada's Social Contract: Evidence from Public Opinion." Canadian Policy Research Network, Ottawa.

Mendelsohn, Matthew and Robert Wolfe. 2001. "Probing the Aftermyth of Seattle: Canadian Public Opinion on International Trade, 1980–2000." *International Journal* 56: 234–260.

Mendelsohn, Matthew, Robert Wolfe and Andrew Parkin. 2002. "Globalization, Trade Policy and the Permissive Consensus in Canada." *Canadian Public Policy* 28: 351–371.

Monroe, Alan D. 1998. "Public Opinion and Public Policy, 1980–1993." *Public Opinion Quarterly* 62: 6–28.

Munton, D. 2002. "Whither Internationalism?" *International Journal* 58: 155–180.

Munton, Don and Tom Keating. 2001. "Internationalism and the Canadian Public." *Canadian Journal of Political Science* 34: 517–549.

Murray, Shoon Kathleen and Jonathan A. Cowden. 1999. "The Role of 'Enemy Images' and Ideology in Elite Belief Systems." *International Studies Quarterly* 43: 455–483.

Nadeau, Richard and Jean H. Guay. 1990. "Un Réexamen De La Loi De Converse Sur Le Lien Entre Le Degré D'information Politique Et La Mobilité De L'opinion." *Revue canadien de science politique* 23: 727–749.

Nelson, Douglas. 2002. "Review of Globalization and the Perceptions of American Workers." *The World Economy* 25: 167–169.

Nie, Norman, Sidney Verba and John Petrocik. 1979. *The Changing American Voter*. Cambridge: Harvard University Press.

Noel, A., J. P. Therien and S. Dallaire. 2004. "Divided over Internationalism: The Canadian Public and Development Assistance." *Canadian Public Policy* 30: 29–46.

Norpoth, Helmut, Michael Lewis-Beck and Jean-Dominique Lafay, eds. 1991. *Economics and Politics: The Calculus of Support*. Ann Arbor: University of Michigan Press.

Norris, Pippa. 1999. *Critical Citizens: Global Support for Democratic Government*. New York: Oxford University Press.

Norris, Pippa. 2000. "Global Governance and Cosmopolitan Citizens." In *Governance in a Globalizing World*, eds. Joseph S. Nye and John D. Donahue. Washington, DC: Brookings Institution Press, pp. 155–177.

O'Rourke, Kevin H. and Richard Sinnott. 2001. "The Determinants of Individual Trade Policy Preferences: International Survey Evidence." In *Brookings Trade Forum 2001*, eds. Susan Margaret Collins and Dani Rodrik. Washington, DC: Brookings Institution Press, pp. 157–206.

Page, Benjamin and Robert Shapiro. 1992. The Rational Public: Fifty Years of Trends in *American's Policy Preferences*. Chicago: University of Chicago Press.

Polanyi, Karl. 1944. *The Great Transformation: The Political and Economic Origins of Our Time*. Boston: Beacon Press.

Popkin, Samuel. 1991. *The Reasoning Voter: Communication and Persuasion in Presidential Campaigns*. Chicago: University of Chicago Press.

Prakash, Aseem. 2001. "The East Asian Crisis and the Globalization Discourse." *Review of International Political Economy* 8: 119–147.

Reilly, John E. 1999. "Americans and the World: A Survey at Century's End." *Foreign Policy* 114: 97–114.

Rodrik, Dani. 1997. *Has Globalization Gone Too Far?* Washington, DC: Institute of International Economics.

Rogowski, Ronald. 1989. *Commerce and Coalitions: How Trade Affects Domestic Political Alignments*. Princeton, NJ: Princeton University Press.

Rowe, David M. 1995. "Politicians, Voters, and Trade." *Mershon International Studies Review* 39: 302–304.

Ruggie, John Gerard. 1982. "International Regimes, Transactions, and Change: Embedded Liberalism in the Postwar Economic Order." In *International Regimes*, ed. Stephen D. Krasner. Ithaca: Cornell University Press, pp. 195–231.

Ruggie, John Gerard. 1998. "What Makes the World Hang Together? Neo-Utilitarianism and the Social Constructivist Challenge." *International Organization* 52: 855–885.

Scheve, Kenneth F. and Matthew J. Slaughter. 2001a. *Globalization and the Perceptions of American Workers*. Washington: Institute for International Economics.

Scheve, Kenneth F. and Matthew J. Slaughter. 2001b. "What Determines Individual Trade-Policy Preferences?" *Journal of International Economics* 54: 267–292.

Scholte, Jan Aart. 2002. "Civil Society and Democracy in Global Governance." *Global Governance* 8: 281–304.

Sigler, John H. and Dennis Goresky. 1974. "Public Opinion on United States-Canadian Relations." *International Organization* 28: 637–68.

Verdier, Daniel. 1994. *Democracy and International Trade: Britain, France, and the United States, 1860–1990*. Princeton: Princeton University Press.

Wolfe, Robert and Matthew Mendelsohn. 2004. "Embedded Liberalism in the Global Era: Would Citizens Support a New Grand Compromise?" *International Journal* 59:2 261–280

Wright, Erik Olin. 1997. *Class Counts: Comparative Studies in Class Analysis*. Cambridge: Cambridge University Press.

Chapter 8

Taking Embedded Liberalism Global: The Corporate Connection

John Gerard Ruggie

Twenty years ago I published a scholarly article that introduced the concept of embedded liberalism.[1] It told the story of how the capitalist countries learned to reconcile the efficiency of markets with the values of social community that markets themselves require in order to survive and thrive. That lesson did not come to them easily.

In the Victorian era, policy concern with the level of domestic employment and price stability was subordinated to maintaining the external value of currencies and, less consistently, to the strictures of free trade. But the growing democratization of national political life made that posture increasingly unsustainable, and the first so-called golden age of globalization unraveled. In the period between the two world wars the opposite was true: the unfettered quest for national policy autonomy – pushed by the political left, right and center alike – steadily undermined and ultimately destroyed an already fragile international economic order.

When a workable balance finally was struck it took on somewhat different forms in different countries, reflecting national political realities: in the US, the New Deal or Keynesian state, and in Europe social democracy or the social market economy. But the underlying idea was the same: a grand social bargain whereby all sectors of society agreed to open markets, which in some cases had become heavily administered if not autarchic in the 1930s, but also to contain and share the social adjustment costs that open markets inevitably produce. That was the essence of the embedded liberalism compromise: economic liberalization was embedded in social community.

Governments played a key role in enacting and sustaining this compromise: moderating the volatility of transaction flows across borders and providing social investments, safety nets and adjustment assistance – yet all the while pushing international liberalization. In the industrialized countries, this grand bargain formed the basis of the longest and most equitable economic expansion in human history.

---

1   John Gerard Ruggie, "International Regimes, Transactions and Change: Embedded Liberalism in the Postwar Economic Order," *International Organization*, 36 (Spring 1982). The essay drew on Karl Polanyi's classic and still unsurpassed account of these wrenching struggles in *The Great Transformation* (Boston: Beacon Press, 1944); for a recent economic history see Harold James, *The End of Globalization: Lessons from the Great Depression* (Cambridge, Mass.: Harvard University Press, 2001).

So what is the problem today? For the industrialized countries, it is the fact that embedded liberalism presupposed an *international* world. It presupposed the existence of *national* economies, engaged in *external* transactions, conducted at *arm's length*, which governments could mediate at the *border* by tariffs and exchange rates, among other tools. The globalization of financial markets and production chains, however, challenges each of these premises and threatens to leave behind merely national social bargains.

The developing countries, of course, never enjoyed the privilege of cushioning the adverse domestic effects of market exposure in the first place. The majority lack the resources, institutional capacity, international support and, in some instances, the political interest on the part of their ruling elites. As a result, large parts of the developing world have been unable to exploit the opportunities offered by globalization for achieving poverty reduction and sustainable development.

Thus, "our challenge," United Nations Secretary-General Kofi Annan alerted the World Economic Forum in January 1999, ten months before the so-called Battle of Seattle, "is to devise a similar compact on the global scale, to underpin the new global economy. ... Until we do," he predicted, "the global economy will be fragile and vulnerable – vulnerable to backlash from all the 'isms' of our post-cold-war world: protectionism, populism, nationalism, ethnic chauvinism, fanaticism and terrorism."[2]

Embedding the global market within shared social values and institutional practices represents a task of historic magnitude. The reason is obvious: there is no govern*ment* at the global level to act on behalf of the common good, as there is at the national level. And international institutions are far too weak to fully compensate. Accordingly, this chapter examines the role of certain social processes and movements in triggering the emergence of more inclusive forms of global govern*ance*. Specifically, I focus on the contribution of the dynamic interplay between civil society, business and the public sector over the issue of corporate social responsibility.

The chapter is divided into two main parts. First, I describe some of the main drivers of the anti-globalization backlash, especially the growing anxieties in the industrialized countries that the social embeddedness side of the equation is losing out to the dictates of globalization. Then I examine the evolution of voluntary initiatives involving civil society and the global business community to promote corporate social responsibility as one means of responding to the many challenges of globalization. In that context, I also summarize the key features of Annan's Global Compact, a UN initiative to engage the corporate community, in partnership with civil society and labor, to implement human rights, labor standards and environmental sustainability in its global domain. The burden of my argument, with due appreciation for the irony, is that the corporate sector, which has done more than any other to create the growing gaps between global economy and national communities, is being pulled into playing a key bridging role between them. In the process, a global public domain is emerging, which cannot substitute for effective action by states but may help produce it.

---

2   Kofi Annan, "A Compact for the New Century," Jan. 31, 1999 (UN, SG/SM/6881).

The Backlash

The globalization backlash has many sources, some better reasoned than others.[3] But three negative attributes of the recent era of global market integration stand out as having animated particular concern.

First, the benefits of globalization are distributed highly unequally. As the IMF's Managing Director, Horst Kohler, has conceded, "the disparities between the world's richest and poorest nations are wider than ever."[4] Large parts of the developing world are left behind entirely. Africa is less integrated into the global economy today than a decade ago, and insofar as it is, it is largely through commodity exports, which works to Africa's disadvantage as commodity prices have fallen steadily.

Moreover, apart from China, income disparities among the world's people, as distinguished from countries, either have not improved significantly during the past three decades or actually may have become worse, depending on how they are measured.[5] Much the same holds for global poverty rates. Even in the United States, the unprecedented boom of the 1990s barely budged the income shares of the bottom 20 percent of households, and then only briefly.[6]

There is no fully satisfactory or universally accepted explanation of the relationship between these disparities and globalization. But their coexistence over an extended period of time, coupled with excessive claims for globalization's beneficence by some of its most powerful advocates, themselves feed criticism and outright opposition, including by a growing number of mainstream economists.[7]

---

3   For a cross section of critiques see Robin Broad (ed.), *Global Backlash: Citizen Initiatives for a Just World Economy* (Lanham, Md.: Rowman and Littlefield, 2002). Also see the excellent analysis by Susan Ariel Aaronson, *Taking Trade to the Streets* (Ann Arbor: University of Michigan Press, 2001).

4   "Working for a Better Globalization," remarks by Horst Köhler at the Conference on Humanizing the Global Economy, Washington DC, Jan. 28, 2002.

5   The difficulties of statistical measurement are formidable. Robert Wade's chapter in this volume addresses the methodological issues and substantive findings, and reaches a pessimistic conclusion; also see Branko Milanovic, "The Two Faces of Globalization: Against Globalization As We Know It," available at www.worldbank.org/research/inequality/pdf/naiveglobl.pdf. On the other side, see Xavier Sala-i-Martin, "The Disturbing 'Rise' of Global Income Inequality," National Bureau of Economic Research Working Paper no. 8904, Apr. 2002.

6   The Census Bureau reports that the share of total household income accounted for by the bottom quintile increased to 3.7% in 1995, from 3.6% in 1993, but by 1997 it had dropped again to its earlier level, where it remained as of 2000. Carmen DeNavas-Walt, Robert W. Cleveland and Marc I. Roemer, *Money Income in the United States: 2000* (Washington DC: US Census Bureau, Sept. 2001), table C, p. 8. Current figures are noted in Louis Uchitelle, "Stagnant Wages Pose Added Risks to Weak Economy," *New York Times*, Aug. 11, 2002.

7   For example, Dani Rodrik has led the way in challenging World Bank claims that trade liberalization itself leads to greater success in promoting economic growth and poverty reduction, arguing that the causality and the sequencing are far more complex. Rodrik, "Comments on 'Trade, Growth, and Poverty,' by D. Dollar and A. Kraay," available at http://ksghome.harvard.edu~.drodrik.academic. ksg/Rodrik%20on%20Dollar-Kraay.PDF.

Second, the backlash is triggered by a growing imbalance in global rule making. Those rules that favor global market expansion have become more robust and enforceable in the last decade or two – intellectual property rights, for example, or trade dispute resolution through the World Trade Organization. But rules intended to promote equally valid social objectives, be they labor standards, human rights, environmental quality or poverty reduction, lag behind and in some instances actually have become weaker.[8] One result is the situation where considerations of patent rights have trumped fundamental human rights and even pandemic threats to human life – at least until that clash became unbearable for the world's conscience over the HIV/AIDS treatment issue in Africa.[9]

Third, for many people globalization has come to mean greater vulnerability to unfamiliar and unpredictable forces that can bring on economic instability and social dislocation, sometimes at lightning speed. The Asian financial crisis of 1997–8 was such a force – the fourth but not the last major international financial crisis in just two decades. Indeed, the integrity of cultures and sovereignty of states increasingly are seen to be at risk. Even in the most powerful countries, people worry for their jobs, wonder who is in charge and fear that their voices are drowned out in globalization's wake.

The long struggle that ultimately resulted in the embedded liberalism compromise suggests that disparities of this sort are socially unsustainable. Unless they are attended to they are bound to trigger some of the "isms" of which Annan warned – disrupting and potentially undermining the open global economy. What is more, the backlash against globalization has particular bite because it is driven not only, or even primarily, by the poor and the weak. Its vanguard includes large numbers of people in the most privileged societies the world has ever known.

Therefore, let us look briefly at some of the issues that trigger people's anxieties about globalization in the industrialized countries, and how much staying power their concerns are likely to have. Much of the debate about whether globalization is adversely affecting the social embeddedness of market forces focuses on its impact on levels of public expenditure and on public policy, especially in areas related to social safety nets; wage and employment levels; and more elusive issues of identity and accountability.

Public Expenditure

Vito Tanzi and Ludger Schuknecht document the evolution of public expenditure in the industrialized countries going back to 1870.[10] Over the course of the subsequent

---

8   For detailed surveys of what gets "regulated" at the global level, and how, see P. J. Simmons and Chantal de Jonge Oudraat (eds), *Managing Global Issues* (Washington DC: Carnegie Endowment, 2001), and John Braithwaite and Peter Drahos, *Global Business Regulation* (New York: Cambridge University Press, 2000).

9   The business community itself felt that the big pharmaceutical companies put themselves in an untenable position. Gardiner Harris and Laurie McGinley, "AIDS Gaffes in Africa Come Back to Haunt Drug Industry at Home," *Wall Street Journal*, Apr. 23, 2001.

10 Vito Tanzi and Ludger Schuknecht, *Public Spending in the 20th Century* (New York: Cambridge University Press, 2000).

125 years, spending grew from an average of 10.7 percent of gross domestic product, to 45.6 percent. The two world wars and the Great Depression accounted for significant increases. But the most dramatic expansion took place between 1960 and 1980, and in that period social expenditures – for education, health, pensions, unemployment benefits and the like – more than doubled on average. This was also the period of the most significant reductions in barriers to trade and monetary flows by the industrialized countries. Research by political scientists as long ago as the late 1970s demonstrated a relationship between the two: the most open economies also tended to lead in social spending.[11] Broadly speaking, this pattern was in keeping with the embedded liberalism compromise of providing a certain measure of domestic compensation for the risks attending greater international openness.[12]

The 1980s and 1990s saw the emergence of growing skepticism about the role of the state, especially in the United Kingdom and the United States. For a variety of reasons, some substantive, others political, prevailing economic theory and public attitudes began to shift in a neoliberal (the preferred term for neo-laissez-faire) direction.[13] Though public spending continued to increase, it was at a slower pace. And it was purchasing fewer social services, in part due to the declining cost-effectiveness of some interventions, and in part because a rapidly rising public sector debt burden consumed an ever greater fraction of overall government spending.[14] A period of reform and retrenchment ensued.[15]

Tanzi and Schuknecht predict a reduction in public expenditure relative to GDP in the years ahead, reflecting less favorable attitudes toward the role of the state (which may be partially off-set in the United States by the effects of 9/11 and corporate malfeasance), coupled with greater fiscal constraints due to demographic shifts, among other factors.

---

11 David R. Cameron, "The Expansion of the Public Economy: a Comparative Analysis," *American Political Science Review*, 72 (Dec. 1978); and Peter J. Katzenstein, "The Small European States in the International Economy," in John Gerard Ruggie (ed.), *The Antinomies of Interdependence* (New York: Columbia University Press, 1983).

12 Garrett seems to think that embedded liberalism should be measurable by some fixed formula linking year-to-year increases in the degree of openness to levels of growing social expenditure, allowing for a time lag. Geoffrey Garrett, "Capital Mobility, Exchange Rates and Fiscal Policy in the Global Economy," *Review of International Political Economy*, 7 (Spring 2000). But broad social frameworks of this sort work as constitutive expectations pertaining to an overall order of relations, not fixed bargains that govern every transaction. For a discussion of this difference in perspectives, see John Gerard Ruggie, "What Makes the World Hang Together? Neo-utilitarianism and the Social Constructivist Challenge," *International Organization*, 52 (Autumn 1998).

13 I concluded my 1982 article with the observation that the greatest threat to embedded liberalism came not from the so-called new protectionism, as was then widely assumed, "but the resurgent ethos of liberal capitalism" ("International Regimes, Transactions and Change," p. 413). Also see Mark Blyth, *Great Transformations: The Rise and Decline of Embedded Liberalism* (New York: Cambridge University Press, 2002).

14 Government expenditure on public debt rose rapidly from an average of 1.4% of GDP in 1970 to 4.5% in 1995. Tanzi and Schuknecht, *Public Spending in the 20th Century*, p. 46.

15 Mary Ruggie, *Realignments in the Welfare State* (New York: Columbia University Press, 1996).

But what exactly is the relationship between these trends and globalization? An increasingly widespread view holds that global market integration induces governments to pursue greater fiscal austerity, ease regulatory and tax burdens on business, and strongly discourage certain policy options if not ruling them out altogether[16] – owing to the relative increase in capital mobility if nothing else.[17] Geoffrey Garrett has examined aspects of this relationship closely – and skeptically – for some time. In a book published in 1998, he argued that social democracy continued to thrive where powerful left-of-center parties were allied with strong and centralized trade unions – irrespective of differences in the extent of market integration.[18] In other words, domestic coalitional politics appeared to be a more powerful explanation of social spending and related policy outcomes than globalization.[19]

But in a recent and more comprehensive statistical analysis Garrett has modified some of his earlier conclusions in at least three key respects. He now finds that year-to-year increases in total trade *do* have a negative effect on government spending, even though historically a country's exposure to trade was an important determinant of fiscal expansion.[20] He shows that increased international financial openness produces a similar result. And he finds that over time the average mix of taxation in the OECD countries has become somewhat less progressive – that is, "more revenues have been raised by tax sources that target poorer people."[21] Foreign direct investment had no such effects.

---

16 Clearly financial market integration has increased the cost of utilizing capital controls. For example, when Malaysia imposed targeted and time-bound controls to limit domestic spillover from the Asian financial crisis, for which it had no responsibility, all the major credit rating agencies downgraded Malaysia's sovereign risk rating – Fitch IBCA to "junk bond" status. Said a spokesperson for Fitch: "We are in no doubt about Malaysia's ability to service its debt. It is a question of willingness to do so" – even though the Malaysian government had done nothing to indicate any such unwillingness. See Rawi Abdelal and Laura Alfaro, "Malaysia: Capital and Control," Harvard Business School, Case 9-702-040 (June 4, 2002), p. 12.

17 Dani Rodrik, *Has Globalization Gone Too Far?* (Washington DC: Institute for International Economics, 1997).

18 Geoffrey Garrett, *Partisan Politics in the Global Economy* (New York: Cambridge University Press, 1998).

19 Of course, we would also want to know if globalization over time affects domestic coalitional possibilities. For one cut at this question see Jeffry A. Frieden and Ronald Rogowski, "The Impact of the International Economy on National Policies," in Robert O. Keohane and Helen V. Milner (eds), *Internationalization and Domestic Politics* (New York: Cambridge University Press, 1996).

20 Geoffrey Garrett and Deborah Mitchell, "Globalization, Government Spending and Taxation in the OECD," *European Journal of Political Research*, 39 (Mar. 2001), p. 147; and Garrett, "Capital Mobility, Exchange Rates and Fiscal Policy," p. 157. Interestingly, Garrett and Mitchell find no signs that this relationship is true specifically of trade with low-wage countries.

21 Garrett and Mitchell, "Globalization, Government Spending and Taxation," p. 159.

The magnitude of these changes remains small and patterns of variation among countries, and across different market segments for the same country, are exceedingly complex. Nevertheless, they may signal a gradual shift in the political economy of industrialized countries, away from an earlier "compensatory" approach to managing the effects of increased openness, toward more of a "competitiveness" model. This would confirm that popular anxiety about globalization, though possibly exaggerated, is not without any basis in fact. Recent moves by the United States Congress to limit offshore corporate tax havens and to couple President Bush's "fast track" trade negotiation authority with assistance to adversely affected workers indicate that even America's lawmakers – seemingly inured to this issue for the past two decades – have begun to recognize its political salience.[22]

Income and Employment

In the United States, organized labor has been among the most ardent opponents of globalization, especially of further trade liberalization. Although third party presidential candidate Ross Perot coined the phrase, labor's concern has been driven by fear of a "giant sucking sound" of well-paying jobs being exported to low-wage countries.

There is little dispute that median family income in the United States has been stagnant for two decades while worker productivity has been growing.[23] And there can be no disagreement that this gap coincides with large increases in trade exposure.

But there any consensus ends. Edward Leamer has developed a sophisticated economic model and presents country-based evidence partly supporting the globalization hypothesis.[24] In contrast, Robert Lawrence and Matthew Slaughter's statistical study leads them to conclude that "trade had nothing to do with the slow increase in average compensation," that low rates of productivity increases in the non-traded goods sector of the American economy have been responsible.[25]

---

22 Congress agreed to spend up to $12 billion over a ten-year period for such assistance, including a tax credit for 65% of the cost of health insurance should workers lose their jobs to foreign competition. Congress also authorized a pilot project for wage insurance to dislocated workers, under which they would receive some compensation for lower wages in a new job. "Promoting the Noble Cause of Commerce," *The Economist*, Aug. 3, 2002.

23 See, for example, Richard B. Freeman and Lawrence Katz, "Rising Wage Inequality: The United States versus Other Advanced Countries," in Richard B. Freeman (ed.), *Working under Different Rules* (New York: Russell Sage Foundation, 1994).

24 Edward E. Learner, "Wage Inequality from International Competition and Technological Change: Theory and Country Experience," American Economics Association, *Papers and Proceedings*, May 1996.

25 Robert Z. Lawrence and Matthew J. Slaughter, "International Trade and American Wages in the 1980s: Giant Sucking Sound or Small Hiccup?" *Brookings Papers on Economic Activity: Microeconomics*, no. 2 (1993), citation on p. 165. One source of disagreement is that Lawrence and Slaughter find no evidence that labor-intensive tradable goods have declined in price (and thus driven down wages). Leamer suggests that a longer timespan must be considered because prices take time to ripple through the economy.

Paul Krugman, among others, has argued that technological change, especially information technology, is the main cause.[26]

Disentangling and establishing these and other factors with any degree of certainty, Leamer acknowledges, "may be inherently too complex for economists to handle".[27] Dani Rodrik suggests that the link between globalization and its labor market effects may be largely indirect, through shifts in relative bargaining power.[28] Globalization makes the services of large numbers of workers more easily substitutable across national boundaries, Rodrik argues, as a result of which the leverage of immobile labor vis-à-vis mobile capital erodes. Thus, in the neoliberal countries workers are obliged to accept greater instability in earnings and hours worked, if not lower wages altogether; to pay a larger share of their own benefits (as has become all too evident in the area of pensions and health care) as well as improvements in working conditions; and to accept more frequent job changes. Along similar lines, Jagdish Bhagwati uses the term "kaleidoscopic" rather than "flexible" to describe the highly volatile US labor markets, thereby better conveying the nervousness they induce.[29] In the more traditional social democracies and social market economies where income levels and employment are more secure, labor is obliged to accept higher rates of chronic unemployment and lack of job creation.

Thus, the impact of globalization on wage stagnation in the US and high unemployment in Europe remains at minimum an open question for the economy as a whole. Of course, it is not an open question for workers in the industries affected most directly by job-displacing imports, who may have to accept lower-paying work. And if domestic compensatory measures erode at the same time, as discussed in the previous section, then labor's opposition to globalization should hardly come as a surprise.

Identity and Accountability

On the eve of the WTO's 1999 Seattle ministerial meeting, the University of Maryland's Program on International Policy Attitudes published a study of Americans' attitudes toward trade, and globalization more broadly.[30] A solid majority expressed

---

26 Paul Krugman, "Europe Jobless, America Penniless," *Foreign Policy*, 95 (Summer 1994); Paul Krugman and Robert Lawrence, "Trade, Jobs and Wages," *Scientific American*, 270 (April 1994); and Paul Krugman and A. J. Venables, "Globalization and the Inequality of Nations," *Quarterly Journal of Economics*, 110 (1995).

27 Learner, "Wage Inequality," p. 311. Addressing specifically the effects of technological change, Learner argues: "To do the job right, one really needs an accurate, complete, world-wide, long-run, general-equilibrium input-output model estimated from data that may or may not be available."

28 Rodrik, *Has Globalization Gone Too Far?*

29 Jagdish Bhagwati, "Trade and Wages: A Malign Relationship?" Columbia University, Department of Economics, Discussion Paper 761, Oct. 1995. Bhagwati's interpretation further stipulates that in such labor markets employers are reluctant to invest in training unskilled workers, putting them at a further disadvantage.

30 "Americans on Globalization," at http://pipa.org/OnlineReports/Globalization/global_ rep.html.

support for trade liberalization in principle. Only 30 percent felt it was going too fast; the rest felt that it was proceeding at the right speed (62 percent) or too slowly (23 percent).

But in practice business was seen to be the prime beneficiary: 61 percent of respondents felt that business was better off as a result of lower barriers, compared to only 25 percent who believed workers were. Overwhelming majorities felt that US trade policy-makers were giving "too little" consideration to "working Americans" (72 percent), "the general public" (68 percent) or "people like you" (73 percent). Furthermore, 60 percent felt that policy-makers paid too little attention to trade's "impact on the environment".

However, overall support for trade liberalization soared (to 84 percent) when respondents were offered the option that the government would help workers adapt to changes associated with increased trade. Moreover, 78 percent felt that the WTO should consider issues like labor standards and the environment when it makes trade decisions; and respondents were fully prepared to support trade sanctions to advance these (and related) social goals. As for globalization – conceived as the broader process of growing interconnectedness in the world – respondents saw it as having a mixture of positive and negative elements, with the positives moderately outweighing the negatives.

In short, the Maryland study makes it clear that the American public is far from being protectionist. But it views the benefits of open trade to be unequally distributed, and safeguards for workers, labor standards and the environment to be inadequate.

In a recent survey of Canadian public attitudes Matthew Mendelsohn and Robert Wolfe further differentiate attitudes toward trade liberalization from attitudes toward globalization. And they conduct a causal analysis relating those attitudes to relevant attributes of the respondents.[31]

Mendelsohn and Wolfe find that Canadians strongly support new trade agreements (65 percent positive responses), including a Free Trade Area of the Americas (67 percent positive). But they are dubious about encouraging more rapid globalization (only 45 percent positive). Moreover, while respondents strongly favored international cooperation and policy coordination – as is typical of Canadians' attitudes – they fundamentally opposed ceding national control over labor and workplace standards (a mere 27 percent positive) or standards for social programs (just 17 percent) – consequences they closely associate with globalization.

The causal chains behind these differences are even more striking.[32] The authors find that Canadians' attitudes toward trade reflect individuals' calculations of self-interest as economic agents – their level of education or skill, for example, and thus

---

31 Matthew Mendelsohn and Robert Wolfe, "Values, Interests and Globalization: The Continued Compromise of Embedded Liberalism," paper presented at the conference on Global Governance: Towards a New Grand Compromise? at the University of Toronto, May 29, 2002, available at http://qsilver.queensu.ca/~wolfer/General/research.html. Also see Mendelsohn and Wolfe, "Globalization, Trade Policy and the Permissive Consensus in Canada," *Canadian Public Policy*, 28, no. 3 (2002).

32 The regression results are reported in tables 3 and 4 of Mendelsohn and Wolfe, "Values, Interests and Globalization."

their sense of personal competitiveness in the global marketplace. But interest-based factors fail utterly to account for views about globalization. So whereas education, for example, is strongly related to attitudes toward trade, it is irrelevant to how the respondents feel about globalization. Instead, responses to globalization reflect Canadians' sense of identity as citizens and their core values concerning the kind of society in which they wish to live – and the respondents viewed the Canadian welfare state as a core feature of both.

If this is true in Canada it is bound to be all the more so within European Union countries, where identity politics is doubly jolted by globalization and political integration – the latter itself being, in part, a response to globalization.

To sum up, the industrialized countries appear to have passed through the 1990s with a fraying of domestic social safety nets, though not a dismantling. But the trend lines have been heading in negative directions. Moreover, anxieties about globalization appear to reflect individuals' fears not only about potential economic risks and losses, but also about losses measured in terms of identity and control. Unless these doubts about globalization are countered, therefore, they can only be expected to grow.

But, as we shall now see, those same anxieties about globalization also have helped generate and sustain civil society initiatives aimed at managing the adverse effects of globalization more directly, without waiting for states or international organizations to get around to acting. I now turn to that subject, beginning with a brief sketch of the expanding role of civil society in global governance.

Voluntary Initiatives

Once upon a time, governance at the international level was entirely a statist affair. Whether the instruments were international alliances, regimes, law and organizations, or transnational networks of national bureaucracies, states both monopolized the conduct of governance and were the primary objects of their joint decisions and actions. That was the foundational premise of the traditional system.

In recent decades, actors and forces for which the territorial state is not the cardinal organizing principle have begun to out-flank the state externally and to gnaw away at its governance monopoly from the inside. They may be driven by universal values or factional greed, by profit and efficiency considerations or the search for salvation. They include global financial markets and production chains, civil society organizations and such uncivil entities as transnational terrorist and criminal networks.

The place of non-state actors and movements remains poorly understood in the mainstream literature, largely because they tend to be viewed, implicitly if not explicitly, through the lenses of an "institutional substitutability" premise.[33] That is to say, if other institutional forms at the international level do not have the potential

---

33 I first flagged this issue in John Gerard Ruggie, "Territoriality and Beyond: Problematizing Modernity in International Relations," *International Organization*, 46 (Winter 1993).

to *replace* the territorial state they tend to be regarded as unworthy of serious consideration: interesting in practice, perhaps, but not in theory. And the fact is that the state is not disappearing, even in the increasingly integrated European Union.[34]

Nevertheless, significant institutional developments *are* evolving at the global level, among them the emergence of what we might call a global public domain: an arena of discourse, contestation and action organized around global rule making – a transnational space that is not exclusively inhabited by states, and which permits the direct expression and pursuit of human interests, not merely those mediated by the state.[35] One of its major drivers is the expanding role of civil society, and the interplay between civil society organizations and the global corporate sector.[36] This institutional development does not and cannot take the place of states, but it introduces new elements and new dynamics into the processes of global governance.

Civil Society Organizations

Real world players have come to recognize the involvement of civil society organizations (CSOs) in several areas related to global rule making – where by "recognize" I mean that the other players regard CSOs' participation as more or less legitimate, and in varying degrees they actually count on them to play those roles.[37] In other words, the roles have become institutionalized – much as, for example, the environmental movement did within the industrialized countries a generation ago.[38]

To begin with, civil society organizations have become the main international providers of direct assistance to people in developing countries, be it foreign aid, humanitarian relief or a variety of other internationally provided services. Governmental entities, such as the United States Agency for International Development, largely have become contracting agencies while CSOs deliver the goods.

---

34 Of course, individual states on the periphery may fail as a result of collapsed internal authority and the usurpation of the state's coercive apparatus for factional or private ends – as discussed in, for example, Mats Berdal and David M. Malone (eds), *Greed and Grievance: Economic Agendas in Civil Wars* (Boulder, Colo.: Lynne Rienner, 2000).

35 For good discussions of the concept of "public domain" – as distinct from, on the one side, the market and, on the other side, its narrower counterpart, the public sector – see Daniel Drache (ed.), *The Market or the Public Domain: Global Governance and the Asymmetry of Power* (London: Routledge, 2001).

36 I use the term "civil society organization" rather than NGO (nongovernmental organization) to include transnational social movements, coalitions and activist campaigns as well as NGOs.

37 For useful introductions, see Sanjeev Khagram, James V. Riker and Kathryn Sikkink (eds), *Restructuring World Politics: Transnational Social Movements, Networks and Norms* (Minneapolis: University of Minnesota Press, 2002); Ann M. Florini (ed.), *The Third Force: The Rise of Transnational Civil Society* (Washington DC: Carnegie Endowment for International Peace, 2000); and Jessica Mathews, "Power Shift," *Foreign Affairs*, 76 (Jan./Feb. 1997).

38 A good comparable discussion may be found in Cary Coglianese, "Social Movements, Law, and Society: The Institutionalization of the Environmental Movement," *University of Pennsylvania Law Review*, 150 (Nov. 2001).

In a normative vein, CSOs play increasingly important roles in generating, deepening and implementing transnational norms in such areas as human rights, the environment and anti-corruption. They do so through their own global campaign activities, but also by direct involvement in official governance forums like the UN's human rights machinery, where the documentation provided by Amnesty International, for example, carries weight precisely because it is detached from any national interest.[39]

CSO coalitions also have become a significant, if still episodic, force in blocking or promoting international agreements. Two exemplars have acquired iconic status. The most celebrated blockage was of the Multilateral Agreement on Investment (MAI), negotiated at the Organization for Economic Cooperation and Development (OECD), which would have been the high water mark of the neoliberal quest in the 1990s.[40] And the most dramatic instance of successfully promoting a new agreement – even participating fully in its negotiation – is the land-mines ban, which was begun, literally, by two people with a fax machine, and ended up helping to produce an international treaty over the opposition of the most powerful bureaucracy in the world's most powerful state: the US Pentagon.[41] More conventional CSO lobbying contributed to the creation of the International Criminal Court. CSOs also are a powerful source of political pressure for reforming international organizations, especially the Bretton Woods institutions and the WTO.[42]

Coalitions of domestic and transnational civil society networks also perform indispensable roles in the defense of human and labor rights, environmental standards and other social concerns within countries where the normal political process impedes or opposes progress in those areas. A key mechanism is the so-called boomerang

---

39 On human rights, see Thomas Risse, "The Power of Norms versus the Norms of Power: Transnational Civil Society and Human Rights," and on anti-corruption, Fredrik Galtung, "A Global Network to Curb Corruption: The Experience of Transparency International," in Florini, *The Third Force*.

40 A global coalition of CSOs made the case that certain of the MAI's provisions on investment protection would enable transnational corporations to challenge domestic environmental and labor standards on the grounds that they had the equivalent effect of expropriation, so that companies adversely affected could claim compensation. Supporting that fear was a 1996 case involving the Ethyl Corporation, which successfully sued the Canadian government under a similar provision of the North American Free Trade Agreement when Canada banned a gasoline additive Ethyl produced, with Canada agreeing to an out-of-court settlement of $13 million. Andrew Walter, "NGOs, Business, and International Investment: The Multilateral Agreement on Investment, Seattle, and Beyond," *Global Governance*, 7 (Jan./Mar. 2001); and Stephen J. Kobrin, "The MAI and the Clash of Globalizations," *Foreign Policy*, 112 (Fall 1998). Both authors stress that factors other than activist pressure also contributed to the MAI's demise.

41 Motoko Mekata, "Building Partnerships toward a Common Goal: Experiences of the International Campaign to Ban Landmines," in Florini, *The Third Force*; and Ramesh Thakur and William Malley, "The Ottawa Convention on Landmines: A Landmark Humanitarian Treaty in Arms Control?" *Global Governance*, 5 (July/Sept. 1999).

42 Robert O'Brien, Jan Aart Scholte, Marc Williams and Anne Marie Goetz, *Contesting Global Governance* (New York: Cambridge University Press, 2000).

effect, first identified by Keck and Sikkink, whereby domestic civil society actors link up with international actors, including other CSOs, states and international organizations, to bring external pressure to bear on the target state(s).[43]

Finally, civil society organizations have become a major force to induce greater social responsibility in the global corporate sector, by creating transparency in the overseas behavior of companies and their suppliers and creating links to consumers back home.[44] The last of these is of greatest interest for the purposes of the present chapter.

Corporate Social Responsibility

The rights enjoyed by transnational corporations have increased manyfold over the past two decades, as a result of multilateral trade agreements, bilateral investment pacts and domestic liberalization. Along with those rights, however, have come demands, led largely by civil society, that corporations accept commensurate obligations. To oversimplify only slightly, as governments were creating the space for transnational corporations (TNCs) to operate globally, other social actors have sought to infuse that space with greater corporate social responsibility.

Civil society organizations have joined issue with the global corporate sector for several reasons. First, individual companies have made themselves targets by doing "bad" things in the past: Shell in Nigeria, Nike in Indonesia, Nestlé in relation to its breast milk substitute products, unsafe practices in the chemical industry as symbolized by Union Carbide's Bhopal disaster, upscale apparel retailers purchasing from sweatshop suppliers, unsustainable forestry practices by the timber industry, and so on. Even where companies may be breaking no laws, they have been targeted by activist groups for violating the companies' own self-proclaimed standards or broader community norms in such areas as human rights, labor practices and environmental sustainability. CSOs seek to induce companies to undertake verifiable change.

Second, the growing imbalance between corporate rights and obligations itself has become a major factor driving CSO campaigns and, as I suggested earlier, it has particular resonance where it touches on life-and-death issues like HIV/AIDS treatment and related public health crises. In that particular instance, the pharmaceutical industry's pricing policy, combined with its insistence on protecting patent rights, prevented access to treatment for millions of poor people

---

43 Margaret E. Keck and Kathryn Sikkink, *Activists beyond Borders* (Ithaca, N.Y.: Cornell University Press, 1998). Also see Daniel C. Thomas, *The Helsinki Effect: International Norms, Human Rights, and the Demise of Communism* (Princeton: Princeton University Press, 2001).

44 Good overviews may be found in Gary Gereffi, Ronie Garcia-Johnson and Erika Sasser, "The NGO-Industrial Complex," *Foreign Policy*, 125 (July/Aug. 2001), and several unpublished papers on their websites (www.env.duke.edu/solutions/colloquia-7th.html/, and www.env.duke.edu/solutions/research-envcert.html). On labor standards specifically, see Adelle Blackett, "Global Governance, Legal Pluralism and the Decentered State: A Labor Law Critique of Codes of Corporate Conduct," *Indiana Journal of Global Legal Studies*, 8 (2001), pp. 401–47.

in poor countries. Civil society successfully framed price reductions as a corporate obligation.

Gradually, however, the sheer fact that the corporate sector, unlike states and international organizations, has global reach and capacity has become its most compelling attraction to other social actors, together with its ability to make and implement decisions at a pace that neither governments nor intergovernmental agencies can possibly match. In the face of global governance gaps and governance failures, civil society – and increasingly other actors as well, including states – seeks to engage the corporate world's global platform to advance broader social objectives. Kofi Annan's Global Compact, discussed below, is based entirely on this rationale.

The universe of transnational corporations consists roughly of 63,000 firms, with more than 800,000 subsidiaries and millions of suppliers.[45] Improving those companies' social and environmental performance has direct benefits for their employees and the communities in which they operate. But equally important is the potential for generating positive social spillover effects. In the developing world, the adoption of good practices by major firms may exert an upward pull on the performance of local enterprises in the same sector.[46] And in the industrialized countries, the gradual diffusion of good practices by major companies' social and environmental performance abroad may lessen the fear that a global "race to the bottom" will undermine their own policy frameworks for achieving social inclusion and economic security at home.

In sum, as a result of pressure from civil society, companies and business associations began to accept, on a voluntary basis and at a modest pace, new corporate social responsibilities in their own corporate domains, and more recently vis-à-vis society at large. The decision by firms to engage is driven by a variety of factors, but above all by the sensitivity of their corporate brands to consumer attitudes.

Certification Institutions

Transnational corporations have adopted scores of codes of conduct and negotiated others within industry associations and with CSOs. Gary Gereffi and his colleagues call these "certification institutions".[47] By now they exist in most major economic sectors, including mining, petroleum, chemicals, forest products, automobiles as well as textiles, apparel and footwear. A recent OECD survey inventoried 246 codes,

---

45 The number of multinationals and their subsidiaries is reported in the *World Investment Report* (Geneva: United Nations Conference on Trade and Development, 2001). It is impossible to calculate the actual number of suppliers; Nike, for example, has approximately 750, and it is at the lower end among comparable firms in the number of factories as a fraction of its revenue base (personal communication from Nike executive).

46 Surprisingly little systematic research has been done on this question, in contrast to the volume of rhetoric it has generated. For a careful study in the environmental area, see Ronie Garcia-Johnson, *Exporting Environmentalism: US Multinational Chemical Corporations in Brazil and Mexico* (Cambridge, Mass.: MIT Press, 2000).

47 See the sources in note 44.

though the total number remains unknown.[48] In that survey, labor standards (heavy concentration in the apparel industry) and environmental concerns (high in the extractive sector) dominate other issues addressed (148 and 145 cases respectively), with some codes including both.

The initial wave consisted largely of unilateral company codes. They made it possible for firms to claim that their behavior was governed by a code of conduct, but without, for the most part, sharing its details with the public. Of the 118 companies with individual codes included in the OECD survey, for example, only 24 indicated any form of public disclosure of company compliance.[49] And company codes are far more likely to address practices found objectionable by industrialized country consumers than possibly more pervasive problems that entail fewer reputational risks – in the area of labor standards, for instance, workplace harassment and child labor dominate, with freedom of association trailing well behind.

Individual exceptions have always existed, such as Levi Strauss, which pioneered a transparent worldwide code for manufacturing and contractors as long ago as 1991.[50] In 2002, the Royal Dutch/Shell group became the first company to combine its social and financial reports into one, believing that investors should see the full picture of the company's performance.[51] In the interval, some branded apparel retailers began to audit supplier compliance with company codes, in many cases using respected third-party instruments like SA8000.[52] Two major standardized systems for reporting companies' social and environmental performance are now on-stream as well, AccountAbility1000 and the Global Reporting Initiative.[53]

---

48 OECD, Working Party of the Trade Committee, "Codes of Corporate Conduct – an Expanded Review of their Contents," TD/TC/ WP(99)56/FINAL (June 7, 2000). Identifying the total universe of cases would require conducting a company-by-company survey, coupled with complementary surveys of industry associations and relevant CSOs – a prohibitive undertaking. Accordingly, the OECD warns that its inventory is neither a random nor a representative sample. In light of these data collection problems, much of the literature focuses on the far smaller but better known universe of sectoral multi-stakeholder codes and certification agreements; see Gereffi, Garcia-Johnson and Sasser, "The NGO-Industrial Complex."

49 "Codes of Corporate Conduct," table 6, p. 35.

50 www.levistrauss.com/responsibility.

51 www.shell.com/html/investor-en/shellreport01/reports2001/frameset.html.

52 SA8000, a system developed by Social Accountability International, covers a wide range of labor rights, health and safety standards, working conditions and compensation issues. It draws on the idea of quality control standards that are nearly universally used in the production of goods, and extends this concept to the treatment of workers. Companies subscribe to the SA8000 code or "management system", and their facilities are audited and "certified" by external auditors, who are themselves trained and certified by the SA8000 governing body. Deborah Leipziger, *SA8000: The Definitive Guide to the New Social Standard* (London: Financial Times/Prentice Hall, 2001).

53 Their attempt is to make social and environmental reporting as routine as financial reporting. Interestingly, the two systems reflect their respective national origins in their orientation: the GRI, a US invention, tries to capture the full range of possibilities by means of a large number of discrete indicators, whereas AA1000, which originated in the UK, is

Other companies are learning that talk is not cheap. Nike, for example, is in the California courts under that state's Unfair Business Practices Act, accused of making misrepresentations, false statements and material omissions in literature about working conditions in its supply chain in an attempt to maintain or increase sales. The California Superior Court ruled that Nike's promotional statements were not protected as free speech but constituted commercial speech, and it allowed an individual consumer's suit against the company to go forward.[54]

The most ambitious and typically the most transparent certification arrangements tend to be sectoral in scope, and to involve several companies and/or business associations along with civil society participants. Their aims range from ensuring that the price paid to cooperatives of small-scale family farmers growing coffee beans in Costa Rica includes a premium for growing the beans in an environmentally sustainable manner (Fair Trade Certified coffee); to ensuring that plywood ending up at Home Depot and other participating home improvement outlets is produced in accordance with sustainable forestry practices (Forest Stewardship Council); to certifying that sweatshirts sold in college bookstores or cashmere sweaters destined for Fifth Avenue department stores and upscale suburban malls are knitted in conditions that meet agreed labor standards and conditions (Workers Rights Consortium, and either the Fair Labor Association or an individual company code with compliance audited by SA8000). A certification institution called Responsible Care – triggered by Bhopal – now operates in the US chemical industry, while the Global Mining Initiative was recently launched in that sector.

Many such arrangements now exist – there are 22 additional certification institutions in the forest products industry alone, for instance, and the US-based Workers Rights Consortium is closely coordinated with European initiatives like the Clean Clothes Campaign.[55] Their rate of increase over the past decade has been extraordinary.

The Global Compact

Kofi Annan coupled his 1999 warning to the world's business leaders about the fragility of globalization with an initiative called the Global Compact (GC). It is *not* a code of conduct – which has been a major point of contention vis-à-vis anti-globalization activist groups.[56] A partnership between the United Nations,

---

more concerned with instituting guiding principles and maximizing transparency. See www. globalreporting.org and www.accountability.org.uk.

54 Harriet Chiang, "Court says Nike must Defend its PR; Free Speech doesn't Protect Labor Claims," *San Francisco Chronicle*, May 3, 2002.

55 Erika N. Sasser, "Gaining Leverage: NGO Influence on Certification Institutions in the Forest Products Sector," paper presented at the 7th Annual Colloquium on Environmental Law and Institutions, Duke University, Dec. 7–8, 2001; and Blackett, "Global Governance, Legal Pluralism and the Decentered State."

56 Activist groups and some mainstream NGOs fear that because it is not a code of conduct, with explicit performance standards and compliance monitoring, the Compact gives companies a free ride. But as the following discussion tries to make clear, the Compact is a

business, international labor and major transnational civil society organizations, the Compact instead seeks to engage companies in the promotion of certain UN principles within corporate domains.[57] The principles themselves are drawn from the Universal Declaration of Human Rights, the International Labor Organization's Fundamental Principles on Rights at Work and the Rio Principles on Environment and Development.[58] Companies are encouraged to move toward "good practices" as defined through multi-stakeholder dialogue and partnership, rather than relying on their often superior bargaining position vis-à-vis national authorities, especially in small and poor states, to get away with less. The Compact employs three instruments to achieve its aims.

Through its "learning forum", it is designed to generate consensus-based understandings of how a company's commitment to the nine principles can be translated most effectively into corporate management practices. The idea is for the UN to publicize these norms, thereby providing a standard of comparison for – and adding public pressure on – industry laggards. The learning forum is still in its infancy and so its performance cannot yet be assessed.

By means of its "policy dialogues", the Compact generates shared understandings about, for example, the socially responsible posture for companies when operating in countries afflicted by conflict. This particular dialogue has explored how companies can conduct impact assessments and reduce the risks that their own behavior may fuel such conflicts; achieve greater transparency in their financial transactions with the parties to conflicts; and devise revenue sharing regimes that will benefit local populations.[59] The results from these dialogues play a normative role in the broader public arena, and they directly inform the UN's own conflict prevention and peacemaking activities.

Finally, through its "partnership projects" in developing countries the Compact contributes to capacity building where it is needed most. Ongoing cases include support for microlending, investment promotion, HIV/AIDS awareness programs

---

mechanism intended to engage companies in the promotion of UN goals, not to regulate them. Regulation is a perfectly valid objective, but it is not the only one that counts. The most vocal critic on this score is an anti-globalization group called CorpWatch, at www.corpwatch.org.

57 The GC participants include the UN (the Secretary-General's Office, Office of the High Commissioner for Human Rights, International Labor Organization, UN Environment Program and the UN Development Program); the International Confederation of Free Trade Unions (ICFTU); more than a dozen transnational NGOs in the three areas covered by the GC, such as Amnesty International, the International Union for the Conservation of Nature, and Oxfam; as well as individual companies and international business associations. For up-to-date information, see www.unglobalcompact.org.

58 The nine principles are: support and respect for the protection of internationally proclaimed human rights; non-complicity in human rights abuses; freedom of association and the effective recognition of the right to collective bargaining; the elimination of all forms of forced and compulsory labor; the effective abolition of child labor; the elimination of discrimination in respect of employment and occupation; a precautionary approach to environmental challenges; greater environmental responsibility; and encouragement of the development and diffusion of environmentally friendly technologies.

59 Consult www.unglobalcompact.org.

for employees in sub-Saharan Africa, devising sustainable alternatives to child labor, and a host of initiatives in ecoefficiency and other dimensions of environmental management. One of the success stories at the Johannesburg World Summit on Sustainable Development was the Global Compact partnership effort to promote investment in the least developed countries.[60]

Companies initiate participation in the Compact with a letter of commitment from their Chief Executive Officer to the Secretary-General, a step that often requires board approval. Since a kickoff event in July 2000, some 400 companies worldwide – based in Europe, the United States, Japan, Hong Kong, India, Brazil, Thailand and elsewhere – have done so.[61]

Organizationally, the Compact comprises a series of nested networks. The Secretary-General's office provides strategic direction, policy coherence and quality control. The participating UN agencies, companies, international labor, transnational NGOs, and university-based research centers do the heavy lifting in the learning forum, policy dialogues and partnership projects.

The Global Compact has triggered several complementary regional, national, and sectoral initiatives. Typically, they take a subset of interested GC participants beyond its minimum commitments. For example, Norway's Statoil and the International Federation of Chemical, Energy, Mine and General Workers' Unions reached an agreement within the GC framework whereby Statoil is extending the same labor rights as well as health and safety standards to all its overseas operations that it applies in Norway including in Vietnam, Venezuela, Angola, and Azerbaijan.[62] A Nordic Global Compact Network has been established, as has a "Friends of the Global Compact" network in Germany, both pursuing additional work programs of interest to their participants. Pilot projects for country-level counterparts – "local compacts" are under way in some 20 developing countries, under the leadership of the United Nations Development Program. In addition, a number of initiatives intended for other purposes have associated themselves with the GC. The most unusual is the multi-stakeholder Committee for Melbourne, which incorporated the

---

60 Ibid.

61 Brand vulnerability, as already indicated, is a key factor driving companies headquartered in the industrialized countries. In addition, some companies in cutting edge industries have found that they cannot sufficiently motivate the very best people with monetary rewards alone, as a result of which they have adopted more elevated social purposes as part of their corporate culture. Indeed, the GC has done best where companies have created mechanisms of internal communication that permit employees to comment on and report how their own work relates to the implementation of the nine principles – Novartis and Volvo being exemplars. On "internal branding" of this sort, see Bernard Stamler, "Companies are Developing Brand Messages as a Way to Inspire Loyalty among Employees," *New York Times*, July 5, 2001. In the case of developing country firms, their rationale for participating also includes a belief about what is expected of aspiring global corporate players, and in some cases a perceived opportunity for them to navigate domestically around the dictates of their own governmental bureaucracies. (Based on interviews with participants.)

62 "Statoil Signs Agreement with ICEM," *Europe Energy*, Mar. 30, 2001.

GC principles into the strategic plan it developed for that Australian city (City Plan 2010), and is encouraging all firms doing business there to embrace them.[63]

As noted, the Compact is not a code of conduct but a social learning network.[64] It operates on the premise that socially legitimated good practices will help drive out bad ones through the power of transparency and competition. The UN General Assembly could not generate a meaningful code of conduct at this time even if that were deemed desirable; the only countries that would be eager to launch such an effort are equally unfriendly to the private sector, human rights, labor standards and the environment.[65] In any event, many of the GC's principles cannot be defined at this time with the precision required for a viable intergovernmental code. No consensus exists on precisely what comprises a "precautionary approach" – that in the face of environmental uncertainty the bias should favor avoiding risk – even though the principle was enshrined at the 1992 Rio Conference. Similarly, no consensus exists, even among advocates, on where, in long and complex chains of relationships, to set the threshold of corporate "complicity" in human rights abuses.[66] Accumulated experience – through trial, error and social vetting – will gradually fill in the blanks.

Moreover, ex ante standards often become performance ceilings that are difficult to change – witness the inability of the US Senate to muster the political will to improve automobile fuel efficiency standards that have not been altered since 1985, long before the prevalence of so-called sports utility vehicles.[67] In contrast, the Compact seeks to peg company performance globally to evolving international community-based "good practices", thereby potentially "ratcheting up" performance on an ongoing basis.[68]

The Global Compact is based on principles that were universally endorsed by governments, thus stipulating aspirational goals of the entire international community. It enlists partners in the corporate sector and civil society to help bridge the gap between aspiration and reality – to become agencies for the promotion of community norms. Thus, the Compact is a heterodox addition to the growing menu of responses to globalization's challenges that engage the private sector – including corporate

---

63 www.melbourne.vic.gov.au/cityptan/infopage.cfm.

64 The distinction between the two approaches is discussed at greater length in John Gerard Ruggie, "The Theory and Practice of Learning Networks: Corporate Social Responsibility and the Global Compact," *Journal of Corporate Citizenship*, 5 (Spring 2002).

65 In contrast, the General Assembly has endorsed Annan's approach to social partnerships, including the Global Compact, in "Towards Global Partnerships," A/Res/56/76 (Jan. 24, 2002).

66 For a good discussion of the difficulties, see Andrew Clapham, "On Complicity," in Marc Henzelin and Robert Roth (eds), *Le Droit pénal à l'épreuve de l'internationalisation* (forthcoming).

67 David E. Rosenbaum, "Senate Deletes Higher Mileage Standard in Energy Bill," *New York Times*, Mar. 14, 2002. The final vote was 62–38 against.

68 This concept is due to Charles Sabel, Dara O'Rourke and Archon Fung, "Ratcheting Labor Standards: Regulation for Continuous Improvement in the Global Workplace," John F. Kennedy School of Government, Harvard University, KSG Working Paper no. 00–010, May 2, 2000.

codes of conduct, social and environmental reporting initiatives, and various other means to promote and monitor corporate social responsibility.

A Global Public Domain

Despite the great progress that has been achieved in promoting voluntary initiatives, their scope remains limited. For example, the Forest Stewardship Council (FSC) has certified 70 million acres of forests, which amounts to a mere 4 percent of the total acreage controlled by timber companies.[69] Similarly, sales of Fair Trade Certified coffee are estimated to have been 30 million pounds in 2001, a tiny fraction of total global coffee sales.[70] Fewer than 200 firms out of a total of 1,500 participate in the US chemical industry's Responsible Care program.[71] Of the 700 companies subscribing to the Global Compact, perhaps no more than a quarter are deeply engaged. And so on, throughout other industry sectors. By themselves, therefore, they do not and cannot constitute the entirety of solutions.

At the same time, these company-based initiatives are significant not only for what they achieve directly, but also because they are triggering broader second-order consequences. Consider some of the main elements and actors.

First, the investment community has shown growing interest, which brings large amounts of capital into play. Instruments for socially responsible investment, like the Domini and Calvert mutual funds, are proliferating, and major pensions funds, including America's largest, the California Public Employee Retirement System, have made socially responsible investment a priority.[72]

Second, the public sector is slowly entering the picture. Several OECD countries – the UK, France and the Netherlands – have begun to encourage or require companies to engage in social reporting, for example, and to promote corporate social responsibility through other means; the European Union has issued a green paper on the subject.[73] And the 2002 World Summit on Sustainable Development would have

---

69 Andrew C. Revkin, "Forget Nature: Even Eden is Engineered," *New York Times*, Aug. 20, 2002; and Michael E. Conroy, "Can Advocacy-Led Certification Systems Transform Global Corporate Practices? Evidence and Some Theory," University of Massachusetts, Amherst, Political Economy Research Institute, DPE-01-07, Sept. 2001. Conroy claims that the total acreage is more than 5 per cent, and he points out that home improvement centers like Home Depot appear willing to pay a premium for FSC certified lumber. Home Depot got into the act in the first place because activists chose to boycott it to gain leverage over the timber companies, which lack sufficient public personae to be vulnerable to consumer pressure. All major US home improvement outlets participate in the FSC.

70 Conroy, "Can Advocacy-Led Certification Systems Transform Global Corporate Practices?"

71 Andrew King and Michael J. Lenox, "Industry Self-Regulation without Sanctions: The Chemical Industry's Responsible Care Program," *Academy of Management*, 43 (Aug. 2000).

72 Amy Domini, *Socially Responsible Investing: Making a Difference and Making Money* (Chicago: Dearborn Trade, 2001).

73 Commission of the European Communities, "Promoting a European Framework for Corporate Social Responsibility," Brussels: COM [2001] 366 final (July 18, 2001). The

been an outright failure were it not for the many public–private partnership projects it generated.[74] Some governments entered these in part to avoid more binding commitments, to be sure, including the United States, which sought to avoid any targets or timetables; but they also look to such partnerships as a means to leverage limited resources, and to learn by doing in the face of high risk and uncertainty.[75]

Where labor is included in voluntary initiatives – as in the Global Compact – it gains a global platform that may help compensate for, and possibly overcome, its stagnant and even shrinking platform at the national level. Indeed, no social partner has made more effective use of the Global Compact than labor.

Perhaps the most significant development politically is the emergence of a new advocate for a more effective global public sector: business itself. Corporate leaders at the frontier of corporate social responsibility issues have begun to realize that the concept is infinitely elastic: the more they do, the more they will be asked to do. As a result, business leaders themselves have begun to ask, *"Where* is the public sector?" Three elite global business groups – the World Economic Forum, International Chamber of Commerce, and World Business Council for Sustainable Development – recently launched governance initiatives, not to *curtail* the public sector but to clarify where private sector responsibility ends and public responsibility begins.[76]

Similarly, in the staggering HIV/AIDS treatment crisis in Africa, as the major pharmaceutical companies have been forced to lower their prices, and as employers such as Anglo American Mines have been obliged to begin gratis treatment programs for their employees – a third of whom are infected in Anglo's case – they have become strong advocates for public sector capacity building in education and public health alike.[77]

Finally, at the end of the day the accumulation of experience inevitably will lead to a desire for greater benchmarking, for moving from "good" to "best" practices and even formal codification, so that some of the "soft law" products of voluntary initiatives are likely to become "harder" law down the road. The advocates will include industry leaders to lock in their own first-mover advantages, or wanting a level playing field vis-à-vis laggards – as happened when several major energy

---

OECD itself has issued guidelines for transnational corporations, but there is little evidence that companies have paid much attention to them; *The OECD Guidelines for Multinational Enterprises, Revision 2000* (Paris: OECD, 2000).

74 Barry James, "Action Plan of Summit Looks Weak to Activists," *International Herald Tribune*, Sept. 3, 2002.

75 Some of these partnerships fall into the broader category of "global public policy networks", tri-sectoral efforts that also include the World Commission on Dams, the Climate Action Network and the Roll-Back-Malaria campaign, among others; see Wolfgang H. Reinicke and Francis Deng, *Critical Choices: The United Nations, Networks, and the Future of Global Governance* (Ottawa: International Development Research Center, 2000).

76 The World Economic Forum plans to publish an annual Global Governance Report, which will assess the respective contributions that various sectors of society are making to solving global problems; www.weforum.org/site/homepublic.nsf/Content/Global+Governance+Task+Force.

77 Julia Finch, "Anglo Calls for Help on Aids," *Guardian* (London), Aug. 17, 2002.

companies lobbied the US Congress for some form of greenhouse-gas limits after President Bush rejected the Kyoto Protocol.[78] Laggards have a harder time opposing standards based on actual achievements by their peers than ex ante standards.

This terrain is fraught with strategic manipulation and the potential for shirking. But it also opens the door to more firmly institutionalizing an emerging global public domain by bringing the public sector into it. Globalization was a one-way bet for the business community: governments were needed to create the space within which business could expand and integrate, but they were not otherwise welcome. The combination of global governance gaps and governance failures, however, created an organizational niche that civil society actors began to occupy, and from which they have been engaging the global business community in the attempt to balance its newly acquired rights with new social responsibilities. Now we are slowly beginning to come full circle: business wants help to channel some of the pressure it faces into the construction of at least minimally effective public sectors, including at the global level. This sets up the possibility of a very different political dynamic than existed as recently as the 1990s.

Conclusion

When we reflect on how hard it was and how long it took to institute the original embedded liberalism compromise at the national level, the prospect of achieving a similar social framing of global market forces seems exponentially more daunting. But if there is one similarity between the two eras, and the two levels of social organization, it is in the respective roles of the private sector as an inadvertent transformational force – be it the hegemony of the great "trusts" in the late nineteenth century, the abysmal failure of financial institutions in the interwar period, or the spread of multinational corporate empires today. The international political arena differs radically, characterized as it is by the absence of government. And so at the global level there will be many more zigs, many more zags, and quite probably many more failures. But our discussion has outlined both a dynamic of possible change and a possible trajectory.

I have argued that, as a result of the expansion of civil society and its engagement with the corporate sector, a global public domain is emerging. I take that to mean an arena inhabited by various actors for whom the territorial state is not the cardinal organizing principle, as well as by states; and wherein a variety of human interests are expressed and pursued directly, not merely those mediated – promoted, filtered, interpreted – by the state. Indeed, some areas of global public policy would barely exist were it not for non-state actors. And in addition to the traditional machinery

---

78 "These companies have concluded that limits on carbon dioxide and other greenhouse, or heat-trapping, gases are inevitable. ... And to plan long-term investments, they want the predictability that comes from quick adoption of clear rules": Andrew C. Revkin and Neela Banerjee, "Energy Executives Urge Voluntary Greenhouse-Gas Limits," *New York Times*, Aug. 1, 2001. The companies included the Royal Dutch/Shell Group, BP, several power-generating companies – and Enron, which hoped to capture the global permits trading business.

of interstate governance, the likes of essentially private certification institutions are becoming significant components of global rule making. But private governance produces only partial solutions, and its own unfolding brings the public sector back in.

It is difficult at this early stage to be more precise, and thus it is doubly imperative not to exaggerate either the virtues or the defects of these institutional developments. In view of the fragility of voluntary initiatives like certification institutions and the Global Compact, it seems highly implausible to depict them as expressions of the rise of global "corporatism", for example, let alone conjuring up the ghost of corporatism's fascist ancestry as a scenario for the global future.[79] At the same time, it also seems at least premature to view them as expressions of cosmopolitan democracy.[80] Greater pluralism, perhaps; but we are a long way from turning rich country consumers, the employees of transnational corporations or even dedicated activists into global citizens. Moreover, the skewed distribution of agential capacity between North and South is too pronounced, accountability problems too pervasive and the distributional consequences of these kinds of global governance instruments too poorly understood for us to believe that they reflect some new stable equilibrium.

What we can say is that a fundamental recalibration is going on of the public–private sector balance, and it is occurring at the global level no less than the domestic. Haltingly and erratically, something akin to an embedded liberalism compromise is being pulled and pushed into the global arena, and the corporate connection is a key element in that process.

Note

Earlier versions of this chapter were presented as the keynote address at the conference on Global Governance: Towards a New Grand Compromise? at the University of Toronto, May 29, 2002; a Miliband Public Lecture on Global Economic Governance, London School of Economics and Political Science, June 6, 2002; and the keynote paper for the theme panel on International Relations Theory and Global Governance, American Political Science Association, Annual Meeting, Boston, Aug. 31, 2002. I am most grateful to participants at each event for their probing questions and constructive comments.

---

79 Marina Ottaway, "Corporatism Goes Global: International Organizations, Nongovernmental Organizations Networks, and Transnational Business," *Global Governance*, 7 (Sept./Dec. 2001). The referent is not corporations, of course, but the system of governance that closely integrated elements of the state, business and peak labor associations to manage the early twentieth-century breakdown of capitalism in several European countries, including Germany and Italy.

80 The major work in this genre is David Held, *Democracy and the Global Order: From the Modern State to Cosmopolitan Governance* (Cambridge: Polity, 1995); and, more recently, David Held, "Law of States, Law of Peoples: Three Models of Sovereignty," *Legal Theory*, 8, no. 1 (2002).

Index